Business in
Britain

Business in
Britain

by Graham Turner

LITTLE, BROWN AND COMPANY — BOSTON — TORONTO

To my friends, Tom and Alan

Acknowledgements

This book would not have been possible but for the generous help of hundreds of people, many of whom are mentioned in the text. I am particularly grateful to those – such as Lord Cole and Sir Denning Pearson – who gave me their time in the evenings, and to those – Lindsay Alexander, Arthur Bryan, Sir Tatton Brinton and Arnold Weinstock among them – who offered me the hospitality of their homes. With a few exceptions, businessmen in this country are now very accessible and many of those referred to in this book have given a good deal of their time, sometimes at short notice.

I am particularly indebted to Professor T. C. Barker and Mr H. W. Richardson of the University of Kent at Canterbury for many extremely useful suggestions on the historical chapters; Professor Barker was also kind enough to let me see the chapter which he has written for Volume I of the *Twentieth Century Mind* (ed. Cox and Dyson) which is shortly to be published by the Oxford University Press. Derek Aldcroft of the University of Leicester and Alan Milward of the University of East Anglia also generously allowed me to see unpublished manuscripts. Any errors of judgement or fact which remain are, of course, my own.

My publishers have given me the sort of friendship and help which alone make tolerable the pressures which a book such as this one imposes.

As for my wife, she has been adviser, secretary and indispensable prop in time of trouble. She has also produced the index.

Contents

CONTENTS

Business in Britain

Introduction

I have been writing this book during one of the greatest periods of industrial change in Britain's history. I confess that it has sometimes felt like it. Almost every month has brought some major piece of reorganization; and the industrial scene now looks very different from what it did when I began work over three years ago.

It has also, of course, been a period in which Britain has been struggling to hold her place in the world; and in that struggle British industry – as in the battle for exports after the Second World War – has again found itself cast in the role of a peace-time army.

Despite its export successes, it still has more of the characteristics of the Home Guard than of a professional fighting force: in many of its parts, it is poorly equipped and organized, and often indifferently led. Furthermore, the problem of transforming it into a unit capable of dealing with the Americans, West Germans and Japanese in world markets has proved to be more profound even than ardent reformers imagined. It is not merely a question of rationalizing its structure or modernizing its plant and equipment – nor, as Labour Ministers now admit, of setting right 'thirteen years of Tory misrule'; what has to be dealt with are problems and attitudes which have grown up during the last hundred years and more.

The task has not been made any easier by the extreme difficulty of awakening the public to perils all too evident to the politicians. Britain is a low-key society not easily roused (to put the matter kindly) and news of the continued decline in her world position – even when spiced with squeezes, a wage and price freeze and a devaluation – has not been sufficient to produce an adequate response at a time when the country's standard of living was improving, even if more slowly than elsewhere. Given this fact, the British have found it difficult to believe that they were engaged in an economic *guerre à outrance* and their reaction to exhortation has been correspondingly sluggish.

Despite the temptation to become entirely absorbed in the rapid movement of events, the more I have looked at the present condition of British industry the more I have been drawn to examine the roots from which it sprang and the environment in which it has developed. In many ways, I believe, the nature of our industrial history helps to explain the present situation.

The first part of the book, therefore, consists of a brief historical survey which sketches the growth of British industry during the last century and the economic background against which it has grown. I found it impossible to write meaningfully about the large companies of today without putting them into some sort of historical context and the first three chapters are partly intended for that purpose. The final chapter in the section examines the environment in which business now operates – and more particularly its relationship with the Government and its agencies, with the banks and with the business schools, the latest attempt to produce a more professional and disciplined industrial army.

The central part of the book is concerned with the condition of British industry today. I have concentrated (though not exclusively) on large companies because of their over-riding importance in terms of the national economic effort and because it is very difficult to paint a representative picture of the activity of small business. There are chapters on most of the major industries, but I have had to be selective and the selection has been partly based on what took my fancy.

Finally, I have drawn together some of my own thoughts and conclusions about the present state of British business. I think there are some grounds for optimism, not only because the nature of our problems is being more accurately diagnosed but also because there are signs of improvement in performance. On the other hand, the fundamental changes which are needed will not take place rapidly and the renaissance of British industry which has been predicted by optimists for the 1970s will be short-lived – if it takes place at all – unless we can achieve a real break-through in transforming deep-rooted attitudes in our society, foremost among them a failure to recognize that industry is the prime force in our national prosperity.

I do not, however, share the view that an increase in efficiency at all costs ought to be one of our goals; and I would not regard the emulation of the sort of societies which exist in America, West Germany or Japan as any sort of achievement. We already have a society which American critics believe to be the most civilized in the world and what we have to do is to improve the quality of our industrial performance without diminishing the many virtues of that society. I believe that our present level of efficiency is so low that we can step it up substantially without reducing detrimentally the high degree of individual freedom which we currently possess.

I have spent over three years examining a wide spectrum of business life in this country and I have deliberately chosen a broad canvas. I am only too conscious of the shortcomings of the result. I would like to have discussed a number of topics in much more detail, I would like to have spent more time on the small business, but something has had to be sacrificed – if only to produce a book of manageable size.

I should add that, although I have made every effort to keep up to date with a swiftly moving situation, there may well have been changes by the time this book is published.

Great Missenden,   GRAHAM TURNER
July 1969

PART 1

The Background and Environment of Business

CHAPTER 1

The End of British Supremacy
1870–1914

In 1870, Britain was the greatest industrial nation in the world. Over half of the world's coal was raised from her pits, over half its pig-iron and forty per cent of its steel came from British furnaces, and almost half its cotton cloth was spun and woven in British mills. Britain produced well over a third of the world's output of manufactured goods. Her export trade was greater than that of France, Germany and Italy put together, and four times that of the United States. The profits which flowed from her industrial supremacy had already begun to spill over into the finance of enterprises round the globe: by 1870 she had perhaps £800m. invested abroad.

In the next quarter of a century Britain was to lose that pre-eminence; and by 1914 she was, in many crucial respects, lagging behind both the United States and Germany. Not that the British economy was either in decline or even stagnant, indeed industrial production doubled between 1870 and 1914; it was simply that others were now moving ahead a good deal faster. Industrial output over the world as a whole went up more than *four* times during that same period. By 1886 the Americans were producing more steel than the British, and by 1893 so were the Germans. A year later, the United States became the world's leading coal producer. By 1914, the Americans were turning out four times as much steel, the Germans twice as much.

The loss of supremacy provoked, as the evidence became plainer, a mounting chorus of dismay during the 1890s and the early years of the new century. Much of the criticism was directed against British businessmen: managers were charged with being conservative and indolent, salesmen with being ignorant of their markets. A stream of newspaper articles and books – such as Williams's *Made in Germany* (published in 1896) and McKenzie's *The American Invaders* (1901) – fulminated about the situation. The mood, certainly of the pundits, was perhaps best reflected by Kipling's doleful line, written in 1897 – 'Lo, all our pomp of yesterday is one with Nineveh and Tyre'.

The critics made many complaints which have a curiously contemporary ring. In 1906, for example, Shadwell in his book *Industrial Efficiency* took to task both master and man, charging that 'the once enterprising manufacturer has grown slack, he has let his business take care of itself, while he is shooting grouse or yachting in the Mediterranean'. As for the worker, his motto had become 'get as much and do as little as you can' and his business was football or betting. 'We are,' Shadwell went on, 'a nation at play. Work is a nuisance, an evil necessity to be shirked and hurried over as quickly as possible in order that we may get to the real business of life – the golf course, the bridge table, the cricket and football field.'[1] Over-prosperity had produced a climate in which 'the Gospel of Ease has permeated the nation'.[2]

McKenzie, writing earlier in *The American Invaders*, had compiled a similar jeremiad. 'We have been too content,' he confessed, 'to rest satisfied with great accomplishments of past generations – we have been a little too prosperous, far too easy-going.'[3] British masters were 'right behind the times . . . There is a stolid conservatism which seems irremovable'.[4] The distinguished Cambridge economist, Alfred Marshall, also writing after the turn of the century, bemoaned the fact that 'many of the sons of manufacturers [were] content to follow the lead given by their fathers. They worked shorter hours and they extended themselves less to obtain new practical ideas than their fathers had done. . . . In the nineties it became clear that in future Englishmen must take business as seriously as their grandfathers had done, and as their American and German rivals were doing: that their training for business must be methodical, like that of their new rivals, and not merely practical, on lines that had sufficed for the simpler world of two generations ago.'[5]

Britain's loss of industrial leadership was not, of course, particularly

[1] Arthur Shadwell, *Industrial Efficiency* (two vols.), Longmans, Green, London, 1906, vol. 2, pp. 453–4.

[2] *Ibid.*, vol. 2, p. 462.

[3] F. A. McKenzie, *The American Invaders*, Howard Wilford Bell, London, 1901, p. 21.

[4] *Ibid.*, p. 428.

[5] Alfred Marshall, 'Memorandum on Fiscal Policy of International Trade' (1903), in *Official Papers of Alfred Marshall* (1926), p. 406.

surprising. She could hardly hope indefinitely to best the United States, with her vast unexploited natural resources, a steady flow of immigrant labour and a home market which almost trebled (from thirty-one million to ninety-one million) between 1850 and 1910. The rapid industrial advance of Germany (unified only since 1871) was a good deal more surprising to contemporaries, many of whom still looked upon France as Britain's great rival in Europe.

But, in any case, the end of Britain's supremacy was hastened by an unhappy combination of economic circumstances. The first was that the years after 1873 brought what has been called 'the most drastic deflation in the memory of man'.[1] By the mid-1890s, the general level of prices had fallen by about a third, and profits either fell or stayed low in many sectors of industry. This persistent downward spiral began to seem endless by the early 1890s, and it undermined business confidence in new investment and innovation at the very moment when it stood in need of support and encouragement. At the same time, tariff barriers were being raised in many vital markets. During the American Civil War, for example, the United States had increased the average level of its duties on foreign goods from eighteen to forty-seven per cent: there was to be no major reduction until 1913. The French and Germans were also becoming protectionist.[2] The barriers were sometimes not insuperable – the evidence suggests that by and large the Germans overcame them more successfully than the British – but their erection merely placed another difficulty in Britain's path.

Nor did the structure of British industry, the legacy of her leadership in the industrial revolution, make it easier for her to face the new economic climate. She was, to begin with, heavily dependent on textiles, coal, and iron and steel; in 1907 these still accounted for seventy per cent of Britain's export business, and although there had been significant developments within them (the cotton industry, for example, had moved towards the production of better-quality cloths) their preponderance was too great to be healthy.

Again because of her early start, Britain had a heavy investment in technologies which became outdated in the last quarter of the century. No doubt conservatism and complacency played their part in the

<hr>

[1] David S. Landes, 'Technological Change and Development in Western Europe, 1750–1914', in the *Cambridge Economic History of Europe*, vol. 6 (1), CUP, Cambridge, 1965, p. 458.

[2] The average tariff levels of the USA, France and Germany in 1913 were thirty-three per cent, eighteen per cent and twelve per cent.

reluctance to invest in newer techniques, but it is worth remembering that businessmen had to choose between persevering with plant which was still capable of making a profit and risking heavy new investment at a time of falling profits and increasing competition. The knowledge that major investment in new techniques might also imply alliances with other companies did nothing to allay the fears of proprietors who had a strong desire to remain independent.

The low level of profit in many British industries and the prospect of higher returns in other parts of the world helped create the massive movement of money into overseas investment which took place during this period; other factors, like the rising prices of primary commodities after 1896, also played their part. The increase was huge; about £880m. in 1870, the total had reached an estimated £4,000m. by 1913. Between 1870 and 1913, no less than forty per cent of all British investment went abroad, and in the period between 1911 and 1913 she was investing twice as much abroad as at home. The contrast between Britain and her major Continental competitor, Germany, is most striking. In the years 1901–5 and 1911–13 only 5.7 per cent of total German investment went abroad; between 1905 and 1914 the figure for Britain was 52.9 per cent. The London Stock Exchange was dominated by dealing in foreign bonds; in 1913, foreign stocks and shares had a nominal value of almost £6,800m., sixty per cent of the value of all securities quoted on the market. London was the centre of the world financial system and the pound sterling was at the height of its power.

Roughly thirty per cent of this flood of foreign investment went into loans to foreign governments, from Costa Rica and San Domingo to the United States and France, and another forty per cent financed the construction of new railways in a dozen countries. The remainder provided capital for water-works and gas-works, for electric light and tramway companies, for the exploitation of gold and diamond mines in South Africa, for the development of tea, cocoa and coffee plantations. As the century went on, a smaller and smaller proportion went to America and Europe, an increasing share to the Empire and to under-developed countries. Banks which had no desire to hold British industrial shares were happy to keep a substantial part of their portfolios in foreign bonds; the Bucks and Oxon Bank's holdings in 1869 included Turkish, Russian, Chilean and Peruvian bonds.

This vast outflow of money not only yielded good returns for those investors who chose wisely: it also opened up new markets for British staples and greatly helped her capital goods industries. By 1914, it was yielding dividends amounting to one-tenth of the national income and making a major contribution to Britain's balance of payments. Unfortunately its attractions also contributed to a serious under-investment at home: enough did not go into keeping British industry up to date. Some historians, indeed, suggest that capital investment was not even sufficient to stop British industry running down slightly.

By and large Britain progressed not by modernizing her economy, not by taking the lead in the new industries and technologies which were emerging in the last quarter of the century – with the notable exception of her last great technical innovation of the period, the iron steam-ship – but by 'exploiting the remaining possibilities of her traditional situation'.[1] Baulked elsewhere, she found expanding markets for her cotton goods in the East; exports of coal almost quadrupled between 1880 and 1913; and, although unable to compete with the United States in steel production, she used her engineering skills in the processing of steel and found new markets for her iron and steel in the under-developed countries. She rode the iron steam-ship boom: in the early 1890s more than eighty per cent of the world's mercantile tonnage was being launched down British slipways, and it was still over sixty per cent when war broke out. Britain increasingly became not only banker but also shipper to the world – in 1900, fifty-five per cent of the cargoes entering American ports did so in British bottoms – and she lived off the profits of her past success, through her overseas investments.

In the years before the First World War there was perhaps, on the face of things, no undue cause for concern. Certainly some of the statistics were reassuring. British coal production had risen from 133 million tons to 287 million tons between 1875 and 1913; her output of pig-iron and steel had gone up from ten million to eighteen million tons between 1880 and 1913; and the number of cotton looms and spindles in operation increased by forty-five per cent between 1885 and 1913. But the bald figures obscured a less happy situation, of which the iron and steel industry is one illustration. It was a field in which Britain had a proud record: every major innovation in the manufacture of steel had either been created or developed by her. Yet in these years her steel production almost inevitably fell behind that of both the Americans and Germans as they began to exploit their massive natural resources.

[1] E. J. Hobsbawm, *Industry and Empire*, Weidenfeld and Nicolson, London, 1968, p. 125.

Britain's relative decline was partly due to the fact that she was very slow to invest in new ways of making steel. For one thing, British ores were not so suitable for the new processes as those of Germany; for another, she had sunk large amounts of capital in older techniques and, while that capital at least looked like remaining profitable, heavy additional investment seemed risky. One industry witness, speaking to the Tariff Commission in 1904, explained that 'a sense of insecurity with the British manufacturer prevents him from laying down new plant. We are so alarmed and disheartened at the approaching foreign competition that we fear to spend money.'

Again, the British market for iron and steel was growing more slowly than those in the United States and Germany – and they, as usual, had the advantage of substantial tariff protection. New investment and productivity went ahead rapidly in both countries; the new British steel plants which were built in the 1890s were only a quarter to a third of the size of those being built by their German competitors. The annual output of American blast furnaces went up thirty-one times between 1860 and 1910, and giant steel empires mushroomed. Andrew Carnegie, who had capitalized his steel business at $1¼m. in 1878, re-capitalized it at $320m. in 1900. While British steel prices went up by roughly a third between 1883 and 1910, the price of American steel came down by twenty per cent, that of German steel by fourteen per cent.

The British coal industry, despite the fact that both output and exports were rising and that many companies had been making handsome profits, particularly in the years before 1902, was also betraying unhealthy symptoms by 1914. Exactly because of its prosperity the industry had not been compelled to become modern in equipment or rational in organization, and although the productivity of British pits was still the highest in Europe, by 1911 they were turning out less coal per miner than in 1871; rising output had been achieved by tapping easily-worked seams, most of which were exhausted. In 1913, coal output was a record, but the industry had more than doubled its labour force since 1880[1] and American coal had become a third cheaper than Britain's.

As elsewhere, many of the industry's problems were the result of Britain's early start. By 1914, probably two-thirds of her coal was being raised from pits projected before 1875, in which the seams were becoming thinner; the Americans, meanwhile, had deposits which were rich, new and easily mined. Furthermore, the geological conditions in which

[1] From 500,000 men to 1,100,000.

British owners had to work often discouraged mechanization; the result was that, while roughly twenty per cent of the coal from American mines was being cut by machine in 1900, in Britain it was less than two per cent. The British industry was also far more fragmented than its competitors. There were over 1,000 coal companies, many consisting of one mine and tiny compared with the big American concerns: by the early years of the new century the Ruhr too was dominated by a dozen giant combines. Rapid concentration in Germany was materially helped by bankers who bought shares in companies and then pressed for mergers. The British coal-owners, on the other hand, were highly individualistic and when, in 1893, Sir George Elliott suggested the formation of a coal trust to cut out inefficiency and wasteful competition, he got no response.

In the case of cotton textiles, the industry was heavily dependent on exports – in 1907, close to ninety per cent of its production was sold abroad – and vulnerable to the creation of indigenous industries; there were even British manufacturers of textile machinery to help the competition on its way. By 1870, there had already been a major change in the balance of its markets: whereas in 1820, over sixty per cent of Britain's cotton piece goods were being sold in either Europe or the United States, by 1860 the proportion had fallen to nineteen per cent and almost three-quarters of the industry's exports were going to the under-developed countries. By 1900, this bias had become even more pronounced – and, indeed, the continued prosperity of British mills rested on India taking three times as much cotton cloth in 1913 as she had done in 1870. (For this, the industry owed much to the efforts of the Lancashire lobby, which helped stave off the effective imposition of protective duties against British goods until 1917.) The industry was also doing a good deal to help itself by the introduction of better-quality cloths. Unfortunately the war dealt it a really serious blow by driving up the price of British goods and encouraging both the Indian industry and other competitors, such as Japan. Even before then, however, the precariousness of its position was plain enough.

It was not only Britain's staple industries which faced problems. One of McKenzie's main complaints in *The American Invaders* was that the Americans had been allowed to acquire control 'of almost every new industry created during the last fifteen years';[1] and in fields like machine tools, chemicals and electrical equipment Britain lost an early lead.

Many of the early advances in electric technology had been British,

[1] McKenzie, *op. cit.*, p. 28.

yet by 1914 Britain ran a poor third to both the Americans and Germans in the manufacture of electrical goods. They each had over thirty per cent of the world market; Britain had only thirteen per cent, although her industry was still earning an export surplus. The British market, moreover, was dominated by American and German companies. Of the four largest manufacturers of electrical equipment, two were offshoots of the American Westinghouse and General Electric companies and a third was a subsidiary of Siemens. There were plenty of perfectly respectable explanations for this situation, some of them connected with Britain's early development as an industrial power. For example, while British cities had in many cases passed through their period of most rapid growth by the 1870s, urban development in both America and Germany was not so advanced and both were able to instal electricity without displacing older sources of energy to anything like the same extent. The existence of so much cheap coal in Britain must also have militated against heavy investment in electricity.

The story of her chemical industry was, in some respects, similar. Until the 1880s Britain was the world's leading manufacturer – in 1878, for example, she accounted for 46.2 per cent of total output, with the United States and Germany poor runners-up at 13.8 and 8.6 per cent respectively – but by 1913 she was some way behind her two competitors. This was in spite of the fact that her industry had continued to grow rapidly, was earning an export surplus in 1914 and that some parts of it – particularly explosives, paints, some fertilizers and heavy chemicals and soap (with Lever Brothers, one of the parent companies of the present Unilever, taking a decisive part) – had flourished. Britain's decline in international terms was partly due to the refusal of her manufacturers to switch from the older Leblanc method of alkali production, in which they had a heavy investment, to the newer Solvay process, and for a long time Brunner Mond, which became part of ICI when it was formed in 1926, was the only company to use the Solvay method. Brunner Mond was granted a licence in 1872, but it was not until 1893 that its main competitors, who had banded themselves together into United Alkali, opened their first Solvay plant.

In the development of the motor car, Britain (like the U.S.) was rather a late starter and, in Europe, it was the Germans and the French who took the lead in work on the petrol engine. The result was that in 1904 Britain's imports of cars and car parts were eight times the value of her exports. Although she caught up fairly quickly, imports still exceeded exports in 1913 and total car production was roughly seventy-five per cent of the French.[1] As for the Americans, they produced 462,000 cars in 1913 compared with Britain's 25,000 and it was an American company – Ford – which was the biggest manufacturer of cars on the British market. One reason for Britain's modest beginning was that her engineers did not lead in the new techniques of mass production. Whereas Henry Ford (in his American operation) had made 1,700 cars with 300 workers in 1904, by 1914 there was still no British firm capable of turning out one car per man per year.

The story of the Argyll company was not wholly untypical. The firm spent large amounts of money on equipping a big works and hoped to move into mass production. In practice, it subjected its cars to repeated testing, built engines by hand and gave the bodywork anything from thirty to thirty-five coats of paint and varnish.[2]

Nevertheless, although scores of companies did not survive for long a motley collection of firms including former cycle manufacturers like Humber, Riley and Rover as well as others which had no pre-motor history at all – Austin, Morris, Hillman and Standard among them – expanded steadily; when war came in 1914 the industry's morale was high, it was overhauling the French level of output and there were all the signs that it was ready to move rapidly ahead. Helped by the introduction of duties on imported cars, the motor industry was to be one of the growth points of the post-war economy.

Compared with her rivals, Britain also moved only slowly to create a less fragmented industrial structure: in Germany major changes were taking place, while in America the 1870s saw the beginnings of the greatest period of industrial amalgamation in history. John Rockefeller led the way with Standard Oil. In 1872 he gained control of oil refining in the city of Cleveland by buying up his competitors; ten years later he had a virtual monopoly of the transportation and refining of petroleum throughout the United States. Similar groupings followed, all aimed at cutting costs and controlling prices. Four great meat packers established a beef trust; International Harvester, another alliance of companies, virtually monopolized the production of farm machinery; there was a tobacco trust, a whisky trust, a sugar trust, a rubber trust. A survey of 1904 showed that 319 industrial trusts had swallowed 5,300 independent concerns, and that seventy-six of

[1] Britain proved very successful in the export of heavy commercial vehicles and motor cycles: exports of the latter were seven times imports by 1911.

[2] McKenzie noted the same situation in the furniture trade, where the Americans mass-produced while the British industry was dominated by little masters.

them controlled eighty per cent or more of the market for their products.

Powerful spurs drove forward this movement towards concentration. The US home market was large, growing rapidly, highly lucrative *and* protected; competition within it was therefore fierce and almost half the sugar refiners in the country had gone into liquidation before the remainder decided to form the Sugar Trust. The swiftly-growing domestic market also meant that companies had to expand rapidly, and since (despite the steady flow of immigrants) labour was scarce, manufacturers spent heavily on labour-saving machinery: the investment in American manufacturing industry quadrupled between 1850 and 1880. The urgent need for capital placed increasing power in the hands of men who were able to raise money.[1] These men, investment bankers like John Pierpont Morgan, were a driving force behind the amalgamation movement.

Once the bankers had invested either other people's money[2] or their own – which they did in large amounts – they naturally wanted to ensure that the investment paid off. They therefore became increasingly involved in the direction of companies and even bribed their owners to give up control by putting forward reorganization schemes which heavily wrote up a company's capital. When a man stood out against them, they would set up a competitive plant and start a price-war, or even threaten to buy up both him and his competitors. The bankers were therefore often in a position to enforce rationalization once mergers had been made; in Britain, by contrast, no outside force existed to compel owners to accept central control and cut out inefficient plants. The 'trust' form of organization also led, in many cases, to the rapid centralization of authority.

Morgan, whose links with other banks and trust companies put him at the heart of what became known as the 'money trust', created US Steel by first threatening Andrew Carnegie with ruinous competition (by building a heavy plant of his own and combining the light steel producers) and then by buying him out for \$447m. US Steel had a capital of over £280m. at a time when the issued capital of Vickers –

---

[1] They either raised loans in Europe or else persuaded the American public to put their savings into American industry.

[2] They found a ready response among the American middle class to the idea of investing in industry; in December 1886 a million shares changed hands in one day on the New York Stock Exchange for the first time, and by 1913 there were reckoned to be $7\frac{1}{2}$ million book-holders of corporate stock.

with wide interests in steel, armaments and shipbuilding – was still less than £5m.:[1] and it controlled more than sixty per cent of American steel production. Morgan also refinanced and reorganized railroads, was a major influence behind the birth of International Harvester, helped finance American General Electric and American Telephone and Telegraph. 'The captains of industry,' says a leading historian of the growth of capitalism, 'were no longer sovereigns in their own right, but now ruled by the grace of the higher power of the investment banker.'[2]

Thus, in a variety of ways, both the pressures of the market and the growing power of the bankers took many American industries out of the hands of the original proprietors. Resistance to amalgamation was also lower because most American companies were young and family interests had not therefore become deeply-rooted. By 1915, America was a nation of large companies. Her society had paid a heavy price. The treatment of labour was often brutal; competition was ruthlessly crushed; and vast economic power was delivered into the hands of a few men. Nevertheless, out of the fire came large and sophisticated enterprises, in which the economies of scale were all the greater because the American market was ready to accept standardized products.

In Germany, similar events were taking place; a rapid growth of population, swift urbanization, the completion of a national railway network and the exploitation of rich natural resources (coal in the Ruhr, iron ore in Lorraine). As in America, the home market was protected by high tariff barriers, and cartels and combinations spread with extraordinary rapidity; the number rose from four in 1865 to 300 in 1900 and 600 by 1911. Very large enterprises were thereby created; Krupp and Thyssen collected the Ruhr and Silesian steel businesses into trusts, and then set about becoming vertical – they ultimately bought their own iron ore and limestone deposits – while the electrical firm of AEG employed 107,000 people by 1910. By 1916, virtually the whole German chemical industry had been grouped into one organization, which became IG Farben. These huge empires were able to produce standardized products and reap economies of scale which stood them in good stead in export markets.

[1] The difference in scale is still marked even when account is taken of the fact that US Steel was vastly over-valued. The American Commissioner of Corporations estimated that its tangible assets were worth only £140m.

[2] George W. Edwards, *The Evolution of Finance Capitalism*, Longmans, Green, London, 1938, p. 168.

In all this, the German joint-stock bankers wielded enormous influence. Unlike the British banks, they were a combination of commercial bank, investment bank and investment trust, and their power sprang not only from the fact that they lent long-term money to companies, but also because investors bought shares through them and allowed them to act as their proxies at company meetings. They became instruments for the promotion and development of companies and for the encouragement (to put it mildly) of rationalization schemes.[1]

Britain's progress was much more gradual, in company legislation as in other respects. Whereas general limited liability had been available in the United States since 1830, similar legislation was not passed in Britain until the Joint Stock Companies Act of 1856. Before the 1850s, limited liability could only be granted by Royal Charter, Act of Parliament or letters patent. The result was that the field was dominated by family business firms or small common-law partnerships. Investors were not encouraged to take a shareholding in companies without limited liability by the knowledge that they might be held responsible for the company's debts with their entire fortunes.

The Act of 1856 remedied this situation. Under its terms, any group of seven or more persons could form a limited company simply by registering a memorandum of association stating the name and objects of the company and the fact that it was limited.

The Act did produce a sharp increase in the number of company registrations, but nevertheless progress was distinctly slow for several decades after its passage. For one thing, limited liability still had a connotation of either financial sharp practice or bad management, and businesses which resorted to it were often thought to do so because their debts were greater than their assets. W. S. Gilbert's jibe was a fair reflection of a generally-held suspicion:

> Seven men form an association
> (If possible, all peers and baronets)
> They start with a public declaration
> To what extent they mean to pay their debts.
> That's called their capital[2]

---

[1] They were also an influence for the appointment of professional managers, chosen not because of family connections but on their technical and business qualifications. This is one reason why, from the earliest days, Germany's industrial leadership contained a higher proportion of professional executives than that of Britain.

[2] W. S. Gilbert, *Limited Liability*.

The figures did seem to show that many of the early limited companies were of a transient nature. In April 1887, the Registrar of Companies believed that about 11,000 companies were actually carrying on business, yet no less than 24,000 had been registered in the previous twenty-five years. Nor, incidentally, did the change to limited liability necessarily mean that shares in a company were offered to the public.

Even if progress was slow, the new law did produce some notable recruits, many in fields like iron and steel and shipbuilding, where heavy capital investment was called for. The Sheffield steel businesses of John Brown and Cammell, and Palmer's Shipbuilding (the latter's decline was to bring massive unemployment to Jarrow during the years of depression after the 1914 war) were among the first to take advantage of limited liability. The Birmingham Small Arms Company followed in 1873, Cunard in 1878 – though no shares were offered to the public until 1880 – Brunner Mond in 1881.

If the progress of limited liability was slow, so too was the growth of the public shareholding in British industry. Innumerable large firms went limited, but issued no shares or debentures to the public. In 1882, the paid-up capital of all the companies quoted on the London Stock Exchange was only £64m. – out of a total of almost £5,800m. of quoted securities – and most of the issues which did exist were in preference shares or debentures. Sizeable issues of Ordinary shares were still rare.

The mechanism for launching a new company onto the market was still, indeed, both primitive and highly speculative, and it was seldom that either merchant banks or joint-stock banks took part in helping promote new company issues. They might receive subscriptions, but that was all. Notable exceptions to this general rule were the promotion of Guinness by Baring Brothers in 1886 and Allsopps (another brewing concern) by the Westminster Bank in 1887. Companies which wanted to raise money on the market frequently handled the operation themselves, perhaps retaining a firm of stockbrokers to advise them on the timing and terms of the issue and to arrange underwriting for it. In other cases, it was left to company promoters of varying reputation and honesty to handle flotations and to try to popularize the idea of investment in equities. One such was Ernest Hooley, a Nottingham lace manufacturer who began his financial career in 1895, promoted twenty-six companies with a capital of £18m. at a gross profit of £5m. but still went bankrupt in 1898. His biggest success was the Dunlop rubber flotation of 1896, where the business was bought for £3m. and sold to the public a few weeks later for £5m.

Flotation could bring anxieties even for companies which were both prosperous and reputable, as the experience of J. and P. Coats, the Paisley sewing thread concern, showed. Coats was efficient enough to have captured a large slice of the American market and at the time it went to the market, in 1890, forty per cent of its world sales were in the United States. Its owners originally proposed a selling price of £6,250,000, but the reaction of the financial Press was far from favourable and Coats had to come down to £5,750,000 and to put three worthy outside businessmen on to its Board, including an alderman of the City of London. In the event, the issue was almost three times over-subscribed.

When Britain's own merger movement got under way, in the last decade of the century, it was modest by comparison with what was happening elsewhere. Many sectors of her industry were largely made up of highly independent family businesses sufficiently long established for family power to have become entrenched, and there was little instinctive liking among her industrialists for merging into larger units despite the long-term threat which the concentration of companies in the United States and Germany obviously posed. Nor did there exist in Britain the powerful spurs which drove forward amalgamations in both those countries.

For one thing, the British market was not so susceptible as the American to the acceptance of standardized products; on the contrary, its consumers strongly preferred articles exhibiting individual character. Britain's overseas customers also demanded products made to their own detailed specification and, unlike the United States, Britain was tremendously dependent on her export trade, on a score of markets all over the world. In 1870 she was selling £17 7s worth of goods abroad per head of the population; the figure for the United States was only £4 9s.[1]

Even if the home market had been proportionately more important, it was not protected; indeed a wholehearted adherence to free trade was widely believed to be a pre-requisite for prosperity, even though there were plenty of doubters by the early 1890s. The first significant breach in the policy did not come until 1915, when Chancellor McKenna imposed duties on a limited range of goods – cars, cycles and watches among them – and it was not until 1931–2 that the great bulk of British industry was protected.

[1] Hobsbawm, *op. cit.*, p. 111.

In this situation, with a home market wide open to foreign competition, the advantages of combination were less obvious than they were in the United States.[1] It is still surprising that more defensive alliances did not take place before they did, but the British industrialist's reputation for stubborn independence was fully earned. In addition, at a time of falling prices and profits, there was little eagerness on the part of many businessmen to seek capital from the public (even if it meant no loss of control) nor indeed did the investing public want to risk its money in British industry when there were better returns to be had elsewhere.

As for the bankers, they played a much more conservative part than in the United States or Germany. They had no wish to hold shares in industrial companies – though many country banks had included railway shares in their portfolios – and while they were ready to provide cheap working capital in the shape of overdraft facilities, they were unwilling to lend money for capital investment. In contrast to their American and German counterparts, they preferred to keep an arms-length relationship. They took no initiative in seeking to create a new shape for British industry, they had no desire to do more than keep their customers solvent and collect their modest interest; they were as parochial, in many respects, as the industrialists they served.

The first major phase of amalgamation in Britain, when it finally came in the 1890s, has been fairly described as 'a mild trend towards mild combination'.[2] Many of the unions then formed were, as we shall see, desperate and half-hearted alliances apparently motivated more by a desire to preserve the status quo than to tackle markets more aggressively. The proprietors who entered into them seemed all too often to regard them as a last refuge rather than a springboard, and sought (often successfully) to retain power for themselves and their descendants. For many, they were also a confession of failure.

There had been one or two significant amalgamations before the 1890s; in 1877, for example, six Scottish grain distilleries had combined to form the Distillers Company and in 1886 the Nobel Dynamite Trust was set up.

The 1890s, however, brought a wave of industrial alliances, stimulated by a variety of forces. For one thing, the long decline in prices and profits, combined with the technical changes which had taken place in

---

[1] The President of the Sugar Trust at the time of its foundation is quoted as saying that 'the tariff is the mother of trusts'.

[2] Landes, *op. cit.*, p. 473.

many industries, forced companies to huddle together into defensive unions. In other cases, efficient concerns which had felt the impact of price wars wanted to eliminate competition. The movement was helped by a period of cheap money, when the yield on Government stocks was so low that investors were willing to accept greater risk for the prospect of a better return. Even so, the effects of the merger movement were concentrated on particular sectors of industry; of the fifty-two largest companies in Britain in 1905, seventeen were in brewing, and ten in textiles.[1]

The wave of mergers in brewing was set in motion by an unusual combination of circumstances. There was a steadily rising demand for beer during the 1880s and 1890s, and little difficulty in raising money on the market, partly because breweries had either local or national reputations and were additionally attractive in that they held most of their capital assets in the form of real property. But the crucial factor which forced them to come to the market for cash and then to seek amalgamations was that, as transport improved and brewing became increasingly mechanized, the ownership of retail outlets grew more valuable as a means of excluding competitors and because of the chance to exploit the retailer's margin. They became all the more valuable when the power to issue new licences reverted to local JPs who, after 1880, refused to grant them as freely as in the past.

A furious scramble to acquire retail outlets began, prices shot up, and large sums had to be raised to finance purchases. In 1892, there were over £50m. of brewery shares on the market, more than the entire 'commercial and industrial' group of ten years before, and by the turn of the century, £175m. had been raised on the Stock Exchange since the Guinness flotation. In that time at least 150 brewing businesses had been amalgamated and absorbed – although large numbers of private breweries still survived – and many of the more acquisitive companies had paid highly inflated prices for property. The result was that a good many had to be financially reconstructed in the early years of the new century.

The brewery mergers were followed by a series of amalgamations in textiles, which began with the take-over by J. and P. Coats of major competitor, Clark; in the same year, 1896, it also acquired control of two other rivals. This made Coats the largest firm in British

[1] Of the largest fifty-four American companies, there was only one in each of these categories.

manufacturing industry, with a nominal share and loan capital of £7.5m. and a market value of £22m.

This union was followed by defensive action on the part of many of the remaining sewing thread manufacturers. In 1897, eleven English sewing cotton companies together with three linen and silk thread firms formed English Sewing Cotton. Coats not only encouraged the union but also invested £200,000 in the shares of the new company. In 1898, thirty-one spinners and doublers of the best Egyptian cotton formed the Fine Cotton Spinners and Doublers Association and in 1899 fifty-nine firms joined together in the Calico Printers Association, which controlled about eighty-five per cent of the British industry.

Unlike the Coats-Clark union, several of these textile mergers took the form of federations with no effective central organization and, far from producing economies of scale, they simply represented the sum of the inefficiency of their parts. Calico Printers, for example, started life with a Board of eighty-four directors and eight managing directors and the terms of the association gave each of the founder companies the right to run their affairs for the first five years without any control from the centre. In 1907, it was discovered as 'a study in disorganization'.[1] English Sewing Cotton had a similar constitution. In neither instance was there any attempt to cut out the dead wood. Since in many cases too high a price had been paid for the individual companies in order to persuade them to come together, the groups very rapidly ran into trouble and reorganization became imperative. In 1902, a committee was set up under Otto Phillipi, a German who had had much to do with making Coats efficient, to give Calico Printers a less cumbrous management structure. It duly recommended a small board of six to eight, with an executive of two to four members. Thereafter, the closure of mills began. A similar reorganization was carried out at English Sewing Cotton, which was by then losing money heavily.

In cotton, the aim was to merge with competitors so as to check price-cutting. In iron and steel, similar processes were at work. The alliance between the two tube-making firms of A. J. Stewart and Menzies and Lloyd and Lloyd in 1902 was expressly for the purpose of 'the extinction of competition'. There was also a series of mergers aimed at achieving vertical integration from the raw material through to the finished product. John Brown of Sheffield, which had already bought coal and iron mines in the 1870s, took over the Clydebank Engineering and Shipbuilding Company in 1899. Cammells, another Sheffield steel firm

[1] H. W. Macrosty, *The Trust Movement in British Industry*. 1907. p. xi.

with hematite mines in Cumberland, merged in 1903 with Lairds, the pioneer iron shipbuilders in Birkenhead. In 1897 a third Sheffield company, Vickers, which had a steel and armaments business, moved into naval shipbuilding by buying the Naval Construction and Armaments Company in Barrow and the Maxim-Nordenfelt Gun Company of Erith. In 1902 it took over Napier, which had interests in both engineering and shipbuilding.

Some mergers took place in industries where there was little or no foreign competition. For example, Wallpaper Manufacturers was a combination of firms with ninety-eight per cent of the market, and Associated Portland Cement brought together thirty-one firms in the cement business; both were formed in 1900. There was one merger which resulted directly from the threat of powerful competition from abroad. In 1901, the giant American Tobacco Company had taken over Ogdens and threatened to launch a massive campaign to capture a major share of the British market. Within a month, thirteen British companies had banded together to form Imperial Tobacco. A bitter price war began between the two groups, but in 1902 a compromise was reached by which Ogdens became part of Imperial, which was given a monopoly of the British and Irish market, while American Tobacco was to be freed from any competition by Imperial in the United States. A separate company, British-American Tobacco, was set up to handle the export business of both concerns in the rest of the world: American Tobacco had both a controlling shareholding and twelve of the eighteen directors of the new company. The arrangement was not long-lived because American Tobacco fell foul of the anti-trust laws in the United States and was ordered to divest itself of its interest in BAT.

It is interesting to note, parenthetically, that American capital investment in Britain started as early as 1856, when five Americans set up a vulcanized rubber factory in Edinburgh, but it was not until the 1880s that U.S. money began to arrive on any significant scale. Much of it went into the electrical industry. Then, in 1911, Ford began assembling cars at a plant in Manchester; Woolworths opened their first British shop in 1909; and both Heinz and Kodak were well established before the First World War. By 1914, somewhere between $75m. and $100m. of American capital had been invested in Britain. The first example of action by the British Government to thwart a possible American take-over came in 1902, when Cunard was given a loan of £2.6m. and was also promised an annual subsidy of £150,000.

There were also mergers in a wide variety of other industries. In chemicals, forty-nine firms which had kept to the outdated Leblanc method of alkali production came together in United Alkali as a last-ditch effort to combat Brunner Mond. Brunner Mond itself began a long series of absorptions in 1895. Guest Keen, with interests in steel and nuts and bolts joined up in 1902 with the Midlands screw manufacturing firm of Nettlefolds (in which Joseph Chamberlain had taken an active part before retiring in the 1870s to devote himself to politics). In 1894 William Lever, the Bolton grocer who had set up the soap business of Lever Brothers nine years earlier, began to take over some of his smaller competitors and in 1901 Lever Brothers became a public company with a capital of £1m. Lever then tried to bring together the ten principal soap manufacturers and, though he failed, by 1911 he had taken over all but two of them. To secure his sources of supply, he also acquired plantations in the Solomon Islands and the Congo. By 1913 the capital of Lever Brothers had risen to £30m.

A steady process of amalgamation also took place in service industries. In 1870 there were still 130 railway companies, but by 1914 only fourteen groups were left and they had reached a working understanding. A series of mergers between joint-stock banks began in the 1880s and 1890s, partly to keep pace with the growth in the size of industry; in the eleven years from 1891 to 1902 there were 114 amalgamations. In 1884 Lloyds came to London, where the Westminster and the National Provincial had both been for some time. They were followed seven years later by the Birmingham and Midland, and in 1896 Barclays was formed by the union of fifteen banks, many of them of Quaker origin.

The shape of modern British industry began to emerge in a variety of other ways. In 1897 Marcus Samuel set up the Shell Transport and Trading Company to supply, transport, store and sell oil in the Far East. The 'Shell' soon found itself at war with the Royal Dutch Petroleum Company and in 1907 the two companies merged, with Royal Dutch taking a sixty per cent controlling interest. In 1909, the forerunner of British Petroleum was founded under the name of the Anglo-Persian Oil Company, and in 1914 Winston Churchill persuaded the British Government to invest £2m. in the new venture to ensure a source of oil under British control. The General Electric Company began life as an electrical wholesaler in London during the 1880s, built its first factory in 1888, made its first commercial electric lamp in 1895 and became a public company in 1900. Courtaulds was floated in 1913, when it had already begun to make huge profits out of rayon.

The period between 1870 and 1914 also saw the growth of multiple stores which, with the exception of W. H. Smith, had been rare before 1870. Jesse Boot started his chain of chemists' shops and began the manufacture of pharmaceuticals for them in the 1880s; in 1896, he had thirty-one shops, by 1913 well over five hundred. J. Lyons was floated in 1894; Home and Colonial in 1895, Lipton in 1898 – both had over five hundred shops by the early years of the new century. The Co-operatives, too, flourished, with turnover multiplying four times to £80m. in the thirty years before the First War. By 1914, Marks and Spencer had 145 shops in its chain.

Nevertheless, despite these amalgamations, British industry in 1914 was still composed predominantly of small companies; the scale of enterprise was increasing, but only slowly. For example, only twenty-nine companies quoted on the London Stock Exchange on 2 January 1900 had Ordinary shares which were valued at more than £1m. Even in 1919 (the valuation was made on 1 January) there were still only twenty-two companies quoted on the market whose issued capital was valued at more than £5m. Only eight were worth more than £10m.; British-American Tobacco was comfortably the largest, valued at £40,850,000.[1]

As for the control of businesses, some areas of British industry were largely in the hands of joint-stock companies by the time war came: they controlled most of the major units in iron and steel, coal and heavy engineering, virtually all the banks and all the larger breweries, and they were dominant in soap, tobacco and in many parts of textiles. Nonetheless in 1914 roughly eighty per cent of all British companies were still private and the typical unit of control remained the small family business. The capital demands of industry were certainly growing, but very often they did not outpace the fortunes of their owners – with help from the banks – before 1914. Nor were death duties the force they later became in driving proprietors to seek public money. Of all the securities quoted on the Stock Exchange in 1913, only eight per cent consisted of shares in British industry.

[1] The runners-up were Coats (£33.19m.); Imperial Tobacco (£29m.); Guinness (£17.25m.); Courtaulds (£16m.); Vickers (£15.54m.); Brunner Mond (£15.42m.) and P and O Steam Navigation (£13.60m.). Information provided by de Zoete and Gorton. The companies were those in the Breweries, Commercial and Industrial, Iron, Coal and Steel and Shipping Sections.

Just as the amalgamation of companies did not proceed at the same pace as in the United States, so too price-fixing and other methods of controlling the market were adopted with less enthusiasm. Rigging the market loses some of its attractions when the market is unprotected and when there is such a multiplicity of small companies, but there also existed a strong belief in competition at the beginning of the period. As prices drifted steadily downwards and profits were squeezed, how-ever, this faith was considerably shaken and in 1890 Alfred Marshall could speak of the 'evil savour' into which the word competition had fallen.[1] This was the background to the spread during the period of a series of defensive agreements and combinations between manu-facturers in a bid to temper competition and control the market; they were also thought expedient as a method of avoiding mergers.

There were, of course, examples of collusion between manufacturers long before 1870. Price-fixing agreements had existed in parts of the iron trade since the first quarter of the nineteenth century, and similar arrangements became much more widespread in the latter part of the century: William Lever said in 1906 that there had been a working agreement on soap prices for the previous thirty years. Again, in the 1870s a Thread Association was set up, but proved to be a flop in its attempt to rig markets because of persistent under-cutting by some producers. At the same time groups of shippers began to fix freight rates through what became known as the conference system and by 1908 a series of conferences controlled every route sailed by British ships with the exception of the North Atlantic. There were also plenty of gentlemen's agreements.

But anti-competitive pacts did not get strongly under way until the 1890s; a US Governmental Committee of 1901 singled out thirty-five British combinations for investigation and found that only two of them had existed before 1890. One of the most notorious formed thereafter was an agreement which began to operate in the metallic bedstead trade in 1901. It embraced a wide range of products and covered five hundred masters and 20,000 workpeople. The basis of the agreement was an alliance between masters and men by which the masters would employ only union labour, the men would only work for employers in the masters' association, and if any firms sold below the agreed list price, his *workers* were to be called out on strike.

One of the vehicles which could be used to control competition was the trade association. A network of such associations began to develop

[1] Alfred Marshall, *Principles of Political Economy*, London, 8th ed., p. 6.

during the 1880s and by 1914 there were a considerable number. They were, essentially, instruments for maintaining the status quo and as such a powerful barrier to rationalization within an industry. They made a particular appeal to the small and inefficient, who were happy to join provided that their domestic markets were protected from invasion by their British competitors, and that prices were fixed at levels which gave satisfactory profits. In this way, sub-marginal enterprises were allowed to carry on business at the expense of the more efficient. After the war, Lord Snowden was to say of the trade association: 'Its purpose in the first place is to keep alive uneconomic concerns which never would be able to stand or survive against the competition of more powerful rivals.' By that time, there were hundreds of trade associations fulfilling precisely that purpose.

Yet, in the boom years before 1914, an optimist might conceivably have taken the view that the slowing-down of growth in the years after 1873 merely represented a (rather lengthy) pause in Britain's progress. Even in 1913 Britain was still – though by a very narrow margin – the greatest exporting nation in the world. She appeared to have gone some way towards completing a remarkable recovery.

Beneath the prosperity, however, there lay problems. Both cotton and coal were over-manned. Furthermore, Britain's export trade was increasingly dependent on markets in the Empire and the under-developed nations, and her salesmen had not made sufficient impact on the rich (and protected) markets of America and Europe.

A number of other factors, more difficult to measure in their influence and many of them rooted in the nature of British society, may have had an impact on Britain's industrial progress. To begin with, she lagged behind her rivals in education. Shadwell registered the fact that by 1870 there were $7\frac{1}{2}$m. children in the State-financed schools of America, whereas in Britain there was accommodation for less than two million in the country's eight thousand-odd voluntary schools.[1] There was the same discrepancy at a higher level forty years later. In 1913, there were 9,000 university students in Britain compared with 60,000 in Germany, although it should be added that this period saw a rapid spread of technical education in Britain. There were four graduates in German chemical works for every one in similar English plants.

Britain was also loath to accept that the teaching of business skills had a place in higher education. The first American graduate business school was set up in 1881 with the foundation of the Wharton School of

[1] *Op. cit.*, vol. 2, p. 407.

Finance and Commerce in the University of Pennsylvania. Harvard decided to substitute a business school for a school of diplomacy and government service which had originally been planned, and in 1908 the Harvard Graduate School of Business Administration was established. By 1920 there were business schools at fifty American universities; Britain did not have a single business school until the 1960s. It is true that the American institutions gained in academic prestige only slowly, but their foundation did reflect a growing interest in professional management, in the solution of business problems by rational analysis and in the use of scientific techniques to increase productivity and profit.

Nor, indeed, did either business or the acquisition of individual fortunes through business have in Britain the prestige which they enjoyed in the United States. In America, the simplest method of acquiring social status was to make money, and profit-making was the most respected of activities, while in Britain, the way to high social status was – and in some respects still is – through the ownership of land. The social progress of many businessmen has been described as 'shirt-sleeves to hunting jackets in three generations'.[1] The mere making of money was not worshipped as a goal in itself, even when taxation was low. The biographer of Sir Robert Waley Cohen, who joined Shell in the early years, makes a revealing comparison between Shell's founder, Marcus Samuel and his Dutch rival Henri Deterding, who became the first boss of Royal Dutch/Shell. He says that 'with Marcus, the making of money was a minor consideration, a means to an end which was exalted'. Deterding, on the other hand, was 'never misled by ideals or principles from the goal of maximum profitability'.[2] Undoubtedly there were Englishmen like Deterding, and Dutchmen like Samuel, but the description does reflect something of the nature of a society where money, far from being a measure of worth, was something not to be spoken about.

The higher orders of society had been taught that there were better things to do with their time than to go into business to make money; building and running an empire were more congenial and meritorious. These attitudes did nothing to help reverse Britain's relative industrial decline in the world. As a leading historian of the professions has put it: '. . . the fundamental antipathy induced by public school education to

[1] Landes, *op. cit.*, p. 563.
[2] Robert Henriques, *Sir Robert Waley Cohen, 1877–1952*, Secker and Warburg, London, 1966, p. 100.

everything commercial made it fatally easy for men from public schools to miss the central fact of England's power – that without her industrial strength, let her empire be never so large, she was nothing more than an over-populated island off the coast of north-west Europe.'[1]

[1] W. J. Reader, *Professional Men*, Weidenfeld and Nicolson, London, 1966, p. 205.

CHAPTER 2

The Struggling Economy
1914–1939

The war of 1914–18 had severely disruptive effects on the British economy, not least because of her dependence on international trade. Imports soared, exports slumped: the sale of cotton goods abroad, for example, was halved in the war years. Britain's financial strength was also undermined; she sold perhaps fifteen per cent of her long-term foreign assets during the war, and ended it with a short-term debt of £800m. and an even larger long-term debt to the United States – for long periods the sole source of supply for much vital equipment. As a result, Britain and America exchanged their pre-war roles; by 1918, it was Britain who was the debtor, America the creditor. London had ceased to be the financial capital of the world, and the proud sterling had lost much of its power and stability.

The war also had a serious impact on both the strength and deployment of British industry. The shortages (and higher prices) which developed as factories changed over to war production encouraged other countries to manufacture for themselves goods which they had previously bought from Britain – India produced more of her own cotton cloth – and gave competitors who were not so heavily committed to the conflict an advantage which they were not slow to seize. The United States (which did not declare war until 1917) took over British markets in South America and the Japanese moved into Britain's most important market, India. Again, while the American motor industry continued to expand rapidly (the production of civilian cars was never halted), the British motor industry was stopped in its tracks at a time when it seemed ready to take off. Between 1913 and 1921, according to one estimate, the total output of US manufacturing industry rose by twenty-two per cent, that of Japan by seventy-six per cent;

Britain's output, on the other hand, actually fell – by 7½ per cent.

The effects of the war on industry were, however, far from being wholly negative. It advanced knowledge of the techniques of mass production and created a far greater willingness to rationalize factory lay-outs; brought the introduction of large numbers of machine tools because of labour shortages; led to an increase in the rate of scientific and technological discoveries and created virtually new industries – such as radio communications – which were to prosper when peace came; and stimulated the production of goods, such as dyes and ball-bearings, which Britain had previously imported.

One of its other consequences was the rapid extension of Government intervention in the economy. Its spending rose from £192m. in 1914 to £1,328m. in 1918, at 1914 prices; new Ministries were set up and the number of civil servants doubled; raw materials allocated and food rationed; industries like coal passed temporarily into the hands of the Government; firms like Vickers had limits set on their profits; Government encouragement of trade associations (easier to deal with than a mass of individual companies) led, among other things, to a diminution of competition.

The war was soon followed by a short-lived boom. Industry re-plenished its stocks and all the pent-up demand and purchasing power of an inflationary war economy was released; exports, too, soared. In 1920, steel output and the new tonnage being built in British shipyards were both a third higher than they had been in 1913. The expansive mood of the time showed itself also in a phenomenal increase in the demand for new capital, as industry geared itself up for rapid and prosperous growth. In the eighteen months after March 1919, when wartime controls on capital-raising were relaxed, no less than £400m. was subscribed for new issues. Investors rushed to share in the boom and company promoters reaped an easy harvest; in 1919 alone, sixty-two cotton companies with an *original* share capital of £2.67m. were sold for almost six times that price. The same kind of speculative mania was evident in other industries.

It all seemed ample justification for the optimism which many businessmen appear to have felt in planning for the peace. Vickers, the armaments giant which had been so central to the war effort, was typical. A year before the Armistice, it had set up a Peace Products Committee to examine the prospects for everything from locomotives to pianos; the committee addressed itself – among matters of larger con-cern – to the merits of 'boy rabbits (squeaking)' and 'girl rabbits (non-squeaking)'. Meanwhile Vickers' subsidiary company, Wolseley, was planning to produce a high-class car, priced at £800, which would see off any American competitor. But although its factories turned over smoothly enough to ships and locomotives, to wooden toys and washing machines and furniture, this was not enough. So Vickers paid almost £13m. for the Metropolitan Railway Carriage and Wagon company, which had already bought out the Westinghouse electrical interests in Britain. It was to prove a disappointing investment.[1]

Nor was it the only company with grandiose visions. William Lever, (since 1917, the first Lord Leverhulme), expressed his confidence in the future by making a series of sweeping acquisitions. In 1919 and 1920 he paid a high price for several of his leading competitors in the soap trade and an even higher one (£8m.) for the Niger Company's West African empire. In the Niger's case, he did not even bother to investigate the accounts.[2]

In the summer of 1920, however, when stocks had been rebuilt and plant replaced, the pressure of demand evaporated: a fall in exports started the slide, cancellation of orders became widespread and industry was brought brutally to its senses. Within twelve months, the tonnage under construction in British shipyards halved from 3.3 to 1.6m.; steel output sagged; and Morris Motors, which had produced 276 cars and chassis in September 1920, turned out only seventy-four in the following January. 1921 was a bitter year: by June, twenty-three per cent were out of work. The level of unemployment was seldom to fall below ten per cent for the remainder of the decade.

It was a grim beginning for a country which was still desperately hoping to recreate the world as it had been before 1914, a world in which she had been a great international money-lender and trader. It was a hope which became ever more illusory. In 1922 the Americans again raised their tariff barriers high – by 1929 the average level of duties in the United States was twenty-nine per cent – and other nations followed. At the same time galloping inflation was taking hold in Europe, and by 1923 the price of a newspaper in Germany was 200,000,000,000 marks. The chaos of currencies and the swift spread of protection were both anathema to a nation which aspired to be at the centre of the financial world and which still depended so heavily on its export trade.

In 1925, as an effort to recreate a more stable framework for world

[1] J. D. Scott, *Vickers*, Weidenfeld and Nicolson, London, 1962, p. 167.
[2] Charles Wilson, *History of Unilever*, Cassell, London, 1954, vol. 1, p. 253.

trade, Britain returned to the gold standard – suspended during the war – with the pound sterling back at its pre-war level of $4.86. One result of making the pound dearer in terms of foreign currencies was that Britain's coal exporters found it even harder to do business in a world in which there was already a glut; and in some export markets, British salesmen had to work with a currency which was almost certainly over-valued against governments which deliberately under-valued their own.

Nor was Britain any more successful in persuading others that free trade was the road to prosperity: her efforts to achieve tariff disarmament were fruitless. As a result, she herself resorted to an extension of the existing import duties and put tariffs on a limited range of goods, including rayon, electrical parts, commercial vehicles and tyres. Even so, by 1929 her tariff level averaged only five per cent and she was still essentially a free trade nation. Only when other countries had resorted to massive protection and her major export industries had all but collapsed did Britain finally abandon free trade in 1932.

The boom of 1919–20, among other things, served to aggravate the problems of the basic industries; encouraging them to take on more labour, it added to their embarrassments when markets began to decline. The growth in world demand for coal (roughly four per cent per annum in the years before 1913) became negligible and while consumption at home held up well enough during the 1920s, British exports fell away sharply from 87m. tons to 48m., and total production from 287m. tons in 1913 to 258m. in 1929. Cotton, too, declined disastrously: in 1929, the export of cotton piece goods was precisely half what it had been in 1913. India, protected now, trebled her own production and the Japanese, paying wages less than a fifth of British rates, had captured almost twenty per cent of the world market by 1929. The markets for British steel and ships also continued to decline: in some years, only thirty-five per cent of shipbuilding capacity was in use. So great was Britain's commitment to these depressed industries that the economy did not fully reflect the boom which was going on in the rest of the world from 1927 to 1929.

The 1920s, however, brought only modest changes in the structure of these basic industries; for a long time, their leaders talked as if the slump in trade was merely a temporary setback. Far too many, indeed, preferred to stay in their trenches until the worst was over and although there was plenty of talk about modernization and rationalization, little action followed.

The coal owners, struggling to remain competitive and often beset by the problem of seams which were becoming both narrower and deeper, preferred to reduce costs by cutting wages rather than by spending money on mechanization; in 1927, not much more than twenty per cent of British coal was cut by machine, compared with seventy per cent in America. The owners also resisted the recommendation of the Samuel Commission of 1925 that inefficient pits should be eliminated; at that time there were 1,480 enterprises, only sixty-nine of which had an output of a million tons a year. In America, by contrast, the average *mine* was producing almost that amount; while in Germany, where centralization had been carried still further during the 1920s in the so-called 'rationalization' of industry, eight trusts accounted for fifty-seven per cent of coal output and ninety-five per cent of steel output by 1930.

The cotton industry was even more fragmented – there were 1,900 firms in the spinning and weaving sections alone – and scarcely more amenable to change. Over-capacity was so great that the spinners, for all their efforts, could not even fix prices successfully; there were always mills desperate enough for business to sell at lower rates. Towards the end of the 1920s, the Bank of England was asked to finance a reorganization of the industry; the result, the formation of the Lancashire Cotton Corporation, did lead to the closure of some mills.

The armament companies which had abandoned current management dogma by widespread diversification of their businesses in the early post-war years, also found themselves in considerable difficulty. Vickers, for example, paid no dividend on its Ordinary capital from 1923 to 1926 and eventually had to reduce its capital and write down its Ordinary shares from £1 to 6s 8d. Other engineers with a preponderance of business at the heavy end of the trade found themselves struggling. English Electric (formed in 1918 by an alliance of four companies) also wrote down its capital and did not really begin to prosper until the years before the 1939 war when the Government asked it to go into aircraft production.

The growth of newer industries to some extent compensated for the losses of the heavy brigade. Rayon, many branches of electrical engineering (including radio), motor vehicles (car production more than doubled between 1923 and 1926) and chemicals moved ahead rapidly. As capital investment in them increased, new techniques and economies of scale brought higher productivity and lower prices; the price of cars fell by an average of twenty-five per cent between 1923 and 1929. In the motor industry in particular, there was also much rationalization during the 1920s: by 1929, eighty of the 130 types of car on the market in 1920 had disappeared and Morris and Austin between them held roughly sixty per cent of the market. By the end of the decade, these new industries were poised to exploit any expansion of home demand.

It was the older industries which felt the severest impact of the global depression which struck in 1929; between 1929 and 1931, coal exports fell by a third, iron and steel by more than half, cotton by half and by 1932 Britain's total export trade had been halved. The overall impact of the slump was nothing like so severe as in the United States, however. The fall in industrial production there was twice as great as in Britain but nevertheless this fall in British export earnings gradually affected home demand and the unemployed rose to almost three million in 1931.

By the end of 1932, however, the first signs of a recovery based on the home market were beginning to appear.[1] The most notable features of this were the increase in house-building (three million houses were built during the 1930s) and the rapid progress of the newer industries. The housing boom was helped forward by a Bank Rate which had been lowered to two per cent; and building firms like Wates, Wimpey, Laing and Taylor Woodrow, which were to be among the giants of the post-war world, established themselves during the 1930s largely by successful speculative developments in the South of England (Laing and Taylor Woodrow had come to London in the 1920s). But the demand for houses (as for much else) was largely stimulated by the fact that the price of food had come down by about a quarter between 1927 and 1933; this meant that those men who were still in work had more money to spare.

Demand for building materials (bricks, cement, metal window-frames) and for household equipment and services – consumer durables, household utensils and electricity – also increased rapidly and firms like the General Electric Company became increasingly profitable as the demand for electric cookers and other products shot up. GEC, which had a capital of £3m. in 1918, more than trebled it by 1935.

[1] The bias towards foreign investment also disappeared. Many foreign bonds defaulted in the depression years and thereafter political uncertainty and exchange controls made lending abroad less attractive. In any case, the Government put restrictions on overseas issue to try to protect sterling. As a result, only twenty per cent of the capital raised on the British market went for overseas issues in 1932–6 compared with forty-one per cent in the later 1920s. The amount invested on the Stock Exchange in foreign bonds was lower in 1933 than it had been in 1903.

Similarly, car production doubled between 1932 and 1938 and six producers – Austin, Ford, Morris, Standard, Vauxhall and what was to become the Rootes Group – controlled ninety per cent of the market.[1] The radio industry, rayon, electricity supply (the demand for which rose by over eighty per cent) and chemicals (particularly paint) all made spectacular progress.

Curiously, the 1930s did not see a really substantial rise in the level of retail sales, but this did not prevent some store chains from expanding rapidly; by 1939, Marks and Spencer had 234 stores, Sainsbury two hundred while Jack Cohen (who had started trading in a Hackney market in 1919) had a hundred shops under the name of Tesco. There were a number of mergers: one of the largest came in 1929 when Liptons, Meadow Dairy, Maypole and Home and Colonial joined to form Allied Suppliers.

As the recovery gathered pace, it spread to some of the older industries, notably iron and steel. The expansion of the motor industry and demand for items like metal window-frames played their part, while a new high tariff and agreement with European producers, restricting their imports to Britain, at least ensured that it could reap the benefit of what was happening in the home market. The aircraft industry, for years held back by the fact that (unlike America)[2] Britain had never provided a really substantial base, also began to boom – partly, but not entirely, due to rearmament. Companies like Hawker, which had built motor cycles to stay out of the red during the slump in business after the First War, expanded rapidly; in 1934, it took over Glosters to give it additional production space and then, in the following year, joined forces with Armstrong-Siddeley (which had already acquired A. V. Roe) to form Hawker Siddeley.

Unfortunately the recovery did not extend in anything like the same degree to many of the older industries; by 1937, coal exports were scarcely above their worst depression levels and total production was still going down, while sales of cotton piece goods abroad was less than half what it had been in 1929. The painful process of contraction therefore continued. From the end of the 1920s, coal owners had been discussing and sometimes operating agreements which – through the regulation of sales by quota and the gradual extension of central selling

[1] Rising car sales was one reason for the prosperity of international oil companies like Shell, whose production went up almost six-fold between 1920 and 1938.

[2] The output of the American industry, on the other hand, rose from sixty aircraft in 1924 to 5,500 in 1929.

– attempted to control the market; the Government was happy to sanction these agreements and the Coal Mines Act of 1930 facilitated their operation. But, although productivity improved as mechanization spread and some uneconomic pits were closed, the industry was in an appalling mess by 1939, with hundreds of small, barely-profitable enterprises. The Government, though desiring reform, took no action decisive enough to achieve it before war came: by then, it seemed unlikely that the industry would ever attract sufficient private capital to redeem it.

In steel, there was also little in the way of reorganization. Indeed, the tariff (which reached fifty per cent at one time) had the effect of freezing the industry in its existing mould, still with far too many small plants, each making a wide variety of products on too small a scale. The industry was riddled with price-fixing agreements and rates were set on the basis of the least efficient producer; from 1937 uneconomic plants were actually subsidized by a levy on steel output on the understanding that they would be closed as soon as new productive capacity was created. There was a fair amount of new investment, but far too high a proportion went into small-scale improvements to existing plants. The output of the average British blast furnace in 1937 was 83,000 tons a year, compared with 210,000 and 123,000 tons in the United States and Germany. Steel remained a high-cost industry.

In other sectors of industry, substantial changes of structure took place between the wars and something like the shape of modern business began to emerge. Large numbers of family companies sold out to the public (in whole or in part) and there was a marked increase in economic concentration. By 1939, amalgamations had created a range of businesses which compared well in terms of sheer size with those of any country outside the United States.

In many ways the most important of the mergers which took place between the wars was the alliance which produced Imperial Chemical Industries in 1926. This brought together four companies, Nobel Industries, Brunner Mond, the British Dyestuffs Corporation and United Alkali, and created the biggest company in British industry with an initial issued share capital of £56.8m. Its basic business was in chemicals, explosives and dyestuffs, but since each of the constituent parts had diversified to a lesser or greater extent, ICI also found itself producing gas mantles, motor bicycles, zip fasteners and locomotive fire-boxes.

One of the motives which led to the amalgamation was a fear that a big American or German chemical combine might step in with a bid for one or other of the companies: IG Farben seems to have had designs on British Dyestuffs, and Brunner Mond was actually talking to the Germans about some kind of joint arrangement. It was also feared that American Du Pont might make an offer for Nobel. Harry McGowan (later Lord McGowan), the boss of Nobel, heard that Sir Alfred Mond and some of his directors had gone to New York and would not be back for some time; he thereupon pursued Mond to New York and the scheme which created ICI was drawn up on board the *Aquitania* on her way back to London.

There was also another sort of logic behind the merger. During the war both Mond and McGowan had decided that, compared with the American and German competition, their companies were far too narrowly based and that the future lay in sensible diversification on a solid national base. ICI satisfied both these requirements, and its basic aim was to exploit the markets not only of Britain but also of the Empire; as its name suggests, it was an expression of latter-day imperialism. If it controlled the Empire, Du Pont and IG Farben could take the rest.

Neither McGowan nor Mond was in favour of a loose-knit federation such as had characterized so many British amalgamations and McGowan, in particular, was an apostle of extreme centralization. The result was that, in the words of the present ICI chairman, Sir Peter Allen, ICI was 'put together like an atomic bomb'. Six executive directors were appointed to run the business from the centre, and a massive new headquarters building was begun at Millbank; by 1935 it had a staff of 1,250, very large indeed for those days. After Mond died in 1930, McGowan became in effect an absolute monarch.

Talks were quickly begun with the American and German combines. After discussions with IG Farben had come to nothing, ICI turned to Du Pont and in 1928 made an agreement for patent and process-sharing. The effective result of this agreement was that ICI stayed out of the United States while Du Pont stayed out of the Empire; there were joint ventures in Canada and Latin America. The arrangement lasted until 1952 when the Federal Trade Commission, which had been looking into the situation since 1938, ordered Du Pont to break off the relationship. Meanwhile, ICI had come to an agreement with IG Farben and Europe was left to it and to Solvay. The Farben agreement lasted until 1958.

With its monopolies in explosives, soda ash and chlorine among other things, its international agreements and the benefit of high tariffs in the

1930s, ICI grew steadily; sales increased from £28.8m. in 1927 to £62.1m. in 1938. Nor did the company ever have to go to the market for capital in this period; expansion was financed entirely out of profits.

Other inter-war mergers did not lead to anything like the same degree of centralization. Guest Keen and Nettlefolds, which expanded its existing interests in steel and bought its way into motor components, was run in an extremely decentralized way; it remained a series of local autonomies loosely held together, many of them controlled by family interests. The business was co-ordinated by a body known as the Birmingham Committee which met once a month in the Queen's Hotel, and the individual companies held their own cash balances until long after the Second War. Similarly, the alliance between two tube-producers and two tube-users which created Tube Investments in 1919 produced what was little more than a holding company; the two tube producers were still rivals and left to run as completely separate businesses. Again, Hawker Siddeley remained effectively (even in the early years after the Second World War) a federation of independent units which competed fiercely with each other under the umbrella of a single financial control.

The other international giant created between the wars, Unilever, was very different from ICI both in its origins and in its markets. By the end of the war, its English root, Lever Brothers, had already gained a dominant share of the soap trade in Britain – Leverhulme controlled perhaps sixty per cent of the market by the early 1920s. Lever had also decided to go into the margarine business in the early years of the war, when there was a danger that butter supplies from Denmark and margarine shipments from Holland would be cut off: the same raw materials, oils and fats, could be used to produce both soap and margarine. After the war, the acquisition spree on which Leverhulme embarked – some of his purchases were so bizarre that the company's official historian says they can be explained only by 'economic madness'[1] – led to considerable anxiety on the part of Lever Brothers' bankers. Leverhulme then called in an outside accountant, D'Arcy Cooper, to placate the banks and help sort out the mess.

Cooper became vice-chairman in 1923 and then chairman after Leverhulme died in 1925. They were difficult years. Lever Brothers paid no dividend on its Ordinary shares in 1925 and 1926; in soap, it

[1] Wilson, *op. cit.*, p. 261. Leverhulme's personal purchases included Wall's sausage and ice-cream company and a chain of retail fish shops, known as MacFisheries. These were to help shape the future of a Unilever yet unborn.

was faced with bitter competition from the American Palmolive company and, in margarine, from the Dutch companies of Jurgens and van den Berghs. But Cooper successfully sold off several of the unprofitable businesses, sales of soap increased and by 1929 the company had made a remarkable recovery. In that year, Cooper extended Lever's African trading interests by taking over the African and Eastern Trade Corporation, joining it with the Niger to form the United Africa Company. By 1929 Lever Brothers was indeed in rather better financial trim than its two Dutch rivals, who had already come together to form the Margarine Union in 1927.

In their products, the two sides did not overlap to any really sizeable extent. The Dutch made soap, but concentrated on margarine and other edible fats, while Lever Brothers, though it was in the margarine business, was primarily a soap manufacturer. On the other hand, both were in the market for the same raw materials. Talks began between the two sides when the Dutch made an effort to buy Lever's margarine business, adding that they were quite willing to get out of soap as part of the bargain. The talks then became more ambitious in scope and in September 1929 the two decided to join forces – 'they fell into each other's arms,' said Lord Cole, the present chairman of Unilever Ltd, 'like a couple of exhausted boxers.'

The new alliance was huge; it had an authorized capital of £130m. and an issued capital of almost £100m. In structure it maintained a perfect dualism; two holding companies were set up, Unilever NV in Holland and Unilever Ltd in Britain – one joint company would have been taxed in both countries – and the Boards of the two companies were to appoint a Special Committee to act as an inner Cabinet for the organization as a whole. Initially, the Special Committee had eight members: four Dutch, four British. In the matter of dividends, too, the Dutch and British shareholders were to receive equal amounts.

The vast and dispersed Unilever empire – plantations, African trading companies, whaling fleets, oil mills, soap and margarine factories, grocery stores, fish shops, ice cream plants – was, in the words of Lord Heyworth, Unilever Ltd's chairman from 1942 to 1960, 'an awful dog's breakfast'. It was one of the Special Committee's jobs to make sense of the alliance.

Significant mergers were also taking place in other areas of business. In 1914, there were still thirty-eight joint stock banks, but, by a series of amalgamations at the end of the war, five – the Midland, Westminster, Lloyds, Barclays and the National Provincial – dominated the field thereafter. In shipping, six lines controlled a third of the business by the 1920s. P and O took over British India in 1914, which gave it a total capital of £15m. and a new chairman, James Lyle Mackay, Lord Inchcape. Subsequently, a buying spree gave it, among other things, a stake in the Orient Line, which had taken an early interest in aviation through a holding in Imperial Airways.

American investment in British industry continued to grow steadily and by 1940 amounted to $540m. Some of it seems to have been fairly tentative at first. Vauxhall was taken over by General Motors as an experiment in manufacturing overseas;[1] it involved an investment of only $2½m., small beer for a company which by 1920 already employed a capital of $575m. Other companies were encouraged to start manufacturing in Britain by the new tariff barriers; both Goodyear and Firestone, for example, began making tyres in Britain in 1928. American investment would certainly have been even greater but for the impact of the Depression in the United States. In 1920, for example, Boots was bought out by L. K. Liggett, the founder of the American Rexall Drug chain, but in 1933 the company repatriated its shareholding and the Boots shares were eventually sold back to the public.

The period between the wars saw the Government either support, reorganize or replace private enterprise in a number of industries. This did not represent any revolution in attitude, since the Government had already put money into individual companies before the war, and had virtually nationalized the telephone service in 1912 through the purchase of the principal telephone company. Its post-war interventions were generally still based on an attempt to make private industry more efficient rather than seeking to replace it.

It turned its attention first to the railways and by the Railways Act of 1921 reduced the remaining companies to four by a process of compulsory amalgamation. Thereafter, competition remained on a handful of services, but what emerged were basically four non-competing monopolies. There was also an elaborate Government control over both fares and freight rates, and no general increase in either between 1920 and 1937. This was hardly the kind of environment in which to develop a commercially-minded railway management, desperately needed when passenger traffic began to decline after the First War and when, in the later 1920s, competition from the bus and the lorry began noticeably to increase. Too little was done to prevent the decline of railway businesses: not enough uneconomic lines were closed.

[1] Alfred Sloan had looked first at Austin, now part of British Leyland.

The Government also took a hand in the reorganization of both the electricity and air transport industries. The development of electricity in Britain had been painfully slow, partly because the system of generation was costly, old-fashioned and in the hands of too many small concerns. By an Act of 1926, the Central Electricity Board was set up to own and operate a national transmission system known as the Grid. The Board was soon spending large sums of money – to the benefit of the electrical industry – and by 1933 the Grid was completed at a cost of £27m. In 1935 it confounded its critics by earning a trading surplus of £1m.

The Government first began to subsidize the pioneer air lines in 1921, and thereafter they were effectively under its thumb. In 1924, four of them – including Daimler Airways and Handley Page Transport – were encouraged to merge on the promise of exclusive backing from the Government in the shape of a £1m. subsidy spread over ten years. The new company, Imperial Airways, was thus created before the German and French national airlines, Lufthansa (1926) and Air France (1933). The part-time chairman of Imperial was Sir Eric Geddes, who was also chairman of Dunlop. In 1934, Imperial was given a substantial Government contract to carry mail, but in general tended to concentrate on the Empire routes; certainly on the Continental services it lost ground to private competitors and in particular to Hillman Airways. In 1935 Hillmans became the nucleus of British Airways, and, two years later, it too received a Government subsidy. Imperial Airways came in for some sharp criticism and it was said that Sir Eric Geddes could not devote enough of his time to the airline. Eventually, in 1939, the Government decided to merge Imperial and British into a new, publicly-owned airline, the British Overseas Airways Corporation.

The Government, understandably perhaps at a time of depression, also gave its approval to a good deal of market-rigging in a wide range of British industries; restrictive practices flourished unchecked and competition disappeared. During the 1930s, indeed, many businessmen concentrated their energies not on cutting costs and improving efficiency, but on creating and operating restrictive schemes with the object of banishing competition. Many trade associations became cosy clubs for the protection of the small and inefficient. (In America, the same trends were evident in the early years of the New Deal, but thereafter businessmen suspected of monopolistic practices were again under attack from the Federal watchdogs.) The various sections of the electrical industry were organized into a number of price-fixing bodies

– in lamps, for example, there was a cartel which rigidly controlled both prices and output; in cement, there was a quota system to back up a long-standing price-fixing arrangement; in rayon, foreign competition was eliminated by a combination of high import duties and international alliances.

'A group of producers today,' wrote a contemporary historian, 'could exterminate all competitors with a programme of vicious price-cutting, rigid tying contracts, exclusive dealing agreements, resale price maintenance, deferred rebates and commercial boycotts; they could then proceed to exploit the public through price manipulation and restriction of output; and all the while not only would they be well within their legal rights, but they could successfully defend their policies in the Courts on consideration of public welfare.'[1]

The fact that the aim of most of the rings was not monopoly profits but comfortable collective survival did not prevent them from having a profound effect on British industry in the years after the 1939 war; there existed a whole generation of British businessmen who had very little idea what competition was, and after the war many of them who had absorbed the atmosphere of the inter-war years were in positions of high authority.

Britain entered the Second World War with an economy which was considerably less dependent on exports than it had been in 1914; whereas, then, the efforts of more than one worker in four had been devoted to production for export, in 1939 the proportion had fallen to one in eight. Between 1929 and 1937, the ratio of exports to national income fell from seventeen per cent to eleven per cent. Britain had also become increasingly dependent on the Empire; even the car industry did eighty-five per cent of its trade in imperial markets. On the other hand, she was a good deal less reliant on the older industries; although, in 1939, coal and textiles still accounted for thirty per cent of exports, the newer industries were beginning to restore the balance, with twenty per cent of sales abroad coming from machinery, vehicles and electrical goods. They were to be all the more important in Britain's battle for solvency after 1945.

[1] A. F. Lucas, *Industrial Reconstruction and the Control of Competition*, Longmans, Green, London, 1937, p. 352.

CHAPTER 3

The Battle for the Second Peace
1939–1969

The effects of the Second World War on Britain's economy were similar in nature to those of the First; but they left her even more vulnerable to the problems of the peace. Exports again fell sharply[1] and Britain was soon paying for overseas supplies either by accepting post-war claims against herself or by selling overseas investments. In February 1940 the Treasury compelled holders of American investments to surrender them against their market value in sterling, and then began to sell them in the United States.

Purchases from hard-currency countries were all the more expensive because, on the outbreak of war, the value of the pound in dollars had fallen by fourteen per cent, and when the Lend-Lease Act was passed by America in the spring of 1941, Britain's net gold and dollar reserves were all but exhausted. Under the new arrangements, Britain was supplied with about $27,000m. worth of goods, but although this colossal debt was eventually settled by a payment of only $800m., she ended the war having sold off £1,100m. of her external assets; increased her external debts by almost £3,000m.; and reduced her gold and dollar reserves by £150m.

The burdens of the war effort had also taken their toll of key industries and services. The railways had been badly run down, and so had iron and steel and electricity generating plant; the output of coal had fallen by twelve per cent; while the shipping industry, in particular, had suffered heavy losses – in the case of P. and O. no less than sixty per cent of its fleet. On the domestic front, three million families were living in bomb-damaged homes.

At the same time, the conflict had not been without its benefits.

[1] By 1945, they were less than forty per cent of their level in 1938.

Between 1936 and 1945, for example, the Government had spent over
£1,000m. on fixed capital for the munitions industry and both the new
factories and much of their machinery (machine tools, for example)
were serviceable for normal commercial production. Similarly, a substantial programme of re-equipment and modernization had been
undertaken in shipbuilding yards, mostly at the Government's expense.
In addition, large sums had been pumped into industry for defence-
inspired research and development projects and, in many cases, their
fruits were commercially exploited after the war. Rolls-Royce, for
example, which had taken a leading part in the development of the
'jet' engine, was also working on a version for commercial use from
1945 onwards and, as a result, held most of the world market in gas
turbines until the late 1950s. Other companies benefited from involvement in the development of radar.

The tremendous expansion which the war effort had called for –
Rolls' labour force grew from 8,000 in 1939 to 57,000 in 1945, its
factories to nine times their pre-war size – left considerable problems,
but at least the switch of manpower into the engineering industry had
directed labour into that sector of the economy which had grown
fastest before the war and which was to be at the heart of the export
drive thereafter: by the 1960s, the engineering industry as a whole
accounted for more than forty per cent of Britain's exports.

With the ending of the war, the struggle to rebuild the export trade
began; in the meantime, Britain was given yet another financial prop
in the shape of massive dollar loans from the United States and Canada.
Her exporters at least began with two major advantages – they had a
lead over the West Germans and Japanese, both still struggling to
recover their momentum, and they found themselves operating in a
sellers' market in many parts of the world. The result was that while
consumer demand at home was held back by a variety of controls –
strict quotas were set on sales of cars and Scotch – exports moved ahead
briskly. Between 1946 and 1948, car output doubled, from 219,162
to 412,290, and the boom even extended to shipbuilding and cotton.
By the end of 1948, exports were running at 147 per cent of their
volume in the last year before the war.

Despite this good start, confidence in sterling – as ever in these years –
was easily disturbed and a relatively small deterioration in Britain's
position produced a major exchange crisis. A mild recession in the
United States affected sales in North America and the first relaxation
of controls at home – the rationing of furniture and clothes was

substantially eased – held back exports still further. As a result, there was talk of British goods being over-priced and of the need for 'currency adjustment'. In the summer, pressure on the pound became intense and in September 1949 it was devalued by thirty per cent – from $4 to $2.80.

For a time, devaluation seemed to be paying off, but the outbreak of war in Korea, in the summer of 1950, helped blow Britain off course yet again. As the Americans began to stockpile, a world-wide scramble for raw materials developed and import prices rose by forty per cent in a year. The panic coincided with an increase in the inflow of goods from Europe as trade restrictions were lifted, and Britain's import bill for 1951 was £1,100m. higher than it had been in the previous year. When she announced her own rearmament programme, early in 1951, both exports and investment in domestic industry suffered, and, when the Persian Government seized the Anglo-Iranian Oil company (which supplied a quarter of Britain's crude oil), precious dollars had to be spent in buying supplies from other sources. This combination of events produced yet another sterling crisis.

Late in the year, the Tories returned to power and quickly brought in a new economic policy. Bank rate was raised for the first time since 1932 (apart from a brief period in the summer of 1939), import quotas were introduced and the stockpiling of raw materials cut back. At first, these measures had little effect and the run on the pound continued into the spring of 1952. Eventually the rearmament programme was scaled down, Bank Rate was raised yet again and domestic consumption was reduced by cutting back deliveries to the home market and by restrictions on hire purchase terms for consumer durables. The pattern for the 1950s had begun to emerge.

The years that followed brought a succession of sterling crises. In 1955–7, 1961 and 1964–9, Britain had to defend her currency against attacks of varying strengths, and found it increasingly difficult to play with conviction her role as one of the world's bankers.

The early 1950s, however, saw the gradual disappearance of controls and rationing. Petrol rationing ended in 1950 (to return briefly after the Suez war), steel rationing in 1953, and in 1954 building licences were abolished and food rationing came to an end. In the same year, the quotas on Scotch whisky were removed and more cars steadily became available for the home market.

The long years of restriction had created an unsatisfied consumer demand of considerable intensity; in 1951, for example, a Hillman

Minx which sold for £600 new could fetch as much as £1,000 on the second-hand market. By the early 1950s, there was therefore an enormous untapped reservoir of spending power waiting to be released, and when the controls were removed, the dam broke. New car registrations on the home market more than doubled between 1952 and 1954 and by 1960 had more than doubled again; refrigerators sales showed an even more marked increase.

This rapid acceleration of demand was given additional impetus by a continuing inflation. The rise in earnings was already running ahead of the movement of prices by 1948, and it continued to increase more quickly than both retail prices and output throughout the 1950s and 1960s. Between 1947 and 1967, retail prices went up 115 per cent: earnings, on the other hand, rose by no less than 235 per cent. Thus, the reservoir of spending power was constantly being renewed and, after the second post-war devaluation in 1967, the problem took on a new dimension: the British began to lose faith in their currency.

The upward surge of earnings and prices far ahead of the rise in output ultimately affected Britain's competitive ability in world trade: in 1961, the Bank of England was already telling Selwyn Lloyd that wage settlements contemplated at that time would give Britain an over-valued currency. Furthermore, heavy demand for goods at home increasingly laid claim to industrial capacity which might have been used for export markets.

Nevertheless, helped by a steady expansion in world trade (which moved ahead at an average rate of about seven per cent a year between 1948 and 1967), Britain managed to keep her head above water during the 1950s. On only two occasions between 1948 and 1963 was she in the red on her trading account. The trouble was that the surpluses were generally modest and – taking the capital side of the account into consideration – there was probably only one year, 1958, in which the current balance was comfortably sufficient to cope with a persistently heavy outflow of capital into overseas investment. Between 1946 and 1959, Britain exported something like £4,000m. and the rate was still running at well over £300m. a year, despite the restrictions put on overseas investment by the Labour Government in 1965 and 1966.

The result was that the margin between confidence and crisis was always too narrow for comfort, particularly since Britain's reserves were not large enough to provide reassurance. If the government wanted to keep the pound at $2.80 and to allow considerable freedom for overseas investment, it had to cut back on demand at home. It was natural in these circumstances that, in the interests of ensuring a margin of safety, it should sometimes cut back so hard that the growth of the economy was impaired. During the 1950s and 1960s, the credit squeeze – with high Bank Rate (it reached seven per cent in September 1957), restrictions on lending and the stiffening of hire purchase terms – became a familiar feature of the economic scene. Indeed, it became so familiar that gradually it took on the appearance of primitive ritual: the doctor, grim-faced, entered the patient's room, applied the leeches and let blood. In this case, enough had to be let to satisfy a highly critical international audience and, in the event, the judgments of modern economic science often proved little more accurate than those of ancient medicine. Nor was the problem of excess demand made any easier by a steady increase in public expenditure over the period, partly due to the fact that several newly nationalized industries were desperately trying to catch up on decades of under-investment.

From time to time, more serious remedies were applied. There was the wage and price freeze of 1948, the Selwyn Lloyd pay pause in 1961, the Wilson wage and price freeze of 1966. These failed to do any more than temporarily halt the march of inflation, and the politicians began to think that perhaps new institutions might do the trick. From 1957 to 1961, the Council on Prices, Productivity and Incomes put its collective wisdom at the service of Government and people; it noted in its first report that while national output had been rising at about three per cent a year between 1946 and 1956, wages and salaries had gone up by an average of eight per cent. The Council came and went and the upward drift continued. Then, in 1965, the Prices and Incomes Board was set up to take a critical look at increases in incomes and prices which were referred to it: it had substantially more both in the way of power and influence than anything which had gone before.

Successive Governments were, of course, not merely concerned with checking inflation. They also wanted to show that the British economy could grow in a healthy way, and their enthusiasm for growth was all the greater because many of Britain's competitors were expanding rapidly. It became a matter of increasing reproach to the politicians that while Britain's growth rate in the 1950s was only 2.7 per cent a year (in terms of real product), the Germans (for example) were moving ahead at 7.6 per cent a year.

By the 1960s, these discrepancies were being increasingly observed, and the German 'economic miracle' more and more a subject for wonder and envy. The wonder was all the greater in that West Germany had not only been in ruins after the war but had also betrayed some of the signs of instability which had characterized her in the 1920s; in particular, her currency system had broken down, the Reichsmark was virtually worthless, there had been a headlong flight into goods and the country was on what was cynically referred to as 'the cigarette standard'.

Yet she recovered with astonishing rapidity. For one thing, despite all the rubble, West Germany had actually added to her capital investment during the war, and the capacity for expansion was already present; for another, the replacement of the Reichsmark by the D-Mark in 1948 (at an initial exchange rate of ten to one) brought a startling transformation, with goods flooding back into the shops; and, finally, a high proportion of West German industry produced capital goods, such as machinery, which were to be in high demand.

Furthermore, West Germany entered the 1950s with a crucial advantage over Britain and her other competitors: although the D-Mark was not fully devalued with sterling in 1949, it was still an under-valued currency. Combined with the underlying strength and balance of their industry, this gave the Germans a substantial advantage in export markets: exporting was a highly profitable activity and, for good measure, the West German Government subsidized it in a number of ways. The export-led boom which followed was also marked by heavy capital investment, which went ahead at a much faster rate than in Britain. During the 1950s, the Germans increased the volume of their exports by 282 per cent; Britain by only sixteen per cent.

Germany had other advantages. Defeated in the war, her military expenditure thereafter was very low, and she had very little in the way of overseas commitments to act as a strain on her resources; nor did she have to bear the burdens of a world currency. The Germans, indeed, were able to give their undivided attention to economic recovery: certainly some of the drive which had once been spent in seeking military and political power now appeared to be transferred to the economic front, and into the struggle for a new sort of *Lebensraum*. As a German businessman put it in 1966: 'Germany today cannot exercise influence on the world by military means. She also has no political power, not even through the European community. . . . We have only one weapon of influence: we have become the second greatest trading – well, exporting – power in the world. That is what exports mean to us. That is why I always feel the spirit rise more within me when we win an export order than when we merely win an order at home.'[1] Since the

[1] In *The German Lesson*, an *Economist* survey of 15 October 1966.

army was no longer so respectable an occupation, many of the best young brains in the country turned to business, and fought the new battle with all the precision of a military operation.

So far as the legendary West German worker was concerned, he had a shorter working week than his British counterpart (in manufacturing, at least) as well as longer annual and public holidays. Nor did he prove particularly docile; West German wage rates have risen more rapidly than those in this country.

What did happen – and this was crucial – was that productivity, in terms of output per man hour, moved ahead approximately twice as fast as in Britain. This was partly because a large sector of West German business consisted of modern industries where capital investment was high and capacity highly utilized. Britain's industrial structure, on the other hand, contained a larger proportion of industries with under-utilized capacity; the cotton textile industry, for example, was saddled with a good deal of idle plant and machinery during the 1950s (at one time, its unemployed capacity was estimated at between forty and fifty per cent) and the same was true, to a lesser degree, of shipbuilding and other industries.

But trade union attitudes also played a key role. In West Germany, where there was in any case full employment, the unions did not obstruct the introduction of labour-saving machinery; in Britain, on the other hand, they not only resisted such changes but also insisted on over-manning in many industries. The simplicity of the German union structure – with sixteen unions, each looking after a group of industries, and only one union in any company – meant that there were few, if any, demarcation disputes; while the fact that labour could air its grievances at regular works council meetings with the management helped keep down the number of strikes. So, too, did the willingness of managements to yield to wage demands rather than risk industrial unrest.

In any event, the Tories became increasingly concerned that they could not produce a performance to match that of either Germany or of other European economies. Indeed, their sense of failure was eventually so overwhelming that they were willing to borrow ideas from the French – and it was the machinery of planning which had been created in France which provided the original inspiration for the National Economic Development Council in 1962. 'Neddy', as it was affec-tionately known, was to provide a forum where representatives of management, unions and Government could talk out their problems, and an office which would not only draw up forecasts and targets but also suggest ways in which the obstacles to Britain's growth might be removed. It was from 'Neddy' that there emerged, in 1963, the idea of a growth target of four per cent a year. By 1965, when the Government was ready to sally forth with a National Plan, it had been decided that 3.8 per cent was perhaps a more realistic aim in all the circumstances, but both the National Plan and the 3.8 target disappeared in a succession of sterling crises which culminated in the devaluation of November 1967.

Curiously enough, many businessmen saw the early post-war years in a very different light than the politicians. True, there was stop-go to contend with, but there was also a sellers' market of unparalleled proportions which persisted for longer than many of them, with memories of the 1920s and 1930s, expected. In some industries it lasted ten years, in others almost twenty, and in retrospect, it seemed like paradise. 'In the ten years after the end of the war,' said one of the managing directors of Tube Investments, 'established pre-war businesses could hardly help making money.' In the electrical industry, much the same was true. 'For a long time after the war,' recalled Lord Nelson, now the chairman of General Electric and English Electric, 'it was simply a matter of allocation, people just got into the queue.' For the biggest of the car makers, the British Motor Corporation (the product of a merger between Morris and Austin in 1951), the hungry home market seemed to last until 1964. 'Up to then,' said a senior director of the company, 'the industry had twenty years when the public would take anything at any time or price. If you could turn out things with an engine and four wheels, you couldn't go wrong.'

The sellers' market did nothing to advance the quality of British salesmanship. 'For ten years after the war,' said Niall McDiarmid, formerly of the British Steel Corporation and before that of Stewarts and Lloyds, 'it wasn't necessary for anyone to sell a ton of steel – and there was a time when we'd almost forgotten that we were still in the business of selling tubes.' It was the same at Cunard: 'we didn't have to learn to sell,' said Philip Bates, a deputy chairman of the company, 'people just fell over themselves to get aboard.'

Furthermore, with a booming home market and the profit margins on export sales constantly being eroded by wages and prices which moved ahead of increases in productivity, many companies did not tackle the difficulties of selling abroad with any noticeable enthusiasm. 'If UK orders could fill your capacity,' said a director of one large engineering company with a very modest export record, 'why on earth would you want to go running off to Timbuctoo?' Equally, there was little incentive for companies to reform ramshackle and inefficient organizational structures; the heyday of the management consultant did not come until the sellers' market was over and companies began to put their houses in order, if only to give critics of declining performance less of a target to aim at.

The protracted life of the sellers' market in the years after the war had, indeed, almost as profound an impact on the ethos of British business life as lack of competition had had before it. But the spirit of the pre-war era, with its absence of competition in many areas of business, lived on in much more concrete ways. For one thing, the network of restrictive practices – the price rings, the market-sharing, the collusive tendering – which had often been created as defensive measures against recession, continued long after the war was over; and the private courts which were operated by trade associations to enforce these agreements continued to punish wayward companies which infringed them. With hindsight, the survival of these institutions in a sellers' world seems ludicrous, but industrialists who feared that there might be a return to pre-war conditions regarded them as a useful form of insurance. Their existence removed another spur to greater efficiency: 'with all these gentlemen's agreements still operating,' said the director of a large engineering company, 'there was no great incentive to efficiency on the factory floor.'

Eventually, the Government decided that something should be done to restore a greater degree of competition on the home market and, in 1956, introduced the Restrictive Trade Practices Act. It came as a considerable shock to a generation of businessmen which had almost forgotten what competition was like.

The 1956 Act was not, however, the first which had demonstrated the politicians' concern at the persistence of restraints on competition. The Labour Government had already, in 1948, passed the Monopolies and Restrictive Practices Act, which was the first piece of modern British legislation to deal with the question of monopoly. The concept of taking action was revolutionary, but the terms of the Act itself were tentative to a degree. Unlike American legislation the 1948 Act did not assume that any barrier to competition must necessarily be against the public interest; it embodied the belief that only investigation could show whether such barriers were good or bad. A Commission was duly set up to inquire into monopoly situations – defined as those where one-third of the goods produced in an industry were in the hands of a single company or a group of connected companies – and into any other restrictive practices referred to it by the Board of Trade. The Commission had to judge whether what it had been asked to investigate was against the public interest: in that case, Parliament could legislate to remedy the situation.

The Commission was not apparently of radical inclination – it thought the electric lamp industry's price-fixing agreement reasonable when taken together with the cross-licensing of patents and the exchange of research and development information – and of the twenty reports which it produced in seven years, only one was followed by a Government Order. On the other hand, the Commission did invaluable work not only in revealing the extent to which restrictive practices existed but also by alarming some of their operators enough to persuade them to abandon their schemes. In that sense, it was a useful preparation for the Act of 1956.

The new Act took a very far from neutral attitude to restrictive practices: it assumed that they were bad unless they could be shown to produce a substantial benefit to the public. Under it, a wide range of restrictive agreements had to be registered, and a Court was set up with the status and powers of the High Court to try cases brought before it by a Registrar.[1] If companies wanted to keep their price rings, they had to satisfy the criteria laid down in the Act; these were severe enough to convince the majority of manufacturers that appearing before the Court would be a waste of money.

By the summer of 1966, 2,580 agreements had been registered and 1,875 of them had been dissolved without reference to the Court. Sir Rupert Sich, the Registrar, said in mid-1966 that 'the mass of price-fixing agreements has now been dismantled and there is no backlog of important agreements awaiting their turn to be referred to the Court'; less than one per cent of the agreements registered under the Act had been found consistent with the public interest. Sich pursued his task with considerable fervour: while he felt that it was not the purpose of most restrictive agreements to earn exorbitant profits, he also believed that they made it less necessary for industrialists to keep a close eye on costs.

At first, there was little occasion for the Court to show its teeth. Only nine defendants ventured before it during its first three years, and eight failed to get through the narrow 'gateways' in the Act. But eventually

[1] The Restrictive Practices Court has three judges and eight laymen and uses outside experts to help it in the preparation of cases.

the Court was forced to demonstrate that restrictive agreements were not only no longer respectable, but also expensive for those who chose to persist in them. In 1965, the case of the Galvanized Tank Manufacturers came before it. They had surrendered a previous price-fixing agreement and given an undertaking that they would not make any other agreement with a similar object. At the hearing, eight of them admitted that they had in fact made informal agreements on the prices they would charge: they were fined £102,000. A group of tyre manufacturers were also fined heavily for a similar offence.

Cases like these showed that many industrialists, far from being willing to play the game by the 1956 rules, were determined to circumvent the Act if they possibly could.

The 1956 Act had left a major loophole on the issue of resale price maintenance. It made collective enforcement of r.p.m. illegal, but had in some ways strengthened the hand of individual manufacturers who wanted to set minimum resale prices for their goods. That loophole was closed by the Resale Prices Act of 1964, which forbade individual companies to fix minimum resale prices unless they could show that it was in the public interest. Again, the majority of companies preferred not to face the Court; and of those who chose to fight, very few won.

Meanwhile on the monopolies front, the Commission set up under the 1948 Act had been reshaped in 1956 and told to concentrate on single firm restrictive practices and monopolies – where the company controlled more than a third of the market for a product. The 1956 Act did not deal with the question of mergers which created monopolies. They could not be held up – merely investigated after the event. The fact was that the wave of take-overs which had started in the early 1950s had not led to the sort of amalgamations which created anxiety on the score of monopoly. The event which alerted the Government to the need for stronger powers was the take-over battle between ICI and Courtaulds in 1961–2, which could have created a monopoly in man-made fibres and which the Government was powerless to prevent.

It was left to the Labour Government to take action, and in 1965 the Monopolies and Mergers Act proved to be much more radical than anything the Tories had had in mind before the 1964 Election. Under the Act, the Board of Trade could refer to the Monopolies Commission any merger which would give the joint enterprise a third or more of the market for a product, or where the value of the assets being acquired exceeded £5m. This effectively gave the Government a delaying power over every significant merger proposal. But, although these were wide-ranging powers, they did not represent any basic change of philosophy; the Labour Government, like the Tory administrations before it, did not believe that monopoly was intrinsically dangerous. On the contrary, it was convinced that a good deal of rationalization was essential if British industry was to be capable of facing full-scale international competition.[1]

It was, indeed, impatience at the slowness with which the rationaliza-tion of industry was moving forward which led to the creation of the Industrial Reorganization Corporation in December 1966, with £150m. of public money at its disposal. The IRC duly helped to arrange some celebrated marriages, including those between Leyland and British Motor Holdings, and between GEC and AEI.

During the years immediately after the war, the State had already intervened in industry on a scale far more massive than anything which had gone before. The coal industry was nationalized in 1946, the rail-ways, road haulage and electricity in 1947, the gas industry in 1948, iron and steel in 1949. The airlines, which had been operated by a single corporation, BOAC, were divided into three in 1946 – BOAC on the North Atlantic and Commonwealth routes; British European Airways, which was given the European and domestic services; and that curious conception, British South American Airways. For some of these indus-tries, nationalization was an event for which they had been well prepared; several were already to some extent under Government control. Two, iron and steel and road haulage, were returned to private ownership by the Tories but, so far as steel was concerned, de-nationalization did not mean the end of Government supervision: the Conservatives set up an Iron and Steel Board which not only fixed maximum prices for the industry but also controlled the growth of its capacity by vetting new investment schemes. In 1967, steel was re-nationalized.

The legislation of 1946–9 left a very large part of British industry permanently in the public sector, and since several of the industries involved – coal and the railways were outstanding examples – des-perately needed substantial capital investment, the nationalization statutes considerably increased the public sector's share of total invest-ment. In 1954–6, new investment in the nationalized industries was already running at between £250m. and £300m., had risen to £400m.

[1] During the first three years of the Act's life, only ten of the 272 proposed mergers which came within its provisions were referred and only three were stopped.

in 1960 and by 1966 amounted to £1,361m., a rate of annual investment equal to that of the whole of private industry.[1]

The Government also played a crucial role in the reorganization of two of the older industries which remained in private hands and which had run into serious difficulties. The first was cotton textiles. Its post-war boom had been kept going for a time by the Korean War, but the collapse thereafter was rapid. Between 1952 and 1963, 1,140 mills were closed: in five years from 1954 to 1959, about a quarter of the industry simply disappeared. The manufacturers struggled to persuade the Government that a limit must be put on imports, particularly from the Far East, but they failed. In 1959, however, the Government decided that it had to intervene to encourage the industry to rationalize itself; the result was the Cotton Industry Act, which paid manufacturers for scrapping redundant machinery and mills and subsidized those who installed modern equipment. There followed what one manufacturer called 'a large measure of suicide' – almost half the looms and over forty per cent of the spindles were scrapped – but the various sections of the industry still remained extremely fragmented: in 1965, for example, there were still 350 weaving companies.

The shipbuilding industry also ran into problems of over-capacity once the post-war building boom was over; by 1960, its order-books had begun to shrink and – as more and more British companies began to order in Japanese and Continental yards – it became plain that British yards had become uncompetitive on both price and delivery dates. Again, the Government (following the Geddes Report of 1966) per-suaded the industry to reorganize itself; financial help was made available to those yards which were ready to become part of larger groups. Amalgamations followed on the Clyde and in the North-East, but one of the Clyde groups (Upper Clyde Shipbuilders) had to ask for a large Government loan in 1969.

The aircraft industry was a rather different case. Here, the Govern-ment became dissatisfied with the industry's fragmented structure partly because it felt new projects were growing so rapidly in cost and complexity that only large organizations could handle them. In 1958, the leaders of the industry were told that rationalization was essential and that the Government would not continue to bear any of the cost of developing civil aircraft if amalgamations were not forthcoming. The

[1] Total public investment had risen from £7,525m. in 1956 (equal to about forty-one per cent of the gross national product at factor cost), to £15,251m. in 1966 (equal to forty-seven per cent of GNP).

threat worked; and eventually, two major groups – Hawker Siddeley and the British Aircraft Corporation – emerged.

The process by which industries were either cajoled or bullied into reorganization by Government pressure represented an intensification of tactics which had been used between the wars. What was unusual in the years after 1945 was the arrival of the take-over bid as a normal weapon of private business strategy. Before the war the amalgamation game was normally played to a very gentlemanly set of rules. Proposals of marriage were made, but if the suitor was rebuffed, he did not usually press his offer. In any case, he was often left with little alternative, since very large blocks of shares were frequently in the hands of either the company Board or its friends.

After the war, the rules changed. Take-over battles were often fought in public and no punches were pulled. Existing managements came under heavy attack and no company, however large or venerable, was safe. Who would have imagined before the war that anybody would ever dare to try and take over the Savoy Hotel against the wishes of the management? Harold Samuel made the attempt in 1953, unsuccessfully as it turned out.

The take-over movement of the 1950s grew out of a curious combination of circumstances. First of all, in the years after the war, share prices remained low and did not value businesses accurately. Shareholders had very little information about the companies whose equities they held[1] and – with their memories of the inter-war years – did not expect a great deal in the way of either dividends or capital appreciation. Share prices, moreover, often failed to take account of the large cash reserves which many companies had accumulated partly out of caution and partly because they had not had time to invest all their retained profits. Nor did they reflect the market value of the freehold properties which many companies owned and which appreciated rapidly in value during the 1950s.

These discrepancies did not, however, escape the attention of a group of shrewd entrepreneurs – among them Charles Clore, Harold Samuel, Isaac Wolfson and the late Hugh Fraser. Even they were perhaps a little surprised at the modest price for which these hidden riches could sometimes be acquired: some businesses yielded up as much in actual cash as it had cost to buy them. The bidders may also not have realized at first that the acquisition of companies could create its own

[1] The Companies Act of 1967 partly remedied this situation by requiring companies to give more information.

momentum, and that the realization of the assets of their purchases would not only make them rich but also so enhance the value of their own company's shares that they were immensely strengthened for the next battle.

The movement began slowly in the late 1940s, when Isaac Wolfson and others acquired stores and shops often at bargain prices. In the early 1950s, Charles Clore began to buy up shoe store chains – Freeman, Hardy and Willis, Dolcis, Manfield and others and then, in 1955–6, came a novel battle, with the Clan Line shipping company bidding for Union-Castle and a committee of shareholders fighting for, and ultimately getting, better terms than those originally offered. In 1958, the City was rent in twain by the struggle for control of British Aluminium between the Tube Investments-Reynolds alliance and Alcoa; in 1959, House of Fraser and Debenhams fought it out for Harrods; and in 1961–2 came the ICI offer for Courtaulds. But even this was all relatively small beer compared with the merger wave which got under way in 1966.

By the early 1960s, however, the motives of bidders were of a completely different kind. Companies were more realistically priced and most did not have either large reserves of cash or ridiculously undervalued assets – in short, bargains were more difficult to come by. The bids which were made after the mid-1950s were generally motivated by a desire to strengthen a company's business in its own or related markets and not with the aim of buying assets on the cheap.

The arrival of the take-over tactic had profound repercussions on the management of companies. They could no longer afford to hoard unused resources, and it behoved them to distribute to shareholders a more generous portion of their earnings: that at least helped to keep the share price high and made them less vulnerable to attack. These factors undoubtedly played some part in the spectacular advance of equities during the 1950s: they virtually trebled in price over the course of the decade. The *Financial Times* index (based on the price of thirty selected industrial shares) had only reached 111·3 (1935 = 100) by the beginning of July 1950, but by 1955 it was standing at well over 200 and in July 1960 reached 315. The major factors in the boom were undoubtedly the rising profits (and dividends) of industry in a period which was for the most part a sellers' market, and a desire to find some hedge against inflation.

The movement was greatly strengthened by the decision of the huge institutional investors to put a much larger proportion of their assets into equities. Before the war, for example, insurance companies had less than five per cent of their total assets in Ordinary shares; by 1954, the proportion had risen to fourteen per cent and to twenty-two per cent by 1967. But there also developed, for the first time, a widespread public interest in the ownership of shares; in this respect, Britain was half a century behind the United States.

By 1969, despite the recurrent economic crises of the post-war years, British business was operating in a healthier climate than had existed since the years before 1914. Cartels had largely disappeared; companies were forced to begin relearning the arts of selling; a revolution in company organization had begun in the later 1950s, with Shell calling in the American management consultants, McKinsey, and others following its example; companies which had never tackled overseas markets in a realistic way were compelled to do so, and the dependence on the old industries had been replaced by a much more balanced export trade.[1] There was a great deal of leeway to be made up, however, and by this time, the efficiency of business was not merely a question of private profit but of the survival of Britain as a front-rank industrial power.

---

[1] In 1967, exports of textiles, coal, iron and steel and ships accounted for only eleven per cent of total sales abroad. Non-electrical machinery accounted for twenty per cent, transport equipment (including cars) for fourteen per cent, chemicals for almost ten per cent.

CHAPTER 4

Breaking the 'Log-Jam':
Whitehall, Banks and Business Schools

The growing impatience on the part of Governments with the performance and efficiency of British industry has led politicians increasingly to the conclusion that it needs to be helped and guided a good deal more firmly than in the past. The result has been the rapid growth of a kind of Little-Jack-Hornerism, with Ministers and their advisers sticking their thumbs into a variety of pies. There has been an ecstasy of exhortation, a rapture of reports, a crescendo of committees, an avalanche of advice; and consent by government has become a more prominent feature of business life than government by consent.

It would be splendid to be able to report that words and paper and earnest good intentions had won the day. Alas, after five years of ardent intervention and dedicated consultation Britain's growth rate is still well below the average for Western Europe, the balance of payments is still precarious and the pound is still a shaky currency. The most noticeable example of growth, indeed, has been among the new bureaucracy of planning, whose various cadres burn up so much energy in advertising their virtues and struggling to maintain their place in the Whitehall Second Division.

So far as the central purpose of intervention is concerned, the so-called National Plan of 1965 is buried fathoms deep in humiliation and failure and its only successor is a document, entitled 'An Economic Assessment to 1972', whose main aims seem to be to fuel the Whitehall talkfest, to keep the memory of planning alive and (most important of all) not to be wrong; it wisely steers clear of predictions but, even so, has more escape hatches than a magician's trick wardrobe. Its hyper-caution is the best possible indication of the depths to which the morale of the planners has sunk after eight years' active service.

On more limited fronts, there have been successes – a considerable upheaval in the structure of British industry has been effectively promoted – but they have scarcely justified the high opinion which the politicians once entertained of their own inspirational powers.

The accession of Labour in 1964 proved to be a watershed in the extension of Government involvement in business. The Tories had become increasingly interventionist during their later years in office, but their efforts were sporadic and did not spring from any consistent philosophy and their purpose was generally either remedial or regulatory – bribing the ailing cotton textile industry to reform itself, for example, or aiming to secure greater competition by attacking restrictive practices and resale price maintenance. True, they also created the NEDC; were ready to direct industry to areas of high unemployment; and even (on occasion) to insist on mergers where national defence and very large sums of government money were at stake, as in the case of the aircraft industry. These, nevertheless, were isolated measures imposed upon a still largely laissez-faire system. The Tories did not intervene because they enjoyed it or believed in it as a general principle; they intervened because they felt compelled to. They conceived their role as analogous to that of a referee who has to blow his whistle from time to time, but prefers to keep out of the way of the players.

The Labour Government, on the other hand, had far more ambitious purposes. It was determined to muscle in on the game because the wholesale restructuring of British industry could, in its view, only be achieved with the active encouragement of the Government; it intended to go into 'partnership' with industry, whether industry liked it or not. Nor was it thinking only in the short term. The new Cabinet included men who believed that it was 'meaningless to speak of the permanent independence of British industry' and that the best hope was to fatten up British companies so that they might wield effective influence in the international mergers of the future. Labour was determined to break with its own bare hands what its leaders called 'the log-jam'.

The onslaught began, logically enough, at the centre – in Whitehall. Its first targets were two departments, the Treasury and the Board of Trade, which were looked upon as bastions of a reactionary order. The Treasury was an old enemy, regarded as scraping, restrictionist and utterly ignorant of the needs of industry; how could it promote growth? The Board of Trade was suspect for different reasons. It was the stronghold of laissez-faire (although it had pushed the car firms into Scotland

and Merseyside), and it tended to play a passive role in its relations with industry: 'we don't want to do what the Board of Trade has traditionally done,' said one Labour Minister, 'that's to say, just sit back and see what happens.' It was also thought to be too much of a rag-bag – everything from administering company law to preventing the import of rotten potatoes – to be able to apply itself decisively to crucial areas of the economy.

There was a fair measure of truth in these beliefs. The Treasury *was* remote from industry,[1] although it had begun to interest itself in planning and growth after the formation of the NEDC, and it *was* an article of faith within the Board of Trade that, by and large, industry knew what was best for itself – 'we were not impertinent enough to think we knew better', said one of its former senior officials. Its industrial divisions, whose task it was to liaise with almost every sort of enterprise from computers to wool textiles, did not always seem precisely sure where that liaison was supposed to lead. Furthermore, since the department saw itself primarily as the guardian of a liberal international trading policy, it also tended to be anti-protectionist on the home front. For decades, the Board had resisted pressure from the cotton textile industry for tariff protection and had been quite ready to leave the computer industry to the mercy of American competition; it was not, it believed, part of its mission to save British industry. This lack of the right sort of crusading instinct did not endear it to the Socialists.

For much the same reasons, the Board had little taste for trust-busting; monopolies at home might give Britain greater competitive strength in international markets.

Since neither the Treasury nor the Board of Trade could be abolished, two new departments were set up to outflank them. The first, the Department of Economic Affairs, was to be a long-term planning ministry (a counterpoise to the Treasury's short-term preoccupations) whose task – in the jargon of the time – was to 'get Britain on the move'. It was to be active where the Board of Trade had tended to be passive, a promoter of growth, a stimulant for change, an energizer, a dynamo;

---

[1] There is now more contact between the Treasury and industrialists, but most of it is at the highest levels. The Permanent Secretary finds himself involved in questions of overseas investment by British-based companies when the sums of foreign exchange required are very large; and also frequently acts as 'the embodiment of the shareholder' in the affairs of British Petroleum, almost half of whose shares are owned by the Government. He is, for example, always consulted about the dividend.

believing in high demand and a high growth-rate, it was a manifesta-
tion of the permissive society in economic terms, the equivalent of the
mini-skirt. To cement the partnership with industry, a group of
advisers was recruited to represent its point of view within the department.

Conveniently enough, the creation of the DEA also solved some of
Labour's political problems. It provided an ideal platform for the
ebullient George Brown and – by creating a second economic department in addition to the Treasury – enabled the Prime Minister, Harold
Wilson, to take a greater hand in economic policy by dividing responsibility between the two.

The second new department was the Ministry of Technology, which
gradually took unto itself surveillance of virtually the entire engineering
industry. Once it had reached full flower, its spirit and intent were
fairly summarized by one of its Ministers, Anthony Wedgwood-Benn,
when he described it as 'a public entrepreneurial enterprise'. Its job was
to act as a goad to industry, 'to prod the tortoise', and at the same time to
protect key sectors of the economy from foreign take-overs; it was both
interventionist and Gaullist. Nor, as time went on, was it afraid to get
its feet wet by reaching conclusions about what would be best for a
particular industry – much to the distaste of some of those at the Board
of Trade. 'With the arrival of MinTech,' said a former Board of Trade
senior official, 'the judgement of the bureaucrat has replaced the judgement of the market.'

Neither of the new departments, however, found life particularly
easy and the DEA could scarcely have been launched in more un-
promising circumstances. It was called upon to focus attention on long-
term growth at precisely the moment when Britain was most heavily
besieged with short-term problems; this was an impossible remit, and
it is not surprising that the DEA has never succeeded in its basic task. It
was also rendered vulnerable by the fact that it had power over neither
money nor people, and that its influence rested almost entirely on the
personality of George Brown and his standing in the political hierarchy;
it was, to a greater extent than any other department, the personal
machine of its Minister.

The DEA lost some critical early battles – the Treasury kept control of
nationalized industry investment as the result of a concordat between
the permanent secretaries of the two departments – but the demise of
the National Plan was its Waterloo. Part of the trouble was that the
Plan became much more than a blueprint for economic growth; it was

intended to embody Labour's promise of a glorious future. In other words, it became a political weapon, which had to be rushed through before Labour went to the country again. The NEDC was asked on a Thursday to give its approval to the Plan by the following Wednesday and George Brown enlisted the support of the Confederation of British Industry after a late-night dash to Sunningdale, where they were gathered. John Davies, then the CBI's director-general, described the mood before Mr Brown's sudden arrival as one of 'non-conviction', but the Minister persuaded them that if they withheld support, they would be striking a damaging blow at the economy. Wrongly, as Davies now believes, they allowed themselves to be convinced. The Plan finally passed away peacefully enough with the deflationary measures of July 1966 and George Brown shortly moved to the Foreign Office. Thereafter, the DEA became and has remained a rump.

Nor was the concept of appointing industrial advisers an unqualified success. They were impressed by the meticulousness of their new Civil Servant colleagues and by the aura of their new surroundings – one told me how flattered he was to have a room which overlooked the Rotunda – but they were not easily absorbed into the Whitehall machine and at first were seriously under-employed. Even when they had found their feet, their advice was rejected quite as often as it was accepted; they had some influence on the level of investment grants, but other measures, such as the regional employment premium, were carried through despite their opposition.

The Ministry of Technology made a hardly more promising start. For a time, indeed, it seemed doomed to be an old crocks' club for seriously wounded industries; it went to the aid of the shipbuilding and computer industries and was closely involved in rescuing Rootes from its financial troubles. Nor was it always able to act according to the bright vision of its founders: Rootes was rescued partly because of the political rumpus which might have attended such a serious loss of employment in Scotland. Nevertheless, the Ministry's influence grew, partly because of the energy of Wedgwood-Benn. It played a significant role in the rationalization of the motor and computer industries and its own Civil Servants credit it with having conceived the idea of the Industrial Reorganization Corporation; this, they say, was originally intended to apply only to machine tools, but was then picked up by George Brown and expanded.

As probably the only Government department in the world which combines responsibility for industrial policy with the management of scientific resources (it controls and finances seventeen Government research establishments), it also had a unique opportunity to direct Government money into channels useful to industry: in 1969–70, research and development expenditure linked to industry exceeded that linked to defence for the first time. Carbon fibres were developed at Farnborough and Harwell. The Ministry of Technology also prided itself on being more 'hard-nosed' about prestige projects – such as the air bus, which was turned down on what is called 'very strict commercial criteria'.

The arrival of two new Ministries had profound repercussions not only on Whitehall, but also on its dependencies. One body which suffered as a result was the NEDC; founded on the theory that rational men talking round a table can produce solutions, it had the stigma of being a Tory creation and, in any case, George Brown was said to prefer talking to the trade unions and employers informally rather than round the Council table. Furthermore, since the preparation of the National Plan had been taken out of its hands by the DEA – there had been a considerable exodus of 'Neddy' men from the Economic Division to the new department – the NEDC was left with very little. To be precise, it retained the 'Little Neddies', committees which were intended to improve the performance of particular industries.[1] Not surprisingly, its morale suffered.

It was not, however, allowed to die. Fred Catherwood, a former British Aluminium man who had become chief industrial adviser at the DEA, was appointed its director-general and, after the death of the Plan, the DEA seemed to take the Council rather more seriously. Cynics might have said that the politicians were fraternizing more because it mattered less; their attendances at the Council's monthly meetings has something of the appearance of a ritual sacrifice at the altar of consultation.

'Neddy', indeed, conveys a strong impression of the absence of power and, if one is to believe some of its leading members, it is both a drag and a spent force. One said that he found attendance at its deliberations 'immensely depressing'; another, denying that 'Neddy' had ever 'ironed anything out', said he personally did not want a forum whose aim was to reach unanimity between groups with naturally conflicting interests and added that he thought it reproduced the worst defects of

[1] The Little Neddies are made up of industrialists, trade unionists, representatives of government and independent members. In each case (and there are now 23 Little Neddies), the Neddy office acts as a secretariat.

Parliament. Certainly, the CBI and the TUC do not need to attend the NEDC to be able to lobby the Government.

Some of its critics would shed no tears if it were disbanded; others believe that it might be useful if it were more independent of the Government (it is invariably chaired by a Minister) and if it limited its work to providing an assessment of the cost of alternative economic policies. At present, in the view of one of Catherwood's former colleagues at the DEA, 'Neddy' is no more than 'a servicing agency for the "Little Neddies" '.

It is true that, like other Whitehall agencies, NEDC depends heavily on the personality and standing of its boss. Catherwood, a lean, earnest and friendly man who moved into Whitehall because he believed that the people who were running the economy had no understanding of 'the industrial facts of life', would strongly dispute that Neddy has proved to be a failure. He concedes that the office has no power, but is convinced that its influence is 'enormous' precisely because it can present a case which is not partisan; he thinks the investigations into specific problems which it commissions (and which account for perhaps half of its £750,000 annual budget) are extremely effective weapons in the Whitehall paper war. Catherwood also believes that being 'in on the net' is invaluable and that much of his most effective work is carried on behind the scenes – 'if I am seen to be fighting in public, then it is clear I have lost the fight.'

Catherwood would add that NEDC has been particularly successful in tackling particular industrial bottlenecks – he thinks its influence has given impetus to the container revolution in shipping, for example – but the sum total of the office's efforts is somewhat unexciting. The same must be said of most of the 'Little Neddies', which have generated a good deal of paper but comparatively little action.[1] The entire 'Neddy' structure is beginning to look superfluous; there are surely less cumbersome ways of achieving effective consultation between the Government and industry.

While 'Neddy' languished (particularly during the early years of Labour rule), the DEA added to activity on the fringes of Whitehall by having two children of its own which, as time went on, attracted considerably more attention than their parent. The first was the Prices and Incomes Board, created in 1965 and intended as a useful auxiliary of the administration in the battle to keep wage and price rises in line with

---

[1] Industrialists can generally only spare a day a month for service on the Little Neddies.

whatever the Government deemed acceptable at any particular point
in time. Troublesome cases could be sent for impartial scrutiny to the
Board, which was to include a trade unionist, a businessman and
independent members, supported by appropriate specialist advice. The
impartiality of the new body was demonstrated by the appointment as
its chairman of Aubrey Jones, a former Tory Cabinet Minister and one
of the most intelligent men in politics; Mr Jones's name was apparently
the only one in a long list circulated to employers and trade unionists
to be received without demur.

It very shortly became plain that Aubrey Jones had no intention of
being circumscribed by the PIB's limited brief and that he was determined to run his own sort of empire, not to say private army, even at the
risk of occasionally embarrassing his sponsors. To begin with, he
wanted to be able to pick his own Board and staff – a Board of objective
and independent-minded people which was 'not too large to control'
and which was capable of looking at problems in an original and
penetrating fashion. He increasingly got his own way on this point and
the PIB became less and less a Jones-Brown Board and more and
more a Jones Board. Even so, the DEA occasionally jibbed at what
it considered his more outlandish suggestions; it would not agree
to the appointment of the chairman of an American company to the
Board.

Mr Jones was to prove an independent servant in other ways.
Although the rules said that the PIB should investigate only those cases
referred to it by the Government, he also wanted to pick references for
himself and was ready to use all his politician's skill to get them. As his
vision of the Board's role expanded this meant the opportunity to
conduct 'efficiency audits' right across the range of society; he wanted to
examine not only proposed increases in road haulage rates but also the
efficiency of the universities. His ambition and zeal did not increase his
popularity; for some, he was becoming too much of a Nosey Parker for
comfort. As one industrialist put it: 'Mr Jones wants to be an impartial
universal scrutineer, whose views we cannot do without.'[1]

It is certainly true that the influence of the PIB has sprung largely
from Jones's own stature and incisiveness: without him, it might have
become a pliant tool of Government. Jones has also been the dominant
force on the Board – one senior member said he did not mind being
dominated as the chairman was such a clever man – although he
strongly rejects the suggestion that he was a one-man band. The fact

[1] Mr. Jones is to leave the PIB to join the International Publishing Corporation.

that he read and approved every report himself (and the Board has now produced well over one hundred) has given the PIB's work one inestimable virtue which the output of some other agencies has noticeably lacked: that of consistency.

It is harder to quantify what the Board achieved under his leadership. It has helped to stimulate the idea that wage increases should be linked to productivity agreements (even if some of these have been unconvincing) and it has delayed some price increases. But its brisk and penetrating reports have had a usefulness quite apart from their value in enforcing Government policy. They have questioned a good many accepted practices on both sides of industry and disturbed the complacency of some of the more comfortable corners of the economy (the clearing banks and the building societies, for example). The PIB, in fact, has acted as a sort of universal consultant, Mr Jones's own vehicle for influencing society. Since it has passed under the control of the Department of Employment and Productivity (the old Ministry of Labour) it has often had a great deal less to do. What the Tories will do to it, should they return to power at the next election, remains to be seen. One of Mr Jones's reasons for leaving was a fear that the Board might be downgraded under a Tory administration.

The second of the DEA's offspring, the Industrial Reorganization Corporation, also seems unlikely to survive unscathed if the Tories come back to power. Although the IRC was slow to get under way – after its first year of existence, people were beginning to ask exactly what it was doing – it has since become the most controversial of all Labour's attempts to speed up the restructuring of industry, and for obvious enough reasons. It has used its power and influence to push through mergers which might not have taken place if the market mechanism had been allowed to operate freely (it is doubtful, for example, whether GEC would have won the battle for AEI without IRC backing); it has used public money to buy shares and achieve a merger which it approved and, in doing so, was instrumental in frustrating the offer of another company which might otherwise have been victorious (it backed George Kent in the take-over of Cambridge Instrument against the bid of the Rank Organization); and, by the novelty of its approach, has created all the alarm which would be produced by a stunt pilot flying a supersonic jet under Tower Bridge.

From the beginning, neither its organization nor its techniques were designed to allay the fears of the doubtful, although the IRC itself feels that, by having a Board composed predominantly of prominent business men, the attempt was made. Ronald Grierson, a former merchant banker who was IRC's first managing director, favoured the idea of a small staff (less than a dozen executives in a total of thirty – 'about as big as the Mission to Peking', in the words of one of them) and recruited them on the basis of ability and personality: in one way, it seemed a throw-back to the cult of the amateur. In the words of his second-in-command, Roger Brooke (an ex-Foreign Office man whom Grierson had first met when Brooke was commercial attaché in Israel),[1] they were looking for confidence and for youth – 'our people must belong to the generation with an eye for the things which need changing'.

The result was that the IRC's staff consisted of men from diverse backgrounds, most of them in their thirties. One was a former journalist; another was hired straight from university; a third was lent by a firm of solicitors; others came from chartered accountancy, merchant banking and the World Bank, and later recruits included a Double First in languages from Labour Party headquarters. None of them was given a title, although Brooke acted as head of staff, and the informality of the organization – according to Brooke – 'saved the need to draw organization charts and write interminable memos'. The recruits were paid salaries comparable with those in merchant banking but very high for Whitehall, although Grierson himself took on the job for nothing because he did not think the Government would have been willing to pay him appropriately and preferred not to haggle.

The idea was that this group of clever and energetic young men should be watched over by a Board of experienced businessmen, headed by Sir Frank Kearton, the chairman of Courtaulds; the young men were to do the ground-work and put up schemes, which were then vetted by their elders. The problem of Board members being privy to mergers which directly or indirectly affected their own companies was met by withholding information from any interested parties to a scheme; Kearton himself, for example, knew nothing of the IRC's investigations into the wool textile industry.

But if the arrival of youth at the helm in such force was disturbing to some – and in the early days Brooke said he sometimes used to take older men on visits with him in order to reassure clients – their *élan*, desire for quick results and willingness to dispense with the usual quantities of paper were equally novel; it was not for nothing that its executive staff were known as 'ops.'. Whereas the Prices and Incomes

[1] Brooke resigned from the IRC in 1969 to take up a new job.

Board, in a different line of country, used a battery of economists and statisticians, the IRC took an altogether different line. 'We don't feel the need for economists,' said Brooke in 1968, 'and we don't believe in great volumes of analysis. It's not a question of analysing the problem – there are plenty of Little Neddies already and 25 reports on everything – what is needed is action.'

Initially, the IRC did commission a number of reports by outsiders, but it was not always entirely happy with their recommendations and Brooke was frank about the fact that they helped the organization achieve acceptance. He was adamant that the IRC's job was to come to a view – even at the risk of being wrong – and then to back it. The view, in his opinion, had to be based not only on looking at production lines but also on an assessment of the key individuals in a company or industry. These methods clearly carried the danger of over-hasty decisions.

The IRC also had (and still has) a strong bias in favour of building very large companies. Brooke, like others in Whitehall, believed that – in key industries – Britain ought to have companies big enough to take the lead in the international mergers which he was convinced were inevitable. The long-term choice in the motor industry, for example, seemed to him to be between selling out to the Americans and joining some sort of European merger. The satisfaction he felt at the creation of British Leyland was based on a conviction that it was strong enough to be the 'lead company' in such a merger. But he also believed that Britain needed as many really substantial companies as possible because international mergers were likely to require some horse-trading – with the French say, being given the leading role in a joint airframe business and a British company playing the dominant part in a computer alliance.

Along with the IRC's ambitious ideas and its somewhat informal style – one report began with a quotation from Lewis Carroll – there went considerable power. Although in some ways it resembles a State merchant bank, it has the ability – which no merchant bank possesses – to 'tramp around the competitors of its clients'. Furthermore, IRC support for a merger – particularly if it includes the magic words 'in the national interest' – has considerable weight not only with reluctant company bosses but also with the big institutional shareholders.

The IRC's greatest strength, however, has lain in the fact that £150m. of Government money was put at its disposal. It has also been widely assumed that, if technologically-based companies do as they are bid, they will keep themselves in line for Government research and development contracts. This combination of factors, together with the remarkable freedom of action which the IRC has been allowed by the Whitehall departments with which it works (the DEA, the Board of Trade and MinTech), has made it extremely influential. Relations between the two sides have not always been smooth – at times, the IRC was sometimes thought not to be forthcoming enough (the Permanent Secretary of one department was not told about the merger between English Electric and Elliott Automation until a few hours before it was announced) – but no serious attempt has so far been made to curb the IRC's vivacity. The general climate of opinion has been favourable to its activities and it has been doing the sort of job which required a free hand if it was to be done at all.

Having built up its confidence and standing, it was soon making its influence felt. This was particularly true after Sir Frank Kearton took over control: he was not disposed to be cautious and was ready to prove that IRC was very far from being a paper tiger. He was also willing to use his own personal authority, and his part in the GEC-AEI battle may well have been crucial. As the struggle went on, and it began to look doubtful if the IRC's candidate (GEC) would win, the IRC took the initiative by letting it be known that it was ready to see the big institutions and explain its case. Within the Corporation, it was widely believed that it was Kearton's impressive performance on that occasion which swung the crucial shares. His successors have been no less adventurous. The IRC has since made take-over bids for companies on its own account and has also been asked to arbitrate between the merits of two bidders. In 1969, its second managing director, Charles Villiers (another merchant banker) said that it was currently discussing mergers with sixty-nine companies in twenty different industries.

In some ways, the IRC was fortunate that it came into the merger business at a time when this was, in any case, flourishing. In 1966, companies spent £535m. on take-overs; by 1968, the figure had more than quadrupled to £2,312m. Many of these mergers would have taken place whether the IRC had been in existence or not, but in a significant number of cases it at least prepared the soil.

On the other hand, its efforts are open to many criticisms. Even former members of its staff concede that it has often failed to explain its point of view adequately to the general public. In the case of GEC-AEI, it gave more information to the institutions than was available to ordinary stockholders; in other, even more controversial affairs, it kept its reasoning to itself until long after the event. There is, furthermore, some evidence that it has been too liberal in the way it has dispensed Government funds; £25m. was made available to British Leyland after the British Motor Holdings-Leyland merger, although the company has not so far shown any sign of capital hunger.

But the basic objection to the IRC's activities is that it has seemed arrogant enough to believe that it could pass judgement on the basis of restricted experience and sometimes limited evidence; 'who the hell are they to say what's right?' was a typical response among the industrialists whose point of view it did not favour. There is little doubt that its ground-work was sometimes not as thorough as it might have been and a former member of its staff confesses to having been unhappy about the 'judgements of Solomon' which it produced; equally, there was concern even within the organization that it should be buying shares in the market in pursuit of a piece of industrial logic whose merit could not be proved.

Nevertheless, its activities have been convincing enough to impel a former Archbishop of Canterbury (Lord Fisher) to rise to its defence in *The Times*; *he* was quite ready, he said, to back the IRC's judgment. My own inclination is that, taking the Corporation's efforts as a whole, the former Archbishop is right; certainly there is little evidence as yet that the IRC has made any major errors in terms of the long-term interest of the economy and it has backed a number of sensible alliances. Time alone will tell. It has also had the merit of not being afraid to stick out its neck and take decisions; this is a rare enough virtue to deserve some applause.

The IRC has done other work which has received less publicity than its merger-making activities but which has none the less been valuable. It has, for example, been used by the Government to evaluate an assortment of industrial projects – the various proposals for aluminium smelters, for example – and it has the right mixture of skills to do this sort of job well.

The influence of the IRC and the weight which Labour has attached to the promotion of mergers has inevitably made the Government less zealous than it might have been in using its investigatory powers and has therefore taken work out of the hands of the Monopolies Commission; there is little doubt that the IRC helped prevent certain very large mergers (that, for example, between GEC and English Electric) from being referred to the Commission for scrutiny. The IRC, indeed, has even found itself in the slightly curious position of promoting a merger between the trawling interests of Associated Fisheries and the Ross Group when the Commission had previously turned down a complete merger of the two companies. In deciding (under the extremely vague terms of the 1965 Monopolies and Mergers Act) whether a particular alliance constituted a prima facie danger to the public interest, the Board of Trade has very frequently preferred amalgamation to investigation.

This situation – with one body promoting mergers and another standing by in the wings to question them – has been almost as confused as it has appeared. Nor has the position of the Monopolies Commission been made any happier by the fact that its field of fire overlaps that of the Prices and Incomes Board, several of whose reports have dealt with monopolistic practices.

Furthermore, while senior Board of Trade officials have been delighted to use their new powers to refer service groups like the estate agents for the Commission's scrutiny, they have not always been entirely happy with the reports which it has produced. On some occasions, they have thought that its recommendations were not stringent enough – since the Board refers very few mergers, it is clearly anxious about the ones which it does send down; on others (such as its report on detergents) that it had recommended a solution which was impracticable.[1] Nor can it influence the Commission once a reference has been made: 'my colleagues and I,' said Sir Ashton Roskill, the Commission's chairman, 'do not bother about what Government policy is.' The only thing which the Government can do is to appoint Commission members in the hope that their views may (to some extent) reflect its own.

By the beginning of 1969, however, the Government was beginning to feel that it was perhaps time to put a mild check on the tide of mergers. It showed its concern by referring to the Commission the proposed alliance between Unilever and Allied Breweries and the take-over bid by Rank for De La Rue: one on the grounds of size, the other because it wanted to take a careful look at the merits of the conglomerate.[2] It also strengthened the Monopolies Commission by appointing new members to it. This return to favour by the Commission may well be temporary: whatever the opinions of the politicians, the

---

[1] The Board of Trade is also sensitive to the criticism that the Commission can be charged with inconsistency, in that each of its reports is prepared by a different selection of its members.

[2] The Unilever/Allied Breweries merger was given the go-ahead (though the companies decided not to proceed) the Rank/De la Rue alliance turned down.

pressure for size is certain to grow because of the nature of the inter-national competition, and it is therefore likely that the importance of the Commission will fluctuate.

The Restrictive Practices Court has also found its scope diminished to some extent by the Labour Government: it has, in effect, suffered from the contradiction between a competitive and a planned economy. The ultimate judgement on some important restrictive agreements now rests not with the Court, but with the politicians and their advisers; it is up to the Board of Trade to decide whether they are in the national interest. Sir Rupert Sich, the Registrar and one of the few men on the fringes of Whitehall who is happy to be called a trust-buster, expresses the hope that the Board will not pick too many losers.

The job of putting industry's case in Whitehall belongs to the Con-federation of British Industry, formed in 1965 to bring together the activities of three separate employers' organizations, the largest of which was the Federation of British Industries. Their activities were given a considerable face-lift by John Davies, a former British Petroleum man who took a substantial cut in salary to become its director-general.

Davies felt that the CBI had become too much like its own sort of civil service, that it spent far too much of its time processing detailed in-quiries from members – 'somebody who made brass screws would ask who were the best agents in Montevideo and what their credit ratings were' – and that it had not taken a strong enough line on major issues like Britain's entry into the Common Market. He was determined to remedy these defects and ready to risk his members becoming 'jolly unhappy' in the process. As a result, the CBI has spoken up with a loud voice on topics like the Common Market and overseas investment. Davies still thinks it is under-powered, however – the Swedish em-ployers, with an economy a fifth the size of Britain's, have a budget twice as large as the CBI's £1m.

Davies has also proved to be a new sort of bosses' man. He formed a close personal friendship with the former TUC general secretary, George Woodcock; is very far from being an uncritical supporter of Edward Heath, the Tory Party leader;[1] and was determined not to be doctrinaire and spend all his time 'belly-aching about Government policy'. In this latter respect, however, his good intentions were scarcely fulfilled; particularly after the departure of George Brown (an expansionist who wanted to see a high level of demand in the economy),

[1] He has, however, now left the CBI to go into politics as a Tory.

he has found himself frequently locked in combat with the politicians.

The results of his protests were mixed. He claimed some successes – modification of the 1967 Prices and Incomes Act, for example – but the CBI's representations have frequently been rejected. The most that the CBI can hope to do is chip away hopefully at the resistant granite of a Labour Government.

Just as the merger boom has brought industry and Government nearer together, so too has it drawn industry closer to the City of London. In one way, the merchant bankers are well suited to take a hand in merger-making: most of them have been given exemption[1] by the Board of Trade to issue circulars and offers without Board approval. They have used this advantage to the full. They rapidly became aware during the 1960s that take-overs and mergers could be an expanding and highly profitable activity and many of them (Schroder Wagg, Hill Samuel, Morgan Grenfell, Warburgs, Barings, Rothschilds and others) developed it alongside their existing business, which already included commercial banking, raising foreign loans, investment banking (Schroder Wagg, for example, handles over £500m. of investment money) and acceptance credit.[2]

This diversification was in the best merchant banking tradition of seizing upon any sort of potentially lucrative business; their smallness and their highly centralized nature, as well as their opportunist traditions, make them remarkably manoeuvrable institutions. 'We make money,' as one merchant banker put it, 'by being on our toes, picking up the crumbs and filling in the gaps.' Another said simply: 'We are parasites,' and when I suggested that merchant bankers were smooth wheeler-dealers, replied that there was nothing smooth about them, that life was too short for smooth operations. He added that he had a reputation for being rude and sarcastic to clients and had never lost one by laying down the law. While other kinds of enterprise like to boast that they are the biggest in their field, a merchant bank's proudest boast is that it was first.

So, although the merger business was likely to 'go up and down like a yo-yo', the merchant banks expanded rapidly to meet the need for

---

[1] Under the Prevention of Fraud (Investments) Act of 1958.

[2] A company in need of cash promises to pay a sum of money in, say, three months' time, the merchant bank 'accepts' the promise, puts its own name to it and then sells it in the discount market. On this particular business, the accepting house make a commission of 1–$1\frac{1}{2}$ per cent.

their services. Hill Samuel, which had had only four people in its Issues and Mergers department in 1963, now has over thirty; similarly Warburgs has doubled its staff in the last three years, Morgan Grenfell in the last two. Some could hardly expand quickly enough: Hill Samuel found itself handling as many as twenty take-over situations at one time. Life was all the more hectic in that so many bids were opposed.

To the combatants, the merchant bankers are able to offer a wide range of services; and, like barristers, they can be hired either for attack or defence.[1] They advise on the term of an offer, set up meetings between the two parties, jolly them along, advise on tactics, do the negotiating, produce the offer documents, vouch for profit forecasts, give advice on raising cash and then raise it. They can also perform an important psychological function in helping relieve a company Board of emotional strain during a battle and then by taking the blame in the event of failure.

The returns can be high, particularly since very little capital is involved. A merchant bank with a sizeable business in issues and mergers might make as much as £1m. in a good year, although individual fees vary enormously. For a large and successful operation, it might collect £250,000 – 'if we win a really big one', said one merchant banker, 'we can always persuade the client to pay more than he should'; if it loses, on the other hand, it may decide to charge only a nominal sum. For a smaller assignment – the successful take-over of a company worth £10m. – it might earn £20,000 in fees. Most of the men employed in merger departments are young, highly paid and tend to be either accountants or lawyers.

But the merchant banks have also been strengthening their connections with domestic industry in other ways. Some bought shares in unquoted companies, offered them financial advice and fattened them up for the market; others were even willing to take on the actual management of companies, to the same end; others again merely offered a financial consultancy service. These developments, which began to gather pace towards the end of the 1950s, were not entirely novel, since one of the Issuing Houses, Charterhouse Investment Trust (set up in 1925) had for a long time been putting money into companies which wanted long-term capital. Charterhouse had also found itself in a situation where it held either a majority or a substantial minority

---

[1] Warburgs claim to be the first merchant bank to defend a company in a take-over battle; this was in the mid-50s.

interest in these businesses and it is now, amongst other things, a diversified holding company.

This level of involvement is still rare among the merchant banks. William Brandt's Sons has bought Jensen Motors and set about re-organizing it in the same way as some American investment banks – who have no commercial banking business – have taken over the management of companies: Lazard Frères moved into Avis, the car rental firm. By and large, however, British merchant bankers prefer to steer clear of becoming involved in management, although they will gladly offer financial advice and even, in exceptional cases, lend out one of their men for a short time: Schroder Wagg, for instance, has loaned one of its staff to Rubery Owen to advise on organization. Some-times, of course, merchant bankers find themselves sitting on the Boards of manufacturing companies, but they do not always enjoy the ex-perience. 'First of all, it's a very time-absorbing occupation,' said one man, 'and it's also intensely boring compared with merchant banking. Nor does that sort of work pay as it should.'

The joint-stock bankers have watched these developments with in-terest, but until recently have left the field entirely to the merchant bankers; 'we are vice-presidents of the missed opportunities league,' said one chief general manager sadly. Two banks, however, have now dipped their toes into the pool. One of them, the National Westminster, has made a number of new issues and claims to offer all the services which a client might get from a merchant bank. It also intends to set about preparing unquoted companies for the market, but has so far made only very modest beginnings and this side of the business is still not large enough to justify a separate department. Certainly the merchant banks are not worried about the sort of competition which the joint-stock bankers are likely to provide in this field. 'Bringing in a joint-stock bank for that sort of work,' said one, 'is like sending for the nursing orderly instead of the doctor.'

The Midland Bank has tried to break into the business in a different sort of way. In 1967 it bought a third share in a merchant bank, Samuel Montagu, and has also set up a subsidiary whose business it is to make loans to companies for between five and seven years, sometimes taking a share in the equity. Midland-Montagu can then take these companies to the market and give advice on mergers and other prob-lems. This venture has also not had particularly exciting beginnings. Other clearing banks have formed similar links but although senior managers at Barclays have been turning over the idea of offering free advice to small companies (and perhaps providing capital and acquiring an equity interest), they are only too conscious that it might take them a long time to prove that they could perform these services as well as a good merchant bank. One of the problems is getting the right sort of men; and many joint-stock bankers are afraid that, if they paid merchant bank rates, they would have the rest of their staff up in arms.

The joint-stock bankers, on the whole, have followed the old saw of sticking to their last, and their last – so far as industry is concerned – means lending short-term money. They say that they do not have the money for long-term lending and that, in any case, this might mean getting 'locked in'; 'we don't want to be in, say, the paint business,' said one chief general manager, 'and if we lent long, we would be.' On the other hand, overdrafts are often allowed to roll over year by year, provided the money is being used for working capital and Barclays, for example, enters into some five-year arrangements – for the price of a commitment fee. When the banks lend for capital purposes, they usually expect to be repaid in a lump sum. To be fair to them, the clearing banks would like to be more adventurous than they are; and if the credit restrictions are ever lifted, they may well become so, if only because they are being goaded into action by the American banks which have flooded into London.

The big institutional investors (insurance companies, pension funds, unit trusts and the like) also keep their distance from industry, despite the fact that their equity shareholdings are often very substantial: the largest of them, the Prudential, tries to keep its holdings in a company below ten per cent, but exceeds the limit in sixty-two cases. This, combined with a knowledge that the Pru's bad opinion can damn a company in the City, gives it considerable potential influence; the present chief general manager, R. H. Owen, says he can never remember a chairman refusing an invitation to visit them.

So far, however, the institutions have scarcely used their influence at all. Indeed, ten years ago, bodies like the Pru and the Norwich Union very seldom even visited companies in which they had big shareholdings; and now, when visits are more frequent, the initiative almost invariably comes from a stockbroker or merchant banker acting for the firm in question. The only occasions when institutions have put pressure on managements has been when the companies concerned were in really serious trouble, although the Pru's chief investment manager, Alastair Murray, says that they are getting round to the idea that it might not be inappropriate to 'give a prod' to a company which is not doing well enough.

The reasons given by the institutions for the passive role which they have so far adopted are simple enough. 'We don't know how to run an industrial company,' said Owen, 'we haven't the expertise and we must remain that way.' One of the Norwich Union's senior investment managers explained that it had holdings in 1,100 companies and could not conceivably know enough to advise the managements of all of them. He added that he did not feel himself to be the champion of any shareholder who was not a policy-holder of the Norwich Union.[1]

In the same way as the Government seized upon the idea of planning to revive a flagging economy, so it was prepared to look favourably upon fashionable remedies for reviving flagging businessmen. What appears to have happened is that Britain looked to see what the admirable Americans had (apart from a huge and well-protected home market) which she lacked. One of the answers was business schools. Enthusiasm for such a solution in itself suggests that the situation must have been regarded as serious. Business schools are about as British as drum majorettes: in fields where they believe success depends primarily on experience and instinct, the British only turn to teaching as a last resort.

Before the Second War, indeed, education specifically for management had scarcely existed in this country. A number of universities (Birmingham amongst them) offered first degrees in commerce which were intended for broader purposes than a career in management, but only two institutions of university calibre (the Manchester College of Science and Technology and the London School of Economics) ran post-graduate courses for managers or potential managers. Technical colleges also provided some courses and a few companies ran their own.

The meagreness of these provisions sprang from fundamental social causes; the most important of these was that there existed a great gulf between the universities and industry. The universities, for their part, were generally hostile to the notion of providing 'vocational training', while most businessmen rejected the idea that formal education could play any part in developing managers. By contrast, the Americans had by 1930 established no less than 200 schools of commerce and business

---

[1] The Norwich Union does have a half-share in a partnership with one of the merchant banks, Kleinwort Benson; its purpose is to take a stake in small unqoted companies which are then prepared for the market.

administration; the quantity may have been more impressive than the quality, but it did at least reflect a demand for educated managers.

Even after 1945, the enthusiasm in Britain for such institutions increased only marginally. A number of independent management courses were set up (the one at Henley, which opened in 1948, offered a twelve-week general course), but the universities kept their distance for the most part and technical colleges were left to carry the main burden of academic management education. In 1951, American universities and colleges were already turning out annually some 4,500 MBAs (Masters in Business Administration); ten years later, less than 200 students were attending post-graduate business courses in British universities.

Since that time, however, there has been a profound transformation. NEDC recommended 'at least one very high-level new school or institution'; and Lord Robbins two, which Lord Franks proposed should be at London and Manchester. Once the fashion had been set, it proved irresistible. There are now thirty-seven business schools and university management departments (the best-known are at London, Manchester, Bradford, Strathclyde, Warwick, Oxford, Liverpool and Durham), most of them heavily over-subscribed;[1] five independent colleges; forty-five polytechnics and 150 technical colleges which, between them, offer no less than 2,000 business and management courses); not to mention institutions run by management consultants and by companies themselves. By the beginning of 1969, roughly 2,300 students were on post-graduate management courses, and perhaps 125,000 managers (eight per cent of the total) attended courses of a week or longer in 1968. So far as sheer volume is concerned, Britain still lags well behind the United States – which produced 15,000 MBAs in 1968 – but the difference is nothing like so great as it was ten years ago.

The new institutions offer a wide range of courses; and many make considerable provision for men already in mid-career.[2] The London and Manchester Business Schools, among others, run two-year degree courses for graduates as well as a variety of shorter sessions at various stages of development; others offer one-year courses for graduates; Oxford has a six-month syllabus for experienced managers; while Warwick offers a first degree in Management Sciences.

Superficially, this mushroom growth appears impressive; in practice,

[1] The London Business School believes it could fill its places ten times over.

[2] In 1967, five out of six students at the London Business School had had experience in industry.

it has created massive problems which are by no means resolved. For one thing, it required the creation almost overnight of a corps of instructors who were capable of addressing themselves to a very different sort of audience from the one to which they were accustomed. For those who came in from industry to teach, there was the sharp intellectual challenge of facing high-quality university graduates, while former university lecturers had to earn the respect of more or less mature businessmen. It was a severe test for many. 'At university,' said Harold Rose, who had come from LSE to be Professor of Finance at the London Business School, 'it is the students who are on trial. At business schools, it is the professors.'

It has been clear from the beginning that the supply of good instructors would be nothing like adequate to meet the explosion of demand, and the evidence suggests that the available teaching resources are of mixed quality and (in many cases) badly overstretched. The signs of strain are worst in some of the polytechnics and technical colleges which, if the critics can be believed, are sometimes regarded as places of refuge from industry. 'Far too many,' said the head of one management department, 'are people who have fallen by the wayside and can't teach.' The shortage of first-class teachers, however, is evident at almost every level.

The fact that business school staffs are paid on the normal academic scales is one reason for the shortage; their salaries do not compare with those available in industry, and business school principals (unlike their American counterparts) are not allowed to break the rules and pay the market rate for men of outstanding talent. The discrepancy in money rewards has had the effect of encouraging business school teachers to turn increasingly to freelance consultancy. The general rule is that they should not give more than one day a week to outside work; by stretching this limit, some are able to double their academic salary and most can add fifty per cent to it.

The business schools were also expected to bridge the gulf between industry and the universities. The problem was more one of attitude than of finance. A good many industrialists were prepared to put up money for such a transparently worthy cause, but there was also scepticism about the practical value of the training provided by the new schools. This has led to a sharp and continuing debate (both within the schools and outside them) about where the emphasis of their courses should lie. What many businessmen wanted was short, sharp, non-theoretical courses for men between thirty and forty years of age, imparting the modern techniques of financial control, marketing and operations research and putting the accent on cost-cutting and profit-consciousness. The academic side in the argument preferred a more leisurely pace and a heavy emphasis on instruction in the analytic tools of management.

Inside the schools, the tension between those who wanted to put the emphasis on analytic work and those who wanted to lean towards vocational training was made all the sharper by the fact that, while some of the staffs had come from business and tended to be biased towards a 'practical' approach, the vast majority were academics who had their professional pride (amongst other things) to consider. They believed in the analytic approach and did not want to risk their re-spectability by doing the sort of work at which their former colleagues might look askance; after all, they might at some stage want to return to their original disciplines. The need to reach a compromise between the two views was clear enough, however, if only because the new schools felt (in the early days, at least) that they had to please industry to succeed: none of them relished the idea of half-full classes.

Once they were solidly established, these restraints were no longer so compelling; a successful school can afford to teach what it likes. In a number of cases (London and Manchester amongst them) the acade-mics have clearly won the day, although the mixture is in each case a judicious one. Both have questioned the Harvard Business School's methods as a model – it uses actual case studies as the basis of a very high proportion of its work and approaches them with a less analytic treatment than is favoured at London and Manchester. They have leaned more towards the Massachusetts Institute of Technology, which stresses the application of mathematical techniques to management problems – although it is not perhaps so theoretical in its emphasis as, say, the Carnegie Institute of Technology in Pittsburgh.

Like MIT, London and Manchester put considerable weight on instruction in the basic tools of analysis and do not see themselves as providing crash courses for 'accountants who want to know a bit more'. 'We are not turning out young men to do a specialist job straight after graduation,' said a professor at the London Business School. 'We are trying to educate rather than train, and we have to give our students a good basis of theory because it's going to have to last them twenty or thirty years. When companies buy our people, they're buying long-term potential – just like the Americans do.' Knowledge of the basic tech-niques of analysis was, he believed, vital – 'a man who is going to identify the critical variables in a situation can't do it except in terms of models'. Grigor McLelland, the Principal of the Manchester school, holds similar views, although he is conscious that his ideas may be considered too theoretical by some. Business problems, he believes, must be analysed by structure rather than content, and he adds that it is absolutely essential to go deeply into basic issues – 'in teaching marginal analysis, for example, you must discuss the empirical work done to establish cost curves in various industries'. McLelland insists that he is doing much more than simply turning out 'back-room boys', but his approach is not one which is universally popular in industry.

Other schools have favoured a different balance. At Oxford, Norman Leyland, who is director of the Centre for Management Studies, believes there is a real danger that business education in this country will become too academic and hence lose touch with the realities of business life. An academic type of training, he thinks, only prevents people from coming to decisions when the facts are inadequate; in business, this is fatal because the facts are seldom anything else.

Leyland is also critical of attempts to pump fashionable techniques into businessmen who may not be equipped to use them properly. 'Ninety per cent of the people who're taught discounted cash flow oughtn't to be allowed near it,' he said. 'In two years' time, in any case, it'll be XYZ instead of DCF and there'll be a one-day seminar at a splendid hotel in Yarmouth.' The first half of the Oxford course is much the same as at London and Manchester, but the students spend the second three months doing a project on their own companies. The aim of the Centre is 'not to train managers to manage, but to help people develop and improve their ability to take decisions'.

Unlike the Manchester school, which is closely linked with the university, the Oxford Centre has retained considerable independence, which it plainly relishes. It gives neither degrees nor diplomas of its own and although students may submit their papers to the university for the award of a certificate, Leyland said he will not allow projects to be shaped so that they can be submitted. 'If the university thinks it's not examinable,' he said, 'then that's too bad.'

Henley reckons to take an approach which is 'markedly more pragmatic'. Its basic recipe is simple enough: gather together sixty or so middle managers between the ages of thirty-three and forty-two and drawn from a wide variety of backgrounds (industry, the banks, accountancy, the Armed and Civil Services, local government, nationalized industry and the trade unions) and allow them to cross-fertilize.

'It is Britain in microcosm', said J. P. Martin-Bates, a former management consultant who is now Principal of the college, 'and in aggregate it represents an enormous amount of experience. We use that experience as much as we can.'

Each course is broken down into groups, called syndicates, and the members spend a high proportion of their time at Henley sharing their experience in discussing together a range of topics. This is partly intended to give them self-confidence 'in the context of the group'. The syndicates also play business games and do case studies. The directing staff, whose principal job it is to set up the course for the students and keep it on the right lines, are for the most part neither academics nor specialists in particular fields. 'We are not experts,' said one man who had joined the directing staff from adult education, 'but we do have a general knowledge.'

Henley makes no reports to employers, awards no diplomas – 'all you are entitled to is the green tie', said one of the directing staff – and Martin-Bates is adamant that it is 'not *only* a place of learning'. Schools like London and Manchester, he believes, do very well the job of adding to the stock of knowledge – 'those who want a good drubbing can get it there' – while Henley exists to improve a man's personal qualities, to act as a finishing school for managers. It is a view which is shared by members of the directing staff: 'our job,' said one, 'is not to provide them with facts. After all, they're not inverted waste-paper baskets.' Henley, however, has broadened its field of operation in recent years. It now offers specialist courses in subjects like quantitative analysis and linear programming and undertakes more research work of its own. Martin-Bates is also trying to strengthen his staff by adding to it men who are specialists in particular subjects.

The Old Boys I have spoken to felt that their time there helped give them self-confidence, allowed them to re-assess themselves and generally exerted a broadening influence upon their lives. 'It's a great place for getting round the table with people from ICI and the RAF,' said a man in the retail trade.[1] Two, on the other hand, were critical about its failure to supply them with more formal knowledge. 'Henley is basically a device for cross-fertilization,' said one, 'and the most you can do by that method is to raise everybody to the level of the best man in your own syndicate. Basically, everyone is pulling themselves up by their own bootstraps.' The College says evidence from surveys show that

[1] Henley could scarcely be in a more congenial spot. It is run from a country house on the banks of the Thames – once the home of W. H. Smith, Lord Hambledon.

this is not a representative view; in any case, the reforms which have been introduced will perhaps make more recent course members feel that a better balance is now being struck.

These differences of approach represent a healthy diversity. Equally healthy is the real effort which is being made in the major schools to pick out from a mass of applicants those who seem to have a genuine vocation for business. Both London and Manchester put all their graduate applicants through the Princeton Test – a $3\frac{1}{2}$-hour examination used by all the American business schools to measure ability to reason in quantitative and verbal terms – but neither a high score in the test nor a First Class Honours degree is any guarantee of a place if the candidate seems unlikely to be suitable for the business life. 'If a man doesn't have the feel of an executive, he's out,' said Arthur Earle, Principal of the London Business School. At Manchester, McLelland looks particularly for people who have a record of independent leadership and who have taken on enterprising jobs in the vacations – managing a beat group, for example. 'Drive,' he said, 'is the dominant ethos.'

On the other hand, this sort of selection is bound to depend heavily on intuitive judgements, and the Principal of one business school admitted that it was much easier to spot the negative than the positive: 'who would have picked out Weinstock at twenty-one?' he asked. Both London and Manchester seem happy enough with the intellectual calibre of the graduates they have been getting, although there is less unanimity about those who come in mid-career. One complaint is that even quite senior executives are ignorant of techniques as elementary as reading a balance sheet and that more advanced work is held up while this is taught. Another criticism is that some students show a marked lack of *élan*. 'They are jolly nice and they work hard,' said a professor at one business school, 'but they are curiously ineffective. You have the feeling that they don't want to beat anybody and many don't have a capacity for getting through to solutions.'

This sort of criticism is relevant to the mission on which many of the business schools feel themselves to be bent: to supply the yeast for British business. The sceptics – and there are still a good many even among the more prestigious British industrialists – wonder just what sort of yeast it will be. None of the new schools claims to be able to teach the entrepreneurial spirit, that urge which impels men to launch businesses and make fortunes. 'If it's drive that's lacking,' said McLelland, 'then I'm not sure the business school is the right place to teach them.' The best they can do, he thinks, is bring entrepreneurial drive into the light of day if it is already latent.

The schools are convinced, however, that it is possible to 'teach' management in the sense that – like engineering – it has principles, a body of knowledge and quantitative tools. These, they point out, are an essential complement to the entrepreneurial spirit; 'all the drive in the world won't help you if you don't know what sums to do,' said Mc-Lelland. The schools also claim that they can teach businessmen to plan for growth, to perceive opportunities for profit and cut out the unprofitable – not to mention giving them instruction in elementary techniques.

But senior staff at some of our leading schools feel that they are wrestling with problems far more profound than the ignorance of individual managers. They believe that what they are being asked to combat is an environment which is profoundly anti-business, compared with the United States. 'We have to create the atmosphere and attitudes which the American schools merely reinforce,' said a professor at London. 'They are swimming with the tide while we are swimming against it.' There is a conviction that, in many cases, indoctrination against the idea of a career in industry begins at school and that many of the values inculcated there – approval of the team spirit, disapproval of individual ambition and of the profit motive – militate against the development of a business-minded society. These attitudes are re-inforced, in the view of one business school Principal, by a deep-rooted commitment within Britain to welfare economics at the expense of creating really productive industry. 'If our society has to choose between higher productivity and an egalitarian tax structure,' said Arthur Earle, 'it goes for egalitarianism every time.' This makes businessmen, in the view of one of Earle's senior staff, far too acquiescent towards Government – 'British industry nationalizes itself' – and far too ready to think of their companies as branches of the public service. In some instances, the ideology being expounded in the business schools has a plainly trans-Atlantic flavour.

The schools are certainly agents for the introduction of American business practices. Not only are many modelled on American institutions but they also use a very high proportion of American literature; eighty per cent of the texts at the London Business School are American and forty per cent of the case studies are based on the experience of US companies. In addition, the leading schools welcome large numbers of visiting American lecturers each year and (at London) even its

Executive Development Programme and its Alumni Association sound American.

Whether they are setting out to change society or merely to leaven the business lump, the new schools have a sizeable task on their hands. Norman Leyland thinks that at the moment we have nothing more than a number of experiments, while John Tyzack, a management consultant who helped found the Staff College of the National Coal Board, believes the leaven will not begin to show results for twenty-five years. The 'log-jam' to which socialist politicians have so picturesquely referred involves deeply-ingrained social attitudes as well as industrial structure.

PART 2

The Big Firms and the Men Who Run Them

CHAPTER 5

Three Giants:
Shell, Unilever, ICI

Only four privately-controlled companies with headquarters in Britain have an annual turnover[1] of more than £1,000m. They are the Royal Dutch/Shell Group, Unilever, British Petroleum and ICI: BP is unusual in that 48–49 per cent of its equity is owned by the British government, although it operates like a normal private company. In terms of sales, Shell, Unilever and ICI rank first, second and fourth among companies outside the United States. (British Petroleum is third.) Shell is also the fourth largest company in the world, headed only by General Motors, Standard Oil of New Jersey, and Ford.

Each of the three attempts to marshal a herd of subsidiary and associated companies: Shell and Unilever, which are Anglo-Dutch enterprises, have 500 apiece, ICI over 350. Shell, with sales (after taxes) of £3,746m. in 1968, is well over half as big again as Unilever (external sales in 1968 £2,306m.) and Unilever, in its turn, is almost twice as large as ICI (£1,237m.) Nor do the numbers of people they employ bear any relation to their comparative sizes. Shell, which is more than three times as big as ICI, has less workers (171,000 to ICI's 188,000 in 1968): Unilever, which is far less capital-intensive than the other two, has 312,000 on its payroll. Each Unilever employee has only £3,304 of capital behind him at the end of 1968, compared with £7,909 for each worker in ICI and £25,300 for each Shell man. Unilever's low figure for average capital employed reveals it as the most labour-intensive company of its size in the world and reflects, among other things, a very large labour force in Africa (about 80,000, many working on plantations producing raw materials like palm oil), while Shell's

[1] After sales taxes, duty and excise.

very high figure reflects a heavy investment in giant tankers, refineries and pipelines.

At a time of increasingly sharp international competition, these are the companies which, because of their size and spread, must match themselves against the biggest American and Continental corporations. Shell always compares its performance with that of Standard of New Jersey; ICI measures its productivity against that of Du Pont; Unilever shapes its organization to combat competitors like Procter and Gamble, the detergent empire whose headquarters are in Cincinatti.

Another effect of their size is to make them at once sensitive and self-conscious. None of them seeks to make much of the breadth of its interests: they prefer to stress their importance rather than their size. Some of the reasons for this are obvious enough: all three have a history of monopoly and cartel which they would rather forget. They are also aware of the traditional British distrust of great agglomerations of power, of whatever sort – and vaguely sense that the giants of industry may have inherited some of the apprehensions once reserved for standing armies.

At one time or another, all three have been under the shadow of nationalization. Lord Heyworth, chairman from 1942 to 1960 of the Special Committee of three which runs Unilever, had to explain to Herbert Morrison why it was 'not on' to nationalize Unilever. ('You could, to him.') As for ICI, it ran a series of advertisements to help stave off the possibility of Government take-over ('ICI has to be as big as it is, to do the very big job that it is doing'). Shell, in a strategic business where nationalization is always on the cards in a dozen countries, knows perfectly well that there are members of the Labour Party who would like to see State ownership of the entire British oil industry; there has also been a proposal to set up a nationalized corporation to take over control of the North Sea gas industry where Shell, among others, has found large reserves of natural gas. These possibilities do not seem to cause it much anxiety, perhaps because they appear very remote, perhaps also because only fourteen per cent of Shell's investment is in Britain – and the British operation is, in any case, one of the least profitable parts of the business.

Unilever, which is in many ways the most sensitive of the three, had in the past a reputation for secretiveness about the extent of its interests which was remarkable even in an age when companies were reluctant to reveal anything more about themselves than the strict letter of the law prescribed. It seemed unwilling to admit even to itself just how wide-spread were its interests. For example, one of its subsidiaries, Silcocks of Liverpool, which produces animal feedstuffs, was for many years referred to *inside the business* only by the code letters 'NW'. Nor is the past entirely dead in this respect. There is still one company within the group (it is not in Britain) which Unilever men normally only refer to among themselves by code letters. In both cases, the reasons for secrecy have been commercial rather than political.[1]

But there is an additional reason for Unilever's sensitivity which flows directly from its Anglo-Dutch parentage. It is afraid that too much debate about the current state of the balance of power between London and Rotterdam may disturb the unity which has been so painstakingly built up. Unilever is still suffering these growing pains, although it is only fair to add that the divisions between London and Rotterdam are far less pronounced than they were ten years ago. Perhaps these fears spring partly from the fact that the business was created as an equal partnership: nobody is therefore anxious to spell out how far it has strayed from this theoretically perfect equality.

Shell has never had to operate under that particular constraint: the Dutch have always been the majority shareholders, and if more seems to happen now in London than in The Hague, they have ultimate control and the right to nominate three of the five managing directors. Certainly the two sides of Shell have now achieved a degree of integration which must be the envy of those trying to create the same forgetfulness of nationality in Unilever.

This is not to deny that occasionally (even since the last war) individual Dutch and British managing directors in Shell have been barely on speaking terms. Furthermore, in the view of one of Shell's former managing directors, the friction between London and The Hague had become so severe by the middle of the 1950s that – without a reorganization such as that which followed McKinsey's arrival in 1957 – there could well have been a national clash. 'It wasn't exactly war,' he said, 'but it wasn't far off.'

Such frictions in Shell were, however, of a different sort to those still latent in Unilever and which the company is at particular pains to

---

[1] The reason for Unilever's concern about Silcocks was simply that, while it sold its animal feeds direct to farmers, another known Unilever subsidiary, British Oil and Cake Mills, was selling through merchants. Unilever was afraid the merchants would be furious if they had discovered that, while one subsidiary was using them, another was competing with them. The fears proved groundless when Unilever revealed that it owned Silcocks.

try and allay. The clashes, when they occurred, were more a question of personalities than of nationalities, and the tensions which built up between London and The Hague in the 1950s were caused by the fact that there were two virtually separate power structures in Shell, divided by geography and unsure of their roles in what had become an extremely confused organizational structure. There is no doubt that Shell has genuinely broken through the nationality barrier, and that loyalties have been submerged in the business to a remarkable degree. 'I have no sense of being a Dutchman except when the problem becomes national', said Jan Brouwer, the senior of the five managing directors. 'I felt no more when the Dutch were thrown out of Indonesia than I did when the British were thrown out of India.' The most recent of the managing directors to be elected is an American, Monroe Spaght, formerly President of Shell Oil, the group's US affiliate: he was one of the three Dutch appointees.

These are not isolated examples, nor are they part of a multi-national pose. There is in Shell a genuine carelessness about nationality (and, for that matter, about race) which applies at least to the senior managers. They even curse each other in a remarkably relaxed and unself-conscious way.[1] In Unilever, on the other hand, the same is far from true as yet. It is worth adding that, considering the appalling difficulties of uniting companies with split nationality, both Shell and Unilever have made remarkable progress. No American company – or, indeed, any other European concern – has had to tackle such a job.

Shell has been helped in this respect both by its history and by the nature of the oil industry. It came into existence in a world which was dominated by the Americans and more particularly by Standard Oil; it has always had either to fight a powerful external enemy or else come to terms with it. In business, as in politics, this can act as an effective unifying force. Furthermore, the whole ethos of the oil business was American. To this day, oil men still talk about prices in terms of cents per barrel,[2] and the conversation of men like Brouwer is sprinkled with Americanisms like 'most any'. In the oil business, there was therefore an external orthodoxy to which the British and the Dutch both had to conform, as well as strong external competition.

---

[1] I only noticed one example of anxiety about national sensitivities. Some of Shell's executives were rather over-emphatic in pointing out that a number of the company's key senior managers are based on The Hague. It seemed to me that they were still a little nervous of upsetting the Dutch.

[2] There are 35 gallons in the oilman's barrel.

In addition, there is the nature of the business itself. It is quite usual for Shell men to spend a large part of their working lives outside their native countries. Gerry Wagner, one of the Dutch managing directors, spent seventeen of his first eighteen years in Shell abroad, and one of the younger Dutch managers had worked successively in England, Spain, the Canary Islands, Tangier, Morocco and Canada before returning to Holland. In these circumstances, it is not surprising if their national identities disappear.

There has been something of the same interchange in Unilever (Lord Heyworth spent a good deal of his early life with the company in North America), but on the whole the business has tended to be rather more compartmentalized than Shell; a man who joined Unilever's African empire, The United Africa Company, tended to stay with it. But the crucial point is that Unilever did not feel the full force of American competition until after the Second World War, when Procter and Gamble began to make serious inroads into its markets; the competitive strength of Procter and Gamble has done more for Anglo-Dutch unity in Unilever than any other single factor. P and G's attack on Unilever's most important markets materially helped to wear down the resistance of those who wanted to retain two separate pyramids of power, one in London, the other in Rotterdam.

The businesses of the three companies are, of course, very different. About eighty-eight per cent of Shell's income comes from oil, the other twelve per cent from chemicals. ICI, on the other hand, has an enormous spread of interests: heavy chemicals, man-made fibres, plastics and paint as well as some quaint legacies from the diversifition pursued in earlier days by its constituent parts – the Kynoch Press, part of one of its subsidiaries, Imperial Metal Industries, is a good example. Unilever has an equally wide range of activity which takes in a multitude of foods, frozen and unfrozen, human and animal, as well as soap, detergents, and toilet preparations. It has the unusual distinction of being the producer of both home perms and curries.

The markets at which they aim are also different. Unilever, which sells perhaps eighty per cent of its output to housewives, thinks of itself as very much a 'Mum' company and is heavily involved in television advertising, plastic daffodils and all the other bric-à-brac of consumer promotion. The company has its own advertising agency, Lintas (short for the Lever International Advertising Service),[1] and spent over £170m. in 1967 on advertising and promotion. ICI, on the

[1] It also has its own market-research company.

other hand, sells very little direct to the public, and its world-wide promotion bill (including films, direct mail and displays) is only £12m. a year. Shell reckons to spend about £25m. annually on promotion of all kinds – half of it in the United States.

The companies' dependence on the British market also varies sharply. While ICI does not much less than half its turnover in the United Kingdom, Unilever's sales in this country account for about a third of its total business, while Shell does only ten per cent of its turnover and makes only five per cent of its profit in the British Isles.

Despite their size, all three were under the effective control of one man for a substantial part of their history, and in two cases until comparatively recent times. Sir Henri Deterding, the Dutch architect of the alliance with the British, was an absolute monarch in Shell until 1936 and Lord McGowan was virtually a dictator in ICI until 1950. In the case of Unilever, one of the tasks which Lord Heyworth set himself when he took over control of the company in 1942 was to make it plain that the Dutch founding families could not exercise power by Divine Right. In his last few years in office, he had been the dominating figure of the Unilever Board, partly by virtue of his knowledge of the business and partly because of the immense authority which he built up over the years.

The days of one-man rule are no more: all three companies are now run by committees. Unilever has its Special Committee of three; Shell has its committee of five managing directors (until fairly recently there were seven); ICI has its Board with a chairman who is not the chief executive – the company has firmly resisted pressure from within and advice from without (from McKinsey) to change this. The present chairman, Sir Peter Allen, is emphatic that ICI is not like the typical American corporation with its chief executive officer. His own role in the company, he says, has 'some element of the Prime Minister with his Cabinet, some element of the cricket captain and his team'.

In recent years, each of the companies has gone through a major reorganization; both Shell and ICI hired McKinsey to help them, Unilever preferred to do the job for itself. In each case, it was a difficult and often painful process. Unilever has spent a good part of the 1960s carrying through its revolution – which essentially consisted in transferring power over the group's most important products in key European countries from national managements to new overlords, known as co-ordinators, whose job it is to ensure that a cohesive policy is followed across national boundaries in defined product areas. At first, opposition to the idea was so powerful that the Special Committee shelved the plan for a year until there were signs that a reform of the company structure along the lines they had in mind would be welcomed. Setting out to change ICI, according to one of the company's former deputy chairmen, was also far from easy. It was 'like sticking pins in a sleeping elephant', he said, and added, 'you need a lot of pins'.

All the companies clearly play a significant role in the British economy. ICI alone is responsible for $2\frac{1}{2}$ per cent of the output of British manufacturing industry and between six and eight per cent of the country's investment in manufacturing industry. Shell earns the attention of the Government for a different reason. It keeps a very large part of its reserves of cash and securities – which amounted to £651m. at the end of 1968 – in London in sterling. It also brings back to Britain the greater part of the foreign exchange which it earns and converts it into sterling, and negotiates each year with the Treasury to fix a sum which it can convert back into foreign exchange for re-investment abroad. The unfortunate thing from Shell's point of view is that this sum is somewhat restricted when Britain is in balance of payments difficulties – a not infrequent state of affairs – and Shell then has to raise funds abroad.

Shell's Helicopter View

Shell's top executives in London hardly regard themselves as part of life in Britain at all, and try to cultivate what they call 'the helicopter view'. 'England,' said one, 'is just as much abroad to us as Venezuela.'[1] Indeed, if one is to believe what some of them say, their residence in the British Isles has become increasingly grudging: they vent their spleen about the British tax system by speculating on the benefits of taking themselves off en bloc to New York, or to some other kindlier financial climate.

Their virulence is made all the sharper by the size of the resources at Shell's disposal. Like Government officials, they use millions and

[1] Shell-Mex and BP which, under joint ownership, markets Shell's products in Britain, is simply the nearest of Shell's associated companies. It is comparable to Deutsche Shell or Shell Italiana (though they are owned hundred per cent by Shell) and is a great deal less important than Shell Oil, the group's American affiliate.

billions as normal units of discussion. 'Six nothings don't overawe me,' said Frank McFadzean, the managing director who is currently in charge of planning. 'It all comes down to simple principles in the end.' Sometimes its officials fall into what sounds to the outsider like blasé grandiloquence. For example Shell, like other oil companies, has taken out catastrophe insurance, to protect it against the impact of major disasters. 'But,' said one of its senior finance men, 'we wouldn't worry about £2m. After all, you don't insure your fountain pen.'

Shell's extraordinarily well-endowed complex of offices on the south bank of the Thames has 3,000 rooms, the largest private telephone exchange in Britain, a swimming pool of international standard, a rifle range, a cinema and four squash courts; and about 4,600 people work there. Yet Shell Centre is only half – though the larger half – of the Royal Dutch/Shell Group's central offices. The other, a good deal more modest in size, numbers and facilities, is in The Hague. Between them, they control the second largest oil group in the world, with over £3,000m. of assets. Shell supplies fourteen per cent of all the oil sold in the non-Communist world; has interests in oilfields in twenty-two countries; owns or has an interest in seventy-eight refineries and 41,000 miles of pipeline; and either owns or has on charter well over seventeen million tons of shipping, a sixth of the world's tanker tonnage. On an average day, Shell has four hundred ships at sea.

It is all a long way from the Shell of pre-war days, when the company was still relatively modest in size and its form of paternalism (except during the worst days of the 1930s) fully justified its nickname of 'Momma Shell'. The oil industry at that time was, after all, fairly predictable. A handful of major companies dominated the world, consulting regularly with each other and behaving very much as if the oil business was a club.

Most of Shell's oil came from Indonesia, Venezuela and Borneo, was refined at source in a handful of installations like the one at Balikpapan in Indonesia, was then shipped in an armada of 180 vessels, most of them between 9,000 and 12,000 tons. Britain was supplied by a fleet of coastal tankers, which landed oil products at a dozen different ports. At this sort of size, it was still possible to manage Shell in a loose and highly personal way. Departments were known by the initials of their bosses, the records of meetings were often kept only in people's heads, there were no budgets and no financial controls worth the name.

Shell, indeed, had never been quite so ascetic or profit-conscious as competitors like Standard Oil of New Jersey (which operates in

Britain as Esso Petroleum). 'We've never been greedy,' said Charles
Hadfield, until a few years ago Shell's finance co-ordinator, and recalled
that when he went about after the war saying that the prime aim of the
business was profit, he was told to 'tone it down a bit'. Shell expected
to make its way in the world by a combination of marketing skill
and political shrewdness, and it recruited the kind of men who were
able to get on well with heads of Governments. Since the company was
also, in many of its parts, what Frank McFadzean described as 'the
commercial branch of the Raj', this meant taking on young men of
pedigree. Hadfield remembers being interviewed by a woman in the
1930s: 'She asked had I been to Eton, and then before I could reply,
said "oh, everybody's been to Eton" and put down Eton. Did I play
polo – "oh, everybody plays polo" and so on.'

Particularly in those parts of the world where the company held
virtually unchallenged sway, life with Shell was civilized indeed.
'We must have had ninety per cent of the business in the Sudan,' said
Hadfield, 'and eighty-five per cent in Malaya – and we'd usually
shut up shop at four and play golf. In Kenya, the ADC to the Governor
was always ringing up and asking four or five of us to come to
dinner.'

After the war, there were problems – Shell had lost one of its major
sources of supply, Indonesia – but selling oil was not one of them; with
a world shortage, Shell had only to find and market it. 'Possession of the
stuff,' said Gerry Wagner, one of Shell's Dutch managing directors,
'was enough to make you money.' Because Shell did not have enough
oil of its own, it had to make good the deficiency by buying supplies
from other producers, like Gulf.

Little had happened as yet to disturb the oligopoly of the pre-war
years. 'We didn't cut each other's throats,' said Harry Bridges, now
head of Shell's operation in Canada. 'In a world where you were short
of supplies, you didn't step on the other man's toes too much.' But, in the
scramble for oil and markets, a good deal was left undone. For one thing,
little attempt was made to introduce either order or logic into the
company's untidy organization; Shell had lost a dictator without
finding a constitution. 'We didn't try to manage anything between
1945 and 1956,' said Frank McFadzean. 'There was a terrible diffusion
of responsibility.'

Nor was there much in the way of forward planning. Prices were
stable, profit margins ample: 'the future,' as Jan Brouwer, the senior
of Shell's five managing directors, put it, 'did not play too much of a

part'. The result was that Shell grew fat and rather self-satisfied. 'We were living,' said Dr Hoog, Shell's manufacturing co-ordinator, 'in a rosy, hunky-dorey world.'

In this sort of atmosphere, Shell, like everybody else, went for a high volume of sales without enquiring too closely into costs. It had long been an article of faith that the group should be represented everywhere, and thousands of outlets were allowed to open up without any real analysis of future profitability. 'Fifteen years ago,' said Monroe Spaght in 1967, 'somebody came along and said 'we'd like to represent you here". "Thank God", we said. Now he has a twenty-year contract and he can tell us where to go.' This overriding passion for volume was perhaps all the more curious in that Shell, unlike BP, was always short of crude oil of its own – and, in these years, not noticeably successful in the search for new sources of supply.

But the era of oligopoly and fat profit margins soon came to an abrupt end. Independent, and relatively unknown American companies like Marathon, Continental and Amerada set out to find cheap Middle Eastern crude and by the mid–1950s were finding it in large quantities. Life was made all the more difficult when the US Government fixed a quota on the import of crude oil to protect the home industry, forcing the independents to find other markets in Europe and elsewhere. The world shortage of oil was turning into a world surplus.

This fact was temporarily obscured by the artificial shortage created by the Suez war. Shell found itself beautifully placed to exploit the situation. It had a major source of supply, Venezuela, which was not affected by the crisis, and it used its advantage to the full. 1957 was the company's *annus mirabilis*: it produced a record profit of £225m. and a return on net assets of over fifteen per cent.

Unfortunately, the end of the crisis brought a glut of oil on the world's markets and a disastrous collapse of prices – by between forty and fifty cents a barrel. Shell's profits fell by almost thirty per cent in one year, its return on net assets from 15.3 to 9.4 per cent. The collapse was a shattering blow to the company's morale, and its repercussions all the more far-reaching because several of Shell's most influential managing directors were men who remembered both the difficult years of the 1930s and the company's desperate shortage of cash after the war. The hatches were battened down firmly in the hope that good times would return. Capital investment was held down – it did not reach its 1956 level again until 1964; projects were mothballed for between six and eighteen months; Shell chartered ships rather than building them; and, by 1963, the company was hiring refinery capacity.

Shell, however, *had* become concerned about its confused organization and in 1957 it invited McKinsey to help sort it out. The McKinsey men found a company which had been growing rapidly but which had never been thoroughly unified; such unity as it had, depended on individual personalities. Now, there was to be an attempt to produce one company, instead of two running side by side. The exercise was known as 'Operation Fasten Your Seat Belt'.

The weaknesses in Shell's structure were plain enough. It was, in the first place, divided at the top. The two offices in London and The Hague functioned as separate entities – in some ways, they might have belonged to different companies – and there were two departments for many functions – personnel, for example. Nor did the managing directors of the Group work cohesively enough to bridge the gulf, and indeed were apt to create their own self-contained empires.

This split was reflected throughout the organization. Both London and The Hague had their own geographical spheres of interest, and each had areas of functional expertise under its control; the geographical dividing lines had been drawn to take account of politics and history rather than on the basis of logic or commercial good sense. Indonesia, for example, was part of the Dutch sphere of interest: Borneo part of the British. But, although Indonesia was in the Dutch zone, the marketing of its products was directed from London – which had traditionally been responsible for the marketing, shipping and finance functions in Shell – while production and exploration were controlled from The Hague. Similarly, although the Argentine was in the British zone, its production and exploration activities were run from Holland.

In these circumstances, it was hardly surprising if general managers of individual operating companies were in doubt as to where ultimate responsibility lay; all too often they were caught in a withering cross-fire of directives from both central offices. The one beneficial effect of the system was that it bred strong general managers; anyone who could survive this sort of confusion, and prosper, was proof against anything.

The reorganization which came into force on April 1, 1959 (a happy coincidence for cynics within the company) corrected a number of these weaknesses. There was to be one, unified central office, and the duplication of departments was to end; in future, for example, there was to be one personnel department, in either London or The Hague. The division of the world into British and Dutch spheres of interest was also largely brought to an end: regional boundaries were to be drawn with the idea of improving efficiency rather than preserving some historic interest. Shell's chemical business was hived off and became a separate operation.

The managing directors, who had often acted independently of each other and, when they met, had done so without agenda or notes, were now to work in unison. But they were also given a more limited role: they were told to spend less time on detail and were charged with developing an overall, long-term strategy for the company. The operating companies, on the other hand, were given even greater autonomy under the new regime: they were, in theory at least, to be sovereign bodies in which the 'mind and management' of the company was to reside. Finally, to allow the managing directors freedom to think and to prevent Shell from disintegrating into a hundred parts while they were doing so, a new race of men, known as co-ordinators, was created. As their name implied, they were given the job of handling the day-to-day affairs of the group.

The title was chosen to avoid any suggestion that the operating units were being managed from either London or The Hague. Some of the co-ordinators were responsible for particular functions, such as finance, others for different regions of the world. They were paid between £15,000 and £30,000 and most of them were to be based in London. All the oil co-ordinators reported to a managing director who acted as Director of Co-ordination Oil (DCO), and all the chemical co-ordinators to a Director of Co-ordination Chemical (DCC).

So much was clear enough; there were however, a number of oddities. The first was that the managing directors were neither to manage nor direct. Once they had conceived the grand strategy, they were given no clear-cut executive power to ensure that the operating units carried it out. On paper, at least, they could convey their views only in the form of advice. (The co-ordinators were in the same position.) The managing directors were cast as philosopher-kings, but on the face of things with no more authority than their powers of persuasion afforded them.

This caution about the terms in which the operating companies were to be addressed sprang from the decision that the 'mind and management' of Shell was to lie with the operating units. Many people may regard this as simply a legal fiction, but fiction or not it is a useful (and legitimate) means of avoiding double taxation.[1]

The reorganization of 1959 represented a first step in the direction of order, but it had obvious weaknesses in practice. In particular, Shell did not find the concept of the managing directors as remote philosophers workable. 'If you are going to have super-geniuses with nothing to do,' said one of the present managing directors, 'then seven is too many.' In fact, the office of DCO proved to be too onerous a job for one man, while others tended to be under-employed. There was also a feeling that the operating companies had been given too much autonomy.

As a result, the organization structure has been progressively modified. The managing directors (now reduced to five) have, to say the least, assumed a more active role. In 1966, each of them (except Brouwer) was given responsibility for a region of the world as well as a number of functional jobs. Now, for example, Monroe Spaght covers the Western Hemisphere, chemicals, marketing and computer services, while McFadzean deals with Africa and the Far East as well as the marine side of the business, supplies and planning, exploration and production. Under the same reorganization, the office of DCO was abolished, to be followed in 1968 by the DCC. But then, of course, Shell was left with the same problem which it had had before McKinsey – namely, how to make sure that the managing directors did not behave like independent satraps. It therefore put one managing director in charge of planning. His job – it is currently McFadzean – is to make sure that there is proper liaison and co-ordination.

While their language in addressing operating companies remains advisory, the managing directors themselves have no doubt about where ultimate power now lies. 'People are sent letters, saying, this is

---

[1] Guarded language is not the only curiosity in Shell. The managing directors were (and still are) members of an organization which, legally and formally, does not exist. 'The Royal Dutch/Shell Group of Companies', says Shell, is simply a convenient way of describing the 'Shell family' and it does not refer to a single legal entity with a centralized management. The Boards of the two *parent* companies, Royal Dutch Petroleum and Shell Transport and Trading, do meet jointly every month, but the gathering has no legal standing. Thus, the committee of managing directors – which, like the Royal Dutch/Shell Group, has no legal existence – has, on paper, nothing to manage or direct except its own staffs. It does not constitute a Board in the normal sense of the word and it does not have a chairman, although one of them is the senior. What the managing directors do, in effect, is to represent the two parent companies and their views are merely, according to the senior member, Jan Brouwer, 'part of the flow of . . . advice and services' to the operating companies.

our advice as shareholders,' said McFadzean, 'but they'll get retold if they don't take it the first time.' 'Put it this way,' said Spaght. 'I'm stood there flat-footed in the door.' Wagner added that the committee of five only used the phrase 'it has been decided that' very occasionally, but that decisions were nevertheless taken. 'It's like discussions with your wife,' he explained. 'If somebody asked if you'd had a meeting with her to decide whether or not to buy a carpet, you'd say "no" – but you did!' The managing directors are now effectively the chief executives of their regions.

Yet, despite their new authority, Shell is still run by a committee; the five, who are paid between £50,000 and £75,000 a year, have equal status, and none has the final voice. At least one of the five vehemently opposes the idea of committee rule because he thinks the presence of five equals creates a temptation to try to reach unanimity before acting, but on the other hand the system works with considerable flexibility. If there is only one managing director in London when a decision is urgently required, he takes it.

Three of the five (McFadzean, Spaght and David Barran) are based in London, though they also have offices in The Hague; the other two (Brouwer and Wagner) spend most of their time in Holland. They meet as often as necessary, but usually twice a week, and there are probably two meetings in London for every one in The Hague. They spend a good deal of their time discussing future strategy and key appointments within the Group.

According to McFadzean, there is never a cleavage along national lines, and a vote has never been taken, In his view a vote would probably have to be accompanied by resignations. 'You simply recognize when the consensus is against you,' he said. 'There must be give and take in an organization like this.'

Before he moved to Shell, Spaght was a research chemist. Behind a mild, reflective manner, he conceals a considerable toughness; in his first six months as President of Shell Oil, he removed five vice-presidents (which he describes as 'a pragmatic experience') and, after cutting back the labour force sharply, took on the unions in a strike which lasted for a year in some plants. In the end, Spaght won and Shell Oil's profits went up 130 per cent between 1960 and 1966, as against ten per cent for the rest of the group. Shell Oil has also out-performed the rest of the American industry in recent years. Spaght took a considerable cut in salary (he was earning $250,000 a year) to take on the managing director's job.

He has a reputation for sharp awareness of the financial repercussions of new policies and feels strongly about the slowness which some parts of Shell have shown in cutting costs and raising profits. When he first arrived, he surprised a good many Shell men by asking them point-blank in the corridor whether they were making money. When I asked him what he thought he had contributed since his arrival in London, Spaght replied that he might have brought 'a greater sense of unhappiness'. To him, as to the evangelist, you are either winning or sinning.

McFadzean is much more overtly aggressive in style. A Glaswegian who ran away to sea before going to University to read law and economics, he talks like a machine gun and feels passionately about the perniciousness of Government interference in business. He worked at the Colonial Development Corporation – an organization which he now calls 'an exercise in buffoonery of the first order' – until he was sacked after a row with Lord Reith. He said in 1967 that he would retire from Shell before he was sixty unless he could raise its return on assets (then nine per cent) to twelve per cent within a few years: he looks like staying – in 1968, Shell's return went up to $11\frac{1}{2}$ per cent.

Brouwer, the senior managing director, represents an older tradition in Shell bosses: he is essentially a diplomat, precise, guarded and with a dry wit. He does not believe that emotion has any useful part to play in the running of a group like Shell. 'If your responsibility is managing a prize fighter,' he said, 'then you can afford the luxury. With a thing as complex as Shell, it is a waste of time.' Curiously, for the boss of an oil company, he enjoys the luxury of a coal fire in his office. David Barran, the chairman of Shell Transport and Trading, the British parent company, has the speech and mannerisms of a typical upper-class Englishman: he also has an extremely quick mind and is a first-rate negotiator. Wagner, the youngest of the five at 53, reached the top after being boss of Shell's company in Venezuela.

The composition and character of the five shows that a new type of man has emerged in Shell. The company still has its quota of congenial nonentities, but the old mixture of dictators and diplomats has given way to a much subtler blend of skills. 'We're not interested now in people who can talk learnedly about political developments,' said one of Shell's co-ordinators. 'We want men to whom a half-cent counts.'[1]

Even so, Shell still needs diplomatic skill. One of McFadzean's

[1] A change of one cent in the price of a barrel of oil makes a difference to Shell's profit, one way or the other, of £7½m.

responsibilities in recent years has been the conduct of negotiations with the Nigerians and Biafrans about Shell's £200m. investment there; errors of judgement in these matters can cost a good many half-cents. Nor was the Nigerian situation in any way exceptional. Shell has to live with the fact that oil is a strategic commodity, and that for nations like Venezuela, it accounts for over seventy per cent of the national income (in the case of Brunei it is over ninety per cent). Even in non-producing countries, an oil refinery has come to be regarded as a national status symbol, and Shell has found itself building a number of installations which could not have been justified solely on commercial criteria. Occasionally, perhaps, the company has been politically over-sensitive: it built a refinery in Denmark because of a fear that the Danes might not be willing to buy oil refined in Sweden. Past experience no doubt makes for caution. Shell's general manager in Cuba, who had had to deal with the Batista régime, was forced to flee the country when Castro took over.

In the first years after the disastrous experience of 1958, Shell's policy was basically one of retrenchment and reform. Its bosses rejected the risks of an expansive capital investment programme in an uncertain world, and decided to squeeze more out of the money which they had already spent. From 1960 onwards they began to make cuts in their labour force, and in the ten years up to 1967 reduced it by twenty per cent, while the company's output doubled. The central office staffs were trimmed as the McKinsey reorganization took effect and there was a substantial improvement in productivity at the refineries. The plant at Curaçao, for example, which used to produce 300,000 barrels a day with a staff of 11,000, now turns out 350,000 a day with only 4,000 people. Shell also began to dispose of some of its properties in overseas countries – houses, swimming pools and clubs were either sold or given away.

The trouble was that all the economies were more than wiped out by other factors. The price of refined oil products fell steadily, from $5 a barrel in 1960 to $4.30 in 1967, royalty payments to the producer countries went up by eleven per cent between 1960 and 1966 and by 1964 Shell's return on net assets had fallen still further to 8.2 per cent: it was at the bottom of the big oil company league.

It might be argued that such comparisons are bound to favour American companies which do a large proportion of their business in the United States, because American company income taxes average only about twenty per cent, against fifty per cent elsewhere. The effect of this discrepancy can be seen by comparing Shell's results with those of Texaco. In 1965, for example, Shell's total income was 232 per cent of Texaco's, but its income tax bill was 653 per cent (£209m. against £32m.). Texaco makes over seventy per cent of its profits in the US: Shell, about a quarter. On the other hand, this was far from a complete alibi. In 1964, BP – which at that time had no business worth talking about in the United States, still earned a better return on net assets than Shell.[1]

By 1963, however, it had become apparent to Shell that austerity by itself was not going to produce a marked improvement in its results. Total profits had risen slowly but they were still below their 1957 level, and there was no sign of the return of easier times. Even though there was a steady rise in world demand for oil (by about seven per cent per annum), supply continued to outrun it and prices to fall. The realization began to grow that if the group wanted to cut its costs further – enough, indeed, to improve its return on assets – it would have to spend heavily.

Its parsimony over the previous years at least meant that it had considerable resources at its disposal; cash reserves, which stood at £320m. in 1956, amounted to no less than £617m. by the end of 1963. In 1964, the company's capital expenditure at last rose above the 1956 figure: from then on, the increase was remarkable. Two years later, in 1966, Shell invested £533m., more than twice the 1963 total. This represented an extraordinarily sharp reversal of policy – an example of stop-go which even post-war British Governments would find it difficult to match. In some areas, it probably paid Shell to wait; in others, it merely fell behind its competitors. In 1968, Shell spent £553m. on capital investment, and expects to continue investing at about the same rate.

A substantial part of the money has gone into the building of giant 200,000-ton tankers. Shell (like others) had not placed major orders for new ships since 1956, and by the early 1960s was chartering roughly two-thirds of its tonnage, a proportion rather higher than the industry

[1] BP now has a strong marketing and refinery network in the US and has made a substantial oil strike in Alaska; the retail outlets will give it about 2 per cent of the US market and do not have to be paid for until the 1970s, by which time the Alaskan oil should be reaching the US market. Sir Maurice Bridgeman, the former BP chairman, told me in 1967 that the company had not entered the American market in the past either because of a shortage of cash or because it had not been sure whether it could obtain enough foreign exchange to finance the operation properly. Presumably it is now expected to pay for its retail outlets largely out of dollars earned from Alaskan oil.

average. This was one example, however, of where it paid to hold off on new investment because, as MacFadzean pointed out, if Shell had decided to build earlier, it would have found itself with a fleet of obsolescent 55,000-tonners. As it was, it placed its first orders for 200,000-ton ships in 1965. The timing proved to be fortunate, the contracts were fixed at good prices, and Shell ordered in such numbers that it is now well ahead of its competitors; no other company had eighteen giant tankers in service at the end of 1968. Although the oil has on occasions to be transferred into smaller ships for lack of deep-water ports, the big ships still give Shell substantial economies of scale, cutting as much as 12 cents a barrel off transport costs.[1]

Shell has also spent heavily on computers – over £70m. so far – in an effort to cut office and refinery costs further, but also to help it take strategic decisions more quickly and efficiently. Combined with an improved flow of information into the central offices, the computers enable the planners to assess much more accurately and rapidly the effect of a change of policy in, say, Switzerland, on operations in Austria, Italy, Germany and France.

Even more important, Shell's luck in exploration seems to have turned. For a time, nothing had seemed to go right for the group: in Libya, for example, it had watched Standard of Jersey strike it rich, while it had spent £10m. and found nothing worthwhile. In Nigeria with BP and in Oman, however, it continued to drill after others had given up, and was richly rewarded.[1] It hopes that Nigeria alone will one day yield it as much as a million barrels a day, over twenty per cent of its present needs. Not only would this reduce Shell's need to buy oil from other companies – it could cut outside purchases (which have already fallen from a third to twenty-two per cent) to an estimated sixteen per cent by 1973 – but would also mean a major saving on transport expenses. It costs only thirty cents a barrel to carry oil from Nigeria to Europe, compared with forty cents when the oil comes from the Middle East.

Shell has continued to find new areas where costs can be sharply reduced; marketing is one such. The pattern was set by what happened to Shell Oil in the United States after Spaght had taken over as President of the company in 1961. Spaght chose to abandon the Shell dogma that the company should be represented as widely as possible

[1] The outbreak of the second Arab-Israeli war hit Shell less hard than other companies because it pushed up chartering costs for smaller ships, it increased the advantage of the big tankers – and helped cover the cost of transfer to smaller ships.

and put the emphasis on profitable rather than universal marketing. If petrol stations were unprofitable, they were closed – even at the risk of losing some part of Shell's share of the market – and new ones were opened in more promising areas.

Shell Oil now has fewer petrol stations than ten years ago – 22,000 compared with 24,000 – but it sells three times the amount of petrol more profitably.

Spaght also reduced the labour force from 38,000 to 32,000 and did away with several layers of management. 'We just simplified the hell out of it,' he said. But other parts of Shell were slow to follow the American example. 'If we'd gone at it like Shell Oil in 1961,' said McFadzean, 'we'd be very much stronger today. For example, we could have closed eight hundred stations in Italy and increased Shell Italiana's profitability.'

Now, however, changes are being made rapidly. In Germany, unprofitable service stations are being closed, distributors bought out, contracts terminated; in Italy, Shell has stopped supplying in certain areas. In Britain, progress has been slower, largely because of the historic proliferation of retail outlets and because the 60/40 partnership with BP (like any other) tends to inhibit drastic measures. 'If anyone asked either of us whether we would link up today,' said one of the managing directors, 'we would just laugh hysterically.' That it has survived at all when other companies have been dissolving similar partnerships might suggest that it is profitable and that no satisfactory way of breaking it up has yet been found.[1]

The trouble is that Shell and BP (which is about forty per cent of Shell's size in overall terms) have interests which differ in many ways. BP is 'long' on crude (it is currently selling about thirty-five per cent of its oil to other companies) and short on marketing outlets : it is therefore reluctant to see any potentially profitable petrol station closed. 'Rationalization initially may mean losing gallonage to our competitors,' said one of its senior executives. Shell-Mex and BP is also more important to BP than it is to Shell : it is one of the largest units proportionately in which BP has an interest and does about one-eighth of the company's business. Shell, on the other hand, is short of low-cost crude, and has too many small outlets for its liking.

The upshot is that, although considerable efforts have been made

[1] BP, too, feels that the partnership is 'an unhappy compromise', but it is unwilling to pull out unless Shell is prepared to give it sufficient stations as part of the bargain, to keep up sales to the level which its share of the present partnership achieves.

to speed up rationalization, neither partner has been able to go as fast as it wished. The trouble, so far as Shell is concerned, is that forty per cent of Shell-Mex's stations contribute less than twelve per cent of its total sales, and that this forty per cent all have annual throughputs of less than 50,000 gallons: Shell believes an average of 50,000 gallons a year is a reasonable minimum target.[1] Spaght puts the Shell view crisply: 'there's too many damn outlets and it's not efficient enough as a system of distribution.' Applying the criteria which he used in the U.S., he would like to close three of the present outlets and open two larger ones in their place. He is quite prepared to see Shell-Mex's share of the market fall temporarily, so long as sales become more profitable in the process.

Progress has been made: a number of outlets have been closed and a surcharge has been put on small 'drops' by road tankers. This inevitably makes life more difficult for the smaller garages, but so far the vast majority have preferred to remain in business; nor can Shell-Mex force the pace too much since a good deal depends on the rate at which existing long-term contracts with dealers in the small stations terminate.

It has frequently been suggested that many of Shell's problems might be solved by a merger with BP. It would certainly dispose of the problem of Shell-Mex, and would also give Shell access to BP's ample supplies of crude oil – a large part of which now goes, ironically enough, to Shell's American competitors, Standard of Jersey and Mobil. Furthermore, a merger would mean considerable staff economies: the equivalent in number of BP's head office staff could probably be dispensed with. But the suggestion is firmly turned down by the directors of both companies, and for very plausible reasons.

Shell's major objection is that such an alliance would give the joint company well over a third of the petrol market in many major European countries, and that such a large proportion of the business would be difficult to improve upon except at considerable expense;[2] it might also, Shell thinks, make the group vulnerable to left-wing political attack in certain countries.

BP makes much the same point, but in relation to the situation which would be created in certain *producer* countries: the joint company would be buying something like eighty per cent of Kuwait's oil and sixty per

---

[1] Shell's major competitor, Esso, sets its sights on 100,000 gallons.

[2] Lord Heyworth, the former chairman of Unilever, made the same point in relation to detergents: 'when you have fifty per cent of the business in a country,' he said, 'it becomes too expensive to get more.'

cent of Iran's output. Furthermore no company with a Government shareholding can operate in Venezuela because of local law, which would presumably mean that – in the event of a merger – Shell would have to sell out its interests there because of BP's big Government shareholding. These are pertinent objections which would remain valid even if the nightmarish problems of the shareholding situation – with the British Government's forty-eight per cent and Burmah Oil's twenty-four per cent holding in BP and the sixty per cent Dutch ownership of Shell – could be resolved.

In any case, Shell is gradually coping with its traditional problem of being short of its own crude oil and is now in a healthy position. The company used to reckon modestly that, as a result of the war, it was four years behind Esso: now it believes that the gap has been narrowed to one. The best way of raising its return substantially, apart from the measures which have already been taken, would be for it to buy one of its American competitors. That would give it what it needs most, a still larger base on the North American continent. In that respect, at least, BP might now prove an ideal partner: the trouble is that the American Department of Justice might not think so.

Unilever's Many Mansions

If the 'helicopter view' is particularly useful at Shell because of the strategic nature of its wares, it is essential at Unilever because of the bewildering range of the group's activities. Ernest Woodroofe, one of the Special Committee of three men which runs Unilever, aptly describes it as 'the most scattered and diverse company in the world'. On the one hand, it is battling with the problems involved in maintaining a large imperial trading enterprise (the United Africa) long after the empire has disappeared; on the other, it is struggling to combat American giants (which fight on a much more limited front) in the most sophisticated markets in the world. As if this were not enough, it is engaged in a dozen other assorted contests in various parts of the world, and has recently given more indication of extending its commitments than of reducing them.

The Unilever Empire

Plantations

235,000 acres in the Congo, Nigeria, the Cameroons, Malaysia and the Solomon Islands, producing palm oil, palm kernels, rubber, copra, cocoa and tea.

Companies

The *United Africa Company* group, trading in twenty-two territories in Africa, plus Bahrein and Abu Dhabi. They own a fleet of ships, the Palm Line, tugs and barges which operate on the River Niger, a group of departmental stores under the name of Kingsway. They are in partnership with companies which sell, among other things, cement, beer, beds and plastics. In the *United States* Unilever owns Lever Brothers, which sells detergents, soap, margarine and toothpaste, and Thomas J. Lipton, which sells tea, soup and ice cream among other things. In *Britain*, it has forty companies, including Batchelors, Birds Eye, British Oil and Cake Mills, Domestos, Gibbs Proprietaries, John Knight, Lever Brothers, MacFisheries, Thames Board Mills, Van den Berghs, Wall's (ice cream and meats), and John West.

Products

In 1967, 17 per cent of Unilever's sales (£437m.) came from margarine and other edible fats and oils; 21 per cent (£515m.) from other foods; 20 per cent (£510m.) from detergents and toilet preparations; 8 per cent (£204m.) from animal foodstuffs; 9 per cent (£227m.) from merchandise and the other activities of The United Africa Company, and plantations; 5 per cent (£129m.) from paper, printing, packaging, plastics, chemicals and other interests.

In Britain

is behind Persil, Omo, Lux, Surf, Sunlight, Pears, Lifebuoy, Quix, Stergene, Sqezy, Domestos, Handy Andy, Vim, Knight's Castile, Breeze, Gibbs SR, Signal, Pepsodent, Sunsilk, Pin-up, Blue Band, Stork, Summer County, Spry, Cookeen, Birds Eye, Vesta, Surprise, Tree Top, Wall's sausages, pies and ice cream, and John West.

World-Wide

Unilever sells detergents and household cleaners in 50 countries, toilet preparations in 44, margarine in 40, ice cream in 15.

Unilever looks, and is, uncomfortably spread and it still bears the marks of its birth as the creation (in its British half) of a successful entrepreneur who latterly showed signs of megalomania.

The control of this far-flung empire has called for a good deal of ingenuity and tolerance (not to mention strong nerves) on the part of the commanders at headquarters. They have had to try and strike a balance between dominating subsidiary companies which in some cases would have preferred (and still prefer) not to acknowledge their relationship with Unilever, and granting its satellites so much freedom that the company's financial stability was imperilled.

The result has been what, at first glance, is a rag-bag of companies, where the degree of autonomy depends either on success or (as in the case of The United Africa Company) on size and tradition; but what is, in fact, a group where power is effectively in the hands of three men and in which headquarters retains a powerful range of sanctions. For one thing, the financial control exercised by head office is unusually stringent. Most of the subsidiaries have to clear their cash position daily through a Unilever account and, equally important, the amounts which even senior field commanders can spend without the Special Committee's approval are very modest indeed. The co-ordinator of the company's detergent business, for example, who is responsible in an executive capacity for operations in all the major European markets, cannot approve any item of capital expenditure costing over £50,000 without its blessing. (In Shell, by contrast, the managing director in charge of Europe can spend up to £1m. without asking anybody.) The Special Committee also retains power over the appointment and pay of executives earning more than £4,800. What is more, companies like Wall's have to report to a product boss at headquarters, and their strategy for yoghourt has to fit in with an overall plan.

These realities are sometimes obscured by the sniping at head office in which some of Unilever's subsidiaries indulge. A number can be so disparaging in their attitude that from time to time, Unilever is reluctant to allow inquisitive outsiders free access to them. Birds Eye and Wall's, for example, are reported to take the view that, while they do belong to Unilever – just – it would be better if the rest of the company were more like Birds Eye (or Wall's) and that, since the main Board know damn all about their business, they should keep their noses out of it.

So, despite the diversity of Unilever's empire, enormous power remains in the hands of the Special Committee, to which the Board delegates all its powers (except formalities like the declaration of the dividend).[1] For the last twenty years, the committee has consisted of three men; these three take virtually all the decisions that matter and once they are taken, they represent Unilever policy. The present trio consists of Lord Cole, Harold Hartog and Ernest Woodroofe. Three is not only a good number from the point of view of efficiency: it also happens to be the minimum which is practicable given the fact of Unilever's Anglo-Dutch parentage. The chairmen of both parents clearly have to be members, and since two would – equally clearly – be an awkward number in case of major disagreement, a third is essential.

The existence of a triumvirate at the top of the business also frees each of the three to travel to the outlying parts of the company – and showing the flag is important in a company as widely spread as Unilever. Lord Heyworth, who became chairman of the Special Committee in 1942, had noted the chaos which frequently broke out when the first Lord Leverhulme set forth on his travels – a steady stream of cables pursued him round the world – and laid it down that decisions should be taken by those members of the Special Committee who happened to be in London at the time. Heyworth also felt that a triumvirate was more difficult to lobby, particularly since none of the three represented any individual part of Unilever; when he first joined the company, the Special Committee had had seven members – which made things far too easy for bosses of subsidiary companies who appeared before it with proposals for new capital investment. 'It was money for old rope,' he said. 'There were so many people shooting questions that you could do just what you liked with them.' With only

[1] It is only on rare occasions that decisions are taken at the weekly meeting of the Unilever Board, which is essentially a way of keeping the directors informed about the overall progress of the business. Unilever's co-equal British and Dutch parent companies – Unilever Limited and Unilever NV, each with its own shareholders and its own head office – give it the appearance of a diarchy. This impression is re-inforced by the fact that when the Special Committee meets in London, it is chaired by Lord Cole, the chairman of Limited, while when it meets in Rotterdam, it is chaired by Harold Hartog, the chairman of NV. In fact, the two companies are linked by a whole series of agreements which ensure that, operationally, the business is run as one – the two parent companies even have identical Boards. The existence of two head offices, however, has its uses; for example, it legally avoids the double taxation (British or Dutch) which would fall upon the company if it had only one head office. The aim of the exercise is precisely the same as Shell's: it is simply that the means are different. Whereas Shell legally avoids double taxation by having central offices which do not manage, Unilever achieves the same result by having two head offices instead of one.

three,[1] on the other hand, there could be complete discipline in the questioning of applicants for company cash: communication was also markedly better.

Since all items of major policy must go through the Special Committee, it meets frequently. Each of the three reckons to spend a third of his time on it, and Woodroofe puts the proportion as high as forty per cent. They have inter-connecting rooms in Unilever House; meetings are held in the one which happens to be most convenient. The men from The United Africa Company see them once a month, the chief product bosses once or twice a month, and they can rapidly summon anybody else. Even the most independent of the subsidiary bosses can be called in at a moment's notice; equally, the Special Committee can be convened immediately for anyone whose business is urgent enough.

A key part is played by the secretary to the committee, a woman – 'we can't be rude to her,' said Lord Cole. She fixes the meetings, allocates the time during which the visiting bosses make their reports, calls in additional people whom she thinks ought to be there, and at the end of meetings circulates the minutes to the two company secretaries, the Board and any appropriate senior managers. Woodroofe claims that this system makes Unilever 'the best-documented company in the world'. With its range of interests, it needs to be.

But the Special Committee's efficiency obviously depends on the ability of the three men concerned to work together with a minimum of friction. In that respect, Unilever are lucky in the present incumbents.

George Cole, so far as the running of the business is concerned, is *primus inter pares*. He can, and on occasion does, exert a decisive influence on both the Special Committee and the Unilever Board. It was Cole who talked the Board into planting a large new palm oil estate at Sabah (North Borneo) when there was still a risk that Indonesia might move into the area. Again, when the company's British detergent business was under investigation by the Monopolies Commission, it was Cole who insisted that the Board should take a firm line with the Government and refuse to offer a voluntary cut either in prices or in its advertising budget.

Cole is a man of middling height, bald, sharp-eyed, rather like an avuncular eagle in appearance. He was born in Singapore and went to school there before joining the Royal Niger Company; his experience includes running the retailing side of the United Africa Company's

[1] Unilever, like Shell, reduced its committee by not replacing members as they retired.

business. It has fallen to him to consummate the work of Heyworth in trying to forge a united company, instead of two national enclaves.[1] Whereas Heyworth challenged the assumption of some members of the Dutch founding families that they should wield influence in the business as of right, Cole has carried through the first part of a revolution which has effectively destroyed the old spheres of influence, with the Dutch taking Europe and the British the rest. The revolution is far from complete, but at least the necessary legislation is on the Unilever statute book; it is arguable that Cole has had to spend too much of his nervous energy prosecuting it.

He has also made a contribution to a certain democratization which has become evident in Unilever in recent years. Cole does plenty of talking in the Special Committee but, whereas Heyworth did all the reporting at Board meetings, individual members now report for themselves. Heyworth was held in considerable awe, and colleagues who chose to disagree with him paid heed to certain well-known danger signals. 'When Geoffrey started rubbing the side of his nose,' said one Unilever director, 'you stopped arguing.' Cole's first reactions can be explosive, but there is a feeling that the opportunities for debate are now greater. The change in atmosphere has also been marked in a number of more trivial ways. For example, the table in the directors' dining room used to be oval, the chairman always sat on the left inside the door, and waiters placed the members at it in order of seniority. When he took office, Cole introduced a round table, and decreed that there should be no fixed places.

These changes are as much a reflection of Cole's own status in the Unilever hierarchy as of any difference in temperament. In his last years, Heyworth had dominated the Board partly because he had been in power long before even the most senior of his colleagues: Frits Tempel, the chairman of Unilever NV in 1956, did not come on to the Unilever Board until five years after Heyworth had been appointed chairman. Many of Cole's colleagues, by contrast, are much closer to him in seniority.

But, in any event, it is doubtful whether Cole could have been the dominant figure which Heyworth was, if only because the business is now so much more diverse. When Heyworth took office, Unilever was essentially a soap and margarine concern – even in 1950, sales of soap, detergents and margarine were over four times greater than those of

[1] Heyworth said his aim was 'to produce an Anglo-Dutch team instead of two nearly balancing factions'.

other products. Granted Heyworth's expertise in both fields, it was a business which one man could still dominate. Since then, it has become increasingly diverse and, by 1967, sales of 'other foods' were greater than those of either margarine or soap and detergents.

Cole's judgements are often subjective and instinctive rather than analytic. He also favours memoranda and directives which, according to one Unilever director, are 'brief but obscure, like Napoleon's constitution for Westphalia'. This occasionally gets him into trouble with some of Unilever's Continental bosses, who like to be given precise instructions which they can then follow to the letter.

Harold Hartog, the chairman of the Dutch parent company, is the only surviving representative of the founding families on the Unilever Main Board.[1] Hartog's of Oss was started by his grandfather as a meat-packing concern, and then moved into margarine but Hartog did not come into Unilever until after the merger and never worked for the family business. Whereas some members of the founding families have, in the past, resisted the unification of Unilever because they wanted to maintain Dutch power over Europe, Hartog has always been a convinced integrationist who believed that national amour-propre had no part in an international business. Perhaps he was influenced by the effect which German nationalism had on the Unilever business in the 1930s and remembers the time when Unilever avoided public mention of its German operation because of Hitler's hatred of foreign companies. (Now there is a Unilever House in Hamburg and Unilever shares are quoted on the Hamburg Stock Exchange.)

A slight and courteous man, Hartog lives in London and has a week-end house in Surrey, but as the boss of the Dutch parent, considers Europe to some degree his parish. The two sides of the business still have their individual management jamborees and while Cole is talking to the British managers at a gathering known as the 'Oh Be Joyful', Hartog is saying much the same things to Continental managers in Rotterdam.

Ernest Woodroofe, the third member of the Special Committee, is a Yorkshireman who took a Ph.D in physics at Leeds University before joining the oil-crushing side of the business. As a former head of the research side of Unilever, he strongly rejects the idea that the company is little more than a gigantic grocer's shop and points out that it spends over £19m. a year on research and development. In the Special

[1] Lord Leverhulme, the grandson of the founder of Lever Brothers, is an advisory director.

Committee, Woodroofe is the most analytical in approach and frequently attacks the proposal under scrutiny.

None of the three limits his interest to any particular part of Unilever – it would make his presence indispensable, apart from anything else – but Hartog knows more than the other two about Europe, and Cole is the acknowledged expert on Africa. Hartog is quite frank that, on some occasions, they do not possess the specialist knowledge needed for the precise assessment of an investment proposal. 'In that case,' he said, 'we have to make our judgement on the basis of the man who's putting up the idea.' This, again, is some reflection of the impact of Unilever's gigantic spread.

The Special Committee does not divide on the basis of nationality, it has never in recent times come to a majority decision and it has never taken a vote; it appears, in fact, to work on the consensus theory which operates in Shell. A major disagreement at this level could be catastrophic and some trouble is taken to project a unity which may be less than perfect. 'If there were disagreement on some small point,' said Woodroofe, 'we wouldn't voice it, because then the decision would seem less firm on the other side of the table.'

One complaint about the Special Committee is that, because it is overburdened, it is slow to make up its mind. Woodroofe admits that it is close to being over-worked, but believes that important decisions are taken very quickly indeed: a good many less crucial decisions are certainly delayed because they have to pass through this narrow funnel.

Another criticism is that the Special Committee keeps too tight a rein on individual subsidiaries. Its financial control is certainly strict, and there is probably a good deal of petty interference from the multitude of committees which still festoon the Unilever organization. On the other hand, successful subsidiaries continue for year after year without the Special Committee making any alteration to the operating plans which they put up.

In the past, despite its smallness and flexibility, the Special Committee has sometimes looked slow on its feet: slow to respond to challenges such as that posed by Procter and Gamble's development of non-soapy detergents after the war, slow too to get out of businesses which did not produce satisfactory profits. (The sale of the Norwegian business as long ago as 1957 is the best example of Unilever giving up a significant area of operation.) Nonetheless, it was a vital link for as long as there remained two virtually separate pyramids of power in Unilever, with the Dutch controlling Europe from Rotterdam, and Britain controlling the rest from London. Just how divided an existence the two sides led – and this until comparatively recent times – may be judged from the fact that even the buying of oils and fats was done separately. The division was marked not only by strong nationalistic feeling but also by some personal animosities.

The years before the war saw only a modest realignment in the original spheres of influence. The one major change was caused by Hitler's accession to power in Germany, the largest market within the Dutch sphere of influence. The profits of the Dutch side of the business, Unilever NV, suffered heavily – in 1933, Hitler ordered margarine production to be halved to protect the German dairy industry – and it was eventually decided that the old division of power was no longer satisfactory. The solution was for the British parent company to sell the American subsidiaries to Unilever NV. In a curious transaction, Unilever Ltd actually lent NV roughly £11m. to buy the American businesses from itself. This also helped compensate the Dutch for their losses during the war, when all the companies in Eastern Europe – including the Schicht group – disappeared into Communist hands.

The two separate pyramids of power continued to function after the war, though Unilever's centre of gravity remained – as it always had been – in London. Not only did the Special Committee (two Englishmen and one Dutchman) almost always meet there,[1] but the Board was dominated by Englishmen, generally in a proportion of three to two, while three of the four regional managements had their headquarters in London.

But the luxury of partition and the duplication of departments could not last forever. Procter and Gamble had already made inroads into Unilever's soap business in the first years after the war by developing and marketing a non-soapy detergent which was far more effective in hard water. Whereas in 1938 Unilever had held fifty-four per cent of the British market against Procter and Gamble's eighteen per cent, by 1950 Unilever's share had slipped to fifty-two per cent while P and G's had risen to thirty-three. By 1964, Unilever was only marginally ahead of Procter: forty-five per cent to forty-three per cent. (In 1967, P and G was slightly in the lead in world sales in terms of tonnage.)

But this was only the first phase of the American advance. The second came when US companies began to manage their overseas operations in a unified way. This monolithic assault exposed grave

[1] Occasionally, the Special Committee meets in Holland, partly to nourish Anglo-Dutch unity.

weaknesses in Unilever. Whereas P and G had universal products and international brand names, not to mention a vast home market, Unilever had different brand names and advertising campaigns for almost every major national market.

This was the result of allowing national managements to borrow whatever brand names and advertising campaigns seemed most suitable. The diversity had become not only uneconomic but also in some cases absurd. In Switzerland, for example, Omo was a soaker, in France it was a detergent. (It was the same with other products. In Holland, for example, Blue Band was Unilever's cheap margarine, in Germany it was the expensive brand.)

The basic trouble was that Unilever was divided into national units, each trying to market a wide range of products and each of them concentrating on what would profit them rather than Unilever as a whole. They were hopelessly ill-fitted to cope with giant American companies like Procter and Gamble, which did not recognize national boundaries and which were marketing only one group of products. Procter and Gamble made Unilever look cumbersome – 'it could turn Tide pink round the world overnight,' said a Unilever director enviously, 'we couldn't move like that'; with a more limited range of products, it was also able to concentrate its promotional effort.

Nor could the regional managements at head office do much to combat Procter and Gamble. They, like the national managements, were trying to cope with a huge range of products, and their power, in any case, was modest. The arrival of the Common Market made Unilever's fragmented structure seem all the more obsolete.

By 1961, it was becoming clear to Lord Cole that fundamental reorganization was overdue. The first tentative effort at reform was to create a group of co-ordinators whose job it was to develop an overall strategy for a given group of products. There was, for example, a detergent co-ordinator; another who covered margarine and other edible fats (known as Foods I); another for frozen and convenience foods (Foods II), and so on. The trouble was that they were given no teeth; they were merely there to provide advice.

Cole then set out to convince first ten men, and then fifty, that the co-ordinators should be given executive power over a group of key countries – Germany, France, Belgium, Holland and the United Kingdom – which would be known as 'executive' countries. The proposal set off a fierce argument. Some of the Dutch directors saw it as a threat to their preserve in Europe, and it was plain to bosses of national businesses that their own power would be considerably reduced.

The initial resistance was so vociferous, indeed, that Cole and the Special Committee retreated temporarily. It might have caused irreparable harm, they thought, to try to impose a solution. Gradually, however, economic logic produced a demand for change from below; at a two-day conference of a hundred senior managers held in Brighton in the autumn of 1965, it was the chairman of the German national Board who argued that major changes were necessary. The first co-ordinators with executive power took office in September, 1966.

There are now six co-ordinators – for detergents; margarine and edible fats; frozen and convenience foods; meat (known as Foods III); toilet preparations; and chemicals. Each of them is expected to span the entire world, but his executive powers are limited to the original countries, plus Italy which has been added more recently. The intention is to expand the executive area until it includes all the major markets of the world outside the United States.[1] It will never take in countries like Ceylon, where Unilever makes its entire range of products in one factory and where it would clearly be illogical to have the plant manager responsible to four different co-ordinators. These smaller markets are dealt with by overseas marketing and technical officers – 'jacks of all trades', in Woodroofe's words – who take advice from various co-ordinators before channelling it to the territory concerned.

The new structure has brought substantial shifts of power. Rotterdam has lost its undisputed control over Europe; although two of the most important co-ordinators have their headquarters in Holland (Foods I and II), the other four operate from London. The national managements, as expected, have suffered heavily and in some countries – Germany in particular – there was at first a serious decline in morale. They still give advice on manufacturing and marketing, they have a say in pricing and the division of TV time, they are also Unilever's front men in the different countries, but power undoubtedly lies with the co-ordinators. By switching from a geographic to a product base, Unilever has taken a major step towards becoming a united company.

It is far too early to judge how successful the co-ordinators will be in matching themselves against international competition. They are at least in power and facing up to some daunting problems. One of their tasks is somehow to reduce the host of Unilever's brand names. They want to make products interchangeable between countries as far as

[1] The United States is a special case for good reasons. See below, p. 138.

possible – 'though we wouldn't put a British sausage into Germany,' said a Unilever director – yet the margarine co-ordinator is faced with a situation where margarine can only be sold in tubs and bricks in Holland, in cubes in France and in cubes and tubs in Germany. Similarly, while a 'butter' flavour can be added to margarine in Holland and Germany, in France it is prohibited. There have already been costly failures in exporting products which were popular in some countries, but have proved unacceptable in others: Unilever's efforts to launch frozen foods and instant coffee in France were both flops. The field of frozen and convenience foods is a particularly difficult one, partly because the range of goods is so great, partly because there is much less uniformity in eating than in washing habits. Nevertheless there are obviously substantial savings to be made, even if only by not building a new plant in Holland when one already exists in Germany.

A second piece of reorganization aimed at unifying the two head offices and eliminating duplicate departments; the process is known as 'Lororization' – Lo standing for London, and Ro for Rotterdam. It began with the merging of the two research operations in the 1950s and, more recently, has been going ahead at a considerable pace. Unilever is shy about saying just how far it has gone, but the company is now in sight of having one head office, like Shell.

These fundamental changes will do a great deal to break down remaining national divisions. Inevitably, however, it will take a long time to 'Lororize' product areas which have virtually become national preserves; Unilever's margarine bosses, for example, are mostly Dutch.

The growing diversity of Unilever's business was another factor which hastened the arrival of product co-ordinators. 'National managements,' said Hartog, 'could no longer act as an effective sounding-board for all their companies.' The process of more rational diversification (as distinct from the undisciplined expansion of Leverhulme's last years) began in the later 1930s. By that time, Unilever had captured large shares of the soap and margarine markets in a number of countries (it was not unusual for it to have seventy-five per cent of margarine sales – and indeed its current share in Britain is nearer to eighty per cent)[1] and there was a belief within the company that the market for soap had reached saturation point in many places.

[1] One interesting feature of margarine sales in Britain is that the Allied Suppliers chain of shops (in which Unilever has a large shareholding) stocks only Unilever brands. Unilever denies that it has ever put any pressure on Allied Suppliers.

Heyworth says that the decision to make a major move into foods was taken in 1943. By then, Unilever had acquired the majority of the shares of Birds Eye in Britain (it did not become a wholly-owned subsidiary until 1957) and in 1943, the company also bought the Batchelors canned foods business. Heyworth says it also looked at Chivers, but felt that the capital structure was too complicated. Unilever thus expanded a base in foods which already included Wall's meat, Wall's ice-cream, John West and MacFisheries.

The new acquisitions represented a major shift in the balance of the company. They took Unilever a step further away from the vertical structure which Leverhulme had erected – where the company grew a proportion of its own raw materials, shipped them in its own fleet, processed them, packaged the result, transported them to retail outlets, and promoted them through its own advertising agency. There were weak links in the chain – Unilever's plantations have never provided a major part of its raw material needs and today do not supply even one-fortieth of those needs. With the move into foods, Unilever has to buy large supplies of agricultural produce; and when it began to manu-facture non-soapy detergents, it also had to purchase large quantities of chemicals, like phosphates, which its own factories could not produce.

The investment in foods was stepped up sharply in the mid-1950s. Unilever had become afraid that sales of margarine and edible fats might actually decline, while profit on convenience foods was good and the market growing: by 1958, forty per cent of married women in Britain between the ages of thirty and thirty-four had jobs. In the event, Unilever's fears were not realized. Margarine sales rose by seventy-five per cent, detergent sales by 120 per cent between 1955 and 1966; but the sales of 'other foods' shot up by 270 per cent.

Hartog holds to the view that while margarine sales may continue to increase, they will do so at only a modest price. In the prosperous part of the world, he argues, people will eat less visible fat for dietary reasons, while sales in the unprosperous part (where consumption of margarine is still rising) will be limited by low purchasing power. As for detergents, Hartog expects a steady, if not dramatic expansion – helped by the growing use of automatic machines, which take fifteen to twenty-five per cent more powder than non-automatic appliances. The major growth areas in the years ahead, he believes, will be in foods, chemicals, toilet preparations and 'disposables'.

If American competition and the increasing spread of the business have

demanded a more unified Unilever, African politics have made the
United Africa Company less of a separate province than it once was.
Cole said that traditionally an Iron Curtain had existed between them
which was largely respected by the parent company. There was always
financial control – which the UAC could scarcely complain about since
it was at times heavily in debt to the parent – but otherwise there was a
minimum of interference. The members of the Special Committee were
also members of the UAC Board, but it was they who crossed Blackfriars Bridge to United Africa House – with its books on Bantu and
sagas of the great explorers in the board-room – rather than the UAC
men who came to them. The UAC justified its somewhat cavalier
separatism by pointing out that they were merchants and not manufacturers. The parent company seemed prepared to stomach this
attitude.

By the 1930s, the UAC had developed considerably from the days
when its ancestor, the Royal Niger Company, had shipped staple goods
like salt, textiles and sugar to West Africa and taken in return raw
materials like palm oil and kernels; it had no choice, because the basis
of the trade was barter and not money. At that time, the company also
employed its own private army, ran the Post Office and (by 1939) sold
50,000 items through thousands of shops and stores. 'We supplied
everything they wanted,' said Lord Heyworth, 'everything from gin to
dry batteries.' In return, the company took ground nuts, cocoa, ivory,
rubber and hides and skins.

During the war, the British Government – which needed the raw
materials for strategic purposes – set up its own marketing boards, and
the UAC bought for the account of the Government. 'You had to be a
genius not to make money in those years,' said Sir Arthur Smith, the
solid Boltonian who is now chairman of the company. 'You could sell
goods at almost any price, because they were in such short supply.'
The UAC earned as much as forty per cent, after tax, on its capital
employed.

The fat profits continued after the war, but there were major political
hazards in the offing as African nationalism spread. The UAC bosses
therefore set about identifying the businesses which would still be
acceptable even if they were run by expatriates. They came to the
conclusion that they could not keep their small shops and stores, and
in the years that followed thousands were sold or written off. From
1955, the UAC began to redeploy its resources.

Immediately after the war, it had begun to set up a chain of department stores. Then it decided to look for areas in which it could manufacture, and sought partners with the necessary expertise. It now makes cement in partnership with Associated Portland Cement; brews beer with Heineken; makes beds in conjunction with Vono; manufactures cigarettes with Philip Morris and acts as agent for Vauxhall cars and Bedford trucks in Nigeria and Ghana. In Nigeria alone, the UAC has forty-four companies. But it still has its own port at Burutu, it still carries goods up the Niger on its own fleet of barges, and it still runs a shipyard to keep them in good repair.

The good years brought in a flood of competitors – particularly in the French territories. The company's business suffered heavily, and its redeployment left it short of a satisfactory return on capital. Nor could it avoid the consequences of the upheavals which have affected the area: the Congo war cost Unilever £2m., not to mention the loss of profits for six years after 1960. What the Nigerian civil war will cost cannot yet be guessed at. By the 1960s, the UAC was earning a meagre four to five per cent (after tax) on its capital employed. For a number of years now, the UAC's performance has depressed the returns which Unilever as a whole has been able to earn, and it is not much consolation to shareholders that the UAC, in Sir Arthur Smith's words, has 'a standing and a role in Africa which you can't put in terms of return on capital'.

The unsatisfactory returns forced the UAC to take a closer look at the profitability of every part of its business; many of its activities, as Smith recognizes, are based simply on tradition. The UAC is aiming to increase turnover from £275m. to £300m. by 1972, and to raise the return on capital to between six-and-a-half and seven per cent. At the same time, Unilever intends to reduce the proportion of its capital engaged in Africa without reducing the total investment.

The difficult times through which the UAC has been passing has not dimmed its determination to function as an independent unit, but the change in its circumstances has forced it to lean more heavily on the parent company. Unilever's manufacturing know-how is useful to it, not to mention its ability to help in resettling expatriates. For several years, the flow across Blackfriars Bridge has been reversed; it is now the UAC men who make the pilgrimage to the Special Committee.

Yet another part of the Unilever empire, its business in the United States (in 1968 its interests in North and South America employed thirteen per cent of its capital and earned the same proportion of its profit), has also kept an arms-length relationship with the parent company, though for rather different reasons. In this case Unilever is afraid that if it is seen to exercise management over its American interests it could be accused of being in business in the United States, and fall foul of the anti-trust laws. Cole insists that Unilever exercises only rights of ownership in the United States and the memoranda which cross the Atlantic are meticulously marked 'for information only'; the parent company fixes the dividend and it can replace the president of the US business, but in all other respects the Americans are left to go their own way.

For the most part, their own way has proved fairly satisfactory but Unilever's foothold in America confers other benefits besides cash. The United States is the land of innovation, particularly in the field of detergents, as the company has good cause to remember.

Unilever's overall performance in recent years has certainly not been particularly exciting. In the ten years ending in 1968, for example, sales went up by seventy-three per cent, profits by only fifty-two per cent. Its return on capital employed in 1968, at 9.3 per cent, was lower than it had been in 1959 – though it had recovered from a low point of 7.9 per cent in 1962.

Cole's reply to criticism is that a company as widely spread as Unilever is bound to show an average rate of return. He and other members of the Special Committee insist that the company's diversity is a source of strength in that, while one part of the business may be doing badly, there are usually compensatory successes on other fronts. They even excuse the UAC's low returns for the last decade by pointing out that it has in the past made up for shortcomings in other parts of the company.

Unilever is presumably stuck with its vast spread – it could hardly dispose of the United Africa Company or any other major part of the group – and with its average returns. But it is arguable that no business, however able its management, can hope to operate on so many different fronts as Unilever, and recent events only seem to emphasize its vulnerability to more specialized rivals; Procter and Gamble has given it a pasting on the introduction of enzymatic detergents, in which it led Unilever by several months. Yet Unilever was test-marketing a brand of its own as long ago as July 1967, and if its bosses had not been persuaded that more time should be given to perfecting it, they could have been out first. Now, they are struggling to catch up, and paying the price in heavy promotion expenditure (£5m. in 1969 in the UK alone). Even if, as is happening, Unilever managers tend to specialize instead of (as in the past) zig-zagging across the range of the group's activities, there is still a danger that diffusion will mean delay.

Unilever's modest progress, indeed, makes one think of the lines from the anthem to the British Empire – 'wider still and wider, shall thy bounds be set' and of the anthem's popular title – 'Land of Hope and Glory'. The danger for a company of Unilever's spread is that there will always be too much of the first and too little of the second.

ICI's Struggle for World Power

Whatever else ICI may lack, it is not brains. It employs about seven thousand graduates and continues to recruit new ones at a rate of six hundred a year. (Shell takes about three hundred a year, Unilever between sixty and eighty.) Nor is it simply a question of volume: the quality is also remarkably high – something like eighty of the annual intake have First-Class Honours degrees, and a number of them also have Ph.Ds. This intellectual excellence is reflected on the main Board: eight of the sixteen executive directors in 1967 were Firsts, and all sixteen had been to university.[1] Half the Board, in the view of Peter Menzies, one of ICI's three deputy chairmen, might easily have become professors if they had opted for academic life. At divisional level, only twelve of ICI's 103 directors in 1967 did not have a degree, and six of the twelve held some professional qualification. Of the 103, thirty-six were Firsts and thirty-eight had Ph.Ds or D.Phils.[2] This gives ICI the most educated management in British industry.

What is more, ICI's recruits generally come to stay. Whereas Ford

[1] This compares with an average of fifty-one per cent for directors of Britain's 102 largest companies. *Management To-Day*, March 1967: 'Britain's Top Directors,' by Robert Heller.

[2] Even in those parts of ICI which regard themselves as being 'earthier' (i.e. closer to the consumer), the proportion of graduates is still high. Only one director of Paints Division, for example, did not have a degree in 1967, while two had Firsts and two Ph.Ds; on the Board of ICI Fibres there were four Firsts and five Ph.Ds or D.Phils.

ICI

Products

12,000 different products of which the main groups are organic and inorganic chemicals; synthetic fibres – nylon and 'Terylene'; fertilizers and pesticides; plastics; dyes and pigments; paints; mining and quarrying explosives; medicines, antiseptics and antibiotics.

Divisions

Mond, headquarters Runcorn Heath, Cheshire. Soda ash – for which ICI has virtually the entire British market; chlorine and caustic soda, where it has 75 per cent. From chlorine comes the basic materials for PVC. Mond also produces lime, salt, chlorinated solvents, aerosol propellants and herbicides. It accounted for 19.2 per cent of ICI's sales in 1968.

Heavy Organic Chemicals, Billingham, Teeside. From naphtha, produces, among other things, ethylene – which goes into polythene, anti-freeze and detergents – and aromatics, basic to nylon and terylene production. 8.4 per cent of ICI turnover in 1968.

Agricultural, Billingham, Tees-side. Has about 50 per cent of the British fertilizer market. Largest ammonia manufacturer in the world. Also produces building materials such as cement and insulated boards. 12.1 per cent of turnover in 1968.

ICI Fibres, Harrogate, Yorkshire. Has at least 50 per cent of the nylon market in the United Kingdom, and is by far the largest producer of polyester fibre. 21.7 per cent of ICI's sales in 1968.

Plastics, Welwyn Garden City, Hertfordshire. Has at least 25 per cent of the British plastics market. Produces polythene, PVC and 'Perspex' among other things. It accounted for 12.3 per cent of ICI's turn-over in 1968.

Dyestuffs, Manchester. Nylon polymer, dyes, detergents. 11.8 per cent of turnover in 1968.

Paints, Slough, Buckinghamshire. Has about 40 per cent of the British retail market, and about a quarter of the trade market. 6.8 per cent of sales in 1968.

Nobel, Stevenston, Ayrshire. Dominates the British market in explosives. Accounted for rather less than 5 per cent of sales in 1968.

Pharmaceuticals, Wilmslow, Cheshire. Ethical medicines, antiseptics, antibiotics, anaesthetics. 3.5 per cent of ICI's turnover in 1968.

ICI manufactures, among other things, Alkathene, Propathene, Perspex, Dulux, Belco, Vymura, Bri-Nylon, Ulstron, Vynide, Terylene, Lightning Zipp Fasteners, Savlon, Flypel, Weedol, Lawn Plus, Verdone.

of Britain, for example, which has improved its record in recent years, still loses something like ten per cent of its graduate intake annually, ICI's wastage rate is less than five per cent a year. Graduates apparently find ICI congenial: indeed, Jack Coates, the company's general manager of personnel, believes it may be rather too congenial in the sense that the turnover is not large enough to maintain what he calls a 'through-draught'.

For the scientist or engineer – and eight out of nine of ICI's graduates are one or the other – the company's attractions are obvious enough. Its research facilities are first class, its managers civilized and highly intelligent, its clubs comfortable and it retains – in many of its parts – the atmosphere of the common room and the laboratory. Even at Millbank, among those who may not have done any chemistry or physics for twenty years, the old Adam is apt to break out. 'People are quite likely to sketch out a benzene ring on the back of a menu,' said Michael Clapham, another deputy chairman, 'and then add a radical or two.' (Clapham, a classics graduate, keeps a scientific dictionary in his desk to help him 'keep up with the words'.)

The company, in fact, provides a perfect bridge into industry for the young science graduate. The danger is that it may attract a large number whose motivations are not entirely commercial and it is noticeable that while ICI men, not unnaturally, look upon themselves as something of an élite, they do not necessarily regard themselves as being an élite of business. 'We think of ourselves as being a university with a purpose', said one of ICI's divisional chairmen. 'We are very similar,' said another senior executive, 'to the Administrative Class of the Civil Service.' The difficulty, as Peter Menzies sees it, is to get young scientists interested in 'things which they may consider vulgar, like selling plastic zip fasteners'. A good many, as Menzies admits, are never converted; enough survive, as the divisional Boards demonstrate.

Another of ICI's merits for the intelligent young man is a lack of authoritarianism and sense of hierarchy. There is a notable (and most attractive) freedom and lack of formality in the relationship between, for example, junior managers and divisional Board chairmen, and an implicit assumption that it is brains rather than rank which really matters. 'I was never under instruction,' said Peter Menzies, who went into the treasurer's department before the war. 'From the day I joined the company, I was part of the "we", I was never an employed man. Right from the beginning, I was telling – or advising – the people higher up what they should be doing – and it's an attitude we deliberately encourage.'

No other company in Britain has anything to compare with the Smoker which is held every year at Norton Hall, one of ICI's executive clubs in the North-East. At the Smoker, junior and middle management turn a cool and humorous eye on the bosses, who are invited to sit in the front row. 'Paul is Love' said the banner across the stage at the 1967 Smoker (Sir Paul Chambers was then the ICI chairman) and the songs and sketches were direct, to say the least. The atmosphere was that of a university soirée for elderly students. Balding executives dressed in green-and-white striped rugger strips acted as scene-shifters and main Board directors sat in the front row wearing 'Oscars' to indicate that they had contributed to previous Smokers. 'You'd never get so many graduates into one room anywhere else outside a university', said one proudly.

No doubt the high incidence of graduates throughout ICI helps to explain a certain intellectual arrogance about which ICI men themselves are apologetic. It may very well have been appropriate to the first thirty years of the company's life. For much of that time, buttressed by monopolies and protected by cartels, it was more often allocating its products than selling them. Its image among the British public was that of a gentle and benevolent giant, its return on capital usually eleven per cent or better; in 1960, it was 13.2 per cent. Since then, the arrogance has looked out of place. ICI continued to grow rapidly, but by the end of the 1950s it had entered what one of its senior executives described as 'the era of fallibility'.

The company had certainly emerged from the war in an extraordinarily complacent frame of mind. Its world was both limited and heavily fortified by self-denying pacts with other companies. It operated jointly with Du Pont in Canada, but it left the United States to Du Pont just as Du Pont left Britain and most of the old Empire to ICI: 'we didn't play around in their backyard', said Leslie Williams, one of ICI's former deputy chairmen. Out of a turnover of £263m. in 1951, ICI's sales in America amounted to less than £2m. Partly because of the old agreement with I. G. Farben, ICI had also not developed a European business worth the name, and sales in Western Europe in 1951 were below £5m. Despite the fact that the company did a substantial business in the countries of the old Empire, only about one-eighth of its total assets was invested abroad in 1950. It was essentially a national company and still remarkably parochial in its thinking.

The balance of its activities, on the other hand, had changed considerably since the early days of the merger. Whereas in 1927 over eighty per cent of its turnover had come from either the heavy inorganic chemicals of what is now Mond Division or from the explosives of Nobel, by 1949 Mond and Nobel accounted for a good deal less than half ICI's total sales. On the other hand, the new products which had developed before and during the war – plastics, fibres, paints and pharmaceuticals – still amounted to less than twenty per cent of turnover.

The company's complacency was also reinforced by the fact that it found itself in a world of shortages. Since a number of ICI's products were, in any case, monopolies or near-monopolies, the arts of salesmanship were, to that degree, superfluous. 'If you kept technically ahead of your competitors – where you had competitors, that is – you could sell the stuff', said one of the senior managers at Millbank. 'We used to believe,' said a former chairman of Mond Division, 'that if the chemistry was right and the engineering was right, the rest would look after itself. We didn't believe in sordid things like marketing.' The indifference was hardly surprising, since the operating divisions were not responsible for selling their own products. They simply manufactured them: the selling – in Britain, at least – was in the hands of a chain of regional offices controlled from Millbank.

The company's attitude to profit could be curiously ambivalent in these years. Sir Paul Chambers, who had joined in 1947, recalls that some directors were embarrassed to go to one annual general meeting in the late 1940s because they felt they had made too much profit. Chambers considered this ridiculous: the profit only seemed high because the company's assets were still being valued on a pre-war basis.

Not that it mattered a great deal what the directors felt in those early post-war days. ICI was run as a dictatorship by Lord McGowan, who remained chairman until 1950, when he was seventy-six. He both spoke and thought of ICI as 'my company', and his manner at the Board table could be brusque and peremptory. 'In introducing a topic, he would simply say "I've decided that . . .", ask for comments and then glare round,' said one who sat on the Board with him. He ran the business on a mixture of hunch and experience, and leaned heavily for advice on outside directors like Lord Weir.

Sometimes his hunches were influenced too strongly by a continuing loyalty to Nobel – he built a new protein fibre plant at Dumfries which cost £3½m. and is now closed – but his contribution to the growth of ICI was immense; he welded the four founding companies[1] into a unity and played a major part in building up the overseas business. If his arrogance and his personal mannerisms did not endear him to all his colleagues – he did not like to ride in the company lift with other people – he was at least open to question by anybody with the necessary courage.

The first real challenge to his rule came from Paul Chambers. Chambers, who became finance director in 1948, was the first executive director to be appointed from outside the company and, as a senior Civil Servant with the Inland Revenue during the war, he had been used to saying precisely what he thought. His first clash with McGowan came when he had the temerity to query some item of expenditure on an overseas venture, McGowan's particular preserve. Thereafter, McGowan decreed that nothing was to be approved until it had been agreed by the finance director.

There were to be other confrontations. At 10.30 each Wednesday morning, Chambers' finance committee met in the Board room, and this was followed by a meeting of directors at noon. On one particular Wednesday morning, McGowan sent his secretary to tell Chambers that he wanted the Board meeting brought forward to 11 a.m. Chambers told her that this was not possible and asked her to convey this information to the chairman. She was afraid to do so, and McGowan duly strode in at eleven. Chambers looked up and said: 'I'm sorry, this is going to take us another three-quarters of an hour. I'll let you know when I've finished.' The rest of the meeting was carried through in hushed silence and one director told Chambers that he simply could not do that sort of thing. McGowan, however, never mentioned the incident again until shortly before he retired, when he told Chambers: 'It was a damn good thing you did. If others had opposed me, it would have been so much better for everybody.' Chambers became one of the executors of his estate.[2]

But this was only one individual's challenge to the accepted ways

[1] Nobel Industries, Brunner Mond, the British Dyestuffs Corporation and United Alkali.

[2] After McGowan retired, he decided he would like to go to South Africa. When he found that ICI was no longer able to pay his expenses, he persuaded Sir Ernest Oppenheimer (father to Sir Harry) to invite him and pay for the trip. Oppenheimer said he would pay 'reasonable travelling expenses'. McGowan thereupon hired a special train to take him and a handful of directors from St Pancras to Tilbury and, after lunch, remarked to the party: 'I hope this will teach that bugger Ernest what reasonable travelling expenses means.'

of the company. Of more fundamental importance was the growth of new areas of business which were ultimately to transform ICI. They were the result of either diversification or of discovery. Nobel Division, for example, seeking a profitable use for its cellulose, had gone first into coated fabrics and then into paints: in 1936, a separate Paints Division was set up. Similarly, in the 1930s the old Alkali Division had discovered polythene, while Dyestuffs had worked on the development of pvc; both were eventually linked with a thermosetting plastics moulding powder company which ICI acquired, and a Plastics Division created. By 1945 it was still only a small business (with a turnover of between £500,000 and £1m.), but like paint it was ready for major expansion. In the same way, the research which Dyestuffs had done into anti-malarial and sulpha drugs, and its decision to manufacture penicillin in the early 1940s, laid the foundation for post-war expansion in pharmaceuticals.

Even more significantly for the future, ICI had moved into man-made fibres during the war. Having acquired the right to manufacture nylon through its patent-sharing agreement with Du Pont, in 1940 it formed British Nylon Spinners as a 50/50 partnership with Courtaulds. In the following year, Calico Printers discovered 'Terylene', asked ICI to help with its development and in 1947 sold its partner the world rights outside the United States. British Nylon Spinners opened a new plant at Pontypool in 1948, which was to be the base for a bonanza comparable with the rayon boom in the years before and after the First War. Sales of nylon grew by fifteen to twenty-five per cent a year from 1952 onwards, and the return on capital reached twenty-five to thirty per cent as nylon swept successively through women's stockings, lingerie, socks, knitwear, sweaters and shirts. Terylene, which took off roughly six years after the nylon boom had begun, also developed an annual growth rate of between fifteen and twenty-five per cent.

These new products not only changed the balance of ICI's business, they also began to create a type of manager who was noticeably different from the production and research-oriented bosses of the 1930s. No doubt the dissolution of ICI's pact with Du Pont in 1952, and the end of the seller's market after the mid-50s played a part in the change. The fibres group, for example, became involved in consumer advertising, refused to trust its fate to ICI's regional selling organization – it had its own sales force from the beginning – and looked with some disdain on the heavy chemical brigade: 'here', said one of its directors, 'it's a business you're running, not pipelines over the Pennines'. But the first real step forward came when ICI re-entered the retail paint market on January 1, 1953.

It had failed badly in efforts to do so before the war, but Leslie Williams, who had come up through the paint side of the business, had no intention of being held back by a conservative Board. He put the word Dulux on an ICI van and spent a modest £40,000 on an advertising campaign with the slogan: 'Say Dulux to Your Decorator'. One of the then directors thereupon told him that he would ruin ICI's paint business. These upheavals, however, affected only a small part of ICI's activities, and a sizeable part of the company still remains technical rather than commercial in its orientation.

Despite these changes, it continued to present a remarkably conservative face to the world. Throughout the decade, it was led by elderly Scotsmen of scientific rather than commercial inclination. McGowan was succeeded by John Rogers, a 72-year-old Glaswegian who had begun life as a lab. boy before joining Nobel, and in 1953 he was followed by another Glaswegian, Alexander Fleck (later Lord Fleck), who was already sixty-four. Fleck, a chemist of considerable distinction, who had begun as a laboratory assistant, was a man of impeccable integrity who was universally loved throughout the company. He was, however, not only more interested in the technical than the commercial aspects of any proposition but also knew little about finance. He did little to educate a Board which was, in large part, commercially naïve like himself.

On the other hand, Fleck restored some sort of democracy to the deliberations of the Board in contrast to the long years of McGowan's dictatorship. His technique was simple. He would go round the table, allowing each man to put his view, and keeping a score-card. If there was a clear majority for the proposal, Fleck would recommend it: if not, he would call for further discussion. This led to long-winded debates, but it brought a new sense of corporate responsibility to the Board and, even if Fleck himself rarely gave a positive lead in commercial matters, he had in Paul Chambers a deputy chairman who was ready to back the new men and new products. Money was not a problem at this stage. The capital hunger of the 1960s was still in the future and for the moment there was more cash than projects. ICI invested in fibres and plastics among other things and, except for one bad year (1958),[1] the return on investment remained above eleven per cent.

[1] 1958 was a poor year for many industries, and particularly for one as closely linked to the fortunes of the UK economy as chemicals.

The easy times were over by the time Fleck retired in 1960, and Paul Chambers, the new chairman, had inherited more problems than policies. The company was internationally weak; technologically conservative compared with the Americans; and its organization was both illogical and out-of-date. To remedy this ICI had to be prepared to spend large amounts of money, to suffer the birth-pangs which inevitably attend the introduction of a new technology and to face a major administrative upheaval.

ICI was still very much a national company. Sales in Western Europe had risen to £35m. by 1960 and in 1958 ICI had linked up with Celanese in the United States in an effort to break Du Pont's grip on the American polyester market, but these were only the first steps forward. The harsh fact was that the company had neither the plant nor the organization to sustain a major attack on the markets of the world.

The crucial need, if that was to be attempted, was a massive programme of plant renewal and extension. It had become cheaper to run ICI's ammonia plants on oil rather than coal in 1956, but it was not until 1958 that funds had been made available to build some small ammonia units based on naphtha feedstocks. ICI's initial investment was modest. Meanwhile it was still running large numbers of small plants – partly a legacy of the wartime policy of dispersal – and in the late 1950s Mond Division was operating plants built during the war.

ICI's organization was just as urgently in need of reconstruction: nobody was quite sure who was responsible for what. The chairmen of the operating divisions could scarcely be held accountable for their results: their sales forces were not directly under their command and their authority was undermined by ceaseless interventions from head office. The functional directors at Millbank felt free to deal directly with their counterparts in the divisions over the heads of the divisional chairman: and the main Board directors who were partly responsible for each division often chose to regard themselves as its effective boss.

Meanwhile the main Board, deeply involved in the affairs of the company's parts, was not free to consider the direction of the whole, and the enthusiasm of many directors was too often focused on running their own empires. The way in which ICI allocated its capital resources was also primitive for a company of its size. The divisions came before the main Board for an annual conference at the rate of roughly one a month: investment projects were judged in isolation and not ranked in any order of priority according to their expected results. Nor was

there any attempt to look at the size and content of the capital programme as a whole, and little opportunity for the Board to be selective:
all it could do was to approve or turn down each proposal as it came
up. In the event the divisions which spent most heavily frequently
failed by considerable margins to meet their forecasts not only on the
completion dates of new plants but also on the profitability they had
predicted for them. These were the more obvious weaknesses, but
there were others.

The regional sales organization was unsatisfactory for a world in
which the company's representatives had to sell instead of merely
delivering in bulk, and in which its new products required intensive
and specialized marketing effort. Its international organization was also
still more appropriate to the age of cartels. There were only two overseas directors, one responsible for the Americas and for Africa south of
15° North, the other for the rest of the world, including Japan, the
Middle East and Western Europe. Finally, the deputy chairmen had
no specific function at all.

This inadequate structure was made all the more cumbersome by
committees of every size and sort which met to discuss every subject
which could be discussed by a committee. 'Often,' said the chairman
of the Paints Division, Peter Overbury, 'they were an excuse to kick
around a topic without actually deciding anything. People tended to
wait for the committee meeting, and even when a decision was taken,
it was often a compromise.'

The election of Paul Chambers to the chairmanship of ICI in 1960
was symbolic of a recognition within the company that radical change
was essential. Chambers was still an outsider to many of the old
brigade: he had never worked in a division, he had never accepted
the preconceived notions of ICI's scientific Establishment, he had looked
with a disapproving eye on its lack of sales expertise. But, as a man who
had spent the years from 1935 to 1940 as a member of the Indian
Legislative Assembly, followed by spells with the Inland Revenue and
the Control Commission for Germany, he also possessed a highly
political instinct: one of the high points of his life had been tearing
the Opposition to shreds in piloting the Income Tax Amendment Act
through the Indian Lower House.

Nor had Chambers' tastes fundamentally changed. 'Where Alec
Fleck would tell you half the members of the Royal Society off the
cuff,' said one of his colleagues, 'Paul could reel off half the members of
the House of Commons.' He took command of ICI as a reforming

politician might take hold of an ailing party machine. He did not merely want to break the company of its introverted habits, to demand from it good marketing as well as good science, he also wanted to put it on the map, to be its leader in a great era of expansion, to make it an international force. The habitual silence of Fleck was to give way to a torrent of speeches from a variety of platforms all over the world. In some of this, Chambers was moved only by his own individual conviction: but, as his election to the chair suggested, he was far from being the only member of the Board in favour of a policy of rapid expansion. On the contrary, others were even more bullish, even more ready to take risks to break ICI out of its restricting mould.

His tactics as chairman were very different from Fleck's. He talked a great deal in the Board room, he was always ready to back a hunch and he sought to manage the Board as a Prime Minister might manage his Cabinet. Instead of asking each man in turn for his opinion, Chambers would do a considerable amount of lobbying before Board meetings and then call on those whom he knew would take a view similar to his own. With a large Board to handle, he made no apology for this sort of manipulation. 'I operate on the principle,' he told me in 1967, 'that, when people listen to the arguments of others, they tend to soften. In my view, the chairman is not a referee, but a captain who has to decide who will bat and bowl where.' He recalled that, in dealing with one particular proposal, he had not called for a vote because he was afraid it might have gone against him on a show of hands.

Not surprisingly, Chambers was to prove a controversial chairman, both inside and outside the company, although with a business of the size, complexity and nature of ICI, it is dangerous to attribute too much power to one man. His tactics in the Board room disturbed some; they felt they were being hustled through unfamiliar territory. His public speeches, and more particularly his attacks on the Government, alarmed others: this was not ICI's discreet way of doing things (after all, Harold Wilson could still nationalize the company). But what was most disturbing of all to some of the old guard was that Chambers had taken ICI into the public arena. If mistakes had been made under Fleck, they might well have gone unnoticed; under the flamboyant Chambers, they were there for all to see.

The first moves were not contentious, they were simply long overdue. In the summer of 1960, ICI set up a European Council which was to examine, among other things, the possibility of manufacturing in Europe: and it also began to step up its effort to sell polyester fibre in the United States. ICI was at last beginning to shake off its Imperial bonds and the results were a judgement on the conservatism and insularity of the past. By 1968, its sales in Europe had reached £174m., almost five times greater than in 1960, and over sixty per cent of sales in the Common Market countries were being manufactured at new ICI plants in Germany and Holland. By 1970, ICI expects to have at least £100m. invested in Europe. In the United States, too, there were notable successes. To Chambers' surprise ICI and Celanese found that they could penetrate quickly and deeply into the American fibre market, and by 1965 they had captured twenty-five per cent of polyester sales. In the following year, ICI America Inc. was set up. By 1968, ICI had almost a third of its assets invested abroad, compared with an eighth in 1950.

An overhaul of ICI's management structure was also long overdue. After the set-back to profits in 1961, Chambers tried to persuade the divisional chairmen that changes in management philosophy were essential. Eventually it was decided that ICI would never change quickly enough without outside influence and the company's deputy chairmen proposed to Chambers that management consultants should be called in – a step which Fleck has resisted : McKinsey were chosen partly because Shell had reported favourably on them. McKinsey worked in ICI for eighteen months and, in the view of Sir Peter Allen, the present chairman of the company, 'they were worth every penny, they really made us sweat it out'.

The new organization which emerged in 1964 was partly what McKinsey recommended, partly what ICI felt was best for itself. (ICI, for example, rejected the idea of an executive chairman.) The result was a compromise, but it represented an advance. The old, obscure lines of responsibility were clarified by giving chairmen of operating divisions a good deal more authority. They gained control of their own sales forces through the abolition of the regional sales organization : they were allowed to spend up to £100,000 on individual projects without reference to the main Board; and, more importantly, they were freed from the interference of marauding main Board directors. The old system of group directors, under which main Board men frequently tried to run divisions from Millbank, was abolished and in future the divisional chairmen were to report for themselves to a four-man committee of the Board called a Control Group, which was responsible for monitoring the affairs of several divisions. A main Board liaison director was appointed for each division, but his function was simply to provide advice and support. He is currently referred to somewhat cynically among the divisions as 'our friend' at head office.

A number of safeguards were created to ensure that main Board directors did not meddle in divisional affairs. To begin with, each executive director of the company was given several jobs. Mr Albert Frost, for example, is not only the company's present finance director, he is also responsible for ICI's business in the Middle East and, in addition, acts as liaison director for the Paints Division. Furthermore, a deliberate effort was made to avoid making a man liaison director for the division of which he had previously been chairman; this involved acceptance of the amateur principle that an able man can do anything, providing he has the right ICI background.[1] New directors who in the old days had arrived at Millbank secure in the knowledge that they could still run their old divisions from afar, were now prevented from dipping their fingers into the divisional pie by being set tasks which they had not tackled before. Needless to say, it was (and is) a painful experience for those who turn up at head office with passionate but parochial views: in the opinion of one high-level company observer, the resulting coma frequently lasts at least six months.

The McKinsey reorganization also led to a more orderly approach to the question of allocating the company's resources. Instead of divisions queueing up to bring their projects to Millbank, the new Control Groups begin to take a preliminary look at all divisional profit and plans capital expenditure budgets for three years ahead in the same month, November. The company's Capital Programme Committee, and subsequently the main Board, then looks at the divisions' spending proposals as a whole (tailoring them to the money available) before the Control Groups approve individual divisional programmes.

These reforms were broadly welcomed throughout ICI. They had the effect of increasing the stature of the divisional chairmen as business-men in their own right. All the division chairmen I talked to were delighted with many of their new-found freedoms – the ability to appoint their own salesmen, for example: they had also been happy to disband a good proportion of their assorted committees and to treat the survivors in a comparatively cavalier fashion – 'we tend to take the decisions and then inform the committee', said one chairman with a smile. But some had a greater sense of freedom from the interference from head office than others. The chairman of one of the big divisions

[1] The effort has not been entirely successful: there are still those 'friends' who were chairmen of the divisions which they now watch over.

based in the north of England said he felt extremely autonomous and had never had any trouble in getting his capital expenditure schemes approved – 'unless you can be shown to be a complete bloody fool,' he added, 'how can anyone in London know enough to query you?' On the other hand, the chairman of a division with its headquarters in the south described his position as one of 'nominal autonomy': he had to spend a great deal of his time preparing papers for head office, he complained. The chairman of a second division was irked that there seemed to be overall company implications in practically everything he did. 'It even covers things like holidays and canteens,' he said, 'and you have to conform to some degree.'

But whatever the degree of freedom they may have achieved from Millbank, the divisional chairmen are also aware that, because of the highly integrated nature of ICI's business, they have become increasingly dependent on one another. 'Before the war,' said one, 'we could live in separate compartments, but now we are in each other's pockets.' No less than fifty per cent of the business of Heavy Organic Chemicals is with other divisions of the company; Dyestuffs supplies Fibres with all its nylon polymer; while Agricultural Division supplies Nobel with ammonia, Dyestuffs with ammonia and nitric acid for nylon polymer and Fibres with methanol for 'Terylene'. When two divisions discuss what are still called 'intra-merger prices', they are expected to combine brotherly love with strict commercial judgement. When the brotherly love falters, the case goes to Millbank for settlement.

The interdependence has reached such a point in some parts of the company that divisions develop joint investment plans. For example, the financial calculations on the new vinyl chloride plants built by Mond Division were done by Mond, Plastics and Heavy Organic Chemicals together. The reason is obvious enough: it is no use building plants to produce the base for pvc without also installing capacity to produce the pvc itself. The chairmen and deputy chairmen of the three divisions now meet together two or three times a year quite independently of Millbank to discuss their mutual problems.

ICI had thus faced the need to extend its business overseas and to reorganize its structure at home. There still remained the more profound problem of expanding the scale of its operations to make them adequate for international markets. Chambers was very conscious that the American chemical industry was investing sums sufficient to produce a new ICI every year, and that the Japanese industry was moving ahead at a rate – fifteen per cent per annum – far in advance of what was happening in Britain. He was also aware of what it would cost to try to keep pace.

ICI's first effort to make inroads into the problem of scale was both controversial and indicative of the nature of the company's dilemma. Having tried, and failed, to acquire Courtaulds by peaceful means, Chambers launched a take-over bid. ICI's stated objective was to create a man-made fibres combine capable of matching the scale of the American and European producers: Courtaulds did not hesitate to point out that it would also have provided ICI with a tied market for its own products.

Whatever the motive, the effort failed. Courtaulds fought off the bid and ICI suffered a serious blow to its confidence and prestige. Chambers was criticized inside the company for the damage he was felt to have done to ICI's treasured image[1] (although in fact the bid followed a unanimous Board decision); Fleck, muttered the critics, would never have involved ICI in such a humiliation. In 1964, ICI exchanged the 37½ per cent of Courtaulds' shares which it had acquired during the battle (plus £10m. in cash) for Courtaulds' fifty per cent share of British Nylon Spinners.

Having tried to achieve rapid expansion by acquisition, ICI set in train a massive investment programme in almost every major area of its operations: it was designed to achieve the necessary economies of scale, to make the switch from coal to oil, and in addition to expand the company's range of products. Up to this point, its capital investment had been running at modest levels and in 1963 was still below what it had been in 1957. (In some ways, what was happening at ICI was very similar to the situation at Shell.) From 1964 onwards, it increased sharply and in the four years from 1964 to 1967, almost £600m. was spent; by 1966, total investment was almost three times what it had been in 1963.

This represented an uncomfortably rapid increase in the company's investment. During 1965, as Peter Menzies pointed out, ICI had spent roughly nineteen per cent of its net investment at the beginning of that year: in 1966, it repeated the dose. 'Not all that money can have been wisely spent', adds Menzies.

Nylon, 'Terylene' and plastics capacity were increased and giant new plants sanctioned to provide the basic raw materials for these products

---

[1] Sir Paul says the criticism came mainly from 'older executives', who were steeped in policies which stemmed from the cartel days when there was a desire to avoid publicity at all costs.

and for a huge expansion and modernization programme for fertilizers. The increase in the size of plant was as startling as the escalation in the capital sums involved. The Heavy Organic Chemicals division's fourth ethylene plant, for example, which came into operation in 1966, was bigger than the first three put together, and the fifth (with an annual capacity of 450,000 tons) was more than twice as large as the fourth. The same sort of increases were taking place at Mond, where giant new chlorine and vinyl chloride plants were being installed, and in the Agricultural Division with a succession of new ammonia and urea plants. Just how essential the replacements were, however, is clear from the fact that when the new chlorine plants (capable of producing 200,000 tons a year) went into service at Mond, they replaced equipment with an annual capacity of only 28,000 tons.

The potential rewards from the new plants were, as might be expected, considerable – one 450,000-ton ethylene plant was reckoned to yield almost twice the return on capital of three 150,000-tonners – although in a technology which was moving as fast as petrochemicals, an investment of this size was bound to be 'a real gambler's throw', as Peter Menzies admitted. For example, an acetylene plant built by Mond which was still not running at full efficiency in the autumn of 1968 was expected to have been dismantled by the end of 1969. But ICI felt it had no choice; it might build big and see its effort capped by others; but if it remained small, it was finished. 'We either spent £100m. on nylon or else got out,' said Menzies, 'and it was the same with ammonia.' This was not merely Chambers' decision: the pressure for the expansion of fibres capacity came largely from Leslie Williams and the men at ICI Fibres, and from Sir Ronald Holroyd and Rowland Wright on the petrochemicals side.

Having taken a gamble of this order, it would have been surprising if ICI had not encountered major difficulties. In both 1965 and 1966, the company was forced to go to the market for loan capital. In 1965, according to Menzies, it underestimated the cost of fibres expansion, and had to raise £50m. at what Menzies then considered the 'extravagant' rate of 7½ per cent. In 1966, with a fall in profits and the need for new capital still increasing, another £60m. had to be raised, this time at eight per cent.

The second thing which upset ICI's forecasts was that the British economy passed into a period of prolonged crisis at a crucial moment. This was critical for a company which was deeply involved in industries as fundamental as clothing.

ICI's planners did not accept the feasibility of the four per cent national growth rate which Neddy had declared to be a reasonable target (although some of its customers were working on that basis), but instead made the assumption that the economy would continue to grow at its average rate in the past. In the event, national growth fell below the minimum for which ICI had allowed. It was the squeeze and global over-capacity which Chambers blamed for the falling off in the increase of nylon sales; in 1966, nylon's rate of expansion was halved and ICI found itself with a considerable amount of surplus capacity.

But there was a third calamity which reflected more on ICI's own judgement than on the policies of the Labour Government. Put crudely, the company tried to spend too much too quickly – at the height of the investment spree, it had planned to invest £4m. a week, a very large part of it in Britain. It was a rate which could not be sustained. 'We tried to grow faster than our resources would take us', said Maurice Hodgson, head of the company's planning department. 'It wasn't just a question of cash, but also of the industry supplying the equipment and of the skilled management available. The trouble was simply lack of experience – we had never tried to do anything like that in the past.' The price of lack of experience when combined with the problems of proving a new technology was high: at one stage, more than £100m. of new plant was over six months late.

ICI's reaction was logical enough: it accepted that it needed to plan better and spend more wisely. One deputy chairman, Lord Beeching, took a close look at the company's planning apparatus while another, Sir Peter Allen, concerned himself with its use of financial resources and the application of what he called 'a little horse sense'. 'A sense of urgency,' Allen reflected later, 'is not a bad thing. The British tend to whistle too much when they're prosperous and perhaps we had whistled too much.'

One practical result of this soul-searching was that in 1966 a much strengthened company planning department was set up. It had a staff of twenty and what Maurice Hodgson called 'an unusually high inspirational content'. With a large Board 'where the urgent can sometimes displace the important', he saw his job as providing better information on key questions of strategy: what fields of business ought ICI to be in, where should it concentrate its capital investment, what performance should it expect? Hodgson's men now assemble all the proposals for future investment which arrive from the divisions, match

them not only against the available cash but also against total resources and then make recommendations. One division chairman told
me in 1967 that he preferred to argue with the Board of ICI for new
cash rather than with the Board of a bank: in 1969, the difference is
probably less pronounced.

Major management changes followed. Chambers, who had decided
no less than six years earlier that he would move to the Royal Insurance
Company in either 1968 or 1969, left the company and his successor
was not Lord Beeching – who was known to want a thorough-going
debate on the whole future of ICI – but Sir Peter Allen. Beeching
resigned from the Board. Allen, with an avuncular appearance and
hobbies which included golf and railways (he has written a number of
books on both subjects, including one entitled *On the Old Lines*), was
widely taken to be a compromise candidate who would soothe ICI's
troubled spirits after the upheavals of the Chambers era.

In fact, Allen's manner is a good deal less avuncular than his
appearance. His handling of the Board and his abrasive attitude
towards those whose performance was less than satisfactory immediately
impressed the company's outside directors. He has proved to have a
shrewdness in delegation and considerable powers of leadership: 'he
can get more out of people than anyone else I know', said one of
his colleagues. 'He is like the conductor of an orchestra who calls in
the right people at the right times.' Whether he will continue to call the
right tune remains to be seen.

Allen has at least been fortunate to arrive at a time when the benefits
of the heavy investment programme are beginning to show themselves,
together with a bonus from the devaluation of the pound in November,
1967. The company's return on capital went up from 8.8 per cent in
1967 to almost twelve per cent in 1968. Menzies, while taking the view
that 1968 will probably prove to have been a good year and that he
expects returns to settle down at somewhere between ten and eleven
per cent, adds that this is not good enough – 'we should really be
earning thirteen to fourteen per cent' – but says he cannot think
of a major international company based in Britain which has done
much better.

The limitations of its British base are, indeed, one reason which ICI
gives for the fact that it has not done better: 'we are limping along
because we live in a ghetto', said Menzies. The problems of a small
home market are particularly severe for a company like ICI which
requires such heavy capital investment. 'To live in today's world,' said

Leslie Williams, 'we have to build plants just as big as those of the European and American giants, but we only have a market of fifty million people.'

The company bosses also tend to blame the British environment for their shortcomings in fields which have nothing to do with the economies of scale. Even the difficulties of making scientists into salesmen are put down in some part to the national character. Similarly, ICI attributes its admitted failure in the past to cut out activities which yield unsatisfactory returns (it is no longer in the retail salt business) partly to the notion that ruthlessness is not a British characteristic. It also makes the point that it must beware of getting on the wrong side of the politicians: 'we may talk about getting out of some product or other, but then the next man from Whitehall will ask why Britain has to import so many chemicals', said Menzies. 'Paying too much regard to the national interest', is one of the reasons given by doubters within the company for ICI's continued heavy investment in fertilizers, which Du Pont dropped some time ago, and which is only now beginning to earn tolerable returns. This produces dissatisfaction – 'you can't play roulette just to satisfy the country's interest', said one deputy chairman – but so far nothing in the way of concrete action.

ICI seems lost between pleasure at being regarded as a national institution, a bell-wether of British industry, and restlessness at the shackles which it feels being British impose upon it. Certainly, despite the fact that sales overseas are now greater than turnover in the United Kingdom, the company still finds difficulty in thinking in the supranational terms which are a common-place at Shell.

Its other basic problem is that it not only doubles in size every ten years but also doubles in complexity, and it has not so far demonstrated that it has a system of long-term planning adequate to cope with its considerable diversity of products and of markets. Allen sees this diversity as a source of strength – 'the great chemical heart-land' of the business, he points out, saw ICI through the crises of 1960–1 and 1965–6, when profits dropped first out of plastics and then out of fibres – but ICI is trying to be a giant in so many fields that without (and perhaps even with) a clear long-term view of where it is going, plus the control to sustain that view over a long period, the company could be faced with some very uncomfortable choices, including the need to get out of a major sector of its business. Rather like the British economy, it seems to be involved in a race against the clock: how to grow quickly enough to keep its place in the international first division.

In the past, the company has had clear policy guide-lines but it has tended to adhere to them for too short a time. For that reason, it has often been more concerned with immediate problems than with long-term principles and it has sometimes seemed to dabble uncertainly in fields where its expertise is inadequate. The £40m. or so which it put into various textile companies[1] in an effort to strengthen firms with able managements and at the same time to provide itself with useful friends – not tied customers, it insists – is often cited as a case in point. One of these partnerships – with Joe Hyman's Viyella – has already ended in divorce. Part of the trouble seems to have been a confusion as to why ICI put up the money in the first place – a confusion which some of the ICI bosses seem to share. But although some of them feel that they probably invested in too many companies, the company is determined to go on promoting the formation of larger groups in textile processing – particularly if Courtaulds shows signs of trying to take over more sizeable textile companies.[2]

ICI reckons that it is big enough in fibres (with major businesses in Europe and America) to weather the severe fluctuations in profits which have occurred in the past and which Sir Peter Allen is sure will occur again; big enough, too, to have passed the point where it needs a link with Courtaulds of the sort which Sir Frank Kearton proposed in 1966.

The company's planners have to make sure that they do not allow ICI to drift into other situations of this type. Hodgson's men have certainly helped to apply a new discipline to the consideration of investment projects, and no doubt ICI will make great efforts to compensate itself for the loss of Lord Beeching, without question the most brilliant long-term planner in the business; whether its Board structure will be a hindrance or a help is a matter for debate. Sir Peter Allen believes the present Board of eighteen (thirteen executives and five outsiders) is ideal and that a company like ICI must operate by seeking a consensus – 'it kills fewer chief executives and very often produces better answers. If you're wrong when you're on your own,' he adds, 'it can ruin the company.' Critics believe that the ICI chairman should also be the chief executive and that it would be much more effectively managed by a small executive committee, in the style of Unilever.

[1] The companies were Carrington and Dewhurst, English Sewing Cotton, Klinger Manufacturing, Lister, Northgate and Viyella.

[2] Courtaulds' bid for English Calico in 1969 produced a sharp reaction from ICI: and induced the Board of Trade to intervene.

On the credit side, the company is making notable progress in an area which is critical to its international competitiveness, that of labour costs. Allen is well aware that ICI still needs fifty per cent more men to produce a million tons of chemicals than the big American companies, but in 1967 sales per employee rose by ten per cent, and by fifteen per cent in 1968. The jibe that ICI carries more passengers than British Rail still has some force – there is a gap of twenty-five per cent between its best and its worst productivity performance – but there are a good deal fewer passengers than there were.

ICI has at least had the courage and the skill to take one great leap forward, and is consolidating its gains. 'ICI excels in calibre,' said one of its divisional chairmen, 'but I feel it still has to prove conclusively that it also excels in effectiveness.'

CHAPTER 6

The State's Industries

The residuum of political controversy has settled so thickly over the subject of nationalization that it requires a conscious effort to think of the nationalized industries as a collection of distinct, let alone highly individual entities. Yet although transfer to public ownership may confer a stigma in the minds of many, it does not (by some sinister process) transform its victims into identical animals, and indeed the nationalized industries include enterprises which are as different in their nature and atmosphere as, say, Shell and Ferranti.

The National Coal Board, for instance, has its headquarters in a green-and-cream institutional rabbit-warren in Grosvenor Place (Hobart House, in my view, carries the idea of austerity for public servants beyond tolerable limits), while BOAC operates from a smart new office block at London Airport whose corridors still carry echoes of Flying Officer Kite and whose lusher style is envied by the men from BEA. The others, too, are housed in premises which seem to mirror the current state of their morale as well as their history. The Railways Board has its home in a cavernous nineteenth-century railway hotel (the old Grand Central) at Marylebone; the Post Office in a gloomy pile on the fringes of the City which, appropriately enough (since the Post Office was until very recently a Government department and had a politician – the Postmaster-General – as its chairman), looks similar to other piles in Whitehall,[1] and whose drabness is relieved only by doormen with pink tail-coats and top hats; BEA in a converted pre-war school. The Electricity Council, on the other hand, is housed amid the clinical splendours of the new Millbank office complex, while gas has celebrated its new-found glamour by moving to Marble Arch. The

[1] It will shortly move to a new office block in central London.

The State's Industries

Electricity Council

Millbank, London. Turnover 1967–8, £1,217m. Net assets, £4,458m. 1,000 showrooms. 221,000 employees.

British Steel Corporation

Grosvenor Place, London. Largest steel business in the world outside the United States and Russia. Turnover, 1967–8, £1,071m. Output, 22.87m. ingot tons. Net assets, £1,058m. 250,000 employees.

National Coal Board

Grosvenor Place, London. Turnover 1967–8, £900m. Net assets, £742m. Output 170m. tons. Also 520m. bricks, 120,000 houses, 296,000 acres of land. 433,000 employees.

Post Office

St Martins-le-Grand, London. Income, 1967–8, £845m. Net assets, £1,945m. 25,000 post offices. 412,000 employees.

Gas Council

Marble Arch, London. Turnover, 1967–8, £589m. Net assets, £1,116m. 1,250 showrooms. 122,000 employees.

British Rail

Marylebone Road, London. Turnover 1968, £517½m. Assets £1,945m. 33 hotels. 77 ships. 339,000 employees.

British Overseas Airways Corporation

London Airport, Hounslow, Middlesex. Turnover, £169m. in 1968–9. Largest airline in the Western world outside the US. 20,000 employees.

British European Airways

Ruislip, Middlesex. Turnover in 1968–9, £108m. 21,000 employees.

British Steel Corporation has taken up where AEI left off, in Grosvenor Place, neatly sandwiched between coal and gas.

The nationalized chairmen are an equally diverse group. They include a former merchant banker, Lord Melchett, at British Steel, and a man who might have aspired to be a Labour Prime Minister, Lord Robens, at the National Coal Board as well as professional gas, electricity and railway-men. The majority are probably Conservatives, and Melchett is still a member of the Carlton Club. In the past, the group has included academics like Sir Ronald Edwards (now chairman of Beecham) and men from private industry like Lord Beeching.

Nor are the differences between the industries limited to their public faces. The variation in size is enormous. The Electricity Council, for example, has net assets thirty-eight times as great as those of BEA (which itself carries more passengers than any other international airline except Pan-American) and sales which are almost fourteen times as great. Similarly, the Electricity Council invested almost £600m. in 1967–8, compared with less than £100m. in the case of British Rail and only £24m. in the case of BEA. The bigger brethren are apt to take pride in their size: Lord Robens remarked jocularly of the chairman of a smaller nationalized concern that 'he might as well be running a sweet shop'.

Some of the nationalized industries are capital-intensive, others labour-intensive. Wages account for about sixty-five per cent of the operating costs of the railways and seventy-five per cent of the postal side of the Post Office, but only seventeen per cent of electricity's running expenses and twenty-seven per cent of the Steel Corporation's. Some face strong foreign competition, others none at all. Roughly a third of BOAC's business originates in the United States, where it has to match itself against Pan-American and TWA; BEA, too, is exposed to full-scale international competition on two-thirds of its business[1] (the remaining third consists of its domestic routes) and British Steel sells perhaps one-fifth of its output abroad. The rest face little or no overseas competition.

Only two nationalized industries – BOAC and the Steel Corporation – have the privilege of deciding (after consultation with the appropriate Minister) what rate of interest to pay the Government on part of their capital. Like limited liability companies, they are not obliged to pay

[1] It should be added that since both prices and routes are fixed by an international air transport body, the nature of the competition which the airlines face is necessarily restricted.

any dividends on this Public Dividend Capital in bad years. The rest pay interest on all their capital at fixed rates. Any surplus which remains is generally used to finance new capital investment.

There are also wide variations in organization and structure. The majority of the nationalized industries are both unitary and increasingly highly centralized, but the Gas and Electricity Councils are still (July 1969) federal bodies, with Area Boards which historically have had a fair amount of freedom conducting their own activities.[1] Whereas the Minister of Power appoints only the main Board directors of the Coal Board and the Steel Corporation, in the case of gas and electricity he also appoints all the members of the Area Boards. This difference in structure has inevitably been reflected in the style in which the different industries were led.

At the NCB, for example, Robens is chief executive as well as chairman and runs the industry in a highly personal way. 'I don't think anybody works for the National Coal Board,' he said. 'My close associates work for me.' The chairmen of the Gas and Electricity Councils, on the other hand, were originally cast as more *primus inter pares*. Sir Stanley Brown, chairman of the Central Electricity Generating Board, one of the Electricity Council's constituents parts, told me in 1967 that he no more thought of the Council chairmen being his boss than the Prime Minister would consider the Speaker of the House of Commons his,[2] and one of the Area Board chairmen regarded the Council chairman as more his leader than his boss.[3] Similarly, until 1965 the Gas Council functioned as a combination of co-operative trade association and talking shop; the Area Boards told the Council when they intended to build new plant, but they were not asking permission to do so. On occasion in the past, Area gas Board chairmen have felt quite free to lobby their colleagues to oppose schemes proposed by the Council chairman, and former officials admit having been contemptuous of the

---

[1] Both, however, are certain to become less federal in the near future. The advent of new sources of gas (Algeria and the North Sea), which are under central control, has already reduced the autonomy of the Area gas Boards, and will eventually take away their functions of production and long-distance transmission of their own supplies. The Gas Council will therefore become an increasingly powerful body. The Electricity Council is to be replaced by an Electricity Authority with more power over the CEGB and the Area Boards.

[2] There is a salary differential: the chairman of the Council is paid £15,000 while the chairman of the CEGB gets £13,000.

[3] Their successors are likely to modify these views in the light of the recent reorganization of the industry.

Council's visits to their districts because it had so little statutory power over them.

Again, while some of the nationalised industries (such as coal and steel) are centred on a series of plants or pits, others (the Post Office and the railways, for example) are of necessity widely dispersed. This, they believe, poses problems for them, not only in maintaining *esprit de corps* but also in transmitting policy down the line. Envious of Lord Robens' success in projecting his image as leader, they put it down to the fact that he can get round the coal mines in a series of whistle-stop tours, while they can hardly hope to keep personal contact with lonely signal boxes and postmen.

Despite common ownership, the nationalized industries are also far from being one big, happy family. As providers of basic materials and services, their relations are inevitably close – the Electricity Generating Board is the Coal Board's biggest customer, followed at some distance by the gas and steel industries, while the Coal Board, the Steel Corporation and the Post Office are British Rail's largest accounts – but often less than cordial. This is all the more evident because their rows are frequently conducted in public: perhaps as publicly-owned industries, they feel this is no less than their duty. A report on the gas industry by a House of Commons Select Committee in 1961 remarked that relations between the Gas Council and the Coal Board had, at their best, been 'wintry'. The same could be said in more recent times of relations between the Electricity Generating Board and the Coal Board; while gasmen bitterly resented electricity boards' tactics in offering householders reduced connection charges if they would instal major electrical appliances. They still find it difficult to resist sly digs at their larger rival; *'we're* not bleeding the country white,' said a senior Gas Council member, in a reference to the huge electricity investment programme.

These have been the most publicized disputes, but relations between BOAC and BEA were until recently far from friendly, and the Post Office has, on occasion, been a good deal less than happy with the service provided by the railways. Even within industries there are profound disharmonies. Area electricity Boards have resented the fact that they could not exercise greater control over their production department, the Generating Board; one chairman accused it of 'thinking only in large sizes' and of being in some ways over-lavish ('too many chauffeur-driven cars'). The Generating Board's chairman, Sir Stanley Brown, emphatically refutes these charges.

Nevertheless, the nationalized industries have a great deal in common. Their functions and sometimes their detailed structures are laid down by statute (which makes reorganization an unnecessarily tedious and long-winded process); their chairman and Boards are appointed by and can be dismissed by politicians, in the shape of the Ministers whose departments watch over them;[1] their capital expenditure has to be approved by the Government and the money is generally raised by the Treasury (although some nationalized industries have now been given freedom to borrow abroad); and not only their investment programmes but also the minutiae of their daily business comes under the scrutiny of cohorts of Civil Servants. If the influence of shareholders is notable by its absence in private business, it is ever-present for the nationalized industries.

Whitehall, indeed, is the focus of their world – the seat at once of their banker, their mentor, their father-confessor and their judge. The chairmen and their senior colleagues are involved in a constant round of meetings with politicians and Civil Servants; some lunch with them, dine with them, and even go to the theatre with them. In some industries more than others (gas for example) a steady stream of Civil Servants tours installations in the provinces.[2] There are investment plans to be scrutinized, projects and negotiations to be examined, major appointments to be settled, public outcries to be abated.

The frequency of intervention has something to do with the way in which a particular industry is organized, with the style of the Minister, with the tradition of the department concerned, but the general rule is that, the worse a nationalized industry is performing, the closer will be the attentions of the shareholders' representatives.[3] Sometimes, indeed, it appears that managers are merely rubber-stamping decisions already taken in Whitehall. 'When the chairman comes back from seeing the Minister,' said a member of one Board which has not been among the most profitable, 'that's it – the Board meeting is a pure formality.' It is obviously a closeness which can be cloying. One former chairman

[1] The Ministry of Power is the sponsoring department for the electricity, coal, gas and steel industries; the Board of Trade for BOAC and BEA; the Ministry of Transport for the railways; and the Minister of Posts and Telecommunications is responsible for the Post Office.

[2] This is not true of all parts of the nationalized industries: the CEGB, for example, maintains an arm's-length relationship with Whitehall.

[3] In the past, one chairman whose concern was doing badly was even told what to put in his annual reports.

said that his main job had been keeping the politicians and Civil Servants off the backs of his managers.

For those who have come from private industry, it is a world which can be infuriatingly slow. 'If I hadn't been in a Government department during the war, I couldn't have stood it for a month,' said Sir John Wall, formerly deputy chairman of the Post Office. 'One project took three days to settle with the manufacturers and the Ministry of Technology, but another six weeks to get the rest of Whitehall into line.' Part of the trouble may be that the scheme which is being proposed has no immediate *political* importance to the Minister concerned, part that – even when the sponsoring department has been convinced – there is always the Treasury, as ultimate banker, to be surmounted.

And, finally, it is a world where personal relationships are crucial, and transcend the letter of the law. 'You can't judge these things on statutory regulations,' said one chairman. 'The real question is how much sympathy exists between you and the Minister. You can't run things if you get on badly with the Minister.' That means not merely establishing personal rapport and mutual self-respect but also learning how to deal diplomatically with the political pressures which inevitably come. Sometimes Ministers will quite blatantly go beyond the powers conferred upon them by law, but often their intrusions are subtler and less direct. 'I wouldn't dream of trying to put pressure on you,' the Minister may say, 'but it would help terribly if . . .' If the chairman turns him down, he may be risking the relationship; if he accedes to the request, he may be allowing a Minister's personal and political interests to take precedence over commercial good sense.

Ministers sometimes like to pose as chairmen of holding companies whose job is simply to keep the ship on the right lines and not try to influence the day-to-day course of management more than they must. They explain the more obvious contraventions of these principles by pointing out that they are often dragged into the arena by Parliamentary questions and by the fact that they are regarded by the public as ultimately responsible. Often enough, the excuse is valid, but it is also true that they are responding to a variety of pressures.

The first springs from the truism that a Minister's seat of power is his Ministry – and that the machine over which he has been given control is normally far more important to him than what goes on at Party conferences. Furthermore, his power in relation to the industry or industries concerned is considerable. He is reading all the policy papers, making all the vital appointments and authorizing investment programmes involving (in the case of the Ministry of Power) well over £1,100m. a year. In these circumstances, the temptation to intervene can prove overwhelming. But it is not simply a question of the exercise of personal power; more complex motives may sometimes determine a Minister's actions.

If his Ministry is the fruit of political power, the root of it is the survival of the Government of which he is a member. For that reason, he has a much tighter relationship with his colleagues in the Cabinet than with the nationalized industry which he has under his wing, and is ultimately more interested in the success of the Government as a whole than in commercial considerations in the short or (for that matter) the long run. A rise in postal prices, for example, may cost votes at a crucial moment. Similarly, a Minister of Power might personally wish to cut back the size of the coal industry more rapidly than his colleagues deem wise: the result might be a slowing-down of pit closures. In ways like these, his decisions may reflect political rather than commercial motives.

As if these cross-currents were not enough, there are also relationships with senior Civil Servants to be cultivated: they can wage war in quite another way. 'If you get on the wrong side of them,' said one of the full-time members of a nationalized industry Board, 'they can bombard you with paper, direct a stream of it at you like water from a hosepipe. Then they keep writing to you once a week, saying we haven't heard from you, have we? Later, when the season for Parliamentary questions comes round, they'll start sending them round to you without any guidance and leave you floundering with a demand for a quick reply. On the other hand, if you stay on the right side of them, they'll just write you a note, saying that this is how they propose to reply and simply try it out on you.'

The chairmen of the nationalized industries are not without weapons of their own, and they have become increasingly adept in their use. One is the effort to stir up public opinion by means of calculated leaks to the Press; in effect, trying to use the public against the Government. This can be particularly effective when Ministers are proving dilatory. 'A Press campaign,' as one chairman put it, 'is a very good way of combating sheer inertia. Ministers get cross when the Press ask them why they are not making up their minds.' Similar tactics might be used when the chairman in question is about to be overruled on an issue – for example, the speed with which the coal industry is to be run down – which is likely to cause considerable unrest in the industry; a newspaper leak *before* the Minister's decision is made public at least indicates that the chairman has fought tooth and nail – even if the politicians have refused to see reason. Lord Robens and Sir Henry Jones of the Gas Council are both skilful in this sort of guerrilla warfare.

One of the most celebrated battles fought by a nationalized industry was the one in which the Gas Council sought to keep down the price it had to pay Shell–Esso for North Sea gas. By putting it about that anything more than a certain price would simply give the oil companies exorbitant profits, it not only put pressure on the companies themselves but also on the Minister of Power; if *he* was willing to settle for very much more than that price, he would be seen to be yielding to the companies and depriving the public of the possibility of lower gas prices. The zest with which the Gas Council conducted the campaign may have owed something to the fact that Sir Henry was known to be furious at the price of 5d per therm which he found himself forced to accept following the first North Sea gas agreement with British Petroleum.

Another weapon (not without its perils) which chairmen can employ is the threat of resignation. Used sparingly, this can be highly effective, partly because good replacements are hard to find; with the level of political interference which exists and at the salaries which nationalized concerns have been able to offer,[1] industrialists are no longer easy to persuade that they should sacrifice themselves in the public service. As one Minister put it: 'When I look round, a short-list of 500 suitable people does not come readily to mind.'

Altogether, the environment of the nationalized industries is very different from that of private business, it requires special, quasi-political skills, and it has restrictions as well as some blessings. In the matter of raising capital, for instance, it is often said (particularly within the nationalized industries) that money is available 'on tap' from the Treasury. But the flow from the 'tap' can also, on occasion, be adjusted to suit the broader economic purposes of the Government in a way which does not happen in private industry. Each of the nationalized industries, in fact, takes a slice of the available cake, and since they either buy their cake or get permission to buy it from the one shop, they are at the mercy of its proprietor: in other words, the Treasury can

[1] Even with the increases granted in 1969, they are still well behind private industry.

reduce their investment programmes as a way of regulating the economy.

In the post-war years, there have certainly been examples of industries which were pushed to the back of the queue and kept so short of funds that their performance was seriously affected: the most notable example was that of the railways in the years before the Modernization Plan of 1954. (The Post Office was also starved of capital, but it was not then a public Corporation.)[1] The irony was that, at the same time, the Coal Board was not able to spend all the money available to it, and was berated by both Ministers and Civil Servants for not investing quickly enough.

In more recent years, the nationalized industries have not generally been kept short of capital and, if there is a consensus among the chairmen, it would seem to be that intermittent cuts are a fair exchange for the freedom to raise large sums. On the other hand, views do vary a good deal about the way in which investment programmes are vetted, both by sponsoring departments and by the Treasury. The process is certainly a good deal more thorough than it was during the 1950s, and there is plenty of evidence to suggest that it needed to be. In that era, for example, no detailed checks were made within the total amount agreed for Coal Board investment – the Ministry of Power took it on trust that the NCB would not submit modernization plans which were uneconomic – and the £1,240m. rail modernization plan was not considered in detail or on technical grounds, nor was it costed in terms of the rate of return on capital. The Ministry of Transport took the view that the railways should run themselves, subject to the most general oversight on appointments and investment.

Now that the scrutiny is a good deal keener, there are plenty of remarks about 'nit-picking' and a frustrated senior official in one of the fuel industries complained that 'civil servants won't take anything on trust – they want everything down on paper, right to the smallest detail'. Sir Ronald Edwards, the former chairman of the Electricity Council, feels however that some nationalized industries expect to get away with less inquiry than they would have to face from their bankers if they operated in the private sector.[2]

---

[1] It became a Public Corporation, with the same status as, say, the NCB, in 1969.

[2] A senior official of one nationalized industry complained that there was *not* *enough* Government interference on matters of real importance. 'There is no shortage of 'phone calls, letters and personal visits from the Ministry,' he said, 'but what the Ministry normally displays is an unerring interest for making itself felt on matters of little or no importance.'

Another grievance which is shared by a number of industries is that when the Treasury turns down a scheme (after it has been approved by the sponsoring department), there is no opportunity of putting their own case to the ultimate banker: it is done for them at second hand by their attendant Civil Servants.

The nationalized industries have also been periodically subject to other sorts of restrictions. They can, for example, either be directed in the way in which they use their resources or at least prevented from exercising freedom of choice. This has been particularly true of the air corporations. BOAC was not able to get dollars with which to replace obsolete aircraft after the war, and later it was encouraged to buy VC10s instead of the Boeing 707s which it would have preferred. More recently, BEA was refused permission to buy Boeings 727s; the Board of Trade's attitude, its management felt, was tantamount to indicating that it could buy any aircraft it wished – provided that they were Trident 3Bs. The same sort of 'persuasion' has been applied to other industries; both electricity and gas have been pressed to use more coal than they would have freely chosen to do, and the Steel Corporation is not free to import cheaper American coking coal.

Again under political pressure, the electricity and gas industries agreed to suspend their advertising programmes at a time when supplies were short. This suspension even affected advertisements for electric storage heaters, though their use did not add to the crucial peak-time load. Before this, the Electricity Council had also withdrawn electric fires from its showrooms for no less than two years, although it knew perfectly well that other retail chains were continuing to sell them. 'It was a case of Caesar's wife,' explained one of the Council's full-time members.

The freedom of the nationalized industries' operations has also been curbed in a variety of other ways. The most notable is that they have never been able to raise their prices without Ministerial approval, although this sort of intervention has no warrant in statute. Nevertheless, it is a caveat which has applied from the earliest years: since 1954, the Coal Board has had an understanding with the Ministry of Power (based originally on an exchange of letters) that it would inform the Minister of any intention to raise charges. In one sense, of course, this is a perfectly justifiable safeguard against the possible misuse of power by industries which enjoy total or partial monopolies, but since some Ministers (in my view, at least) have put other factors before economic good sense, it has had the effect of subsidizing other sectors of the economy, and of condemning the industries concerned to uncommercial operations. These interventions would have been more comprehensible if the nationalized industries had been prone to demanding regular increases in rates; in practice, they have normally only been sought as a last resort. If anything the nationalized industries have been too timorous in pressing for higher charges.[1]

Ministerial interventions can be costly to the industries concerned. In 1952, for example, the then Minister of Transport turned down a request for an increase in rail charges even although it had been approved by the Transport Tribunal: the cost of this refusal to the railways, according to the Ministry of Transport, was £6½m. In 1956, they were allowed only half the increase they had asked for: the cost was £8.4m. Similarly, it has been estimated that the Coal Board lost about £300m. of revenue in the post-war years because prices were kept artificially low,[2] while Post Office charges have regularly lagged far behind the general increase in costs and prices.

Nor are a number of the nationalized industries allowed the usual commercial flexibility in operating their rate structures. The Steel Corporation has to publish its prices and cannot discriminate between customers; the electricity industry is prohibited from showing what is called 'undue preference' in the statute; and the Post Office, whose rates were for a long time published by Parliament, is in very much the same position and has not, in the past, been able to compete successfully for the big mail order contracts. Again, these regulations may be reasonable for monopolistic enterprises, but it is clearly unreasonable to judge them as normal commercial businesses when they are shackled in so many ways.

If these restrictions inhibit aggressive commercial policies, the fear of critical questions being asked in Parliament actively promotes a spirit of caution. Questions are a regular hazard – the Ministry of Power had six hundred in 1967, 120 of them on the coal industry – and they can deal with the most trivial subjects as well as matters of major public concern, such as the security of electricity supplies. As a result, many officials take up defensive attitudes. 'It's just like living in a goldfish bowl,' said a full-time member of one nationalized Board, 'and you

[1] The Prices and Incomes Board now has to approve any price increases which the nationalized industries wish to make.

[2] Professor W. A. Robson, Professor of Public Administration at the London School of Economics: *The Times*, 26 August 1968, 'Improving the return on State-owned assets'.

don't take chances as readily as you might in a private industry.' Since promotion often depends on avoiding public protest, however trivial, local officials also tend to keep their heads down.

The chairmen of nationalized industries do, however, have a considerable say in appointments to their Boards, although the power rests ultimately with the Minister. The normal procedure seems to be that, when either side favours a candidate who is unacceptable to the other, they try to reach a compromise. It is rare for a chairman to be over-ruled, but it has happened.

When it comes to the recruitment of people from outside the industry, on the other hand, Ministers have often had to settle for second, third or even fourth-best. The attraction of becoming something of a public figure is often not enough nowadays to lure the highest-calibre executives away from private enterprise; despite Ministerial flattery and the prospect of a title and an occasional television interview,[1] many have preferred to run their own show rather than have their hands held by politicians and Civil Servants. The nationalized industries have also not been able to compete on salary, except in the ranges up to £4,000 a year.[2] Above that level, those who have climbed back over the wall into private industry have often been able to double their money.

Some of the salaries paid have been little short of ludicrous. Before the Post Office became a nationalized industry, for example, the head of its telecommunications side – responsible for a five-year investment programme of £2,000m. and with an annual income not far short of £500m. – was paid only £6,300 a year. There have also been strange discrepancies between industries. Before the 1969 salary increases were implemented, the full-time member of the Gas Council who was responsible for the entire North Sea gas operation – exploration, storage and pipelines – was paid below the middle of the £7,500–£9,000 range; the chief public relations official of the Steel Corporation was reputed to receive £8,000. No doubt the PR man was worth every penny of his salary, but if he was, the full-time member of the Gas Council was surely being under-paid.

[1] 'Being head of a nationalized industry, and a public figure,' said one former chairman, 'appeals to some of our worst instincts. If you have a taste for showmanship, it gives you plenty of opportunities.' Ministers rank 'PR flair' as one of the most important qualities for a good nationalized chairman.

[2] The politicians' most fruitful hunting-ground in recent times has been among wealthy merchant bankers, who can comfortably afford a spell of public service. 'I did it for the same reason that I'm a JP and a tax commissioner,' said Sir Giles Guthrie, former chairman of BOAC. 'This is just rather bigger.'

Furthermore, although the chairmen do not lead uncomfortable lives, some of them (as public servants) do feel a compulsion to exhibit an austerity which, however modest, would not be mirrored in private industry. For example, Sir Henry Jones, anticipating a considerable loss for 1967–8, sold his official Bentley and bought a Ford Executive instead. The men at BOAC also restrict themselves to Executives, while other chairmen who secretly covet a Rolls or a Bentley content themselves with the humbler Austin Princess. These attitudes are also reflected at lower levels; the chairman of one Area electricity Board is driven around his home city in a Chamois because 'it looks less ostentatious'.

Historically, the nationalized industries have been expected to bear the cost of providing services which made losses but which met society's needs. In the early years after the war, with the railways still making money and a desperate shortage of coal to dispel any worries about uneconomic pits, it did not seem an onerous burden. In any event, this was what these newly-transformed industries were there for (or so both their architects and the public assumed); to provide a public service at the lowest possible cost, to be the servants of their new owners, the people.

Their financial philosophy was equally imprecise. In the majority of cases, the nationalized industries' only obligation was to break even taking one year with another, and to make some contribution to their own reserves. Since, generously enough, the nationalization statutes did not indicate which year was to be taken with which, or over how long a period, it is hardly surprising if chairmen did not feel too harshly driven to produce large profits in the short term. Indeed, since they were regarded (and regarded themselves) as public servants above all else, profit was not only far from uppermost in their minds, but could also be an actual embarrassment when the public did not easily understand the need to build up reserves. When the West Midlands Gas Board made a surplus of £500,000, for example, there was an immediate outcry for reduced prices.

Yet, despite the vagueness and the confusion, most people expected the nationalized industries, in some mysterious way, to produce a transformation of the assets which they had acquired: for some it represented the fulfilment of a golden vision, for others the realization of their worst fears. In retrospect, it seems a ridiculous expectation.

To begin with, the state of the industries which were acquired was, without exception, deplorable: all were in urgent need of rationalization and modernization. The railways were seriously run down, and the

Reid Report of 1945 commented on the backward state of the coal industry: both were suffering from decades of under-investment. Similarly, BEA started its life with a fleet of ten Dakotas, capable of carrying so few passengers that it was virtually impossible to make a profit, while BOAC's fleet included Liberators and Lodestars – the remnants of war. The difficulties of reorganization were also immense; there were 1,045 gasworks, over 800 coal companies and 537 electricity undertakings, and each collection had somehow to be welded into a rational structure.

It was not merely a problem of refurbishing plant and equipment; there were men and attitudes to consider. Many of the industries which were nationalized already had serious management problems of long standing – they had not been attracting enough able young men for many years. The railways, gas and electricity industries provided safe jobs, but they were hardly the sort in which the ambitious could make their fortunes. Many of the gas and electricity undertakings were, in any case, tiny affairs and managed by local bureaucrats rather than businessmen, most of whom were entirely unsuited to controlling larger-scale enterprises. The coal industry was desperately short of good mining engineers; while the Post Office was seldom first choice among graduate entrants to the Civil Service and 'got good people only by accident', according to Alan Wolstencroft, formerly managing director (Posts). The air corporations had a different kind of problem; when building up their businesses after the war, they had to recruit a large number of people who knew nothing about operating an airline.

In many industries the shortage of good managers was made worse by nationalization: a number of the abler railwaymen, for example, who did not like the prospect of public ownership, departed. Most of the organizations which were nationalized, furthermore, lacked (in whole or in part) a strong commercial tradition. Nor was this surprising in the light of their history. Some, like gas and electricity, had been carrying social burdens from their beginnings; they both, for example, had an obligation to supply anyone within a certain distance of their mains. In addition, both they and the railways had had their charges under varying sorts of public surveillance for some time, and their profits were effectively restricted. This helped create organizations dominated by engineers, and in which marketing skills were notable by their absence. Many of the chief engineers of gas and electricity undertakings regarded the marketing of appliances through their showrooms as a not very respectable adjunct to their other activities: the result was that most showrooms were basically service centres and in a 'dreadful' state at nationalization, according to one of the principal officers of the Gas Council.

The climate in the years after nationalization did not encourage more enterprising attitudes. Coal was in such short supply that it sold itself. The Ministry of Power laid down priorities for its allocation and had to give permission for the export of every single ton; until 1956, the NCB's salesmen were Fuel Supplies Officers of the Ministry. In the same way, electricity Boards spent the first twenty years after the war struggling to match demand and provide adequate safety margins, and Sir Ronald Edwards said at the 1968 annual meeting that it had been the first year in which they had been able to go out and sell electricity. The Post Office has still not caught up with demand and has still a waiting-list of 80,000 for telephones. Bill Ryland, the Chief Executive, is frank about the fact that, because of this, they have not been able to develop 'the commercial type, the man who puts the customer first'.

The Post Office, like a number of other British industries, seems to avoid using the word 'sell'; it prefers to talk about 'stimulating demand'. Only now, twenty years after nationalization, are the railways, electricity and gas beginning to look hard for more men with commercial instinct.

In one sense, indeed, nationalization had the effect of absolving the executives of the industries concerned from whatever commercial obligations they may have felt before. They must have found it easy to convince themselves that they had been called to some higher (and less demanding) service. Certainly, in the early post-war years, those heads of nationalized industries who did not believe that they were part of some greater national or international purpose were rare indeed. Keith Granville, now managing director of BOAC, remembers how shocked he was to hear Lord Douglas (then chairman of BEA) say that his job was not to do good for Britain, but to run BEA. BOAC at that time was not only expected to help prop up the British aircraft industry but also act as a spur to a variety of Commonwealth airlines. Granville says that, in that era, they seldom took a decision simply on the basis of what was good for BOAC.

By the second half of the 1950s, however, vague objectives and bright hopes were no longer enough. Coal and the railways had begun to make losses, and their morale was at a low ebb. Their managements, like those of other nationalized industries, did not know what they were supposed to be aiming at, they had no yardsticks by which to measure their efficiency and they had to bear the cost of loss-making services.

The demand for clarification and reform became steadily more insistent. The Herbert Committee on the electricity supply industry, reporting in 1956, had recommended that the managers of the industry should make their decisions on commercial and industrial considerations alone and that, if Ministers wanted them to ignore these factors because of some wider national interest, they should issue a directive to that effect and thus take a responsibility which was properly theirs. In 1960, the Select Committee's report on the British Transport Commission went even further: it said that if the Government wanted the industries concerned (and particularly the railways) to provide services on general social and economic grounds, then the Minister must say so and, if these services could not be run profitably, the cost should be provided, in advance, out of the public purse.

Pressure for a more commercial approach was also coming from within the nationalized industries themselves. Sir Ronald Edwards, who had joined the Electricity Council as part-time deputy chairman in 1957, put up a paper to his colleagues in the same year which argued, amongst other things, that they should be aiming at an eight per cent return on their assets: at that time, the best of the Area Boards was making about five per cent. Edwards had come from a background which was both academic and commercial. In the late 1920s, after joining a firm of chartered accountants, he had helped build up one of the first specialist tax departments in London and was later associated with a firm which, as he said, sold everything 'from Christmas cards to contraceptives'.

His paper was rejected by his new colleagues. Edwards was suggesting that they should seek higher prices in order to achieve a higher rate of return: this, they thought, was wrong in such an important public service as the electricity industry. When he pointed out that even the steel industry looked for an eleven per cent return on its capital, one official was shocked into remarking that Professor Edwards was surely not suggesting that steel was as important as electricity? Nor were the Council impressed by his argument that, by keeping electricity prices low, they were effectively influencing the market in their own favour. To them, electricity was a religion and a sacred trust; to him, a business like any other. Yet, although the paper was rejected – more in sorrow than in anger – it had considerable influence, and not only within the electricity industry. Alarmed by the mounting losses of some of the nationalized industries, a group of senior economists at the Treasury was already thinking in the same direction.

Eventually, in 1961, the Government produced a White Paper which attempted some clarification of the financial and commercial obligations of the nationalized industries.[1] The White Paper emphasized that they were all commercial undertakings (despite the fact that they had social duties) and decreed that financial objectives should be agreed with each of them so as to give management both an incentive and a yardstick. This was duly done, with the carrot placed at distances appropriate to the health of each donkey. The English and Welsh Electricity Boards were given the job of making a gross return on assets of 12.4 per cent, while British Railways was told to reduce its deficit and to break even as soon as possible.[2] The White Paper left many questions unresolved – although the State industries' social obligations were acknowledged, there was no mention of compensatory payments – and it was merely a first tentative effort at remaking the public sector in the image of the private.

In the same year Dr Beeching arrived at British Railways. Although his remit was to try to make the business pay, his brand of evangelism was as strange to the natives as that of Dr Livingstone had been a century before. As William Thorpe, now vice-chairman of the British Railways Board, put it: 'Nobody knew where the hell we were going. Beeching was like Montgomery – he asked "where is Alamein, where are we going to fight from?" He was the first man to sit down with a non-emotional approach and really analyse the problem.' The climate was also changing elsewhere. BOAC, which had run up losses (after interest and tax) of over £64m. in the previous three years, was told by the Select Committee in 1964 that what it had lacked was a single-minded determination to promote its own commercial advantage: in other words, it had allowed itself to be kicked around by the Government.

In 1967, a second White Paper appeared. By that time, the nationalized industries were investing at the rate of £1,700m. a year,[3] roughly

[1] Cmnd. 1337.

[2] The existence of targets can be a useful weapon in the hands of a shrewd chairman; they provide a clear-cut justification for making a surplus and if the Government is seeking to impose restrictions which, in his view, make it impossible for him to reach the target return, he can at least insist that they take responsiblity for the policies which led to the shortfall, and may even be able to deter them altogether.

[3] They currently employ more than 2m. people, and contribute about eleven per cent of the gross domestic product.

double what they had been spending five years before, and the Government was concerned (among other things) that there should not be a misallocation of available resources between public and private institutions. It therefore laid down a test rate of return of roughly eight per cent on new investment, comparable with the average figure for low-risk projects in the private sector. It also said that nationalized industries should relate their prices to the cost of goods and services which they were providing, and indicated that subsidies would be forthcoming to help some of them meet the cost of loss-making services provided on social and economic grounds.

The railways can now either claim a grant on loss-making lines or apply for closures; the gas and electricity industries are paid for burning more coal than they otherwise would; and the Coal Board has been subsidized for deferring the closure of uneconomic pits. BEA, however, has not been compensated for its loss-making Scottish services, nor have electricity, gas and the Post Office[1] been subsidized for their uneconomic operations in rural areas.[2]

This was one of the ways in which the Labour Government sought to rescue its predecessors' creations (abandoned to the Tories shortly after birth) and to put them on a more genuinely commercial basis. It also authorized massive capital write-offs for BOAC (£110m.), the Coal Board (£415m.) and British Railways (£557m.) – leaving the taxpayer to carry the interest burden – in a further effort to help them pay their way.[3] Even so, the return on capital earned by the nationalized industries as a whole is still much lower than the average for private industry. In their best years, their gross yield is about half that for private enterprise, their net yield (after depreciation) about a third. Only BOAC, helped by the capital write-off, does better than the average for private concerns.

Nevertheless, the regular exhortations to a more commercial approach has tended to drive the old-style, service-at-any-price public servants either out of office or underground, and they have been superseded by people who are not insulted if they are described as commercial animals. In other words, it is now fashionable for the chairman

---

[1] If the rural costs of the postal service were roughly the same as they are in towns, the Post Office thinks it would save about £15m.

[2] Some chairmen, however, are not eager to claim subsidies because it probably means a further reduction in their independence.

[3] The Tories had allowed the British Transport Commission to write off £1,192m. of its capital in 1963.

of a nationalized industry to talk and behave like a thoroughly business-like fellow, while (of course) still exhibiting a concern for the cares of the people. This change of emphasis has helped to blur the distinction between the public and private sectors to some extent, a result which both the politicians and many of the chairmen applaud.

Lord Robens, for example, is president of the Advertising Association and the Coal Board has linked up with a number of private concerns in joint ventures over the last few years; gas, electricity and the railways have all run television advertising campaigns as professional as anything produced by private industry; Sir Ronald Edwards used to say he believed in profits and wanted £100m. on the books;[1] the British Steel Corporation is hopefully aiming at a fifteen per cent return on capital – in two or three years' time; the railways are considering going into the petrol and service station business in a big way; and the Post Office is delighted to have a target of its own – 'like the Bell Telephone Company'.

Beneath the glossier façades, however, many of the chairmen and senior managers – taking them at their own assessment of themselves – are undecided to which camp they are supposed to belong. There are few like Keith Granville who regard themselves as 'pure business-men' and only members of the public sector for the purpose of raising capital. More typical is Sir Henry Jones of the Gas Council, who thinks of himself as a mixture of businessman and public servant – 'an inter-mediate animal' – and Bill Ryland's definition of his own position and aims makes plain the gap which still exists between most nationalized industries and private business: 'I think of myself as a businessman first – that consists of putting meaning into the concept of service first and then marketing, actually selling something to people.'

Closeness to Whitehall often helps to destroy the illusion of being part of the commercial world. One of the principal officers of the Gas Council remarked that, while the people in the Area Boards could be 'ninety per cent businessmen', being at headquarters brought contact with the Ministry of Power, which 'warps any idea that you are engaged in a competitive business'. At the other end of the scale from BOAC is British Rail, and for discernible reasons: if railwaymen described themselves as businessmen after the huge losses which they have made over the last decade, they would be condemning themselves out of hand. They have therefore thought of themselves as public servants – the

[1] The electricity industry has the rare distinction of never having produced a deficit in the twenty-one years since nationalization.

present deputy chairman told me that he had been heartened to meet three young men who had joined the railways because they had become 'fed up with the product' and wanted instead to have a sense of public service – although there is now more emphasis on commercial-minded-ness at the top than there was.

The same confusion of motives emerges when the officials of national-ized industries are questioned about the objectives of their businesses; the answers only serve to bear out Lord Beeching's point that while private industry has a single, clear and unchanging primary aim (the maximization of profit), the objectives of nationalized industry are not only 'more numerous, more ambiguous and less distinguishable from qualifying conditions' but also fluctuate from year to year and from Government to Government at the whim of parliamentary and public opinion. The answers also convey the impression that the new com-mercialism is a somewhat superficial growth in a number of industries; while a handful of managers talk about profits and meeting their targets, the majority still seem to be far more concerned with objectives which spring directly from the public service concept.

Ryland of the Post Office, enthusing that it now had a yardstick of efficiency, described that yardstick as 'the best service you can provide, as cheaply as you can', while one of the principal officers of the Gas Council believed its central purpose was 'keeping prices down'. Whatever the Treasury might think, he added, continuity and expan-sion were far more important than profit. Profit was important only to the Chancellor and he even contested the view that being in the red had a bad effect on an industry's morale. In his opinion, a modest deficit of £5 or £10m. did not matter.[1] These views, although unlikely to be held in BOAC, BEA or the Steel Corporation, are probably more widely shared elsewhere than would appear at first sight.

Conviction about the need for a more deep-rooted commercialism may increase as competition between the fuel industries becomes fiercer and as a new generation of managers filters through in the rail-ways, but the ambivalence of the nationalized industries is nevertheless likely to remain unresolved for a number of reasons.

The most important is that control from Whitehall will continue – even if the politicians were ready to yield up their personal power, they will not (in the foreseeable future) be ready to relinquish their influence over industries whose activities have such a bearing on the

[1] Sir Henry Jones comments that this view does not represent the policy of the Gas Council!

state of the economy. Nor are changes in organization likely to alter this. It would remain a fact of life under the Ministry of Nationalized Industries suggested by the Select Committee in 1969, and it would (in my view) persist even if the Tories returned some of the nationalized industries to private ownership. Certainly, their fingers have been only marginally less itchy in more recent years than those of the Socialists when it has come to poking around in the nationalized industry pie. I do not think that the greater degree of interference noticeable in more recent times can be put down mainly to the arrival of a Labour Government. It has much more to do with the fact that the nationalized industries entered the 1960s without a philosophy and had to be given one by one group of politicians or another; with the sharp increase in their capital investment at a time when national resources were scarce; with the need for mediation between the fuel industries once it was evident that we might find ourselves with a surplus of energy and consequent duplication of investment; and with the emergence of two indisputable invalids, in railways and coal. There has been markedly less interference in BOAC's affairs since 1964 than there was before Labour came back to power.

There are dangers if this high level of interference persists. Until now, the nationalized industries have been able to find leaders of reasonable calibre – in general, their quality has improved with the years – but they may find increasing difficulty in doing so. The recent struggle to find a new chairman for the Railways Board could easily be repeated in other industries. This is all the more dangerous in that the State concerns, even more than private business, demand robust leadership if they are not to become flabby and degenerate monoliths.

Nationalized Performance

There is no nationalized equivalent of the headline 'Bumper Year for Shell'. Perhaps because their results frequently justify this lack of appreciation, even the occasional praise they receive – the Prices and Incomes Board, for example, complimenting the Gas Council on its efficiency – is greeted with barely-concealed astonishment.

British Rail, taken into public ownership in 1947, vies with gas as the public's favourite butt. After being led by outsiders for most of its life

(Lord Hurcomb, General Lord Robertson of Oakridge, Lord Beeching), it is now headed by two dyed-in-the-wool railwaymen, Sir Henry Johnson and Mr William Thorpe.

They have taken command of an industry whose morale, in Thorpe's words, has been 'not just rock bottom, but half-way down the waste-pipe' after five years (1963–7) when it piled up losses of £674m. They are hoping to make a surplus of £10m. in 1969 with the help of subsidies which amount to £72½m. and the hiving-off of a sundries freight business which had been losing money at the rate of £20m. a year. Even allowing for the subsidies the arrival of a surplus is the end of a long and dispiriting road: 'We've been due to break even within five years for the last fifty, or that's what it feels like,' said Thorpe.

The railways seem to have suffered from just about every malaise, imposed and self-inflicted, known to industrial man. To begin with, they have been subjected to more organizational nonsenses than any other nationalized industry. From 1953 until 1962, for example, they were simply the largest division of the British Transport Commission, which was also responsible for docks, inland waterways, hotels and London Transport; this meant that an organization employing 649,000 people had no separate management of its own, a patently absurd state of affairs. At a lower level, the regional general managers were given enormous power – 'they were God in uniform', in the words of a member of the present Railways Board – and this helped delay the unification of the system: the overlap in the jurisdictions of the four railway companies on which the regions were broadly based[1] was not eliminated for more than a decade after nationalization. Furthermore, the workshops in each region (British Rail is the only network in the world which has its own manufacturing subsidiary, making wagons, coaches and rails and assembling locomotives) continued to duplicate each other's work.

Nor were the general managers sufficiently encouraged to engage in fundamental thinking by the presence of regional Boards composed largely of part-time outsiders to which they did not belong and some of the members of which were wont to spend time asking pointed questions about the lateness of the 5.50 on the previous Wednesday.

More basically, neither the early post-war Governments (both Labour and Conservative) nor the leaders of the industry itself seem to have given much thought to the sort of railway which was needed after

[1] The Scottish lines were amalgamated into a separate region and the old London and North Eastern Railway was split to form the Eastern and North-Eastern regions.

1945; the tacit assumption (no doubt influenced by the vital role which the railways had played during the war) was that it would continue at its pre-war size. The result was that the 1954 Modernization Plan proposed to refurbish the entire system; the motor car and the lorry (whose challenge had been delayed by petrol rationing and export quotas) might as well not have existed for all the account the planners took of them. Branch lines which were closed a few years later were equipped with expensive multiple diesel units. Similarly, the marshalling yards which were built up and down the country proved to be white elephants when the whole pattern of the railways' freight operations was reshaped after Beeching's arrival. The total cost of the Plan, estimated originally at £1,240m., had risen by thirty-four per cent to £1,660m. by 1959.

When it was quite clear that things had gone seriously wrong – with the deficit steadily increasing – the railways' organization and *modus operandi* were apparently so complex that diagnosis was extremely difficult. Lord Beeching was later to describe the railways as 'a very simple business', but outside medicine men who examined the invalid could not isolate the cause of its groans. The Select Committee confessed that it found it hard to discover just *where* the losses were being incurred, and the Ministry of Transport was unable to help: 'it is very difficult to get an answer to that,' said the then Permanent Secretary.

Despite the fact that the loss-making areas have now been identified,[1] this air of bafflement has not entirely disappeared, either inside the railways or among outside observers. For one thing, since costs are recorded by area, region or division, it is difficult to pin down the overall cost of any activity. In 1968, the Prices and Incomes Board turned down a request for an across-the-board increase in fares and appeared to be unpleasantly surprised both that the railways did not know more about its own business and that the proposed increases were not related to any specific plan to reduce the deficit or break even.

One reason why the handful of bright young men in the industry still appear to be struggling to analyse precisely what does happen is that the railways have traditionally been dominated by operators who aimed to run a really comprehensive service but were often none too sure what it was costing. When timetables were modified, the alterations were usually justified in terms of better service or better utilization

---

[1] The losses have been heaviest on commuter services into London and the large provincial conurbations; on cross-country services between cities; and on the wagonload and sundries freight businesses.

of stock, but the implications in net cash terms were not spelt out. This lack of attention to financial discipline was made worse by railway managements often being sharply divided by function, with nobody to take an overall view except at the most Olympian level. Thorpe recalls that, in one of his former regions, the operating staff were compelled to lay on excursion trains which cost £200 to run and yielded only £90 in revenue, because the commercial staff did not want turnover to fall.

Nor is it yet certain that these fundamental faults have been corrected. The railways are to have their first-ever corporate plan in 1969, and managers are now using all the fashionable words, but inside critics believe that there are still too many who are simply 'playing at trains', interested in technical advance but not in tight financial management: 'they talk about discounted cash flow,' said one man, 'but they're not really interested.'

When Beeching arrived in 1961, he found a mass of statistics, many in the form prescribed by nineteenth-century railway Acts, but traffic costing was not being used for management. 'It was still the era of limitless service,' he said, 'and there were vast numbers of people who had no conception of the cost of the jobs they were doing.' He tried to educate them. When he went on tour, he would ask those who accompanied him to add up the cost of the rolling stock standing idle in the stations through which they passed. Once, on his way to the office from his home in East Grinstead, Beeching himself counted fifty-two stationary banana vans. When he arrived, a member of his staff wanted to order 1,000 banana vans, at a cost of £1m. Beeching asked if they would pay. No, replied the suppliant, but bananas were regular business and the people who wanted them had been customers for years.

The banana vans were not built and Beeching became increasingly concerned about the fleet of a million wagons which stood around the railway system being used as a means of cheap storage by 'regular' customers. Their average turn-round time was fourteen–fifteen days (which meant that they were being used only twenty-five times a year) and they were involved in $4\frac{1}{2}$ marshallings per journey. He also gave impetus to the programme of closures, although the effect was delayed by public opposition. Only three hundred miles of track had been closed between 1954 and 1958; 3,800 miles were closed between 1963 and 1967.

Beeching was not always, however, an outstandingly successful picker of men (even allowing that the railways presented him with a very limited choice) and although he introduced some much-needed organizational reforms (regional general managers were made chairmen of their Boards), a great deal remained to be done when he left. Nevertheless Beeching gave the railways a sense of direction and self-awareness which they had previously lacked. Furthermore, despite the savings which he and his successors achieved by reducing the labour force and the size of the operation, no less than £95m. of the £115m. saved between 1962 and 1966 was swallowed up by rising costs and wages.

Despite the large sums invested in the railways (£1,400m. in the decade up to 1967), the fact that no significant impact had been made on the size of the deficit was also a grave reflection on the effectiveness of the industry's watchdogs at the Ministry of Transport. The section which deals with the railways has been trebled in size over the last few years and is now clearly determined to make up for past errors by poking its nose into the railways' affairs at frequent intervals. The Ministry's view is that the railways can only hope to stay out of its pocket by improving their efficiency.

The new deal has got under way brightly enough: the subsidies have begun to flow (applications for grants have been made on 250 of the 400 passenger services) and the railways now has a Board which is supposed to be concentrating on long-term strategy instead of being regaled – as it was in the past – with lengthy reports on wagon control.

What effect all this will have remains to be seen. The latest White Paper[1] talked about a rail network of 11,000 miles (it was almost 17,000 in 1963), but few people either inside or outside the railways believe that this figure represents bedrock. Senior members of the Railways Board, including Sir Henry Johnson himself, think that it is likely to be lowered to Beeching's estimate of 8,000 miles after the next election. Johnson says he will shed no tears: he wants a railway of economic size.

This, in itself, is fairly revolutionary language for a railwayman to use (the majority are as preservationist by nature as those members of the general public who fight hearty rearguard actions when lines are threatened with closure), but Johnson and Thorpe still have to prove that they can produce a really clear-cut analysis of the railway's problems and a long-term plan for solving them. In many ways, the two men are rather too much alike to form an ideal combination, and pessimists within the railways are not convinced that it will prove radical or penetrating enough. They are unlikely to change the military

[1] Cmnd. 3439, November 1967.

atmosphere of head office, with its separate messes for chief, senior and junior officers: railway traditions die hard.

The railways, however, are only at the beginning of a profound upheaval and although some old problems have been solved, new ones will shortly appear. When Local Passenger Transport Executives[1] take over as contractors for commuter services in the big conurbations, the railwaymen will have fresh problems of diplomacy on their hands. Nor can the Freightliner services – at present earning less than a quarter of the £20m. which is their target – of themselves be the railways' salvation. The only consolation is that the extent of their sickness has at last been realized.

BOAC and BEA could theoretically compete against each other all over the world; there is nothing in the statutes which restricts their operation to any specific area.[2] In practice, although they do compete on certain routes – Beirut and Tel Aviv, for example – they are limited by tradition and by the type of aircraft they fly. BEA has no aircraft which would be any good to BOAC and vice-versa and its chairman, Sir Anthony Milward, says that if the airline did have VC 10s, it would make 'a fantastic loss' on them. Occasionally, there has been horse-trading: in 1958, BOAC was allowed to fly through any point in Europe (after consulting BEA) in return for an extension of BEA's routes to Beirut, Tel Aviv, Cairo and the Persian Gulf.

The size of their respective parishes makes them very different animals, even if one disregards the BEA view that BOAC men – as inheritors of the Imperial Airways tradition – lead easier lives and are usually to be seen with cigars in their mouths. BEA is the largest short-haul operator in the world, with an average flight length of only 350 miles; BOAC's average is 1,677 miles. Similarly, while BEA's average single fare is only £12, BOAC's is £80, and whereas BOAC carries 1½m. passengers for an income of £150m., BEA handles five times as many for an income which is only seventy per cent of BOAC's.

BEA is also, of course, a much more intensive operation than BOAC;

[1] Transport Executives have already been set up to cover Merseyside, Tyneside, Greater Manchester and Birmingham.

[2] The report of the Edwards Committee on Civil Aviation (May 1969) proposed the setting-up of a new National Air Holdings Board, of which BOAC and BEA would be subsidiaries. Edwards also proposed closer collaboration in fields such as marketing and engineering.

it reckons to make sixteen departures an hour compared with BOAC's sixteen a day and on a summer Saturday runs something like five hundred flights ('You can't get pompous on that', said Milward). Because of the separate existence of BOAC, it is also the only major European operator which does not fly world routes and since (on a general rule of thumb), it makes money on journeys of over five hundred miles and losses on anything shorter, earning an overall profit is all the more difficult. It believes that many of its rivals cover themselves on the longer routes and that only Finnair and itself have regularly made money on Europe.

Milward, who came to BEA via the textile industry and the Fleet Air Arm, illustrates the difference which distance makes: 'London to Moscow, 1,500 miles non-stop, we can make nice money with a Comet only thirty per cent full. On the two hundred miles to Paris, we lose nice money with the same Comet sixty-five per cent full.' (BEA loses far more on the Paris run – partly because of handling charges at the French end – than the £300,000 annual deficit it incurs on its Scottish services.) Nor is BEA's job made any easier by the sharp 'peaking' of traffic: the number of passengers in summer is twice what it is in winter and on the Channel Isles service the summer-winter ratio is as high as eight to one.

BOAC not only has the chance to make money on the Atlantic (although its returns are affected by sharp competition and by the high cost of its American installations), but also on the much more profitable routes to the Far East and Africa. Like the shipping companies, it is grateful for the Imperial heritage; competition in these areas tends to be isolated and, according to Keith Granville, its managing director, 'we have them all over a barrel'. BOAC's return on gross assets – taking the original cost of the aircraft – is twice as high on its African sector as on its trans-Atlantic business, well over twice as high on the Eastern routes.

Curiously enough, however, it is BEA which has the more successful long-term record. It lost heavily for the first seven years while it was learning the business, but has made some sort of profit in all but three of the last sixteen years. While it is perfectly true that neither its profits not its return on capital have ever been exciting, this is hardly surprising in view of the way in which its activities are circumscribed – and it has succeeded in becoming the largest carrier in Europe, with over a fifth of the total business in passengers and freight. BEA's more recent hard times have been partly due to Government restrictions on travel: an airline which exists mainly to carry British passengers and goods abroad (over half its business originates in the British Isles) can hardly fail to be affected by a £50 travel allowance. The inclusive tour operators have also stolen some of the cream from its scheduled summer services.

Taking a longer perspective, a number of factors have worked in BEA's favour. Its management history has been remarkably stable and one of its early bosses, Lord Douglas, set a tradition of firmness in dealing with the Government. It has to be added that BEA's special requirements allowed Douglas to be a regular patron of the British aircraft industry without suffering commercial penalties; for the size and range of aircraft which BEA wanted, there were few American or Continental alternatives which were markedly more economic than home-grown products. It was a case of patriotism without tears. Not until the recent case of the Boeing 727/737s did BEA and the Government have a major disagreement over aircraft procurement: as a sop, the Government has agreed to compensate the airline for the reduction in its competitive ability due to the delay in the Trident 3's availability.[1]

BOAC, on the other hand, has had a chequered and often unhappy history. It has suffered from too frequent changes of leadership (nine chairmen between 1939 and 1964, most of them part-timers, some of them too ready to give in to Government pressure); from disasters like that of the Comet which cost it money and a lead over the Americans which, Granville believes, might have made it the world's premier airline; from aircraft, like the Britannia, which suffered considerable teething troubles; from confused objectives; from inadequate management and some bad luck.

Imperialism and patriotism have both cost BOAC dearly. By 1963, for example, it had lost over £15m. on its associations with other (usually Commonwealth) airlines; these alliances were formed in the hope that they might create a useful market for the British aircraft industry as well as contributing in some undefined way to Commonwealth unity. (The case of Kuwait Airlines was rather different: there, BOAC was acting as a tool of the Government's foreign policy.) In the event, the only compensation for these losses came in the shape of extra business directed to BOAC by its allies. BOAC also lost heavily

---

[1] The aid will take the form of a transfer to a special account of £25m. from BEA's interest-bearing capital of £117m. The £25m. will not bear interest and will be transferred in pre-determined amounts over the next four years to the profit and loss account.

on its South American routes, which it appeared to continue out of a sense of national duty.

Its allegiance to British aircraft (whether by choice or direction) has also proved expensive; their operating costs in the years since the war have almost invariably been higher than those of their American counterparts. This was true of the Comet, the Britannia and the VC 10. The standard VC 10, for example, had the same weight and power as the Boeing 707, but only three-quarters of the seats, while the Super VC 10 consumes twenty-three per cent more gallons per hour than the comparable Boeing. BOAC reckons that the Super's first eight passengers go towards off-setting both the high purchase price and the extra operating costs.

The losses of the early 1960s – when BOAC was particularly hard-hit by excess capacity following the arrival of the big jets on the Atlantic – duly produced a new broom in the shape of Sir Giles Guthrie. Guthrie regarded himself as a company doctor whose prime task was to make the airline profitable as rapidly as possible: he had no intention of shouldering the problems of the British aircraft industry. He was ruthless – 'an icy mind, a slightly icy nature and the hardest worker here', according to one of his colleagues – and he had the inestimable advantage of being independent and wealthy enough to invite the Government to find itself another chairman if it did not like his style. He threatened to resign only once.

Guthrie cut BOAC's staff by between 2,000 and 3,000, reduced the size of its order for VC 10s and dropped the South American routes. Under his rule, BOAC also freed itself from its imperial burden; 'these days, when anybody tells us to foster Bongo Bongo Airways because there's a big British investment,' said Granville, 'the answer is, sorry, old boy, it's no damn good to us.'[1]

Guthrie's reign (which ended in 1968) produced large profits in 1967 and 1968, but still leaves BOAC with problems. For one thing, the airline is even now overweight in terms of staff (it flies just over five million miles with a staff of 19,500 while Panam, which flies three times as far, has a complement oly fifty per cent higher); on Granville's admission, it needs to improve its selling and runs third to Panam and TWA on the North Atlantic; and it has had its difficulties with the pilots. For the moment, it has a part-time chairman again and, in the absence of a full-time successor who is both as independent and

[1] BOAC still gives some help to what Granville calls 'emerging airlines' but on a strictly commercial basis.

successful as Guthrie, it is clearly vulnerable to renewed Government interference.

The *Post Office* is the latest recruit (1969) to the ranks of the public corporations. It is made up of two parts which, in some ways, sit incongruously together. Its postal side grows at a snail's pace (one per cent below the annual increase in gross national product) whereas its telecommunications business is one of the most rapidly expanding in the country, currently doubling in size every ten years.

Indeed, it is likely to continue to expand at that rate, since only twenty-nine per cent of British homes now have a telephone, compared with eighty per cent in the United States. The telephone men are also hoping that they will be able to push up the domestic calling rate: at present, although the increase in trunk traffic is as rapid as anywhere in the world, the average British householder makes only twelve calls a week, a quarter of the American average.

The telephone service is still suffering from the blunders and omissions as well as the restraints of the past. In the years during and after the war, the Americans and Swedes (who operate two of the most efficient services in the world) were investing heavily in the electro-mechanical type of switching equipment known as cross-bar; Britain invested little and clung to obsolete equipment. Then, in 1949, the Post Office made what a senior official described as 'a colossal error' by attempting to leap-frog cross-bar and instal electronic exchanges. Only in 1963 did it acknowledge that it had tried to move ahead too rapidly by taking whatever cross-bar equipment it could lay its hands on and incorporating it into the existing system.

By that time the Post Office had already been caught out by an 'explosion' of demand for telephones. It was short of equipment and its efforts to close the gap were not helped by a system of tendering which often favoured firms quoting the lowest price, irrespective of their capacity to deliver on time: the basic principle was '$\frac{1}{2}$d off and never mind if it's two years late', according to one senior executive. Roughly a thousand of the 1,200 contracts placed during this period were completed late.[1]

Small electronic exchanges (handling about 2,000 lines apiece) are now being delivered at the rate of about one hundred a year, but since 4,000 of Britain's 6,000 exchanges are of that size, Ryland does not

[1] This situation could not be blamed entirely on the industry, which faced substantial problems in expanding output so rapidly.

expect the entire system to be operated electronically before the year 2000. He is hoping, however, that his forecasters will be able to get their estimates of demand more nearly right than in the past, when they were calculated on what he calls an 'unstimulated' basis. A Marketing Department has now been set up and includes people recruited from outside.

The postal side of the GPO is suffering from an entirely different sort of headache: its problem is to maintain its very high standard of service in a labour-intensive business where its resources are already fully stretched. The introduction of mechanized sorting techniques – seventy-five post offices which handle three-quarters of Britain's mail will be fully mechanized by 1975 – will yield savings of perhaps £12m. a year, but the postal service is still expected to need a labour force of about 200,000.

There are other problems. One is that since many Post Offices almost fall into the category of ancient monuments – a large number were built before the turn of the century – they have been depreciated right out of the assets, and when rebuilding is done, interest charges go up sharply. However, even if the postal side of the business finds it hard to reach its target return, it will have the consolation of knowing that the American postal service loses more than the GPO's entire annual revenue.

Both Ryland and Wolstencroft are determined that their liberation from the Civil Service strait-jacket shall produce a more business-like operation. They can remember when their expenditure had to be voted each year by Parliament, and when any incentive to make money was nullified by all the Post Office's revenue going straight back into the Treasury's coffers. Now they hope to be able to offer more competitive salaries and to reward efficiency instead of 'paying £40 a year for living twelve months and maintaining the status quo'. One part of their heritage will not be easy to escape. The Post Office unions have, over the years, extended their power into every part of the GPO's life: they expect to be consulted on questions of management organization and even tea breaks are fixed at national level.

The renaissance of *gas* is remarkable by any standards. In 1960, it had all the marks of a dying industry. Total sales had risen by less than one per cent a year over the previous decade, domestic sales had actually fallen, gas was being outsold by electricity and a good many gasmen were worried that total sales would actually begin to decline. The root of the industry's troubles was dependence on an expensive raw material, coking coal: in 1960, 87 per cent of its gas was derived from a coal source – 'coal,' as Sir Henry Jones put it, 'had us by the throat'. Since (unlike electricity) none of its uses makes it irreplaceable – all its functions can be performed by other fuels – the industry had either to find new sources of gas or face the prospect of a lingering death.

In the event, it found several sources. One was a way of making gas from oil; a second was Algerian natural gas, imported in the form of liquid methane; the third, and most important, was the discovery of natural gas under the North Sea. These discoveries completely transformed the old balance of power between gas, electricity and coal. They dealt coal a severe blow – the gas industry has halved its coal consumption since 1956, and less than a third of Britain's gas now comes from a coal source[1] – and they also gave the electricity industry something to think about by bringing gas prices down while electricity's continued to move upwards. Sales of gas to domestic consumers doubled between 1961 and 1968 (the increase in sales to industry was negligible) and the gasmen found themselves, year after year, underestimating the rise in demand.

This radical change also began to transform an organization which, until then, had probably been the most parochial of the nationalized industries. Unlike electricity, which already possessed a national grid by the time it was taken into public control, gas was based on works which – because coal gas was produced at very low pressure – could supply only a limited area; their output was accurately called 'town gas'. The new processes, however, did not have these limitations. The plants which made gas from oil were more powerful and produced gas at higher pressures, while natural gas from Algeria and the North Sea provided a source of supply completely independent of local production. The completion of the Algerian deal in 1961 was the beginning of the end of the separatist power of the Area Boards, and the Gas Council has conducted all the North Sea negotiations on behalf of the industry.

The transformation also came just in time to prevent the gas industry from turning into a rearguard action fought by career gasmen and recruits from local government, but with little in the way of new blood. It is still far too ingrown, but its revival has given it a new glamour and Dennis Rooke, who is in charge of the North Sea operation, says he is bombarded by chemical engineers and geologists who want jobs. A

[1] The proportion is still declining.

high proportion of his staff comes from outside the industry, and Rooke himself is a very new sort of gasman. Appointed a fulltime member of the Council when he had barely turned forty and lacking wide connections in the industry (Sir Henry Jones describes it as 'a very friendly affair'), Rooke was thought by many people to be too young for the job. However, he was a protégé of Sir Kenneth Hutchinson, the former deputy chairman, who did as much as anybody in the industry to encourage a new sense of aggression. Rooke admits to being occasionally brusque and blunt and conveys the flavour of the more competitive private enterprises more than anybody else I met in the State industries.

He is also one of the men who believes that the gas industry has to sell its ware much harder than in the past. Although its traditional emphasis on service and safety was justified because coal gas contained carbon monoxide and breakdown often meant 'Boy Scouts running all over the place', in the words of one Council member, it was accompanied by a failure to penetrate the industrial market and adequately to exploit its own shops, some of which acted in the past as cash collection and service centres but offered neither attractive appliances nor salesmen. Since (again unlike electricity) virtually all gas appliances are marketed through the industry's own retail outlets, this neglect simply squandered potential business. The design of its appliances is now markedly better, but some of its shops still do not have salesmen and a great deal remains to be done before they can be compared with the best private enterprise chain.[1]

Sir Henry Jones is aware of their shortcomings. Appointed chairman in 1960, Jones is a fourth-generation gasman – his great-grandfather was an engineer in Chester as long ago as 1830. An ex-Harrovian, who took a First in mechanical sciences at Cambridge, he was dubbed 'the gentleman gasman from Harrow' by one Minister of Power, but under his leadership the gas industry has not been so pliant as it was in the depressing days of the 1950s. 'He plays the part of a calm chap devoted to his industry,' said the chairman of another nationalized concern, 'but he's sharper than you'd think.' Gas now has a more exciting future than any of the other State industries.

One useful service performed by the arrival of High-Speed Gas was to assist in shaking the *electricity industry* out of its apparent complacency during the 1950s. Gas had become an object of derision among electricity men, and for obvious reasons. From 1953 to 1963, their own sales

[1] Over half the showrooms have been modernized during the last six years.

were moving ahead at more than nine per cent a year, it was regarded as almost a law of nature that demand would continue to double every ten years and, as the Herbert Committee remarked in 1956, it was easy enough for the industry to jog along without too much effort. Its senior officials concede that there was also little pressure to economize in the use of capital, both because of a strong public desire to see the industry build up a safe margin of capacity and because it seemed better to spend 'a little extra' rather than risk the damage which might be caused (to electricity's image as well as to industry) by shortage of supplies – particularly with labour costs relatively low.

After 1963, the situation began to change. The annual increase in demand flattened out – in the years from 1963 to 1968, it was roughly half what it had been during the previous decade – and although this could be put down partly to lack of growth in the economy, the electricity industry had nevertheless spent over £3,500m. between 1962 and 1968 on capital investment, and by the end of that time found itself running into a plant surplus. There were also more particular troubles, among them late deliveries of new plant and teething troubles with generating sets which had jumped from sixty to five hundred megawatts within a decade. The result was that obsolete equipment had to be kept in operation. The industry counter-attacked vigorously enough – it sharply increased its share of the domestic central heating market – but it did not reach its target rate of return in either 1967 or 1968.

The steady withdrawal of gas as a coal user also left the field clear for a head-on clash between the electricity industry and the Coal Board, which wanted to safeguard its future by ensuring that new power stations were coal-fired. This royal battle of monopolies generated heat but little light. Lord Robens claimed that the costs of nuclear stations were being kept secret; the Central Electricity Generating Board replied that it had no detailed knowledge of coal costs, that (as the purchaser of sixty-five million tons annually) it was the residual legatee of the Coal Board's total costs, that other (and smaller) customers were getting coal cheaper, and that it was allocated coal from dear pits because it was powerless to switch to other fuels.

Electricity first 'discovered' that it was using coal uneconomically in the year 1964–5 and was pressed by the Government to continue to burn as much as possible; the Council agreed to tilt the scales by telling its computer that oil was twenty-seven shillings a ton dearer than it really was, but – despite Government exhortation – it would tilt them no further. This, it believed, was a justifiable subsidy: electricity needed a healthy coal industry. The upshot is that the CEGB will still, in 1975, be using the same quantity of coal as it does now, but only three-quarters of its needs compared with the present eighty per cent.

The CEGB, of course, has critics within the industry. Not only do many Area Boards feel powerless before such a juggernaut, they also resent what they consider to be intellectual arrogance: 'they think all the brains are on their side, all the clots on ours', complained one chairman.[1] The CEGB, for its part, puts down the resentment to jealousy because it has the more interesting and advanced technical work, and it believes that if Area Boards made up their minds that their job was selling rather than engineering, they would be better off.

The fact that this resentment has not come out more into the open in the Council chamber is partly due to the personal respect in which the CEGB chairman, Sir Stanley Brown, a lanky and imposing Mid-lander, is held within the industry, partly to a conviction that Brown inevitably knows more than they do about the problems of generation. Sir Stanley describes himself as 'extremely independent without being offensive or disruptive', and (as the spender of two-thirds of the in-dustry's huge investment programme) keeps in the closest touch with the Council's chairman. He is not worried by the prospect of plant surpluses; a seventeen per cent margin is not, he argues, unduly safe and 'if we were above it for two or three years, it wouldn't be a tragedy'.

Marketing has not been one of the industry's strong points, and the more commercially-minded Area Board chairmen admit it. 'In the past,' said one, 'we have had too many amateurish engineers doing the job and we've been too dinosauric. We've operated more like a thousand corner shops than a massive national chain and we've lost out to other multiples, who've actually bought cheaper than we have.' For a long time, Boards closed their showrooms on Saturday afternoons, the best time for husband-and-wife purchases of appliances. Boards which have taken a closer look at their sales organizations have also uncovered some unpleasant facts about their effectiveness in selling to industry. One Board which called in outside consultants found that its 'salesmen' had become little more than processors of applications and forms, and were told by the consultants that three-quarters of its staff were not fit for the job.

---

[1] This relationship will be changed once the reorganization of the industry takes effect. The CEGB will lose much of its power and the Area Boards will probably not be represented on the Authority.

The situation has markedly improved in some areas – notably the North Western, South Western and Eastern – but not in enough. The North Western Board, for example, hived off its shops into a separate operation in 1967 and put a professional marketer in charge. It does not (like some other Boards) allow sub-areas to buy what they like – its sales staff are told to sell what it buys centrally – and is not prepared to throw itself into convulsions to indulge the wilder whims of customers: 'If a woman wants blue knobs and purple spots on her cooker, she will have to wait.' Other Boards have shown comparable initiative, but too many still regard their showrooms as a side-line. The industry has also begun to use its market power with manufacturers much more effectively than in the past, with a National Marketing Office 'channelling' demand on items like refrigerators and storage heaters towards particular models.

Sir Ronald Edwards, who left the industry in 1968, gave it brisk and effective leadership, although one Area Board chairman said he rather hankered after someone (like Lord Robens) with a rougher, tougher style for dealing with the CEGB and the Government. Edwards, however, had to drive what Lord Mills once called 'the statutory boneless wonder', while the Coal Board's statutory organization gives Robens immense power. The industry will certainly need a tough leader in the years ahead: the battle with coal is likely to go on, competition from gas will become harsher and the size of the industry's investment programme, though it is now declining, makes it perpetually vulnerable to outside attack.

The *National Coal Board* has been fortunate in finding, in Lord Robens, a man capable of guiding it down a steep downhill slope. Robens is naturally combative and he has what seems to be a genuine emotional attachment to the industry. Leaders of other nationalized industries marvel that Robens' dedication allows him to ignore what they regard as self-evident truths – 'he can very easily dismiss the economic logic of the situation from his mind' – but they are also impressed by the force of his personality: 'when I'm with him,' said Sir Ronald Edwards, 'I almost want to buy coal.' Robens would add that the only economic logic which matters is that the end of coal would mean the end of cheap energy in Britain.

Of all the nationalized chairmen, he has the greatest physical presence – he is quite plainly a gaffer. Nobody, not even his closest associates, refers to him as 'Alf'; even in private, it is 'the chairman'.

The proletarian image may be good for the workers, but Robens is nothing if not businesslike. He flies around the coalfields in a Dove (bought against advice) and, when he believes that somebody has let him down, he 'blasts hell out of them', in the words of a colleague. He is one of nature's bombardiers.

Robens has had to suffer some acute disappointments. When he first arrived, in 1961, he had high hopes of preserving an industry which produced 200m. tons of coal a year; in the Government's view, its output is unlikely to be much above 120m. tons by 1975. The number of miners has been halved since 1957, the number of pits since 1950, and in some years the industry has contracted at twice the rate of the railways; in 1968, 57,000 men left the mines.

The Coal Board's problems have been made all the more difficult by the fact that its best pits – in the East Midlands – are in an area where labour is scarce and expensive, while its worst pits – in Scotland – are sited where unemployment had traditionally been high. Its social burdens are therefore considerable, and it cannot even contemplate the possibility of closing pits purely on the basis of commercial expediency. It also has £58m. tied up in 120,000 houses, and makes a loss of £300,000 a year on them because the rents it charges are historic rather than economic.[1] The contraction of the industry has had only one obvious benefit; it has seemed to knock much of the militancy out of the once-powerful miners' union, which realizes that strikes simply increase the danger of more conversions to oil.

It is all a dreadful come-down after the 1950s. Then, the Government was frequently on its knees to the industry; now, the position is reversed. By 1959, coal stocks had built up to 36m. tons and, as Derek Ezra, the deputy chairman, remarks, 'when the market turned, we had to adapt ourselves rapidly to a new situation'. (Stocks are now about 24m. tons.)

What particularly grieves Robens, however, is that the decline has continued despite all the efforts which have been made. Mechanization has pushed up productivity by seventy per cent since 1955, and Robens has now set his sights on an average output of five hundred tons from every shift at the coal face. He has been less successful in tackling the problem of the industry's retail outlets, of which the Coal Board directly controls only three or four per cent (they are largely in the hands of some 12,000 merchants). The NCB has now gone into partnership

---

[1] Half the houses, which were built before the war, still do not have bathrooms; the NCB spends roughly £500,000 a year on improvements.

with several of the larger distributors (including one, ironically, who also distributes oil), and it has cut down the number of coal depots, but it has not yet been able fully to rationalize the flow of coal from pit to market. For example, a study of Bury and Rochdale in 1967 showed that the two towns were getting their supplies from no less than ninety-nine different collieries, one in four of all the remaining pits; the number has now been cut to fifteen.

The Coal Board has tried to protect its main investment against the decline of coal by diversifying or (as the Board prefers to put it) extending its operations. Something like a twelfth of its business is now in non-mining activities. The unfortunate thing is that some of them make poor money. The NCB's coke ovens, although profitable, have suffered from a changing market, and its brick-making business, the third largest in the country, has part of its production capacity in the Midlands, too close to the flettons for comfort or profit. The Coal Board, however, makes a handsome profit on processed fuels like Phurnacite and Multiheat and on tar by-products like Synthaprufe. The result is that the £60m. invested in non-mining is currently producing an annual return of nearly £6m.

The NCB intends to put perhaps another £100m. into diversification, with the aim of producing profits of £20m. a year to protect it against the danger of losses on coal.[1] It has linked up with Conoco and Gulf in the search for North Sea gas; formed a partnership with J. H. Sankey (subsidiary of an American paper company, St Regis), which distributes solid fuel appliances and does a sizeable turnover in building supplies; dipped its toe into concrete and chemicals; and manufactures brick panels for systems building.

The *British Steel Corporation*, which accounts for about nine-tenths of Britain's steel production, could hardly have been formed in more unhealthy circumstances. It was born, in 1967, at a time when world capacity exceeded demand (the situation changed markedly in 1968), and when the return on capital of the nationalized companies had declined from 17.3 per cent in 1958 to 1.9 per cent in the year before nationalization. Even its exports were sold abroad below home market prices, with, in many cases, little expectation of making more than a contribution to overheads. It was scarcely surprising that the Corporation should make a loss of £12m. in its first full year of operation.

[1] One or two of the Coal Board's area managements are set targets in terms of a deficit.

Its new masters have not been helped in their early efforts to manoeuvre themselves out of this situation by the nature of the assets which they took over. Many of the industry's plants are both too small and badly sited in view of the fact that Britain already imports more than half its ore and will import an even higher proportion in the years ahead. The Corporation has seventy blast furnaces where twenty would do, and none of its production comes from plants with a capacity of four million tons a year or more, compared with twenty-three per cent in the United States and eleven per cent in Japan. Its productivity is consequently low – only ninety tons per man-year compared with about two hundred tons for the Japanese industry. It is also saddled with expensive long-term ore contracts and a fleet of ore carriers which is out of date: while the Japanese are already using 150,000-tonners, only one of BSC's fleet of sixty-five ships is over 25,000 tons and twenty-one are less than 11,000 tons. The appropriate ports have not been ready to receive bigger carriers and ore has had to be transshipped into smaller vessels in Rotterdam, which is costly and looks ridiculous. However, a new deep-water ore terminal has now been built and should be capable of taking 150,000-ton carriers within a few years.

Nor has its history (distant or recent) endowed the steel industry with strongly competitive instincts. The Iron and Steel Board, set up in 1953, was given the job of fixing maximum steel prices, but they were often set at levels which permitted the less efficient to survive.

The Steel Corporation also inherited a mixed bag of management talent. Fear of renationalization had done nothing to help recruitment into an industry which was already short of first-class men and in which bosses often remained in office long after the normal age of retirement. Nationalization caused a further loss of good blood – some retired because they were opposed to State control, others because they were not offered the jobs which they wanted – and the loyalty of many who remained was uncertain for a time. As one present member of the Board admitted: 'A lot of us sulked in our tents before we realized we had to make a go of it.'

The process of welding the dissident and the dismayed into some sort of cohesive force is still going on. The first stage was to set up regional, multi-product groups as an interim measure in an effort to break down the old company fiefdoms. Some of the groupings were particularly untidy; Colvilles (in Scotland) and Summers (in Cheshire) had scarcely had to speak to each other in the days of private ownership and cynics among them suggested that the Scottish and North-West Group (into which both were put) should set up its headquarters on the summit of Shap. The regional bodies have now disappeared and the suggestion is that they should be replaced by a small number of single-product divisions, with all the key decisions on things like investment and pricing being taken at headquarters. When a settled organizational pattern has at last emerged, it should help to dispel an air of confusion which has been evident at the centre, partly because few people seemed quite sure what they were supposed to be doing, or how far their power extended.

An upturn in steel demand in 1968, the agreement of the Treasury to a scheme which allows the BSC to pay a variable interest on much of its capital and the recovery of Lord Melchett from a long illness have all helped to put fresh heart into the Corporation. It is now embarked on an investment programme of £1,000m. which will include the development of at least three complexes capable of producing five million tons of steel a year each (at Port Talbot, Lackenby and Scunthorpe) and linked to deep-water ore terminals. The Steel Corporation, like so many of the nationalized industries, has been left to deal with the sins of past generations.

CHAPTER 7

The American Presence

One of the recurring themes of American history is that of a European conspiracy designed, in one way or another, to undermine the strength and liberty of the nation. The bogeys were scheming European politicians or bankers, the victims the American people. By a curious irony the last quarter of a century has brought a reversal of roles. If a succession of European prophets of doom is to be believed, the Americans are the schemers now, with corporate armies determined to turn Europe into a subject continent. The manner of the conquest is held to be all the more insidious because it is obscured by the material prosperity which accompanies it; instead of the trinkets of the slavers, there is the dollar to keep the natives' pay packets full while their hands and feet are bound.

So far as Britain is concerned, this latest generation of prophets has formidable statistics at its disposal:

– American investment in the UK has multiplied by seven times since 1950, from £300m. to well over £2,000m.[1]
– American subsidiaries in Britain account for seventeen per cent of exports, thirteen per cent of capital investment, ten per cent of manufacturing sales, and employ one worker in every seventeen.
– American companies have captured a commanding share in a variety of important markets – over half the cars and tractors produced in Britain, more than a third of the petrol, between eighty and ninety per cent of the cheaper cameras and over eighty per cent of the washing machines, eighty per cent of the semi-conductors for integrated circuits

[1] This is roughly twice Britain's investment in the United States; whereas most of our money is in stocks and shares, the Americans have put theirs mainly into plant and machinery.

TABLE I – TOP TEN AMERICAN INVESTORS IN BRITAIN, 1968

Company	Industry	Capital employed (a) (b) £mn	Net income (c) £mn
Esso Petroleum	Oil products	310.4	8.5
Ford Motor Company	Motor vehicles	216.2	7.9
F. W. Woolworth	Retail distribution	159.4	36.5
Vauxhall Motors	Motor vehicles	126.6	9.0
Gallaher	Tobacco	116.3	16.1
Standard Telephones and Cables	Electrical equipment	64.1	8.9
Rootes Motors	Motor vehicles	62.1	−9.0*
IBM	Computers, etc.	49.4	12.4
Mobil Oil	Oil products	49.3	0.3
H. J. Heinz	Food products	38.4	6.9

(a) In Britain.
(b) Net tangible assets plus bank borrowing.
(c) Before interest and tax.
  * Loss.

TABLE II – WHERE AMERICANS DOMINATE

Over 80% of output.
  Boot and shoe machinery, carbon black, colour films, custard powder and starch, sewing machines, tinned baby foods, typewriters.
60–79%
  Agricultural implements,* aluminium semi-manufactures,* breakfast cereals, calculating machines, cigarette lighters, domestic boilers, potato crisps, razor blades and safety razors, sparking plugs.
50–59%
  Cake mixes, cosmetics and toilet preparations, electric shavers, electric switches, ethical proprietaries (drugs sold to National Health Service), foundation garments, pens and pencils, motor cars, pet foods, petroleum refinery construction equipment, tinned milk, tractors, vacuum cleaners.
40–49%
  Computers, locks and keys, photographic equipment, printing and typesetting machinery, rubber tyres, soaps and detergents, watches and clocks.
30–39%
  Abrasives, commercial vehicles, floor polishers, instant coffee, lifts and escalators, portable electric tools, refined petroleum products, refrigerators, washing machines.
15–29%
  Greeting cards, industrial instruments, materials handling equipment, medicinal preparations, mineral drinks, mining machinery, paperback books, petro-chemicals, synthetic fibres, telephones and telecommunications equipment, toilet tissues.
* Including the contribution of Canadian-financed firms.

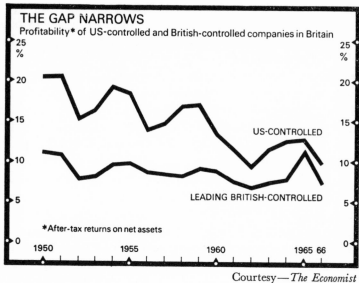

THE GAP NARROWS
Profitability* of US-controlled and British-controlled companies in Britain

US-CONTROLLED

LEADING BRITISH-CONTROLLED

*After-tax returns on net assets

1950   1955   1960   1965 66

Courtesy—*The Economist*

and more than forty per cent of the computers, are produced by American-owned firms. The scale of America's technological effort threatens to overwhelm British companies in many crucial fields of industrial innovation.

– American subsidiaries in this country are moving ahead more rapidly, on average, than British manufacturing companies; their capital investment and sales are growing more quickly, and they are earning more on their investment, although the gap is narrowing.

In theory, the American tide could easily be checked: use of the Treasury's powers under the 1947 Exchange Control Act would stop more American companies from buying their way into Britain. In practice, such prohibition has not been applied, and not merely for the reason that Britain cannot afford to provoke retaliation in the richest market in the world.

To begin with, a good part of America's investment in Britain could scarcely be described as seminal for the future of industrial development: US domination of the baby food market, or razor blades, or baked beans, or cosmetics, may provide statistical fodder for the chauvinists, but it can hardly be expected to provoke violent retaliation from any sane British Government. The Americans have by and large not attempted to buy up the technological heights of the economy, and they know perfectly well that bids for companies like General Electric and English Electric, ICL, British Leyland or Plessey, would not be greeted with approval in Whitehall. Since the war, in any case, American expansion has largely come not through take-over bids but either by developing companies which they had already acquired or by setting up new subsidiaries.

Any balance sheet of the results of the growing American presence, moreover, must register the fact that the benefits for a country like Britain are considerable. American investment helps keep a sluggish economy expanding; American management skills are disseminated at unofficial business schools like Procter and Gamble and Ford; dying businesses are snatched from the brink of the tomb by American saviours; the intermittent purchase of British companies brings an inflow of dollars most welcome to a country still short of reserves.

On the debit side, although the dangers of domination are real enough (particularly in view of the slowness of Europe to produce a concerted response to United States economic strength), the specific disadvantages of the American presence here and now are either impossible to resist without a retreat into economic isolation, or difficult to quantify. There is as yet, for example, no clear-cut evidence to show that imports of raw materials and parts by American subsidiaries has an adverse effect on Britain's trade balance when set against their export business; rather the reverse.[1] Again, it would be nice if Britain had greater technological strength, but she has not, and since technology (in the Western world, at least) has no frontiers, she is compelled to accept the consequences of American power and respond to it as best she may with her own resources and ingenuity, and with such European alliances as she can make. We are not helots yet, and in any event comparatively rich helots are better than comparatively poor ones.

The further point is made that decisions taken in Dearborn or St Paul or Dallas may act against Britain's national interest, however defined. There is no evidence that they have yet done so,[2] and at the very least the Americans would be loath to let installed industrial capacity stand idle. When work has been moved out of Britain by

[1] It has been calculated that the net balance of payments contribution of US firms in Britain is about £285m. 'The Role of American Investment in the British Economy', J. H. Dunning, PEP, 1969. Dunning warns that more research still needs to be done on the subject.

[2] It is worth adding that decisions taken in Britain by British companies could act in precisely the same way. One cannot, for instance, imagine the British Government welcoming a decision by Guest, Keen and Nettlefolds to produce all its own steel in Australia, and thus make the task of the British Steel Corporation even more difficult than it already is.

companies like IBM, it has generally been replaced with activity of a higher technological order. If the charge is that American companies go to Europe (or Japan) to buy components, the answer is that British companies are guilty of the same offence. Nor is there any evidence to show that American subsidiaries are less amenable to political influence than British companies of comparable size. Certainly if the diligence with which many of them cultivate British politicians is any reflection of their attitudes, they are *more* likely to want to act in a politically acceptable way than many British-owned enterprises. Ford and Vauxhall allowed themselves to be directed away from the south-east to Merseyside just as BMC went to Scotland.

None of this is to argue that there are not dangers in the extension of American power in the British economy. In the short term British Governments are certain to resist strongly the takeover of companies which they regard as strategic, and the Americans – if past form is any guide – are unlikely to make the attempt. In the long term, a good deal will depend on the efficiency with which companies like General Electric and English Electric and British Leyland perform, and on their success in building European alliances.

Fears of American domination have increased as both the size of US investments has multiplied and the manner of control over them tightened. In the early post-war years, many American companies – even some of those which had overseas operations before 1939 – tended to be preoccupied with the booming market at home. Europe was still a mass of separate markets, large and small, and (for many) not important enough in terms of overall corporate sales or profits to warrant any degree of priority. They were certainly not significant enough individually to attract the ambitions of the ablest American executives. These even avoided jobs in US-based international divisions, which were sometimes used as laybys in which the long-serving and the worthy could be deposited.

Largely for reasons of self-interest, therefore, America's corporate colonies in Europe were not intensively cultivated by their parent companies. The result was that the American effort in Europe was uncoordinated and, for long periods, largely unremarked. In many cases, subsidiaries in different countries competed with each other, duplicating sources of supply, products and (in some instances) research and development.

Towards the end of the 1950s, this situation began to change markedly. The formation of the Common Market offered the prospect of a vast and united sales territory comparable in size to the United States. Equally important, the European market in many products had begun to move ahead faster than the American domestic market, and gradually became more and more significant as a proportion of total sales. In 1963, Esso's sales in Europe exceeded those in the United States for the first time. IBM and Texas Instruments (which makes semi-conductor components, including integrated circuits) were growing in Britain at the respective rates of thirty-five and twenty-five per cent per annum compound, a good deal faster than their parent companies. Dow Chemical, which set up its first manufacturing plant outside America in 1955, was within ten years doing a quarter of its business abroad. Sterling Drug, whose business outside the United States had been negligible in 1960, was by 1967 earning a third of its total income overseas: its European business, Sterling-Winthrop, grew four or five times as quickly as that of its American parent.

For some companies, like Esso, Europe had suddenly become a super-entity in terms of technology just as much as in sales and growth. The company was involved in the construction of trans-continental pipe-lines and was increasingly planning its supply pattern on the basis of European needs. These developments called for the closer co-ordination of national managements.

Circumstances so dramatically changed brought a revolution in the attitude of American corporations to Europe. Investment was stepped up and corporate chief executives who had spoken to the heads of their overseas operations only infrequently now began seeking them out.[1] The surprising thing was that the machinery of tighter control was assembled so slowly. IBM had had a European organization in Paris since the mid-1950s, but the formation of European headquarters in other companies did not begin until 1965. Thereafter, Union Carbide set itself up in Lausanne, Monsanto and International Telephone and Telegraph in Brussels and Dow Chemical in Zurich, while Ford and Esso came to Britain. (Esso's European oil headquarters is in London, its chemical base in Brussels.)

The establishment of these forward bases also brought overseas postings for detachments of senior American executives: Europe was no longer peripheral. As at Ford of Europe, the four full-time executive

[1] Gilbert Jones, the former president of IBM's overseas organization, the World Trade Corporation, said in 1966 that for years before he seldom went into the office of Tom Watson Jun., the chairman of the Board; by 1966 he estimated that he was spending twenty per cent of his time with Watson.

directors of Esso Europe (formed in 1966) are all Americans,[1] and so (at one time) were the four area managers of IBM Europe.[2] (IBM Europe has been headed by a European for considerable periods of its history, but between 1962 and 1965, its chief executive was an American, Todd Groo.)

There were a number of perfectly sensible reasons for these importations. For one thing, the operation often meant moving a chunk of the company's international division (if not all of it) to Europe, and the men who had done the job in New York or Dearborn were naturally first choice to do it in Brussels or London. They knew the form at corporate headquarters and they had status; if difficulties arose, they would know which strings to pull. Most of the resident European bosses had had nothing like the same experience, and they also carried other disadvantages. For example, if an Italian were to be appointed European overlord, there was a clear danger (felt and admitted by the Europeans themselves) of jealousy and squabbling. It was this, in part, which had caused Kodak's European operation to founder between the wars, and which led to serious difficulties within IBM Europe in the 1950s. The Americans, therefore, rather like the British in India and Africa, were in the happy position of finding themselves cast in the role of benevolent neutrals; it was a natural setting for the policy of divide and rule.

For the Europeans the arrival on their doorstep of those who are jocularly known as 'the beaks' at one American subsidiary was not always a pleasant experience. At Ford, as we have seen, the formation of a European headquarters was the natural culmination of a process of closer American control which had begun in 1961. At IBM, it had already led to the creation of a highly integrated European operation by the early 1960s. At Esso, it represented the culmination of efforts at greater co-ordination which had been going on for several years. In each case, it represented a diminution in the freedom of the British subsidiary: but some saw blessings as well as grief in the new order.

The Esso men in Britain, for example, took comfort from the fact that they (initially, at least) retained a degree of autonomy in running their own affairs which was unusual for an America subsidiary – Esso

[1] Just how important Standard Oil of New Jersey considered Europe to be may be judged from the fact that Nick Campbell, the President of Esso Europe, came from the Jersey main Board, while R. H. Milbrath had been executive director of Esso International, which handled supplies for the European markets.

[2] Only one now is an American.

does not normally consult headquarters before making price changes on its products, and it had taken an option on land for a new refinery at Milford Haven before it mentioned its intentions to New York; they were also encouraged by the thought that, whereas previously the operation (when based in New York) had been made up almost entirely of Americans, there were now a fair proportion of Europeans operating at supra-national level. (Only 127 of Esso Europe's staff of 560 were Americans in 1968.) They expect Europeans to hold all the top jobs within a decade.

In addition, there were some immediate practical advantages. Their superiors, for example, seemed both brisker and more understanding in the West End of London than they had been in New York, perhaps partly because they were more closely identified with Europe and less with corporate headquarters. Matters which had previously taken two months were now approved within two weeks, and instead of submitting investment proposals to a Board Advisory Committee in New York which covered the whole world – and were therefore, in the words of an Esso director 'always wrenching their minds around' – they could set them before men whose attention was exclusively devoted to Europe. Nor did it escape the bosses of Esso that, since the European headquarters was only a stroll across St James's Park, lobbying was a good deal easier; they felt less inhibited in the presence of men whom they met every week than by an annual confrontation on the other side of the Atlantic. On the other hand, they do regret the lessening of contact with the Jersey main Board.

Yet, although the British company retained a considerable amount of autonomy – and conveys a greater sense of freedom from American pressure than any other US subsidiary which I visited – there is another side to the reckoning. Jersey's effort to allay any disappointment that all the top jobs should initially go to Americans – the fact that the European part-time members of the Board accompany the Americans on their periodic visits to individual countries helps to avoid any impression of a trans-Atlantic inquisition – cannot disguise the fact that national plans will now have to be more carefully tailored to meet the requirements of a tightly integrated European operation. Nobody questions the need for greater co-ordination, but it will inevitably reduce British Esso's freedom of manoeuvre. From a purely British point of view, this has to be balanced against the hope that Esso Europe will eventually act as a springboard which propels Europeans into top corporate jobs.

The effects of progressive European (and global) integration on the independence of a British national management are apparent in IBM (UK), which does not have its European headquarters in London and which has never been master in its own house to anything like the same degree as Esso.

The British managing director, indeed, is in some respects a supreme example of the sub-postmasterial role in which British heads of American subsidiaries can be cast.[1] He reports to one of the four European area chiefs, who in turn report to the head of IBM Europe; he reports to the head of the World Trade Corporation who finally reports to the main Board. Every significant move by the British company has to be filtered through the various layers of the Paris headquarters before it even gets to the World Trade Corporation in New York, which itself is 80 miles away from corporate headquarters at Armonk, in up-state New York. The former bosses of IBM (UK) will surely be psychologically equipped to become commanders of the first settlements on the moon.

Even within his own territory, IBM's British chief executive has his lines of authority crossed at a dozen different points. His plants do turn out some final products (such as the 1130 small scientific computer) but they also provide parts for the 360 range of computers, which are assembled in France, West Germany and Italy. Work is moved into and out of Britain at the behest of the World Trade Corporation: the British chief executive may argue, but may not always prevail. There is also a continental liaison for sales. All IBM's business with Ford in Europe is channelled through an Englishman living in London, while the account manager who deals with Shell is a Dutchman living in Holland, and there are men in Paris who are responsible for supporting sales to particular industries – public utilities, insurance, telecommunications and automobiles.

So far as research and development is concerned, Britain has the largest IBM laboratory outside the United States within its parish, at Hursley in Hampshire, but Hursley essentially is not a British operation at all. Projects are allocated to it by a Systems Development Division based in America to which it reports (via an American based in Nice) for functional and technical guidance; the logistics of the operation are under the control of the British managing director only to that degree.

[1] This remark is not intended as a criticism of the present holder of the job, E. R. Nixon: of all the English managing directors of American subsidiaries whom I met, Nixon was among the most independent-minded.

It was the head of the subsidiary of another American company who was quoted in 1963 as saying that 'the Americans treat us as if we were junior management'; the chief executive of IBM (UK) could be forgiven if he were to echo the sentiment.

These, however, are the results of a policy of integration which has been evolving for ten years or more, and it is effective for a company whose product lends itself admirably to a policy of dispersed development and assembly. Yet most British bosses of American subsidiaries like to stress how autonomous they are, and how liberal an attitude the Americans take towards their activities.

Clearly, the amount of autonomy varies from one company to the next, and is influenced not only by the policies of different corporations but also by factors such as the proportion of total turnover which the subsidiary in question provides and by the standing in the United States of its chief executive. The degree of confidence in the leadership is generally reflected in the amount of freedom granted; Sir Patrick Hennessy was generally able to persuade Ford at Dearborn that he knew best, and control over products and operating plans tended to be light. Ernest Amor, the former chairman of Kodak, said that he would have been free to open the company's British plants to the trade unions if he had felt it was necessary, despite the fact that it was contrary to Kodak's normal practice. It is worth remarking that the degree of autonomy which exists in different subsidiaries does not necessarily bear any relation to the number of Americans employed by it: IBM, for instance, only has about half a dozen, but is tightly regulated.

The amount of freedom allowed to American subsidiaries in Britain does not in some respects compare with that given to the subsidiaries of companies like Shell. In the first place, many of them have very limited discretion in the spending of money – and there are certainly very few who, like the head of Ford of Britain, are allowed to spend up to £250,000 within an agreed budget. Dr John Powell, the managing director of Texas Instruments Limited (who, incidentally, has two Americans reporting to him) may spend only amounts up to £12,500 without reference to Dallas; in a major pharmaceutical company, the limit is £5,000, despite the fact that the group covers the whole of Western Europe and that its chairman is also the first non-American vice-president of the parent company. Even when the man in charge is an American, and a senior American at that, it seems to make little difference. Lee Gehrke was formerly the treasurer of Minnesota Mining and Manufacturing at its St Paul headquarters and is now managing director of 3M in Britain, but he cannot spend sums over $10,000 without asking his old colleagues. These are often felt to be ludicrously low limits by the men who are asked to observe them. English directors who work for subsidiaries where the financial freedom is much greater are irked at their inability to 'take a flier'; in the more restricted environments, the sense of frustration can be considerable.

It is worth adding that American parent companies very seldom keep their subsidiaries short of cash for any expansion which can be justified by the prospect of good returns; Kodak was cautious in its investment in Britain during the period of the first post-war Labour Government, but no other company to which I spoke could remember a period when it had been subject to rationing. Nor is the provision of cash a long-winded process; large sums are often made available at very short notice. A former senior executive of Ford of Britain recalled that Dearborn had once agreed to the spending of £1m. on the basis of two telephone calls.

The close watch on the use of cash is also reflected in an intense interest in the annual profit plans of each subsidiary company. Each year, every American corporation either despatches its top brass to Europe or else summons the chief executives of the subsidiaries to the United States, and a para-military ritual of plan-vetting and target-setting begins. The men from Texas Instruments Limited, for example, begin the process by meeting a deputation from Dallas in September, usually in Rome or Nice. They then go to the United States in December for a week, when the agreed plan for the years ahead is put before the parent Board. Similarly, the chairman and managing director of British Kodak spend a day with the main Board in Rochester, while an American management team, headed by the president or chairman of the Board visits 3M in Britain each year to look at results and plans. The Americans are essentially concerned with maximizing profits, but they are seldom interested only in short-term returns: Texas Instruments, for example, ploughed back all the profits of its British operation for the first ten years and Ford's massive investment programme in recent years (for very low rewards) shows that Texas's approach is by no means unique.

Research and development is another of the fields over which American corporations maintain the strictest control; in the not too distant past, many of them exercised that control by keeping their technology within the continental boundaries of the United States. More recently there has been some liberalization, but so far it has been meagre in the majority of cases. British Kodak, which provides between seven and ten per cent of total corporate sales, primarily carries out development and service on existing products; and although Kodak earns about a quarter of its annual income overseas, its international operation gets only seven per cent of total spending on research and development.[1] This is fairly typical.

IBM, on the other hand, has begun to place some of its projects at a string of laboratories outside the United States, largely with the idea of trying to tap a wider reservoir of brains. The laboratory at Hursley, for example (which employs seven hundred of the 15,000 IBMers involved in R. and D.), was responsible for the development of the 360/40 computer. Nevertheless, almost all the most progressive research work is reserved for centres in America: IBM's Advanced Systems Development Division has only one outpost in Europe.

Since it is these laboratories which give birth to new ranges of computers for the world market, this is not in any way surprising. There is tremendous in-fighting within IBM for control of the best projects, which are allocated by a committee sitting in Yorktown, and, naturally enough, the people closest to the committee are able to exert most pressure upon it. Furthermore, the man in charge of the corporation's Systems Development Division is judged primarily by the profits made on domestic (i.e. US) sales, which still account for two-thirds of the whole, and any cuts in R. and D. budgets are therefore more likely to be made in the European operation.

So far as the actual products are concerned, many American corporations keep an even tighter control over their subsidiaries than they do in the matter of finance. The British managing director of IBM, for instance, may not change a nut or bolt in any of the assemblies for which he is responsible without consulting the control centre for the product – the vast majority of which are in the United States. Procter and Gamble, another highly centralized company, has to be informed about the slightest change in the manufacturing processes used by its British subsidiary. In the case of motor companies like Ford and Vauxhall, there is a constant interchange of ideas as new models are developed; the parent companies are concerned to know whether they have the right technical features and whether they are aiming at the right

---

[1] Some of the American drug companies in Britain have a more liberal record in this respect, both in the amount which they spend on research and development, and in its nature.

segment of the market. 3M, which has a gigantic spread of products,[1] regularly sends out teams of experts to look at the various product ranges of its overseas companies. Its traffic sign specialists, for example, will arrive in London, report on that part of the British operation, and then move on elsewhere.

As sales in Europe have grown, however, there has been an increasing tendency on the part of the big US corporations to pay more attention to what their European commanders had to say about new products. IBM, which for a number of years designed its computers for the American market and was delighted if (coincidentally) they fitted European needs, now takes into account what IBM Europe says it wants. It has been encouraged in this course by past mistakes. It chose to halve the sales of forecasts made in Europe for the 1401 range of computers; the Europeans proved to be more nearly right, and their forecasts for the 360 range were accordingly taken much more seriously. IBM's attempt to develop all the software for the Passenger Airline Reservation System in the United States also proved to be an error of judgement. In doing so, the corporation planners forgot that BOAC's operations are very different from those of the American domestic airlines, and eventually an international group was set up in London.

In Kodak, much the same process has been taking place. In the past, products were developed to suit the needs of the U.S. market; the overseas companies commonly took parts from the American model and it was launched in Europe six months later. Although the Instamatic was developed in the United States, the European companies were closely consulted and the camera was manufactured simultaneously in Rochester, London and Stuttgart.

On the question of appointments to senior posts within their British subsidiaries, American corporations normally want to be consulted both on the choice of new Board members and heads of departments, but they are apt to lean heavily on advice from the subsidiary's chief executive. On the other hand, a frequent grumble among the senior British managers is that when a difficult situation arises, the Americans are often not content to leave the problem in foreign hands. Their instinct is still to move in reinforcements from corporate headquarters: a gunboat can do what the local levies cannot. This lack of confidence, where it is displayed, is strongly resented. Nevertheless, British

[1] They include magnetic recording tapes, abrasives, adhesives and industrial plastics. 'Scotch' Brand Pressure-Sensitive Tape is 3M's best-known product in Britain.

managing directors, sometimes find it useful to be able to call in specialist help from the parent company. Esso asked for the temporary loan of fifty American supervisors to help build its refinery at Fawley: the refinery was completed ahead of schedule. Equally, it is sometimes deemed wise to bring in an American to take charge of the construction of a new plant on the principle that he will be able to summon up additional help from the United States in the event of serious snags and that – as one managing director put it – 'only an American can shift an American'. Equally, British chief executives are usually quite free to reject politely those whom they feel are too aggressively American – perhaps by virtue of a pronounced Mid-western accent – or those who cannot acclimatize themselves to life in Britain. They are then quietly repatriated.

In view of all the controls which American corporations normally enforce and the labyrinthine game of international business politics which subsidiary commanders have perforce to play, it might be thought surprising that British businessmen should want to work for US companies at all. They can speak their minds freely enough, but have no ultimate power. Yet many, on the contrary, find it extremely satisfying as well as materially rewarding and, indeed, once they have worked for an American company, they tend to regard the atmosphere of British firms as lethargic and uninspiring. On the other hand, they find the pace of life in American subsidiaries exhilarating if demanding – 'in an American company, everybody is going'; visits to the United States and access to American corporate know-how prove stimulating; in a number of concerns – Kodak and Texas among them – there are no trade unions, which tends to reduce labour problems substantially; experience of American management techniques is invaluable; and, perhaps most important of all, they are given promotion not – as so often in British companies – on the basis of age and faithful service, but on effort and merit. E. R. Nixon, now managing director of IBM (UK), was given the job at the age of forty, although he was not one of the seven men then reporting to the chief executive. Similarly, Laurie Spalton was second-in-command of one of Sterling Drug's four European companies when he was told to merge the four and take charge of the entire operation.

Rightly or wrongly, British managing directors also feel that they have a special relationship with their American masters because of the fact of a common language. This, they believe, causes the Americans to pay more attention to their views than to those of, say, the West Germans or French. They add reluctantly that being British is often a definite disadvantage when it comes to the pursuit of the most senior posts in their parent companies; then, they say, you need to come from the right national stable as well as speak the right language.

Inevitably, there are other dissatisfactions. Most British men do not take kindly to the evangelistic atmosphere of American business life, whether in the form of hymns at breakfast meetings or the complete sacrifice of a man's private life on the altar of corporate glory. 'Even the most energetic Englishman,' said one managing director, 'won't buy this business of total dedication to the company. I feel that in giving myself seventy-five per cent of the time I'm doing quite enough.' He added that loyalty to organizations did not exist in mature men and that the Americans were only able to achieve it because of their lack of a critical nature and their immaturity.

For men like this, working for an American subsidiary and living in England is an ideal compromise. They feel that they have all the advantages of being employed by an efficient organization and none of the disadvantages of living in a society whose customs and values they may even despise. They are quite prepared to forego the prospect of a 25 per cent increase in take-home pay in return for the more relaxed atmosphere of life in Britain.

Their general view of the abilities of their American superiors is a favourable one: they are held to be not only more dedicated, but also more objective and more single-minded in their desire for profit. One man, however, complained that he finds it extremely hard to communicate with many of the senior officers of his parent company, despite the common language, while several berated the Americans for their alleged parochialism – 'the most parochial nation on earth', 'major international decisions should not be taken by a man born in the Mid-West who has never left the United States' – and are exasperated at having to spend so much of their time explaining why things are different in Britain. Many Americans, for their part, find some of their British subordinates too narrow and nationalistic in their thinking.

Again, some British managers react violently against the ceremonial with which they feel obliged to receive important American visitors – the flowers to be placed in the suite at Claridges, the preparation of the plant for the official tour of inspection. 'The bull when the president of the international division comes over here has to be seen to be believed,' said a man who was once a manager with a US company. 'Painting this and whitewashing that, it's like the Queen visiting the Guards depot at Caterham.'

These are symptoms of a more fundamental malaise, compounded of a natural dislike of subordinate status and a feeling that they are likely to remain third-rank executives because of their nationality. This may very well be less than fair to the Americans, but it is true that while there are relatively few US companies which have not yet been able to grow satisfactory British leadership at national level, the number of Englishmen who have climbed far up the ladder of the big US corporations is modest indeed. They have had more success in the smaller companies: Colin Baxter, a former Unilever coordinator, is now president and chief executive of Mars, and there are a number of others who have become main board directors by way of international divisions, but the most senior posts which Englishmen have so far captured in IBM outside Britain are those of systems engineering director in the World Trade Corporation and head of marketing in IBM Europe. No Englishman has ever reached the main Board of Ford and only one has reached the main Board of Standard of Jersey despite the fact that both have been established in Britain for over fifty years.

The feeling that there is little chance of ever reaching the top inevitably leads to executives who work for the less autonomous subsidiaries sensing that they are both mercenaries and eunuchs, and likely to remain so. Those who cannot live indefinitely with a situation in which they do not carry ultimate responsibility eventually leave, and this (together with the high pressure of life) accounts in large part for the relatively high turnover of senior executives from some companies. 'I preferred to work for an American company until I got to the director stage,' said one man who resigned from the Board of a large American subsidiary company. 'At the top level there is not the ultimate satisfaction of knowing that you are taking your own decisions, and that is really why I left.'

A fair proportion of British executives (if my sample is a reliable guide) frequently ask themselves whether they *ought* to be working for American companies at all, and harbour a suspicion that, in some obscure way, they have become quislings. One man admitted to having a guilt complex, and others showed clear signs of it. Almost all the men I met were eager to point out that their company made a positive contribution to Britain's balance of payments; one asked how he should go about starting a 'Keep Britain Great' campaign;[1] most tell themselves that they are helping to bring advanced technology and

[1] The London headquarters of the 'I'm Backing Britain' campaign were in the offices of an American company.

management to Britain, and that the country is better off as a result. They also argue that they are doing a necessary job in educating insular Americans, even though at this stage they may only be the tail trying to wag the dog.

For the most part, they remain steadfastly British in appearance and manner: none of the people I met had been Americanized to any significant extent, although some freely used the jargon of American business – 'demotivating', 'centres of competence', 'tactical action programmes', 'product customer centres'. Some, indeed, while accepting one-class restaurants and the absence of a whole range of cherished status symbols, deliberately set their faces against transatlantic patterns of behaviour of which they disapprove. One managing director insisted that, when his company moved, it should go to the sort of place which did not encourage employees to lead the inbred social life which he had observed around many of its plants in the United States.

The Americans, then, have achieved a deep penetration of the British (and European) economy, and they are rapidly learning the arts of conquest with discretion. Many of them hope to merge so successfully into the European business environment that even their own employees forget they are working for an American company.[1] The majority of American subsidiaries now have British managing directors, and there are few Americans left who still surround themselves with the standard European exploration kit: iced water flask, central heating at full bore, reproduction antique furniture, sales graphs, piped music and coloured photographs of the family and homestead in Dubuque. American subsidiaries also generally work hard at the job of becoming good business neighbours. Du Pont, for example, invariably visits other employers in an area where it intends to build a plant to assure them that it does not intend to poach their workers by paying higher wages.

But now that Europe has become so important, even the largest corporations can no longer afford to treat their overseas operations as a sideline; they must rapidly face up to the need to become international businesses. Although some US corporations have been making the right sort of noises and even the right sort of appointments – the chief executive of Texas Instruments has said that it must have a European presence on its main Board, Jersey now has a Venezuelan at its top

[1] This hope is not so far-fetched as it might appear, particularly in old-established subsidiaries. One British managing director of an American subsidiary said that after he had listened to a man from another company speaking at an industry meeting, his first reaction had been 'Bloody American'.

table and a Frenchman (Jacques Maisonrouge) is president of IBM's World Trade Corporation – men like Jan Brouwer of Shell (who instinctively thinks on a global basis) are still far too rare on the US business scene. The environment does not help: Americans are not easily weaned from their absorption with a massive home market. Yet if they want to continue to expand in sophisticated countries which are awake to the dangers of a major increase in US market strength, they would be wise to think in terms of a sizeable devolution. The Europeans in IBM talk of a day not, they hope, far distant, when its main Board will be sixty per cent American and thirty per cent European, with the remaining ten per cent for the rest of the world. That day is still a long way off in most corporations; even such international representation as has been achieved is too often regarded as something of a public relations exercise.

Once these fundamentally parochial attitudes have been reversed, moreover, the Americans should begin to attract a much higher calibre of European businessmen than they can now expect to retain in any numbers. At present some of those who remain with them are men who are happy to accept subordinate status almost indefinitely, and therefore lack that desire for ultimate power and responsibility which is the mark of the front-rank businessman.

From the British (and, indeed, the European) point of view, the closest watch now needs to be kept on the extension of American business power – not from any narrowly chauvinistic attitude but as a practical precaution against possible disruption of the national economy. The arrival of highly integrated European operations, with their own headquarters, surely makes it sensible for governments to want to be kept closely informed of major policy changes by American subsidiaries in this country. In Europe's present disarray, it is too much to hope that this sort of surveillance would be effective on a continental basis: it must therefore be carried out nationally. No action may be called for, no pressure required, but information should be sought and a single department in Whitehall made responsible for keeping an eye on the activities of US subsidiaries.

CHAPTER 8

Families on the Mat

Despite the steady decline of family power in British industry, there is still in Britain a strong affection for the family business. Many workers believe that they will be 'better looked after'; non-family managers who can reconcile themselves to the fact that they are unlikely ever to hold the top job feel more secure from ruthless attack. The assumption is that the family's established wealth (and reputation) will incline it towards benevolence and away from short-term economic considerations; that the family boss, in other words, will act as an industrial substitute for an idealized Lord of the Manor. A young Cadbury executive put the case succinctly before the merger with Schweppes: 'There is a very high consideration for the individual here which you won't get in a completely professional company.'

Even Lords whose families own only a small proportion of their Manors act as if these loyalties exist among their employees. The Costain family now owns less than ten per cent of the voting share capital of the building firm of Richard Costain. Yet, in a centenary Bulletin, produced in 1965, there appeared this item: 'What happier ending could there be to this brief account of the Costain story, than the news that another Costain has arrived. A son, Nigel John, has been born to . . . '

Sir William Carr, chairman of the News of the World organization, appealed to similar emotions in successfully defending the company (his family then owned less than a third of the voting shares) against a take-over bid from the Pergamon Press in 1968; Pergamon's offer was worth considerably more than the current market price. 'Many shareholders,' Sir William told the meeting, 'have held shares since before the beginning of the 20th Century, and they are not complaining.

The News of the World employs 8,000 people and *looks after* 20,000 or more people in the families of workers . . . What is cash, money, when you have had so much other out of life as well.' Sir William said that if the alternative plan he was proposing went through, 'I will have the privilege of remaining as chairman of this company – a position held by my father and grandfather.' (He has since resigned.)

Families continue to retain dominating positions in companies in which they no longer have a majority shareholding. The Guinnesses, for example, have a good deal less than a controlling stake in the Arthur Guinness brewing business, but they have half the seats on the parent Board and the atmosphere is that of a family estate: portraits of Guinness women and Guinness children as well as Guinness chairmen adorn the walls at the Park Royal plant in London, and the ships which carry Guinness across the Irish Sea are named after Guinness wives – 'Lady Gwendolen', 'Lady Grania' and 'Lady Patricia'. Similarly, the two founding families of the Tate and Lyle sugar and molasses group now own only nine per cent of the voting share capital, but ten of the Board of nineteen are either Tates, Lyles or their relatives and the chairman has always been a member of one or other family. It is doubtful whether the descendants and relations of Lord Marks and Lord Sieff own as much as fifteen per cent of the equity of the Marks and Spencer stores group, but they hold five of the seven top jobs and seven out of the twenty seats on the Board.

Even when family holdings have become minimal, it is not uncommon to find descendants retaining powerful positions in the company. There are, of course, the Clark brothers at Plessey, and there are three Andersons and Geddes on the Board of Peninsular and Oriental Steam Navigation, the world's largest shipping company, although together they have less than one per cent of the P and O equity. The Orient Line, in which P and O bought a half-share in 1919, was managed by Anderson Green, a family business run by the Andersons and their cousins, the Geddes, who also owned a majority share in Orient's equity. Sir Donald Anderson, now the P and O chairman, moved across to the parent company in the 1930s, and when P and O absorbed the Orient Line altogether in 1960, two further Andersons (Sir Colin and Sir Austen) and one Geddes (Ford) were offered seats on the P and O Board. Sir Austen and Sir Colin have now retired, but a second Geddes (Lord), a first cousin of Ford and a second cousin of Sir Donald, joined P and O in 1957.

But there are a number of large companies which are still controlled by family shareholdings, and they tend to be concentrated in particular areas of business. In the stores field, for example, Sir Isaac Wolfson and his family and the Wolfson Foundation have just over fifty per cent of the voting shares of Great Universal Stores; Sir Hugh Fraser exercises through trust and family holdings in Scottish and Universal Investments a substantial control over the House of Fraser (which includes Harrods in its department store empire); and the Sainsbury food stores and shops still belong to a private limited company which is entirely in the hands of the Sainsbury family.

Families are also extremely powerful in the building and contracting industries.[1] Sir Godfrey Mitchell, his family and their charitable trusts control more than half the voting shares of Wimpey, which is the largest construction business in the world outside the United States, while the Laing family and trusts hold roughly eighty per cent of John Laing, the second largest construction company in Britain. McAlpine, which is either third or fourth in the league, is a partnership whose shares can only be held by working partners, and the partners (with a single exception) have always been McAlpines: the exception was a relative. The sixth largest company, Wates, is another private company entirely in the hands of the Wates family.

Other large family companies are scattered across a variety of industries. Over fifty per cent of the voting power in Whitbread, which owns breweries and about 9,700 public houses and off-licences, rests in the hands of the Whitbread family and trusts. British and Commonwealth, one of the biggest shipping companies in the world, is controlled by the Cayzer family, while Pilkington Brothers, the fourth largest flat-glass manufacturer in the world, is the biggest private company in Britain and remains firmly in the hands of the Pilkington family.[2]

Family control, not surprisingly, is a good deal more common among

[1] Sir Maurice Laing, a director of John Laing, has a view about why families are so dominant in the construction business. He writes: 'To run a successful contracting organization, it is necessary for the top men or group of men to be entrepreneurs and this calls for a class of person who must inevitably be more "authoritarian" in his methods of management and who in turn does not like being "bossed about" by anybody, not even his shareholders!'

[2] More than fifty per cent of the Pilkington shares (including employee trusts) are in the hands of members of the family still active in the business, together with their close relations. Virtually all the shares, apart from some substantial charitable or employee trusts, are beneficially owned by descendants of the founders of the company in 1826.

smaller companies. Apart from Yorkshire woollens, other parts of the textile industry which have only recently been touched by rationalization – such as the traditional carpet industry – are still largely in the power of families: the Brintons, the Tomkinsons, the Antons and the Naylors still have control of their own companies in Kidderminster, which is the main centre of the traditional industry. In pottery, the Wedgwood and Johnson families together have what amounts to a controlling interest (the Wedgwoods have forty-two per cent, the Johnsons eight per cent) in a company which, in its own field, is now comparable in size to any in the world.

The principal objection to family businesses has always been that promotion within them was not on the basis of merit, and that the top jobs were reserved for members of the ruling house. The criticism is still valid for a large number of companies, but there has been a considerable change of practice in recent times, partly because family-run companies have found it extremely difficult to attract talented outsiders when seats on the Board were not open to all and partly because family talent has often faded with the passing of the generations.

Wedgwood, for example, which appointed its first non-family directors in 1945, now has a non-family chairman (Arthur Bryan) and a majority of non-family directors. Pilkington, which appointed non-family directors before the war, also has a balance on the Board, although five of the seven members of the executive committee are Pilkingtons; at Sainsbury there is the same balance between family and non-family. There are four Whitbreads in a Board of thirteen, three Laings out of eight, four Cayzers out of ten at British and Commonwealth, while Sir Godfrey Mitchell (now in his late seventies) is the only member of his family on the Wimpey Board.

There are very few companies of any size where the Boardroom is still exclusively a family preserve. McAlpine and Wates are the most notable examples and both seem faintly apologetic about the fact, if unrepentant. Robin McAlpine said jokingly that McAlpine was 'like the Great Auk, it ought to have been extinct a long time ago' while the late Norman Wates, formerly Wates' chairman, admitted that they practised 'nepotism in excelsis'. Wates tries to satisfy the ambitions of non-family managers by offering them seats on subsidiary Boards; while there, they often help to train Wates on their way to the top. Among the smaller companies, the number of exclusively family Boards is higher, but again more and more have been forced to open their doors since the war.

A mere counting of heads in the Boardroom of course, does not necessarily reflect the real power situation within a company, but in a good many cases non-family men play a very prominent part in the actual running of businesses. Colonel Whitbread, for example, now has little to do with the day-to-day management of his company, and it is effectively run by outsiders. The same is true at Wimpey. Sir Godfrey Mitchell says jokingly that he never sees an estimate now, and that when there is nothing else to do, he puts up his feet and reads *The Times*. At Cadbury before the Schweppes merger non-family men formed a majority (3-2) of the Board's Executive Committee, and although the chairman of the company, Adrian, was a fifth generation member of the family, two of its other members, Bob Wadsworth, in charge of the foods division, and Charles Raeburn, the finance director, often carried a good deal more weight than many of the main Board family directors. If Wadsworth agreed with a policy suggestion, Cadbury generally took the view that it was the right thing to do.

There was no evidence for the existence of a Cadbury caucus – where major issues might have been discussed before they went to the Board – either within the Board or outside it. Cadbury seemed to see as much of Wadsworth and another director, Peter Gregory, outside working hours as he did of any member of the family, and said he had no intimate relationship with any other serving member of the family. He occasionally discussed problems with his father, but since Laurence Cadbury had retired, he regarded these talks as purely informatory.

There were other hopeful signs at Cadbury. With Adrian's arrival, it had become less stuffy and non-Cadburys were no longer promoted to the Board only at an advanced age, as a reward for long and faithful service. Peter Gregory had been made a director at the age of 36. On the other hand, being a Cadbury was still regarded as a *sine qua non* for certain key appointments, partly because of an effort to maintain the tradition of paternalism within the company, partly because it was deemed to be good for the external relations of the business.

The chairmanship was one such job, and although Adrian had been chosen over the heads of several Cadburys with longer service than he – the election was made at a meeting in a Stratford-upon-Avon hotel which was attended by non-Cadbury directors – nobody seems to have questioned the implicit assumption that only Cadburys could be candidates. Adrian Cadbury also believed the family name could be an advantage on the personnel and sales sides of the business, but added that if two equal candidates presented themselves for any job other than the chairmanship, the firm's policy was to appoint the non-Cadbury.[1] (Whether the choice, even though made by non-family executives, could be completely dispassionate in an atmosphere still pervaded by family tradition, is a moot point.) The managing director of Courage Barclay, the brewers, who is not a member of any of the founding families of that company, also thinks it invaluable – from the point of view of relations with tenants – if public houses can be visited by a Courage, a Barclay, or a Simonds.

On the point of family chairmanship, Lord Pilkington takes a similar view to the one which was held by Cadbury. Although he foresees an increasing proportion of non-family directors – the odds against new Pilkingtons getting to the top have, he believes, lengthened from 2–1 on to 100–7 against – he still thinks the chair should remain a Pilkington perquisite for the present because 'the name matters to many of the work-people and when we have plants or customers abroad'. Trying to keep the chair in the family, however, could sometimes simply mean rewarding the longest-serving director, regardless of his ability. Pilkington itself has to face the sort of succession problem which occurs even in the most fruitful of families.

As for the effect on the workers of the end of family chairmanship, it is difficult to assess whether it results in any loss of efficiency, either in the short or long term. There is no sign of it at Wedgwood, which has moved ahead with considerable speed since Arthur Bryan took over. This is not to deny that there can be considerable resentment when workers are no longer able to deal direct with senior members of the family. There was evidence of this at Cadbury, where reorganization had led to responsibility being pushed further down the line and, as a result, workers' representatives no longer had such open access to the chairman.

The influence which non-family directors wield at Wedgwood is not in any way unusual. Guinness, for example, has operated for well over half a century on the theory that the running of the business should be largely left to top-class outsiders imported from Oxford or Cambridge. The last member of the Guinness family who was managing director of the company (apart from Lord Boyd's short spell of office in the 1960s) retired in 1902. The active members of the family reckon to keep in close touch with their managers, but seldom oppose them on major decisions: the family turned down one of the diversification

[1] At Brintons, one of the largest carpet firms in Kidderminster, the shareholder's son is given the job in case of a dead-heat.

schemes proposed by the management in the 1950s, but that is the only occasion in recent years when there has been a significant clash of wills. No doubt the succession of bright young men which has served Guinness has not only provided brains for the business but has also freed those of the family who were so inclined to give some of their time to other interests.

Much the same thing happened with the previous generation of shipowning Cayzers. The three members of the family – the late Lord Rotherwick, Sir August Cayzer and Major Harold Cayzer – all had other pursuits, either in politics or in the country, and left the operating side of what was then the Clan Line very much to their staff. Again, there was some resemblance to a country estate, with managers in the place of agents.

At Pilkington, the situation is very different from that at Guinness. A great deal of executive power remains in the hands of the family directors (the chairmanship of all the key policy committees falls to either Lord Pilkington or his second cousin Arthur) but the chairmen of most of the operating divisions are non-family and one of the people whose advice Lord Pilkington seeks most frequently is Terence Bird, chairman of the flat-glass division. Furthermore, although it is effectively Lord Pilkington himself who picks Pilkington's outside directors, he does this to an agreed specification of the Board's needs and the Board as a whole discusses and votes on any possible inside candidates; Lord Pilkington says that his views have by no means always prevailed. So far as Wedgwood is concerned, the three family directors play no part at all in the day-to-day running of the business.

Nonetheless, something in the nature of a family caucus does still seem to exist in some of the larger companies. At British and Commonwealth, although the non-family directors are given very considerable responsibility, the four members of the present generation of Cayzers (Sir Nicholas, Anthony, Bernard and Lord Rotherwick) do fairly frequently hold family meetings in Sir Nicholas's room. At Sainsbury, while members of the family assert that there is the fullest equality at the Board table, they add that 'certain decisions' can only be made by family directors. Until fairly recently, only Pilkingtons had access to the company's cost and profit figures. This is no longer true, but when counsel is taken on questions of tax, the information comes through the family shareholders.

There is no doubt that the existence of any sort of family caucus can only help to make non-family directors into second-class citizens, whether they resent it or not. What is more, even when they are given wide-ranging executive power, there is still a sort of Gentlemen–Players relationship between them and the family which is noticeable to the outsider. On the other hand, it is rare for inequalities to be made overt. Companies with all-family Boards, however, often have dining rooms which are the preserve of the family; one firm which I visited – Johnson Brothers, a large manufacturer of earthenware which was taken over by Wedgwood in 1968 – had at that time both senior and junior family messes. Non-family staff were invited to eat in the senior dining room from time to time.[1]

In many family-owned businesses, non-family directors also have to cope with the intricacies of family politics. This may simply mean unexpected visits from small shareholders who expect to be treated like visiting royalty, but it can also involve the bridging of deep rifts between factions of the family. In one well-known family company, which has now merged with another, fist fights in the office were not unknown, and there was certainly a cordial dislike between some members of the Tate and Lyle families for a good many years after they had merged in 1921: there were separate sales organizations until the early 1940s. It is by no means unknown for outside chairmen and managing directors to be called into family businesses not merely to try to make them more efficient, but also to bang together the heads of feuding owners.

Another aspect of the same hazard is the presence on the Boards of family companies of incompetent relations of the ruling house. Whatever the other benefits of working for a family business, the presence of such men can be both an embarrassment and a drag on efficiency. Very often, the solution seems to be to ignore them or to limit their power of interference as much as possible. The snag is that, where the titular head of the business is weak, he is apt to bring in weak outsiders.

Fortunately, most sizeable family businesses have become much more selective in their methods of recruitment from the family ranks, and there are very few which are still bound to take in sons, whatever their abilities. When Wedgwood decided, some years ago, to see what family talent was available, it called in outside consultants to judge the merits of the applicants. Cadbury, like a number of other large businesses, always tried to 'sieve out the duds' in the days of family control

[1] Johnson now has its first non-family member of the Board; he joins the family directors for lunch.

and it both turned down family suitors who wanted to join the company and got rid of family managers. Members of the family who asked for a job were told that they were welcome to join the company, but they were also told how far they could expect to progress inside the organization: the Cadbury view was that they could fit in perfectly well as, say, middle managers. (Tate and Lyle, by contrast, wants members of the families to be either at the top or nowhere, although a descendant of one of the families is currently head of operational research.) In the majority of firms, the rule seems to be that a job will be found for close relations, but that (in theory, at least) there is open competition from that point on.

So far as interference from family shareholders is concerned, there have been some notable instances of where they have been able to bring about significant changes in a company's business: for example, Wedgwood did no business in Germany for twenty years because Mrs Cecil Wedgwood's husband was killed in the First World War.

This sort of interference is now apparently non-existent in the larger firms, both because big family businesses tend nowadays to try to behave like public companies and because shareholdings are often either widespread or in the hands of trusts. Adrian Cadbury says that the charitable and benevolent trusts which between them hold about ten per cent of the Cadbury-Schweppes equity behave rather like outside institutions: they have, he says, 'a general air of goodwill, but there is no nonsense about standing with us if they think we are not up to the job.' In a good many companies, most of the shareholders are elderly and, when they attend annual meetings, do little more than listen politely or express their appreciation of the Board's efforts. Particularly in the smaller firms, shareholders' meetings can be very short and uneventful. The 1966 meeting of T. and A. Naylor, who make carpets in Kidderminster, lasted just three minutes. It was attended only by the director, the company secretary and a representative of the *Financial Times*.

On the other hand, a fair number of Wedgwoods regularly turn up at the annual meeting in Barlaston, but they seem to be more interested in the continuation of the firm and its traditions than in large dividends. One elderly lady always asks about the welfare of the workers and there is considerable interest in what is happening to Barlaston Hall, the eighteenth-century house which stands on the Wedgwood estate. According to Arthur Bryan, the only question asked about dividend payments in recent years has been whether they were not too high and whether a larger share of the profits ought not to be ploughed back into the company. In most sizeable family businesses, in any case, dividend policy tends to be conservative, particularly when capital is often urgently needed for expansion and when the cost of borrowed money is high. In these cases family shareholders seem to exert as little influence as their counterparts in public companies: they are simply told what they can have in the light of the needs of the business. On the other hand, they are often divided into groups, which are watched over by the family director with whom they are most closely related: for companies where the family is only a minority shareholder, a shift in affection can be vital in the event of a take-over bid.

A more general criticism which can be made of family-owned businesses is that, because they are to a lesser or greater degree isolated from the pressures of the market, they do not need to concern themselves so urgently with either growth or profitability. While families have been at the heart of some of the great growth companies of recent times (the Marks and the Sieffs at Marks and Spencer, the Aishers at Marley Tile), it is also true that some family businesses have chosen to remain small rather than, on the one hand, take public money, or, on the other, open their Boardrooms to outsiders. Ferranti is a classic example of the first case, Wates and McAlpine of the second.

Wates deliberately restricted the expansion of its business in the 1950s until the latest generation of the family was ready to move into commanding positions in the company and initiate a new phase of growth. McAlpine, for its part, had always limited its activity by refusing to take on contracts when there was no family partner available to take responsibility. Robin McAlpine believes that if they had chosen to become a public company, there would have been too much for the family to look after. It should be added that Wates and McAlpine are probably the two most profitable large building and contracting businesses in Britain.

There was no deliberate limitation on size at Cadbury, although the older generation in the company did find it difficult to understand the concern among the younger directors about its rate of growth, even when it had clearly reached a plateau in the later 1950s and early 1960s. Similarly, some of the Wedgwoods would undoubtedly have been content if the company had remained small and efficient; Sir Tatton Brinton, of Brintons carpets, said he feared 'over-expansion' because it might mean loss of contact with the work-people; and one of the directors of Johnson Brothers in Stoke said (before the Wedg-wood take-over) that they were more interested in survival than in size – 'being the biggest is strictly for the birds'.

This caution or lack of urgency about growth is sometimes accom-panied by a comparative indifference to the maximizing of profits, particularly among those who are themselves comfortably off. Sir Tatton Brinton, for example, does not agree with younger directors who say the company should make high returns its first priority. Brinton's attitude is not untypical of the small, prosperous family busi-ness: 'We are here to make carpets as pleasantly as possible, and to make a profit without sacrificing the provision of a good and civilized life for the work-people. Human beings are first on my list. I've always been well off and I don't want to make a million quid.' Similarly, Sir Harry Pilkington said that money for its own sake had never interested him and that he wished he felt more strongly about making profit, while Sir Maurice Laing believes that, although making money is necessary, making money for its own sake is a sordid affair. Some change of attitude is evident in companies which have put a proportion of their shares on the market. The Antons, who control the Victoria Carpet Company, said that now some of their shares were publicly owned they had to pay more attention to profit.

It is easy to be cynical about indifference to money and profit, coming as it does from men who are not only wealthy themselves but who also have businesses with profit records which would often stand comparison with the performance of any other firm in their industries. Nevertheless, there is (in my view) clear evidence of a marked lack of ambition which is admitted by the men concerned and which was described by the managing director of another company as 'the English weakness'. One cannot imagine many American businessmen confess-ing, as this man and others did, that they have to struggle to work up any enthusiasm for making money!

Attitudes towards raising public money (among those who have not already done so) tend to vary from business to business. McAlpine and Wates, like Ferranti, contemplate the prospect with horror. 'We would hate every minute of it,' said Robin McAlpine. 'At the moment, we don't have to think of the shareholders – if we make a mistake, that's that.' Lord Pilkington, however, says that Pilkington intends to remain a private company only so long as it is able to raise enough capital for the growth of the business and to cover the cost of buying out share-holders who sell to meet death duties: the family, he contends, would never hold up the expansion of the business in preference to going public.

On the other hand, among the smaller businesses which have already sold out a proportion of their shares, the prospect of take-over does not seem to be altogether unwelcome. In one company, where the family still has roughly sixty per cent of the shares (although more and more are being sold as relatives die off), the managing director believes they will only continue as a family business for perhaps fifteen years, unless they make a collective decision to sell in the meantime. At least one of the directors would be prepared to sell his own shares for a good offer. David Naylor, the managing director of T. and A. Naylor, agreed that the shareholders of several companies might be better served if more mergers were to take place, although he thought the work-people of firms like his own would prefer to remain part of a family concern.

Many family businesses still pride themselves on their benevolence. So far as the Cadbury component of Cadbury-Schweppes is concerned, there are athletic clubs for men and girls, three swimming pools, an open-air lido (which Cadbury employees can use at reduced rates), squash courts, 120 acres of playing fields, a concert hall for drama and light opera and a magnificent surgery for dealing with accidents in the factory. Cadbury employees also occupy about a third of the houses in Bournville, which is administered by a separate, non-profit-making Village Trust. At Guinness's Dublin brewery, the company spends £70,000 in providing free health treatment for workers and their families – it is known locally as the Guinness Health Service – and there were handsome pensions for all employees (two-thirds of the final wage) as long ago as 1900.

In St Helens, the Pilkingtons used to run a school, started local recreation clubs, have given generous donations to local hospitals and, more recently, bought the town's Theatre Royal (which was about to be sold to Mecca), and modernized it at a cost of £150,000: the company now subsidizes it to the tune of between £20,000 and £25,000 a year. At Wedgwood, there are a number of houses at low rents for employees and ex-employees (terraced houses could be had for as little as 11s 5d a week in 1967), but the war frustrated the family's intention of building a second Bournville. Even in companies where the benevolence is not so obvious, there is plenty of evidence of a genuine concern for the welfare of employees. Brintons has provided what has virtually been guaranteed employment for life and although Sir Tatton concedes that 'this cradle-to-the-grave stuff' does not necessarily lead to maximum efficiency, he likes to think of the company as 'a happy ship'. Other manufacturers in the area contend that Brintons simply drives wage levels higher by the generous rates it pays.

The decline of the family business is bringing profound changes to traditional centres of family power such as Kidderminster and Stoke. The result is all the more marked in Stoke because the pottery industry is heavily concentrated there and also because the industry has attracted few outsiders to an area which is still one of Britain's industrial by-ways.

Before the war, it was made up of hundreds of small businesses often run with antiquated methods from antiquated premises by family bosses or their hired managers. The majority were artists or artisans rather than businessmen. Many were also profoundly provincial: even the heads of comparatively large companies found it distasteful to have to travel to London. They talked about the cussedness of clay, did their costing with the stub of a pencil on the back of an envelope (with the help of guidance from the prevailing economic wind) and hoped that the results would look reasonable at the end of the year. The handful of efficient companies, like Wedgwood, shone like stars in the gloom.

In the early years after the war, little changed. The number of firms did fall, as death and inefficiency took their toll, but many soldiered on, bolstered by high demand and parsimony, by the need to earn a living and perhaps by a desire to stay in Stoke's social swim. Without their tiny factories, they were nothing: with them, they were Mr X, potter, and a name, if not to be reckoned with, at least to be included on the membership and invitation lists for a variety of local institutions and celebrations. There is the Ancient Corporation of Hanley, which has no municipal power but which has an Annual Venison Feast and chooses its own Mayor each year; and there is the Burslem, Longport and Cobridge Association for the Prosecution of Felons, a survival from the days when there were no police, which now devotes itself to charitable work and holds an annual dinner.

There is also the British Pottery Manufacturers Federation, with its popular club and its innumerable committees – twenty-three in all, covering everything from Infringement of Shapes or Designs to Disinfected Straw. Even officials of the Federation find it difficult to say exactly what the purpose of half the committees is, but a good number of the surviving potters are only too delighted to sit on them – and the more ardent think nothing of giving up two days a week to work on several of them. Some simply relish the status which they feel activity within the Federation confers; others hope for practical advantages for their businesses.

Although the days of price-fixing by trade associations are over, the Federation still works in a way which serves to help small and inefficient companies. Financed by levies based on the turnover of firms, it is therefore most expensive for the larger businesses, which need its services least. Yet even the more efficient potters do not feel able to break completely free of the Federation. This is partly because they believe that the Government likes trade associations and partly because any suggestion that they might withdraw inevitably brings a deputation of potters bent on persuading them that they 'owe it to the industry' to continue in membership.

For the smaller men there are undoubtedly benefits. The Federation makes joint industry appeals against rating valuations and is an instrument for putting pressure on the Government. The smaller companies also seem to use it as a management consultant, seeking advice on everything from marketing to labour relations. For these reasons, among others, they continue to huddle round the Federation for comfort.

Despite the efforts of the Federation, there has been a further reduction in the ranks of the potters in recent years as costs have risen and competition become sharper. Many have simply gone out of business, others have been taken over and become part of larger groups. A number have been amalgamated into Allied English Potteries; Wedgwood has acquired Johnson Brothers, William Adams, Susie Cooper and Coalport China; Doulton has taken over Minton; Spode has been bought by the American Carborundum, Enoch Wedgwood and Crown Staffordshire by another US company, Automatic Retailers of America; Meakin and Midwinter have merged.

For many, these amalgamations have come at the end of a long struggle to remain independent. The Spode business had been run before the war by Ronald and Gresham Copeland together with a man called Hewitt. The Copelands were country gentlemen with large houses, a sense of civic duty and a taste for shooting and fishing who worried more about the quality of their products than about their profitability (which was, as a result, disappointing). After the war, a new generation of Copelands (Spencer and Robert) took over. They brought in successively an outside chairman and an outside accountant (the firm had not had one previously) to strengthen the management. By Spencer Copeland's admission, these outsiders saved the company from extinction, but profits continued to be low. Now the Americans have taken over, a new breed of manager has moved into the company with five-year profit and expenditure plans – the details are 'classified' – and although the Copelands remain in the company, their power is considerably reduced.

Johnson Brothers had run into rather different problems. It had concentrated fairly successfully on medium-priced earthenware and had built up a turnover of well over £2m. a year, a large proportion in export markets. Its fame in Stoke was considerable: local saying had it that 'the earth is the Lord's, but the potteries belong to the Johnsons'. Unfortunately, the company had failed to modernize adequately or rationalize its scattered factories, many of which were in very old buildings, and it had not moved into fine china, although it was conscious that china was a growing market with far better profit margins than could be got in earthenware. It was also short of a number of professional skills: it had no designer of its own and it had decided against appointing an accountant because the Board was afraid he might not be fully employed.

By 1967, the price of modernization – which Johnson recognized should have begun considerably earlier – was clearly going to be very high, probably not less than £3m., and it became evident to the family both that their resources were not sufficient to meet the cost and that, in any case, earthenware alone was unlikely to earn the kind of returns which would justify such heavy investment. They therefore sold out for cash and eight per cent of the Wedgwood equity.

Despite all these changes, there are still perhaps 120 potters in existence. Most of them are men who attended local schools, were commissioned in one or other of the world wars, now live in or near Stoke and cling to a small family business. Their profits are often pitifully small – even taking into account the earnings of highly lucrative companies like Wedgwood, the average earnings of members of the Federation is probably no more than five per cent on turnover, less for those companies which make only earthenware. Many are hopefully waiting for a take-over bid, although they are painfully aware that some would find it hard to sell their sites even as car parks.

Tom Simpson was a small potter who survived more successfully than most. Despite the fact that he was in his early seventies and had already had two coronaries, when I met him he still handled the entire production and financial sides of the business. His son, who is commanding officer of the 5th/6th Staffordshire Regiment, was the sales-man;[1] the other director of the company is Simpson's wife. Simpson himself was Mayor of the Ancient Corporation of Hanley in 1967 and died while speaking at the Annual Venison Feast.

He worked in an office which was almost like a living-room, with a table neatly set with tablecloth and knife and fork, an ancient radio set and pictures of his forbears. His family had been in the potting business, on and off, since 1590. One of his less fortunate ancestors was a man known as 'Double-Rabbit' Simpson, who was jailed in 1678 for digging clay on somebody else's land.

Simpson's factory was twenty feet lower than in 1900 due to sub-sidence, the company had paid no dividends for the previous seven years because of heavy capital expenditure (it had spent £30,000 on a new gas kiln), and he grumbled about the fact that he could not get enough workers, but Simpson arrived at eight o'clock every morning and the company then had a turnover which was probably close to £250,000.

Wedgwood, by contrast, has now almost reached the two-part target which Arthur Bryan set himself when he took over in 1963: to become a company with a turnover of £10m. and to earn a profit of between £1½ and £2m. Its sales in 1968 amounted to £12m., and the profit was almost £1.4m.

Wedgwood has always been among the most progressive of the potters. It has had a good costing system since the 1920s (it now has a team of half-a-dozen accountants), was the first potbank to have an electric kiln, opened a brand-new factory at Barlaston in the 1940s, and has had a profit-sharing scheme for its four hundred top staff and workers for twenty years. They have had something to share in; after-tax profits quadrupled between 1949 and 1965.

Bryan, who was brought in after sixteen years with the company (three of them running Wedgwood's American subsidiary), has no technical qualifications at all – a matter for remark among the more traditionally-minded potters – but he does have a trans-Atlantic passion for profit which is rare in Britain.

Family authority has not, at first sight, suffered such a sharp decline in Kidderminster as it has in Stoke. The twenty or so carpet companies in the town are, on average, much larger than the potters, and the years after the war were a time of almost unbroken prosperity. (Indeed, even during the depression of the early 1930s, unemployment in

[1] He is now managing director.

Kidderminster never rose above five per cent.) The result is that many of the founding families are still in the saddle.

Yet, even in comfortable Kidderminster, there have been substantial changes in the pattern of power. Families like the Antons and the Naylors have had to sell off some of their shares to meet death duties; a Worth is still chairman of Bond Worth, but an outside managing director, John Murray, has been recruited, and Tomkinsons has had an outside chairman, Norman Lancaster, since 1963.

In that year, Sir Geoffrey Tomkinson died. His son Kenneth said that both he and others felt that no member of the next generation was sufficiently outstanding to take over leadership of the company: hence Lancaster. Outside management consultants were also brought in to re-allocate areas of responsibility between the various family directors, of whom there are four, and so try to eliminate some of the rivalries which had existed previously. Lancaster now has the most influential position in the company; Kenneth Tomkinson sees him frequently and major issues are discussed with him before action is taken. Tomkinson says that what Lancaster recommends goes for ninety-nine per cent of the time, because of his broader experience and his ability to get the support of his directors.

As Tomkinson suggests, the days of family power in the company may be numbered: not only is there a dearth of younger Tomkinsons of an age to be ready in time, but he also has a feeling that whether he wants the firm to remain in family hands or not, economic circumstances may well dictate differently. At Naylors, too, the days of family control seem to be numbered. David Naylor is responsible for the works, for engineering, for purchasing, for labour relations and for finance and there are no other Naylors on the immediate horizon.

Elsewhere, families are still firmly in control. At the Victoria company, Charles and James Anton – who were joint managing directors from 1933 to 1969[1] – are gradually being succeeded by their four sons (here again, consultants have been called in to redefine responsibilities) and the succession is safe enough. Perhaps the next generation of Antons will not be quite so conservative as their predecessors. Victoria has not even had an overdraft at the bank since 1927: its bosses have preferred to run the business out of retained profits.

At Brintons, which is probably about three times the size of Victoria (it has a turnover of about £10m.), the Brinton and Woodward families

[1] James is now Chairman and Managing Director; Charles resigned from the Chairmanship in 1969, but remains on the Board.

own virtually all the shares, although the holdings are split between forty individuals and trusts and nobody now has more than eight per cent. Tatton Brinton has been joined by his son, Topham, who is in his late twenties, and his cousin John's nephew, who is in his early thirties, but since 1955 there have been a number of non-family directors: everybody, says Brinton, must have a field-marshal's baton in his knapsack. One of the company's four managing directors is non-family and, like the other three, is empowered to take any decisions which come up when the others are away.

Brintons, which was founded in 1783, is one of the most successful companies in Kidderminster. It earns an average of 10–11 per cent on turnover, designs and builds most of its own looms and spends money neither on advertising nor on going to exhibitions. Tatton Brinton is firmly of the opinion that carpets sell not on brand but on colour, design and quality and he prefers to spend his money on a good sales force.

Carpet Manufacturing, another successful business, was no longer controlled by families before its merger with John Crossley – Carpet Trades Holdings; only perhaps twenty per cent of the shares could have been influenced by the Board. But the chairman and managing director of Carpet Manufacturing, Peter Anderson, was a descendant of one of the two families which formed the company by a merger of 1890, and the joint managing director, J. M. Carpenter, was a descendant of the other.

This placid little world has been upset by a number of untoward developments. One has been the success in Britain of a new carpet technology and the emergence of the tufted carpet, by which yarn is tufted through a piece of backing cloth and then locked in with a latex backing. To many of the Kidderminster men the whole business at first seemed cheap and nasty and they poured scorn on some of the cheaper tufteds – 'bits of sacking with five o'clock shadow' – but although they considered it degrading to tuft carpets rather than weave them, they noted that tufteds had taken a large share of the American market[1] and decided that they had better at least cover themselves.

Four of them (including Brintons and Carpet Manufacturing) formed Kosset Carpets in 1954 together with one non-Kidderminster company, with the idea of scaring off the smaller fry,[2] and other firms

---

[1] Now ninety per cent.

[2] Two of the original Kidderminster companies have now sold their shares to other members of the consortium.

followed. The rise of tufted, which has now captured roughly half the British market, represented a real threat particularly to manufacturers like Naylor, who had concentrated on low-priced Axminsters. On the other hand, companies like Carpet Manufacturing, which do little if anything below the medium price-range, have not been seriously affected. Several of the companies which have scrambled into tufted are now not only anxious about being able to make their investment pay adequate returns but also nervous of putting major new investment into weaving plant.

Another disturbing development for some of the carpet companies has been the emergence of more powerful wholesaling groups. Manufacturers like Victoria, which have traditionally depended almost entirely on the wholesaler, have found the new groups cutting into their profit margins. This has left them wishing they were more like Brintons, which sells eighty-five per cent of its production direct to the retailer, and Carpet Manufacturing, where the proportion is ninety-five per cent.

Sir Frank Kearton, the chairman of Courtaulds, is another cloud on the horizon; the carpet industry is on his shopping list and a number of Kidderminster companies are clearly vulnerable to attack (not to mention the willing sellers). But if Kearton did attempt the sort of rationalization which he has helped to carry through in Lancashire textiles, it would almost certainly be a thorough-going affair. He would not want to antagonize customers for his fibres unnecessarily (and fifty per cent of the raw material used by Brintons for its Wiltons and Axminsters is man-made fibres) by competing with them in the finished product. He would therefore probably want to take over a number of companies at the same time.

In Kidderminster, as in many other areas of British industry, family businesses face increasing pressures; tougher competition, death duties, the need for expensive new investment. Many have already disappeared under these pressures, and others are functioning less and less like traditional family businesses. The family empire does not need the strictures of the meritocrats to destroy it: it is being steadily swept away by the forces of nature.

CHAPTER 9

Front-Line Troops:
The Retail Trade

All business partakes to some degree of the nature of war. In retailing, the similarities are simply more apparent. The battleground is public and the tactics, at least in terms of the movements of goods and prices, are observable by all. The 'troops' commonly wear some sort of uniform – even at the Marks head office, the staff dining-room is a sea of dark suits at lunch time – and there is more than a trace of the martinet in many store bosses. 'This is not a Christian name business,' said Sir Bernard Miller, the John Lewis chairman. 'We have to be more formal because we're always on parade.' Furthermore, whereas in the headquarters of many large manufacturing companies it would be difficult to tell whether they made or sold anything at all or were simply Government departments, the offices at Tesco are apt to be littered with half-opened samples while at Sainsbury there is a pervasive smell of cheese.

Nor are retail company headquarters concerned only with high strategy, with the monitoring of performance and the approval of budgets. Lord Sainsbury, who controlled the chain's trading policy for thirty years before his retirement as chairman in 1967, was personally responsible for fixing prices in more than two hundred stores. He had daily meetings to discuss price changes by competitors, area bosses were constantly ringing up with the latest intelligence (at John Lewis, ordinary members of staff are used as 'spies' to keep an eye on what the competition is doing), and on Thursdays and Fridays he met the buyers to discuss strategy for the weeks ahead. To Sainsbury, retailing was a continuous war, with the men in the stores as front-line troops.[1]

The war has perhaps two essential features. It is, first of all, a

[1] The battle reaches its height on Saturday: up to forty per cent of Marks's and Debenhams' trade is done on that day.

The Retail Trade

Co-operatives

Over 25,000 retail outlets, annual sales of about £1,090m., divided between over 500 societies with memberships varying from less than 1,000 to more than a million. Food, clothing, furnishings, shoes, coal and funerals. The retail outlets are served by wholesale societies which between them have sales of roughly £600m. and own over two hundred factories, workshops and warehouses as well as 37,000 acres of farmland. Over 280,000 employees.

Great Universal Stores

Tottenham Court Road, London. Turnover in 1968–9, £382m. Approximately 2,750 shops and stores and warehouses of which 630 are men's clothing shops, including Hector Powe, Neville Reed, John Temple, Hope Brothers, and Willerby; 850 ladies fashion shops including Jax and Paige; 525 furniture shops including Cavendish-Woodhouse, Times Furnishing and Astons. Other shops include Burberrys and The Scotch House. Largest mail-order business in Europe, with sales of roughly £140m. a year. Also clothing, bedding, furniture and footwear factories. 50,500 employees.

Woolworth

Marylebone Road, London. Turnover £295m. in 1968. 1,134 shops and stores. Biggest retailer of toys, stationery, detergents, frozen foods and glassware.

Marks and Spencer

Baker Street, London. Turnover in 1968–9, £317m., £224m. in textiles, £76m. in foods. 29,000 employees (including 12,000 part time).

Allied Suppliers

City Road, London. Turnover in 1968, £228m. 2,100 shops – names include Lipton, Home and Colonial, Pearks and Maypole. Also runs forty-four launderettes, sixty-two restaurants, thirty-eight hairdressing salons; and manufactures sausages, jam, canned foods, pickles, soft drinks in its own factories; tea on its own estates.

Boots Pure Drug

Nottingham. Turnover (including Timothy White shops) £212m. in 1968–9. 1,900 shops – 85 per cent of business in chemists' goods, 15 per cent in other areas.

Tesco

Waltham Cross, Hertfordshire. Turnover in 1968–9 £191.4m. 800 supermarkets and stores. 24,000 employees including part-timers.

British Shoe Corporation

Park Street, London. Subsidiary of Sears Holdings. Turnover in 1967–8, £159m. 2,000 retail shoe shops including Freeman, Hardy and Willis, Manfield, True-Form, Saxone, Dolcis and Lilley and Skinner. Also the Lewis's chain of departmental stores, and Selfridge's. 46,000 employees.

Sainsbury

Stamford Street, London. Turnover in 1960–9, £165m. 244 super-markets and shops.

Fine Fare

Welwyn Garden City, Hertfordshire. Turnover in 1967–8, £122m. 1,140 supermarkets and shops. 20,000 employees. Division of Associated British Foods, controlled by Canadian millionaire, Garfield Weston.

United Drapery Stores

Kensington High Street, London. Turnover in 1968–9 £117.2m. Over 1,000 retail shops and department stores. Just under six hundred men's tailoring shops, including John Collier and Alexandre, and the Richard Shops ladies fashion chain. 32,000 employees including part-timers.

Debenhams

Welbeck Street, London. Turnover in 1967–8, £105.1m. 106 department stores and the chain cf Cresta shops; including Debenham and Freebody, Harvey Nichols, Marshal and Snel-grove, Swan and Edgar and Affleck and Brown. 31,700 employees, including part-timers.

House of Fraser

Glasgow. Turnover in 1968–9, £109m. Sixty-three department stores and shops, including Harrods, Dickens and Jones, D. H. Evans, John Barker, Pontings, Derry and Toms, Rackhams, Kendal Milne and Binns. 27,700 employees, including part-timers.

John Lewis Partnership

Old Cavendish Street, London. Turnover in 1968–9, £90m. Sixteen department stores, four specialist shops, twenty-five Waitrose supermarkets.

fast-moving affair. Tesco, for example, turns over its grocery stock once a fortnight, and a department store group like Debenhams reckons to turn over its hosiery between six and twelve times a year. Most food chains run weekly or fortnightly 'promotions'; and fashion lines for the young can be born and die within three weeks. Secondly, the battle is fought out not in great, set-piece encounters on a single field, but in hundreds of running skirmishes up and down the country.

The extended lines along which the stores have to fight means that their managements are also bound to be widely dispersed. Even in firms which are closely controlled from the centre, the local commanders – in the shape of store managers – are of considerable importance, but since 'trade' has never enjoyed a high status in British business life, many of the large chains find it impossible to recruit enough people of the right calibre. Joseph Collier, who built up United Drapery Stores, told me before he died that he was unhappy with at least half the managers in the company's thousand stores.

The scattered nature of the retailing operation as well as the need for continuing economies of scale – particularly in the buying of merchandise – put a premium on efficient central control. Equally, the need for a large number of on-the-spot decisions and the fact that the retailer must be ultra-sensitive to changes in fashion, taste and social habits, underlines the crucial importance of personal judgement. It is a soil in which dictators, benevolent and otherwise, have flourished. A good many of the large chains – Boots and Sainsbury among them – were built into businesses of national significance by autocrats.

Boots, indeed, retained an organization which had been shaped on the basis of one-man rule for decades after the man in question had died. Even in the 1960s, when Boots had over 1,300 stores, the group's managing director was still expected to handle an enormous range of problems. He was chairman of a shop-fitting committee which dealt with the plans for all new branches as well as all alterations to existing ones; he was head of an executive committee which dealt with the renewal of every lease, every retirement from the business and every managerial appointment; he also spent a good deal of his time making improvements to the company's pension scheme.

Nor interestingly enough, do many retail Boards seem to feel the need for the sort of extra-mural advice and criticism which is provided in large manufacturing businesses by outside directors. Indeed, they take pride that their Boards are made up of 'active directors': there is, they say, no place in the retail business for non-combatants.

As a general rule autocracy seems to have paid off. Certainly the failure to exercise tight central control has borne heavily on the companies concerned; the slowness of department store chains like Debenhams to introduce the central buying of goods has been one cause of a serious loss of ground to competitors like Marks and Spencer. When central buying for stockings was eventually introduced, it was found that the group's stores were dealing with no less than 117 different manufacturers. The co-operatives have also lagged behind partly because of the same sort of dispersed effort: a study of twelve retail societies showed that they had seventeen different sources of supply for their hosiery and at that time evidently preferred to buy for themselves rather than let the Co-operative Wholesale Society do it for them.[1] Allied Suppliers, for its part, has tried to resist the challenge of Tesco with a conglomeration of shops trading under no less than fourteen different names, not to mention a high degree of resistance to full unification within the constituent parts of the business.[2] Even now, the group does not have a thorough-going policy of central purchase: its Scottish stores still largely buy for themselves.

By contrast, John Lewis has been applying the principles of central purchase to its department stores for over forty years: and Marks and Spencer, Boots, Tesco and Sainsbury buy either all their goods or (in the case of Boots) virtually all of them from the centre. Even a business like Great Universal Stores, with groups of shops in different sectors of the retail trade, has gathered together all its purchasing under the wing of a Merchandise Corporation, whose directors include the chairmen of all its retailing divisions.

Another feature of the retail trade is a pre-occupation with business philosophies. 'The thing which holds Marks and Spencer is a philosophy,' said Lord Sieff, Lord Marks's partner in building up the chain, 'and we have to know our philosophy, the principles of which rest largely on an emotional consideration of our relationship with society.' The Co-operative ideology – it is known by its adherents as 'the Movement' – is based on ownership by the members and direction by the representatives. The son of the founder of John Lewis wanted it to be a

[1] The CWS says it now has a successful hosiery marketing scheme and that through joint marketing ventures between the CWS and retail Co-ops, a number of non-food lines sold by the retail Co-ops has now been rationalized.

[2] Two of the major companies in the group, Pearks and Maypole, kept their central staffs separate from those of Lipton and Home and Colonial until 1964 – although the group was first formed in 1929.

business which provided 'not only something to live by but something to live for'. To that end, he turned his workers into partners in 1928: surplus profits were to go to them in the form of an annual bonus. Retail groups are apt to regard themselves as more than mere commercial bodies. Marks, for example, thinks of itself as both a national institution and an instrument of social change.

In some cases, the philosophies thus expounded are clearly intended to perform wide-ranging internal functions: everything from ensuring justice for the workers to providing guide-lines for policy in a world of changing tastes and dispersed resources. But the public projection of trading philosophies also has an external value in a business which deals directly with millions; their practice helps to attract customers. They are certainly deemed to have more value than advertising. Marks spends less than half of one per cent of its turnover on what it calls 'communication with the public', and John Lewis does little or no newspaper advertising.

Marks and Spencer has made its way by aiming at consistently high quality and by practices such as a known readiness to take back (without question) any goods which are found to be unsatisfactory or unsuitable. John Lewis claims to be 'never knowingly undersold' and undertakes to refund the difference in price to any customer who can show that she could have bought the same goods at a lower price elsewhere. The Co-ops built up their sales by offering a dividend on purchases. Tesco marches under the banner of cut prices and takes as its advertising symbol Sir Save-a-lot. Harrods, part of a chain which goes in for co-ordinated buying only on what Sir Hugh Fraser calls 'more general merchandise', proclaims itself in its telegraphic address, 'Everything, London'.

The chains of stores and shops which now dominate the arena are the survivors of a succession of retailing revolutions. The first major revolution of size brought the rise of the department store. Between 1900 and 1939, their share of retail trade rose from one to five per cent: since then, it has not increased. The second upheaval which, in its early stages, was a revolution of numbers, saw the rapid increase of the chains. This was a longer and more enduring process: the multiples have increased their share of retail trade from four per cent in 1960 to well over thirty per cent today.

As the chains grew in strength, there was a steady increase in the size of their outlets. The full impact of this second revolution of scale was not felt until building restrictions were removed in the 1950s. The years from 1956 onwards saw the steady advance of the supermarket.[1] In that year, there were only one hundred in Britain; now there are more than 3,000, and they have already changed the face of the food trade. In 1963, they accounted for less than five per cent of retail food sales; now they have captured well over twenty per cent of the market.

Largely because of the low profit margins on food, supermarket operators such as Tesco then began to turn themselves into something much closer to department stores, but with a very large self-service element. Tesco, for example, now reckons to do as much as twenty per cent of its business in fields other than food – clothing, domestic hardware and furnishings, and consumer durables. It feels confident enough of this diversification to have opened stores quite separate from its food supermarkets. To call this 'one-stop shopping', as Tesco (and others) do, is a ridiculous exaggeration, but it is certain to cause headaches for some of the provincial department stores.

The history of Marks and Spencer – in contrast to that of Woolworth – has been one of increasing specialization. In 1926, when the chain first went public, Marks sold – among other things – toys, gramophone records and music, jewellery, books and sports equipment. By 1932, over seventy per cent of the items listed in its prospectus had been dropped, and the winnowing process continued throughout the 1930s. Yet the number of stores in the chain rose from 126 in 1927 to 234 in 1939 (many of them occupying superb High Street sites), there were 150 extensions to existing premises and turnover increased almost twenty-fold. This phenomenal rate of growth was possible because of rapid expansion in the sale of textiles and food, which by 1939 accounted for almost ninety per cent of M. and S.'s sales.

Behind the simple fact of specialization lay a fundamental change of trading philosophy. Simon Marks had decided that it was foolish to try to serve the whole market, and sought instead to make a unique contribution in his chosen fields of clothing and food. The fact that he had turned the chain into replicas of the dollar store in 1927 – five shillings was the maximum price – gave him a sharp incentive to push his volume up and his prices down. Marks and Israel Sieff set out first of all to break the grip which the Wholesale Textile Association held over manufacturers. Sieff was turned away three times from a company which is now one of M. and S.'s largest suppliers, and a good many

[1] The current definition of a supermarket is one which has 2,000 square feet of selling space. This is now regarded as being little more than a large cigarette kiosk by companies like Tesco.

manufacturers traded with Marks under a numbered account, but in the end it succeeded.

Simon Marks then began to feel increasing concern about variations of quality in the cloth which the chain received from its suppliers. The artificial silk which it bought was known only by letters and numbers. 'V15, V16, V17, Vee don't know', complained Marks, and M. and S. gradually began to lay down the most precise specifications for all its merchandise. A Merchandise Development Department was set up, which soon acted very much like a management consultant with teeth. It preached to suppliers the benefits of mass production and the need for economies of scale, and offered help in solving their production problems. The rewards for those who were prepared to co-operate were large and regular orders. This sort of persuasion rarely failed and Marks, dealing with an industry which was fragmented and short of management, inevitably became more and more involved in the manufacturing process without actually making take-over bids.

In some ways, the growth of Sainsbury closely resembled that of Marks. It too expanded rapidly; new branches were being opened at the rate of ten a year for much of the inter-war period. It too specialized, this time in perishable foods – fresh and cooked meats, bacon, dairy produce and poultry. It too was moved by the same sort of radical and puritan principles which inspired Marks and Sieff and which resulted in shops which were clinical in their simplicity.[1] It too aimed for a limited market: 'we have always looked for the quality-conscious woman, not the slovenly housewife who has run out of money by Wednesday', said Lord Sainsbury.

Lord Sainsbury's father, John Benjamin Sainsbury, was the architect and absolute dictator of the business. He made use of a considerable talent for property development by building terraces of shops in the London area and the adjacent counties, taking the best site for himself and letting the rest. But the company's expansion was limited by a decision that daily deliveries of perishables were not practicable outside a radius of 120 miles from London, and by a gentleman's agreement with another chain which prevented Sainsbury from moving into a town which the other had colonized first.

Tesco had very different origins. Its founder, Jack Cohen, was a

---

[1] Their very lack of flamboyance has probably been an important factor in attracting customers of all classes. Marks's store at Marble Arch takes roughly 5,000 cheques a week (in a country where cheques are still very much a middle-class currency) and is favoured by visits from a catholic section of the Royal family.

market trader who made his first profit by the sale of surplus NAAFI goods after the First War. For a short time, he turned wholesaler to other market traders, but lost so much in bad debts – £4,000 in one year – that he decided to revert to the retail business. This time, Cohen moved one stage beyond the market stall and bought six open-fronted shops, used sugar as a loss-leader and – helped by the fact that small shops were practically being given away – built up a chain of 114 outlets with his own capital. He was the Barnum of the retail trade, with an instinct for showmanship and the street trader's easy patter.

Not all the food multiples fared so well. Allied Suppliers' annual profit fell from £1.8m. to £1m. between 1931 and 1939. The department store groups also had mixed fortunes. The Debenham family relinquished all interest in the business in 1928, and for the next twenty-two years it came under the chairmanship of Sir Frederick Richmond. Richmond had previously run two of the group's upper-crust stores, Debenham and Freebody, and Marshall and Snelgrove: devoted to what had been the carriage end of the trade, he was scarcely the man to give Debenhams the aggressive leadership which it desperately needed.

Its power before the 1914–18 war had been based on a sizeable wholesaling and manufacturing business at home and abroad;[1] its store chain included three of the most fashionable in London. The jewel Debenham and Freebody, had a staff of six hundred in the store and 3,000 in its workrooms, submitted presentation dress designs to Queen Victoria and looked upon Harrods and Selfridges as upstarts. In 1921, Debenhams was a giant; it had a capital of £7m., compared to the £850,000 on which Marks and Spencer went public in 1926.

The inter-war years, however, saw a rapid disintegration of its wholesaling business: clothing manufacturers began to buy their own cloth direct from Bradford, and the overseas warehouses were closed one by one. To offset this decline, Debenhams invested heavily in provincial department stores by acquiring Drapery Trust, with over fifty outlets. In the short term, Debenhams only seemed to have added to its problems. It received no dividend from Drapery Trust in 1932, and in 1934 its capital was written down. In the longer term, part of its troubles stemmed from the fact that it owned a group of stores stretching across the whole range of the trade. This would have made central buying difficult, even if it had been considered, which it was not. Furthermore,

---

[1] Marshall and Snelgrove and Harvey Nicholls fell into Debenhams' hands because of their heavy debts to its wholesale business.

there was little effort to rationalize the organization; when new acquisitions were made, they were allowed to carry on much as they had before take-over. In a good many cases, the old proprietors were left in office and, unless profits actually fell, nobody interfered with them.

Debenhams, in fact, was a loose confederation of stores presided over (managed is too strong a word) by a group of modestly wealthy men who did not succeed in pulling it together. The group, indeed, suffered from a shortage of management at all levels. It had no recruitment policy worth the name and never seems to have made any effort to tap the universities. By 1947, Debenhams' profit was roughly half that of Marks and Spencer.

John Lewis was everything which Debenhams was not. It carried no burdens or glories from the past: in 1928, it owned only three stores. It specialized, in dress and furnishing fabrics, offering four hundred colours in one particular range. It introduced central buying in 1928, and eventually separated buying and selling completely – unlike Debenhams, where the buyers were also heads of departments and, as such, not only bought goods but were also responsible for selling them. Furthermore, Spedan Lewis, the son of the founder, broke what was virtually new ground for the retail trade by going to Oxford and Cambridge universities for his managers. Some of those who joined (including the present chairman) were encouraged neither by their shocked relations nor by appointments boards, and Lewis's own father violently disapproved: the idea of languid young men with fancy accents in his stores roused him to fury. Nevertheless, Spedan Lewis's Learnerships provided the group with the beginnings of an excellent management team. Techniques such as five-year forecasting and budgetary control were introduced in the 1930s, when they were virtually unknown in other parts of the retail business and Lewis's expanded steadily.

It picked up a bargain job-lot in 1940, in the shape of Selfridges Provincial Trust – fourteen stores for a mere £30,000 – and it set off on what (before the war) was no more than a flirtation with the grocery business by acquiring thirty small shops.

After the war, John Lewis – like a number of other groups – preferred organic growth to acquisition so far as its department stores were concerned. It occasionally added to its chain, but for the last sixteen years it has bought no new department stores and now has less than it did in 1945. It has preferred to spend what money it had on developing its existing outlets and (after 1953) on breaking into the supermarket business. Similarly, Marks and Spencer has only built seven new stores in the last thirty years (six more are due for completion in 1969) but since 1952 it has refashioned old premises and doubled their selling space. Sainsbury, too, has achieved its expansion of turnover (only £13m. in 1938) from roughly the same number of shops. Boots, which had 1,200 shops in 1939, has built new outlets and closed old ones, but (until the acquisition of Timothy White in 1968) its expansion had been largely built on a pre-war base.

On the other hand, the end of the war brought with it the rise of store empires which had scarcely existed at its outbreak. Property was still going for a song and it was perfectly possible to buy a group of shops and sell the freehold to an insurance company for more than the original purchase price. Those who exploited this situation were able to build up huge chains in a very short time.

Sir Isaac Wolfson's Great Universal Stores consisted, in 1939, of a mail order business and a handful of shops. By the spring of 1954, GUS owned 870 shops, mainly in furniture and clothing. Nor did the pace slacken. Wolfson swept on into women's fashions, men's outfitting and footwear, and by 1957, owned 2,000 shops. The logic of his empire was to be found mainly in its profits, which were sixty times higher in 1957 (at £21.6m.) than they had been twenty years earlier.

The growth of United Drapery Stores was less dramatic but still remarkable. It had ended the war with a few department stores and a small credit business. In 1946, Joseph Collier, its managing director, picked up the first of a series of what turned out to be bargains – he was offered Banners of Sheffield for £160,000. Collier bought it without even taking stock, and was shortly offered £350,000 for it by the Sheffield Co-op. He sold the freehold of Arding and Hobbs, another department store, to the Royal Liver for more than he had paid for the entire business; and, having bought the chain of Richard shops and the Heelas department store in Reading, sold Heelas to John Lewis for more than he had paid for the two companies combined. Collier then moved briskly into men's tailoring – taking over 50 Shilling Tailors in 1952, Alexandres in 1954. As in the case of GUS, there was no particular logic about the acquisitions when taken as a whole; both groups were effectively retail conglomerates. Charles Clore, on the other hand, concentrated on footwear, and rapidly built up the British Shoe Corporation, with 2,000 shops.

By this time, the first of the post-war revolutions was well under way. There had been isolated experiments with self-service before the war –

Debenhams opened a self-service store in Plymouth in 1926, but closed it again when suppliers refused to supply after difficulties in getting people convicted for shop-lifting. However, it was generally believed that, whatever might be happening in America, the conservative British public were not yet ready to shop for themselves.

After the war, it seemed as if little had changed. Jack Cohen of Tesco, who had visited California in 1932 and seen people going through turnstiles to buy goods laid out in the open air, went again in 1946 and, when he came back, took out the counters from his St Albans shop. Nine months later, Cohen put the counters back again. Within a year, he had tried a second time and this time the counters stayed out.

In many ways, Cohen was a natural propagandist for self-service. He had always been essentially a man of the market, a fast cash trader who had no personal relationships with individual customers: to him shops were market stalls with roofs. The progression to self-service was there-fore a natural one. Cohen came to believe that his sort of shopper did not have time for service and aimed to attract working-class people who wanted neither attention nor credit. 'I have millions of customers,' he said in 1967, 'and I don't know one of them.' Cohen began with other advantages. He was not (like Allied Suppliers) hampered by owning a huge chain of small shops, he did not have a large staff to consider and since (unlike Sainsbury) provisions accounted for only a small propor-tion of his sales, he did not need to instal refrigeration when he removed the counters. (Today, of course, Tesco is fully equipped with refrigera-tion.)

Some of the progressive Co-operative societies had moved even more quickly – in 1950 Co-ops accounted for ninety per cent of all self-service shops – but Sainsbury only opened its first self-service shop in 1950, and thereafter moved at the rate of a handful each year; even in 1968 a good deal less than half its outlets had been converted.[1] Allied Suppliers was no quicker. Its Board seems to have continued in the faith that self-service would not come to pass: and that, even if it did, they could take their time about it. The result was that, although Allied's first shop was converted in 1949, only 250 out of 4,400 had made the change by 1957. Later, the pace increased; by 1967, over half the 2,400 shops which remained were operating on self-service.

The revolution moved into its second phase with the coming of the

[1] It is worth adding that Sainsbury now does seventy per cent of its turnover through self-service outlets; its slowness in conversion was largely due to the fact that many of its old shops had been too narrow in frontage to be suitable for conversion.

supermarket. Tesco, having put windows into its small, open-fronted shops, soon began to look for bigger premises. It was interested in low rents and prepared to risk taking sites off the High Street – Cohen and Hyman Kreitman, his son-in-law who was in charge of the property side of the business, were confident that the customers would come if the cut-price offers and the publicity were right. A series of take-overs carried Cohen outside London (he is now planning his first move into Scotland and waiting for a good opportunity to break into the North-East), but he always banked on self-service and size. By 1968, his chain of eight hundred included 375 supermarkets (250 of them with 5,000 square feet or more) and Kreitman says he would not consider opening a new store with less than 10,000 square feet and that 20,000 square feet is ideal.

Fine Fare, a subsidiary of Garfield Weston's Associated British Foods, moved rapidly (for a time too rapidly) to keep pace with Tesco and by 1968 had over five hundred supermarkets. Others lagged seriously behind. For a long time, indeed, the chaste Sainsbury group refused to use the word supermarket at all (it now says quite unequivocally that it has 101 of them); and just as the Allied Suppliers' Board had doubted the future of the self-service store, so – as men who had grown up with the small shop – they also found it difficult to believe in the super-market. The result was that Allied Supplies dissipated its effort by trying to keep open far too many of its small outlets and allowed Tesco to move into the sites where it should have been.

Allied began to change its ideas after Malcolm Cooper, the solicitor who still heads the company, took over as chairman in 1958. Cooper weeded out the shops with low turnovers – anything less than £450 a week – and that in itself meant the end of 1,500 outlets. But, although Allied now has over five hundred supermarkets, it also retains almost 1,000 with counter service, and the comparison with Tesco on average sales per outlet is revealing: the Tesco average is roughly £6,000 a week, Allied's only £1,770. There are also wide differences in the wage bills of different groups. Tesco's labour costs amounted to only seven per cent of its sales in 1967–8, but in the case of the Co-ops (with their widespread manufacturing empire and their massive labour force of 280,000), to no less than fifteen per cent.

Boots, too, found itself with too many small shops and a high labour bill. In 1956, when a new development programme was drawn up, it had over eight hundred shops with sales of less than £50,000 a year. Within ten years, this had been cut to four hundred by closures and

expansion, and although there is still an enormous variation in the size
of Boots' shops (from £20,000 of sales a year to £1½m.), the average is
now roughly £100,000. As a multiple chemist, however, Boots has not
been able to move into self-service to anything like the same degree as
the grocers, and its labour bill in 1967–8 amounted to seventeen per
cent of turnover. Its average sale (before its merger with Timothy
White) was also low, at about five shillings[1] (compared with fourteen
shillings in supermarkets, twenty-two shillings in department stores and
£4 in shoe shops) and, as its former managing director, Francis Cock-
field, put it: 'You have to sell a hundred bottles to make as much
[profit] as on one pair of shoes.'

Once the supermarketeers had established themselves in the food
business, the temptation to extend their range into fields where the
profit margins were considerably higher than in food became overwhelming,[2] particularly as they could build second storeys on to their
supermarkets at no additional cost in land. Tesco has now opened a
four-floor supermarket with 37,000 square feet of selling space in
Crawley; it includes a restaurant and a hairdressing salon. Fine Fare
is moving in the same direction, but its range does not yet, for example,
include furniture. Furthermore, the Fine Ware clothing and hardware
which it offers in over two hundred of its supermarkets have, until
recently, been part of its grocery operation. By the end of 1969, it
expects to have fifty Fine Ware stores in separate premises.

Other food chains, again, have been more cautious. Allied does not
believe that it has the expertise to move into non-foods, whatever the
profit margin, and the one hundred or so shops which do offer pots and
pans and cheap items of clothing have introduced them largely because
there was space to be filled. The chain does only three per cent of its
turnover outside foods. Sainsbury, too, was extremely reluctant to go
into non-foods and seems at first to have moved into them cautiously
because it was conscious of the danger of diluting its image as a quality
food store. But, since sales of perishable foods are not growing so rapidly
as those of other commodities, Sainsbury is looking more to non-foods

---

[1] This figure may now have changed.

[2] The comparison between the profit margins of those chains which do most of
their business in food and those which are mainly outside food is revealing. Woolworth earned 13.3 per cent for 1967–8, United Drapery almost thirteen per cent and
Marks and Spencer regularly has margins of over twelve per cent. Tesco, on the other
hand, made 5.3 per cent on turnover in 1968–9 while Sainsbury's and Allied's margins
on their trading profits were less than three per cent.

for its growth. They presently account for perhaps four per cent of its turnover.

As the supermarkets expand their activities, the areas in which they overlap with the department stores and with chains like Marks and Spencer are bound to grow. Their non-food sections, however, are still in the early stages of development and they have not yet attained the all-class acceptability which M. and S. has achieved. If and when they do, battle will be joined more seriously.

Marks and Spencer is a formidable competitor for anyone: it is an example of a supremely scientific business run on lines of classic simplicity. It is also the nearest in atmosphere of any company which I visited to that of a religious sect or ideological group. It rests, as they do, on a body of principle, developed over the years and carefully adhered to ('Simon Marks said . . .') and, apart from these tablets from the mountain, there is the same air of conviction among the faithful, the same desire to lead the people a little nearer the Promised Land. It seems appropriate that the chain's brand name should be Saint Michael. Marks's men, not surprisingly, are conscious that outsiders may think them brain-washed. Lord Sieff, now the president, replies: 'It is the worship of true ideals.' At Marks, you are somewhere between the folk-lore which commercial success has created and the ideology which produced that success.[1]

The first of its principles is that of specialization. After a period during and after the war when it had to open restaurants and sell boot polish simply to fill up space, Marks is back to textiles and food in the proportion of 73:27. So far as brand names are concerned, M. and S. carries only one – its own. Nor will it offer any item on which it cannot make a contribution in terms of price and quality, or on which it cannot make a satisfactory return on capital (it likes a gross profit margin of twenty-six per cent). Marks does not sell anything purely as a service to the public: if you have a 12½-inch or 18½-inch neck, that is your misfortune. The decision to move out of children's books is reputed to have been taken after Simon Marks had picked up a volume in one of the stores and asked rhetorically: 'What can we do for Robin Hood? It's already been written,' and eggs were at one time abandoned because M. and S. was not satisfied with the return. They have now reappeared.

[1] The topic which men from Marks are asked most frequently to debate at universities is the proposition that 'Marks and Spencer have done more for humanity than Marx and Engels'.

Specialization has certainly produced its benefits in terms of volume. Marks sells over seven million shirts a year, a third of all the bras sold in Britain, and two-fifths of the ladies' briefs. Marks also reckons to be the largest greengrocer in Britain: it sells more than £3m. worth of bananas a year alone.

The second Marks' principle is one which has been practised almost from the beginning. There is a complete separation between buying and selling: buying is done by head office, selling by the men in the stores. The Marks' headquarters in Baker Street contains fifty buying departments, of which the seven textile groups are the most important. Each of the seven has designers at its disposal and, with the suppliers, they evolve new ranges of clothes. The Board gives its verdict before contracts are placed.

But it is the degree of Marks' involvement with its suppliers which, perhaps more than anything else, makes it unique. Again, the basic principle is clear: Marks, having played such a large part in deciding precisely what sort of goods it wants and (in the clothing field) even in creating them, wishes to buy not merchandise but the use of production capacity over which it can exercise fundamental control. One of its executives put the point clearly: 'We regard ourselves not just as a merchandising organization . . . we have really developed into a pro-duction organization in that we share with our manufacturers the many problems and responsibilities of production and distribution.' In other words, the suppliers are – in more senses than one – in Marks' pocket. Any firm which accepts a Marks' order in some sense loses its autonomy: since it is Marks which has to pay the bills and fire the bullets, it also expects to be able to lay down the law.

To begin with, there are detailed specifications for everything – between two and three hundred altogether. Carrots must be straight and within half an inch of a certain size; for apples, the tolerance is only one-eighth of an inch. Bananas must be entirely free of blemish. Marks' Food Technology Department, having isolated the breed of chicken which it wanted, specified exactly how the birds were to be killed, plucked, stored and packed.

As for clothing, the specifications lay down types of thread, types and sizes of needle and stitch formation and density, not to mention the way in which the finished garment should be pressed and folded. Marks also insists on a specific number of quality inspection stations on every production line. In addition, there are minimum performance stan-dards for every sort of garment: a Marks' shirt must be able to stand up to fifty launderings. Every part of every garment (including the thread) goes through the Marks' laboratory to be tested for strength, shrinkage, colour fastness and so on; three-quarters of the testing is done before the merchandise goes into production. The result is a remarkable evenness of quality.

Where suppliers find themselves unable to meet these rigorous standards and still earn the sort of money which Marks thinks they ought to be making (Marks expects its dictatorship to be mutually beneficial), there are teams of experts at Baker Street ready to move in and help them sort out their problems. There are production engineers who can do anything from developing production planning and control schemes to linear programming, food technologists to advise on crop improvement and handling. Sometimes they fail – not every supplier has adequate management even with Marks holding his hand – but they can reel off scores of case-histories where costs were cut and profits improved. They also act as evangelists for new management techniques and labour-saving machinery, some of which they develop for themselves: for example, they devised an electro-static method of greasing bakery tins which was at once hygienic and saved on both fat and labour.

The stores themselves are spacious and devoid of frills. They express not only a desire to hold down costs but also Simon Marks's revulsion at what he called 'those supermarket slums'. Alone among the big stores, Marks eschews Christmas decorations, has austere window displays (nothing so garish, or expensive, as a model) and offers neither fitting rooms (which would add to staff costs and, hence, to the price of goods) nor – except in large stores – enquiry desks, which might occupy the best selling space. On the other hand, it cossets its sales girls both while they are employees and after they leave. There are comfortable dining rooms and lounges in the stores, not to mention hairdressing salons, and Marks has even begun to offer cervical smear tests not only for its women staff but also for the wives of male employees. Long-service employees get a year's wages as a tax-free gift when they retire and former employees are looked after by the store in whose area they live. They are offered free lunches and free chiropody for life, their pensions are reviewed each year in the light of increases in the cost of living and they are visited regularly to make sure that they are well provided for: where there is genuine hardship, it is not at all unusual for Marks completely to redecorate the woman's home or buy her a new cooker. Marks' wage bill represents only six per cent of its annual sales – lower even than Tesco[1] – but its welfare services are an additional cost. It is one of the paradoxes of M. and S. that, while it insists on high profit margins, it seldom thinks only in terms of profit. Unlike Tesco or Woolworth, it does not pay its store managers on the basis of either profit or increased sales, but by the turnover group into which they fall.

Yet, for all the precision of the system and the thoroughness with which any new venture is scrutinized, Marks – as a business which sells ten per cent by value of Britain's clothes – depends on the personal judgements of its leaders. At one time, those judgements often emanated from Simon Marks himself. Marks even imposed his own taste and prejudices on the stores: M. and S. clearly reflected his basic conservatism about clothes, his membership of the white-shirt-and-grey-flannel-trousers brigade. Marks could not understand why people wanted trousers without turn-ups.

This personal involvement of the Marks' chairman in the fashions sold in its stores has become legendary. In Simon Marks's day, complaints that M. and S.'s pyjamas legs were too short were apt to be met with the reply that the chairman was a short man. When Lord Sieff succeeded him, the length of the girdle on Marks' pyjamas was put down to the fact that 'Israel had trouble tying his bow'. But Simon Marks's conservatism paid off because it accurately reflected provincial taste. Michael Marks, the founder of the business, had his headquarters first in Leeds and then in Wigan, and M. and S. has never been so seduced by the metropolis as to forget either its origins or where its largest markets lie. 'Most of our stores are in places like Wigan', says Lord Sieff, 'and middle-aged people in Wigan do not wear yellow shirts.'

Leadership in Marks has now passed to a group of men, a good many of whom are not descendants of the founding families. It has had to make the transition from a brilliant autocracy to something much nearer to committee rule; no longer are decisions taken on *a priori* grounds as they were in Marks's day. The fact that it has made the change so successfully is partly because of the degree to which Marks's successors were imbued with a common ideology.

The inculcation of the Marksian philosophy was helped by the fact that, at the heart of the business, were a group of men closely bound together by family ties and, in some cases, by deep friendship.[2] Marks

---

[1] It is only fair to add that Marks is selling merchandise which, on average, is much more highly-priced than Tesco's.

[2] The only period when M. and S. had outside directors was between 1935 and 1945: they were eliminated by age.

and Sieff, in Sieff's own words, were 'one body . . . we worked together for sixty-five years and married each other's sisters to make sure we weren't separated.' Another of Marks's sisters married Harry Sacher, and the two Sachers at present on the Board, Michael and Gabriel, are their offspring. Alec Lerner, another former director, married one of Marks's daughters, while Sieff himself has a brother (Edward), two sons (Marcus and Michael), two nephews, a grandson and a grand-nephew in the business. The families see a great deal of each other socially and have retained a remarkable unity.

Marks and Spencer's strength also stems in part from the marriage between trading instinct and intellectual power which has marked its Board ever since Marks and Sieff joined forces full time in 1926. Sieff had an economics degree from Manchester and had worked closely with Chaim Weizmann in the cause of Zionism while Harry Sacher, who joined the Board in the same year, was a barrister who became a leader-writer for the *Manchester Guardian*. The outcome of this alliance of talents has been profound. For one thing, it has produced the sort of stringent self-criticism which Arnold Weinstock has been desperately trying to introduce into the electrical industry. As one Marks' executive put it: 'This is the business of nag, par excellence.'

But neither Marks nor Sieff was content that the ideology should be shared only by the Central Committee of the Party; they wanted all the sales-girls to be converts. Not only did they treat their staffs with genuine consideration, they also drew them into the making of decisions: Simon Marks frequently wanted to know what junior sales assistants thought of the new lines they were discussing. The brainwashing and the benevolence have worked, and Marks and Spencer has become the most successful realization in Britain of the Jewish ideal of the business-as-family.

The Marksian ideology is unlikely to change much, in the foreseeable future at least. Although the average sales of its stores is well over £1m. (almost twice that of Debenhams' outlets), it believes that a large number are still too small and owns 1.8m. square feet of space around its present sites which has still not been developed. The Marks' Board takes the view that once the number of stores exceeds 250, the business might in any case become dangerously impersonal. Nor does M. and S. anticipate making any fundamental changes in the balance of its business: the proportion of sales held by food may increase to something nearer thirty per cent, but that is all. It has become what must be one of the world's best-run businesses, and the main preoccupation of its bosses is to keep it that way.

The retail and wholesale Co-ops, by contrast, have not been notably successful in recent years. For the last decade, the movement has been struggling to bring itself up to date and some progress has been made, but instead of what the Co-op should be – an organization using its massive market power as effectively as M. and S., and on a scale almost four times as great – it is still an uncoordinated giant, a collection of societies large and small, efficient and inefficient, with a relatively small number of supermarkets and modern stores and a multitude of tiny shops in antiquated premises. If any organization cries out for immediate and compulsory rationalization by order of the Government, it is the Co-op.[1]

Since 1959, its sales have been stuck somewhere between £1,000m. and £1,100m.: while the turnover of the multiples has been racing ahead, that of the Co-ops has been virtually stagnating. Their share of retail trade has fallen from twelve per cent in 1950 to about nine per cent now; their return on capital has slumped from nineteen per cent in 1958 to two per cent in 1967, and the average dividend paid by retail societies fell from 11¼d. in 1960 to 6¾d. in 1967.

The Co-ops appear to have lost much of the sense of purpose and the missionary zeal which inspired the birth and growth of the movement. This is not altogether surprising. The society which called it forth has disappeared and it has failed to modify its philosophy, its trading practice and its public face sufficiently to keep pace with its rivals, some of whom now seem to be carrying the torch of service to the consumer more effectively.

Many co-operators seem drawn in two directions at once. On the one hand, they want to emulate the success of chains like Tesco and M. and S.; on the other, they feel that they ought in some way to be different from them. The trouble is that they do not seem quite sure how. The result is that, although the old dogmas remain, the convictions which gave them power have lost much of their force, and many of the Co-ops present a depressing picture of static substance and struggling spirit, despite pockets of high efficiency and the brave efforts of reforming groups.

The movement's most obvious weakness is its apparent inability to match the pace and unity of its rivals. In short, there are still far too

[1] The Co-ops agreed in 1969 to begin discussions which might lead to a merger of the retail and wholesale societies.

many retail societies, each of them free to go its own way; and their links with the wholesale societies – which should be their source of greatest strength with their tremendous central purchasing power – are too tenuous. The retail societies now buy only about half their goods through the CWS and its Scottish counterpart.

So far as the number of societies is concerned, there has been anxiety within the movement since the end of the last century about the duplication of investment by Co-ops in adjacent areas. Pressure for a reduction in numbers has increased sharply during the last decade, reinforced by the straitened circumstances in which the Co-ops have found themselves: an Independent Commission under Hugh Gaitskell recommended in 1958 that there should be no more than three hundred societies and in 1968 the Co-operative Union put forward a plan based on the idea of fifty retail societies. Although the number of societies has come down very substantially, the hard fact is that – more than ten years after Gaitskell – there are still something like five hundred, eighty-seven of them with less than 1,000 members.

Each of these societies is free to buy its goods wherever it wishes; if it does not like what the wholesale societies have to offer, it can go elsewhere. It is rather as though Marks's individual stores were to begin buying half their own merchandise independently of headquarters and telling the men in Baker Street what they could do with half their offerings. The effects of this unbridled autonomy can be seen from the results of a study published by the CWS in 1965 in the report of its joint reorganization committee. The study showed that twenty-four grocery shops belonging to sixteen societies in the Newcastle area stocked, between them, 11,812 lines drawn from 1,200 different suppliers. No less than 5,332 of these lines appeared only in one shop, and only fifty-one of them were stocked by all.

This situation cannot be laid entirely at the door of retail societies who choose to scatter their orders outside the movement. There does seem at times to have been some loss of rapport with the wholesale societies (efforts are being made to restore it), despite the fact that the CWS Board is elected by the retail societies and that the CWS pays them a dividend on their purchases.

Nor has the co-operative movement any central body empowered to impose reform: each of the retail societies is a sovereign body. The most which the Co-operative Union or the CWS can do is to exercise persuasion. The result is that the retail societies are still trying to fight national store chains from a base which is more or less parochial.

Many of them also suffer from a style of management which, while it conforms to the co-operative principle of government by members for the benefit of members, can also severely inhibit their efficiency. They are run by committees of management (now often called Boards of Directors to match the prevailing fashion), whose job it is to oversee the activities of paid officials. These committees of management are unpaid, generally elected by two per cent or less of the membership and often include Co-operative Guildswomen, Co-op employees – milk roundsmen and shop managers, for example – and the ideologically committed. Committees so constituted are not perhaps best-fitted to give dynamic or enlightened commercial leadership. They normally divide themselves into a series of sub-committees, each dealing with a particular part of the society's business. They sometimes concern themselves with the most trivial issues and since their members frequently lack professional management skills, they do not find it easy to exercise really effective control over departmental bosses.

This handicap, combined with a cosy and paternalistic attitude towards staff, means that bad management by officials can go undetected and unpunished. The fact that the movement has tended to be trade-union dominated is also partly responsible for its high wage costs and labour force.

Fortunately, many of the larger societies have been giving an increasing amount of power to their paid officials. In the London Co-operative Society, for example, the chief officer now has clear control both over policy and over day-to-day management, and departmental managers report to an executive committee headed by him and not to sub-committees of the Board of Directors. The improvement in performance to date has scarcely been dramatic, but some small shops have been closed, managers have been told plainly that they will be dealt with if they do not perform adequately, new men have been brought in from outside, and the atmosphere is more business-like than it was.

But the granting of greater executive power to paid officials is far from certain to bring the thorough-going change which is often needed: the Co-op is an extremely inbred movement and many of the officials which it has produced, though diligent, are of modest management calibre. It has been reluctant to take in outsiders no doubt partly because they might not be imbued with the right principles, and this resistance to external influences has also hampered the development of effective profit budgeting and sales forecasting. Low salaries and the

Co-op's unexciting public image have, in any case, discouraged incomers. As one co-operator remarked: 'We have not been recruiting nearly enough of the right people for the last twenty or thirty years and it's no good offering an outsider £3,500 to run a society with a turnover of £3m. which has groceries, dairies, coal yards and funeral parlours when he can get more by becoming manager of the local Tesco supermarket.'

Until recently, many of these criticisms applied with equal force to the CWS. Even in 1965 it had a Board of twenty-one, the members of which were not only directors of the whole enterprise but also managers of parts of it. As in the retail societies, the CWS Board divided itself into a mass of sub-committees and sub-sub-committees: the Finance Committee had two sub-committees apiece. Everything had to be approved by one or other of these committees before it went to the Board.

How ineffective this bureaucratic mass had become is plain from the state into which the CWS had fallen in recent years. Although it still produces perhaps thirty per cent of the goods which it sells to the retail societies in its own factories and on its own farms, these establishments have often been far from efficient. Many are in old buildings, expensive to run; they have frequently been under-utilized, producing a wide range of goods in very short manufacturing runs; and even where a CWS product could not compete successfully in the shops against national brands, it has been retained to keep people in jobs. Furthermore, the CWS has in the past marketed its goods under a huge range of brand names which confused rather than attracted the shopping public. In these circumstances it was not surprising that retail societies turned to outside suppliers. Their other complaint has been that some CWS buyers have not seen the inside of one of their shops for years and therefore are not sufficiently acquainted with what has been going on in the retail business. (The salary levels for buyers are certainly poor compared with outside concerns.)

The CWS also became a sort of casualty station for societies which had become or were becoming insolvent. Since it was invariably the biggest creditor, it was an obvious saviour. These then became part of an organization called Co-operative Retail Services, originally started by the CWS to open up new parts of Britain – such as rural Wales – to co-operative trading. In 1967, CRS was doing a retail business worth £68m.

By 1967, the CWS had become so convinced that fundamental reorganization could be delayed no longer that it imported a chief executive to help implement changes. Philip Thomas, who was re-cruited from Garfield Weston's Associated British Foods, immediately set about a radical restructuring of the entire business. He brought in a number of other outsiders, disbanded the mass of committees and set up what amounted to a small, executive Board. He also closed un-economic factories and began to rationalize the production of those which remained. Although the CWS made the biggest trading loss in its history in 1967, these changes had begun to bear fruit when Thomas was killed in an air crash. The CWS has appointed one of Thomas's close colleagues to succeed him.

Thomas died at a time when both the CWS and many of the retail societies seemed to be on the brink of major changes, but whether the impetus which he helped to create will be maintained remains to be seen.[1] Apart from its structural weaknesses, the Co-ops are still suffering from decades of inadequate thinking. A high proportion of their members come from higher age-groups; over seventy per cent of their business is in foods, where profit margins are thin; they are urgently in need of capital for redevelopment; a large number of small shops need to be closed; the rationalization of the CWS factories has only just begun; and, equally important, their high labour costs must somehow be reduced. If their record is any criterion, not enough of the retail societies are run efficiently. The decline in their share of retail trade, on the other hand, seems to have been arrested, and reform has begun, but the Co-ops will have to move quickly if they are to survive at their present size.

The department stores, for their part, have also come under attack from the multiples, and they have been fighting to hold on to their share of the market. The John Lewis Partnership, however, far from appearing embattled, has done outstandingly well over the last decade and is now hard on the heels of both Debenhams and House of Fraser in terms of annual sales. But for lack of capital and perhaps at times a lack of adventurousness, it would almost certainly have overtaken them. The Partnership's profit margins (before tax) also compare favourably with theirs; it earned 7.7 per cent on turnover in 1967–8, compared with 6.4 for Debenhams and 5.9 per cent for the House of Fraser.

The chairman of the Partnership, Sir Bernard Miller, puts its success down to 'being peculiar in the way we are', to the spirit which shared ownership inspires. The attractions to the shopping public of an under-taking never to be knowingly undersold are obvious, but so far as the

---

[1] The CWS raised its profit to £4.1m. in 1968, on sales of £510m.

spirit is concerned, it may be more apparent to the insider than to the outsider. The group's staff turnover is still high (thirty per cent per annum as against a national average for retail establishments of forty per cent); a straw poll among those who use the stores gives the impression that, while its assistants do not adopt the queenly airs common in some other department stores, they do not seem so deeply identified with the business as the Marks' girls; and, although the chairman can be sacked by the partners if he behaves unconstitutionally, there is still an authoritarian style to the management which Miller himself appears to acknowledge to some extent when he says flatly that they are not 'a soft-centred Owenite lot . . . those who don't make the grade, go'.

Furthermore, while the words employee, staff and managing director are not used at John Lewis, there are partners and there are senior partners. The senior partners have a dining-room of their own, and when it comes to taking holidays in one of the Partnership's camps and guest houses,[1] there is a country house in Hampshire which is reserved for partners with a certain level of responsibility. The reason for this segregation is understandable – the senior partners say it allows them to let down their hair – but it again reinforces the impression of a two-class system.[2] Even the famous Partnership bonus is not quite so splendid as it sounds. It is only recently that a part (and a relatively small part) has been paid in cash, and a high proportion comes to the partners in the form of fringe benefits like sick pay and a discount on purchases; the partners are compelled to invest the remainder in John Lewis five per cent Preference stock, but since currently they fetch only about 10s 6d on the stock market, for every pound of nominal value, they hardly represent a bargain.

Althogether, John Lewis's version of industrial democracy is rather more muted an affair than at first appears. The reasons for its success are largely to be sought elsewhere.

The appeal of its stores, to begin with, is focused on the middle-income brackets, on 'people who want merchandise in good but not extravagant taste'. In that sense, John Lewis is a sort of commercial

[1] Perhaps twenty per cent of the partners spend their annual holiday with the firm. It claims to offer them the best shooting and fishing in England.

[2] Sir Bernard Miller writes: 'In any large business organization, there must be enormous differences in living standards, social attitudes and interests between a high earning management and the average weekly wage earner and that they should tend to live their lives separately is quite as much in accord with the wishes of the latter as of the former. The Partnership has never set out to be egalitarian since that can only mean levelling down.'

equivalent of MRA. The average turnover of its stores (they range from £1m. to £16m. a year) is higher than that of other groups; the sales of its smallest outlet (Caleys of Windsor) is just over £1m., which is about the average for all Debenhams' stores. It has also carried its central buying operation further than any other big department store group. Roughly sixty per cent of its merchandise is common to all its stores and even at Peter Jones, probably the most expensive store in the group and thought of by Miller (rather over-expansively, in my view) as 'a Harrods-type store', ninety-five per cent of the goods are centrally bought. The Partnership, unlike some other groups, has a strong central management team which tries to make sure that it keeps its eye firmly fixed on its market and that the stores conform to the trading policy which it lays down. In that sense, it is the nearest thing in the department store world to Marks and Spencer.

John Lewis would also claim, and with justice, that the quality and depth of its top management – and not just at head office – also sets it apart from the other big groups. Certainly the proportion of graduates among its top 150 managers (no less than 120 are university men) probably cannot be matched by any other business in Britain apart from ICI. Eight of the twelve members of the Central Board were at either Oxford or Cambridge; the deputy chairman, Paul May, took a First in Greats at Oxford. It is not surprising that John Lewis prides itself on being something of a club which provides 'the intellectual company of the Civil Service combined with the interest of a business organization', and if the Partnership is both rather smug and a little inbred, the in-breeding at least springs from a healthier strain than those which exist in some other department store groups.

Debenhams' progress has been a good deal slower in many respects. It emerged from the war with an elderly and conservative Board which was concerned about the possibility of another Depression while groups like GUS were expanding rapidly. They braced themselves for a bump which never came. Debenhams also, unlike John Lewis, remained wedded to a policy of extreme decentralization for a good many years; until 1958, its stores ran very much as individual units.

When John Bedford, who had joined the group during the slump, became chairman and managing director in 1956, he faced a frightening range of problems. The first was that Debenhams was trying to serve virtually the whole market: it had everything from Debenham and Freebody to suburban and provincial stores selling relatively cheap merchandise. There was also (and still is) a tremendous variation in the size of its stores, from huge emporia like the one in Southampton (with 110,000 square feet of selling space on the ground floor alone) to a tiny store in Andover. Furthermore, because of the piecemeal way in which the group had acquired its outlets, in a number of towns they plainly overlapped. In Norwich, for example, there were four Debenhams stores, three selling a more expensive range of goods, one serving the lower end of the market.

So far as the trading policy of the group was concerned, central buying had scarcely begun, although Bedford had introduced it over a limited range of merchandise during the early 1950s in an effort to fend off the challenge of Marks and Spencer. He had to fight a battle against the entrenched power of individual store managers (who were reluctant to yield any of their autonomy to head office) and also against the resistance of store buyers whose territory he was invading.

Bedford has not only made new acquisitions but also begun to rationalize Debenhams' outlets in towns where there was duplication: it now has two stores in Norwich, instead of four. He also set out to narrow the range of goods offered by the group. Debenhams now sells neither the most expensive nor the cheapest merchandise and in its new stores, such as the one at Guildford, it offers a range which Bedford describes as 'Middle A to Middle C'. This is a perfect example of the tendency of the department stores to trade down as the multiples have traded up.

Bedford also began to make slow but steady progress in the introduction of central buying. The first major decisions on this front were not taken until the 1960s, but by 1968 over half of Debenhams' turnover was coming from merchandise centrally bought. This involved a profound change in the structure of power within individual stores (the buyers became departmental heads and found themselves selling goods which others had bought); it frequently also had a depressing effect on morale. Bedford also undermined the autonomy of individual stores by appointing regional bosses to cover all the stores in a particular area, and by putting them on the main Board.

But Debenhams' problems are far from over. For one thing, the transition to central buying will not be complete until 1970, which implies both continued upheaval and heavy expense. The head office staff has been strengthened, although Bedford himself, who has appointed all the present Board, remains very much the decisive force in the company. Unlike John Lewis, however, it has not until recently gone in for university graduates in any numbers – 'if we've six, we're lucky', said Bedford in 1967. 'The retail trade doesn't attract Firsts in Greats.'[1] There has been an apparent absence of flair in some of Debenhams' stores. Debenham and Freebody, for example, used to offer rather staid merchandise and acquired a provincial aunt image; Bedford says it has now been 'completely reorganized'. He believes fervently in the future of the department store, but Debenhams – which made less profit in 1967–8 than it did in 1964–5 – still has to show its paces.

The retail trade has passed through major upheavals, but it has been cushioned from more violent change by the conservative shopping habits of the British public. Out-of-town shopping, for example, is still in its infancy, with sixty-eight per cent of people walking to the shops and only seventeen per cent going by car. If that habit really took hold, it might mean more fundamental change than anything which has yet happened.

---

[1] In 1968, Debenhams recruited five graduates: another five in 1969.

CHAPTER 10

Brewers and Builders

The brewers and builders share a distinction rare among major British industries: on their home territory, they are almost completely exempt from foreign competition. They have also, between them, faced only one foreign invader, in the shape of E. P. Taylor, the Canadian brewer of Carling lager. Taylor, who wanted his beer to sell round the world like Campbell's Soups, gingered up the brewing business very considerably and built himself a British empire of useful size which was later absorbed into the larger body of Bass Charrington.

The brewers are protected from external attack by barriers both natural and man-made. To begin with, Britain is the only country in the world which favours ale as its staple alcoholic drink and this immediately reduces its vulnerability to penetration by lager-drinking nations. Despite all the money which has been spent on promoting lager, it has captured only $3\frac{1}{2}$ per cent of the market in England and Wales (in Scotland, curiously, its share is nearer twenty per cent). Tastes in beer, in other words, do not transplant easily. Nor, in many cases, is it an economic proposition to ship beer over long distances (even if it took well to travel, which it does not) : since, as one brewer put it, 'we're only selling water, wind and crown corks', the price-weight ratio is against it.

Even if these natural barriers were not sufficient discouragement, the really successful foreign invader would still have to find some method of breaching the tied house system: English brewers own 58,000 of Britain's 75,000 public houses (though only about half of total outlets), and they do not give up shelf space to competitors, domestic or otherwise, without an adequate *quid pro quo*.[1] The existence of the tied

---

[1] The tied house may only buy the owner's beer. Any other beer – Guinness, Bass or Double Diamond, for example – has to be bought through the brewer-owner.

Brewers and Builders

Allied Breweries

St John Street, London. Turnover in 1968, £293m. 8,300 public houses, 1,700 off-licences, 100 hotels. Double Diamond, Skol, Long Life, Ansells, Ind Coope, Tetley Walker, Harveys, Cockburn's Port, Babycham, Whiteways and Gaymers ciders.

Bass Charrington

Grosvenor Gardens, London. Turnover in 1968, £282m. 11,500 public houses, 1,600 off-licences, 204 hotels. Bass, Worthington Tennent, Carling Black Label.

Whitbread

Chiswell Street, London. Turnover in 1968, £162m. 8,600 public houses, 1,140 off-licences. Mackeson.

Guinness

Dublin and Park Royal Brewery, London. Turnover in 1968, £137m. Harp lager, Nuttalls and Callard and Bowser confectionery.

Watney Mann

Palace Street, London. Turnover in 1968, £129m. 6,700 public houses, 1,750 off-licences, 50 hotels, 9 motels. 37.6 per cent of International Distillers and Vintners (Gilbey's Gin, J and B Rare Whisky, agents for Hennessy, Smirnoff).

Courage

Southwark Bridge, London. Turnover in 1968, £102m. 4,450 public houses, 500 off-licences, 60 hotels.

*   *   *

Wimpey

Hammersmith Grove, London. Turnover in 1968, £200m. – £100m. in housing.

John Laing

Page Street, London. Turnover in 1968, £100m.

Sir Robert McAlpine and Sons

Park Lane, London. Turnover in 1968 (estimated), £90 to £100m.

Taylor Woodrow

Park Street, London. Turnover in 1968, £71m. excluding associated companies.

Richard Costain

Westminster Bridge Road, London. Turnover in 1968, £86m.

Wates

Norbury, Surrey. Turnover in 1968 (estimated), £55m.

house system[1] might also act as a deterrent to overseas take-over bids in another way. British brewers have over sixty-five per cent of their total assets in pubs and hotels. and most foreign brewers would probably hesitate to become so deeply involved in the property business.[2] (Courage has nearly fifty architects and surveyors on its permanent staff.)

Building and contracting is a discouraging prospect for different reasons. It is a high-risk, labour-intensive industry which suffers from considerable over-capacity and it is also a field in which overseas companies have little to offer in the way of superior technology; its most valuable assets are people rather than machines. In any case, most of the potential competitors are based in countries which have had their own building booms to keep them busy since the end of the war. When they venture abroad, they prefer to go to under-developed parts of the world, rather than compete in a market which has its own highly-developed industry: the big British construction companies are large even in global terms. Furthermore, family power in public companies like Wimpey and Laing (not to mention private businesses like McAlpine and Wates) would doom take-over bids to failure.

This unusual immunity from outside competition on the home market has had a different impact on the two industries. Before the Second World War, the brewing business was one of the most somnolent in the country. Most brewers operated from a local or regional base and there were only a handful of beers (Guinness, Bass and Worthington for example) which could claim to be nationally known. With little or no real competition in many areas (the licensing laws and resistance from publicans combined to keep the number of outlets fairly static), it was scarcely a bracing environment in which to work. The industry, in any case, tended to be production-orientated; even twenty years ago, Guinness rolled out its barrels onto the quay in Dublin with the attitude that, if anybody wanted them, they could come and fetch them. The power of families was still very considerable and, perhaps because of its connection with the products of the land,[3] perhaps because many brewers had become local squires, the brewing life had a certain snob-appeal. It therefore served to attract a sprinkling of ex-military gentlemen with plummy voices and well-bred young

[1] The Monopolies Commission found in 1969 that the system operated against the public interest, but could see no practical alternative.

[2] In the United States, brewers are not allowed to control retail outlets.

[3] Brewers usually refer to the retail outlets which they own as 'tied estate'.

men who were looking for congenial positions where they would not be expected to over-extend themselves.

Even in companies which made a point of recruiting brains, it was not exactly a harsh existence. Life at the Guinness brewery in Dublin before the war was 'almost offensively easy', according to its present managing director, Dr Arthur Hughes, and the pace does not seem particularly hectic now. Nevertheless, brewers were able to convince themselves that only men steeped in the business could possibly succeed and even today, when outsiders have taken a number of the industry's senior posts, brewers are happy to retail stories of 'tip-top chaps' from the outside world who were not able to make the grade.

But the last fifteen years have brought profound changes. For one thing, the development of pasteurized beers with a much longer shelf-life has extended brewers' horizons by allowing them to distribute their wares over a much greater area. (The shelf-life of more traditional products has also been lengthening rapidly: that of Guinness has quadrupled in the last fifteen years.) The feasibility of national distribution (even at the cost of national advertising) was a major force behind the wave of mergers which began in the 1950s. But there were other, equally potent factors. The ambitious Canadian, Eddie Taylor, was one. The link between Ind Coope, Tetley Walker and Ansells in 1961 was only one of those which sprang largely from a determination that the British brewing industry should not be controlled from Toronto. Again, death duties helped bring many of the smaller brewers to their knees. Hereward Swallow, Courage's managing director, says that they have been a major factor in the take-overs in which his company has been involved.

The result was a rapid restructuring of the industry. There was a further sharp decline in the number of independent brewers – only one hundred are left compared with one thousand at the turn of the century – and empires grew swiftly. Mitchells and Butlers, which in 1961 had only 2,300 outlets in the Midlands, became the nucleus of Bass Charrington; by 1968, the group controlled over 13,000 pubs and off-licences. Before Ind Coope began its series of take-overs in 1957, it owned only forty pubs in the London area: its creation, Allied Breweries, now has over 10,000 outlets. The seven largest groups presently account for seventy-three per cent of the industry's output.

Other factors also helped. Mr Charles Clore's take-over bid for Watney made the industry uncomfortably aware that its properties were under-valued in its books. The growth of sales through off-licences, clubs and supermarkets has forced it to reconsider its marketing policies, and the fact that beer consumption has been growing at the rate of only two per cent a year has driven it to think more seriously about the potential of overseas markets.[1] It has also taken a very firm grip on the wine and spirits trade, where growth is greater even if profit margins can be slimmer. Roughly a quarter of Bass Charrington's sales come from wine and spirits, a third in the case of Allied.

So, although the brewers often retain their traditional façades – Courage has its headquarters in a converted row of brewers' houses where Samuel Johnson once worked, while Whitbread too is still based on the original brewery house, decorated now with stags' heads and hunting prints to celebrate Colonel Whitbread's hobbies – the reality which lies behind the façades is much changed. The industry may still be – as one managing director put it – 'a very, very happy show', but it is a much less relaxed show than it once was.

This is partly due to the arrival of a number of outsiders, like Alan Walker, the chairman of Bass Charrington, who was in the sugar business until 1956. So far as Walker is concerned, 'it doesn't matter whether you are making sugar, bolts and nuts or beer, the management skills are the same'. To most of the brewers, this is still heresy, but even the most conservative has had to face the need for a fundamental reappraisal of traditional attitudes. Many have taken computers and organization charts warmly to their bosoms: 'if you can't draw it,' says Swallow, 'it won't work.'

The building industry has not suffered any such profound upheaval; there have been no mergers involving the largest companies. This can be put down largely to family control, sustained perhaps by a continuous construction boom, but it is also has something to do with this being an industry in which the economics of scale are not so apparent above a certain size. There are savings to be made in head office staffs, in plant departments and in regional organizations, but large companies involved in house-building as well as civil engineering are commonly involved in several hundred contracts on different sites at any one time,[2] and their effort is inevitably widely spread. Amalgamations would only increase the spread.

The founding families have generally favoured putting their sons to

[1] Beer sales have doubled in Italy in the last ten years, in France during the last fifteen.

[2] Wimpey currently has about five hundred contracts under way in Britain alone.

work at the earliest possible age: there are few, even today, who would disapprove of Sir Malcolm McAlpine's dictum that the best training for construction bosses was to 'put 'em under a digger that needs repairing'. Frank Taylor, Taylor Woodrow's chairman and managing director, built his first pair of houses with the aid of a bank loan at the age of sixteen, and most of the McAlpines had joined the business by the time they were seventeen. Apart from one member of the fourth generation, none of the McAlpines had had any technical or professional skills or qualifications, and only one has been to a university. The most noticeable exception to this rule is to be found in the more recent generation of the Wates family, a number of whom have been to either Oxford or Cambridge, and continued at British or American business schools. But, again, none has been trained as a civil engineer.

Until the Second World War, almost all the companies which now dominate the industry were primarily speculative house-builders; only McAlpine has not built any houses since the 1920s. It regards them as 'fiddly things, a hell of a lot of little units all over the place' and prefers to concentrate on civil engineering and major buildings, such as office blocks and hotels. McAlpine was large by the turn of the century – it was handling £2m. contracts at a time when Wimpey was concerned only with minor road works in the London suburbs – but it has now been outgrown by both Wimpey and Laing. In 1938, private housing accounted for sixty-five per cent of Wimpey's sales and seventy-five per cent of its profits; in the cases of Taylor Woodrow and Wates, the proportion of turnover was closer to eighty per cent.

The war years, the Labour administrations which followed (with their bias in favour of public housing) and building restrictions helped to bring about a fundamental change in the nature of all these companies, and in some instances speculative house-building became an activity of relatively minor significance. Taylor Woodrow, for example, came out of the war as a builder of airfields and power stations; in 1968, housing accounted for only eight per cent of its business. In the same year, Laing was building scarcely more private houses than thirty years before, and they represented only three per cent of its turnover. Wimpey and Wates have also become markedly less dependent on speculative house-building: it accounts for only a third of Wates's business and a sixth of Wimpey's, although public housing pushes up the proportion of total sales from home-building to two-thirds in the case of Wates and about a half in the case of Wimpey.

Indeed, all the big companies have become more deeply involved in contracting – motorways (Laing had built 123 miles by the end of 1968), atomic power stations, town centre developments, offices, factories, and town halls – and a number of them have put money into building materials and into an increasingly diverse range of activities.

Contracting had obvious enough attractions. The sums involved could be very large (McAlpine won a number of twin atomic reactor contracts worth over £20m.); the profit margins were larger, even if the risks involved were greater; large projects allowed the concentration of management and resources by contrast with the dispersed effort involved in running a string of housing estates; and, finally, they involved neither the increasingly difficult struggle to keep land stocks topped up nor the increasingly tedious process of getting building approval for land, once obtained.

Wates reckons that, instead of the two-year stock of land which was sufficient before the war, it now needs four years' supply on which permission to build has been given. Nor is this surprising since eighty per cent of the land on which Wates was building in 1968 had been the subject of appeals to the Ministry of Housing by local authorities who opposed development. Naturally enough, many companies do not want to keep large amounts of capital tied up in land for long periods.

Their speculative instincts were sometimes, in any case, diverted by the arrival of a boom in commercial property: they wanted to make sure of landing the building contracts involved and, in addition, to share in the handsome profits being made by many of the property developers. Laing, which had already built up a useful portfolio of factories and shops in North London before the war (it still has roughly 110 factories on its rent-roll), decided in 1954 that it would go in for property development as well as property-owning. It looked for its own sites, formed a series of property companies with financial partners (it now has between fifty and sixty altogether), and invariably takes a share in the equity of the finished project. The properties which it owns include the Bull Ring in Birmingham and the St George's Hotel in London. Wates, like Laing, also built up a portfolio of shops and office blocks before the war, and in 1935 began buying up large areas of inner London in the belief that re-development schemes were eventually inevitable; after the war, it extended its holdings and now has a rent roll which, according to Norman Wates, the late chairman, amounts to over £1m. Taylor Woodrow, by contrast, did not set up its own property subsidiary until the early 1960s, because it felt it was basically a contracting business.

Others who preferred not to operate alone, however, formed links with property developers. Wimpey went into partnership with the legendary Harry Hyams in 1957, exchanging – as the Wimpey chairman, Sir Godfrey Mitchell, put it – its own name and money in return for Hyams's expertise. Hyams's job was to find the sites, Wimpey's to supply the bridging money and do the building. Wimpey took a forty per cent share in Hyams's company, Oldham Estate, and eventually Hyams joined the Wimpey Board. But the link with Hyams did not, of course, prevent Wimpey from making other alliances: it owns fifty per cent of the new Euston Centre, through Balgray Investments. Similarly, McAlpine has formed a number of joint property companies, including one – Edger Investments – where it is in partnership with the millionaire solicitor, Gerald Glover.

The chairmen of building and contracting companies are rather apt to play down the importance of their property ventures: Sir Godfrey Mitchell describes Wimpey's investments as 'little side-lines'. The builders have, indeed, had mixed fortunes in their property ventures – apart from their usefulness in providing work; Wimpey, for example, has not yet begun to earn significant returns from its investments, although it could eventually receive very useful dividends from Oldham and Balgray. (Sir Godfrey Mitchell says only that the income will be very welcome in meeting rising costs.) Similarly, although Taylor Woodrow has a property investment of £4.7m., in 1968 it had hardly begun to pay off. Laing and Wates, on the other hand, have been earning useful returns from their investments for some time.

Most of the big companies have been expanding at considerable speed. Laing has trebled its turnover in the last seven years, Taylor Woodrow in the last ten; in other cases, growth has not been so swift, but still impressive. Unfortunately, profit records have often been nothing like so impressive. The profit margins of those companies which publish their results have declined in recent years to levels which are uniformly and (in some instances) disastrously low. Wimpey made 3.4 per cent on turnover (before tax) in 1967, Taylor Woodrow, 3.1 per cent, Costain, 1.6 per cent, Laing, 0.74 of one per cent.[1] Laing, which in 1967 made a profit (before tax) of £851,000 on a turnover of £100m.,

[1] It is worth adding that the profit margins of many big American construction companies are also extremely low. Wimpey believes it is doing well if it makes from 2½ per cent to 3½ per cent on turnover.

had earned over £3m. on a much lower turnover three years before. Wates and McAlpine, which almost certainly have the highest profit margins among the largest companies, do not publish their results.

Some of the reasons for these poor margins are plain enough. Competition is fierce and there have been plenty of contracts which have either made heavy losses or earned only minimal returns; business has fallen back in some sectors in recent years, leaving a good deal of over-capacity and forcing companies to quote low prices or run the risk of losing contracts; labour costs have soared; and there have been some specific disasters, such as Laing's attempt to launch a system building project at a time when supply was greater than demand. It opened three factories to build the components and budgeted for an output of 10,000 units a year. In the event, it produced only 10,000 in three years and had to close one of the factories. The overheads were huge, and so were the losses: to the end of 1968, they amounted to 'many millions'.

But it is also true that there have been more general problems, some of which spring from the dispersed nature of contractors' operations, others from the fact that several have allowed their activities to become extremely diverse – partly with the idea of spreading their risks. Overheads is one of the problems with which Wimpey has been battling, none too successfully so far. It has a staff of 9,000 and overheads have risen from four per cent of turnover (£440,000) in 1944 to 5½ per cent (£10½m.) in 1968. Part of the difficulty is that the company has twenty-one regional headquarters, opened after the war to provide work for all the men who were returning. All are profitable and most are a source of strength (Wimpey does £165m. of its business in Britain) but they also add to the problem of overheads.

It may be significant that the two companies which have restricted themselves either geographically (as in the case of Wates) or in the type and quantity of work which it undertakes (as with McAlpine) should also earn what are probably the best margins in the industry. It was an earlier generation of the Wates family which decreed that the company should stay as close as possible to the Bank of England, and later generations have adhered so faithfully to the concept that sixty per cent of its turnover is now earned in the London area. Although it became national during the war, Wates drew in its horns thereafter and limited its extra-metropolitan activities to the Birmingham area and to Ireland. This concentration of effort enables it to make good use of both its management ability and of a pool of staff labour which it seems to cherish more effectively than most of the other companies.

McAlpine's activity is split evenly between civil engineering and building work. It has only five hundred people at head office and even though it usually has a staff of between fifty and seventy-five on its big sites, its overheads are probably lower than those of either Wimpey or Laing.

A greater spread of outlets, on the other hand, is something which all the big breweries except Guinness have recently been seeking most earnestly.[1] They were basically of two types. There were the large, locally-based brewers, selling over a limited area – Mitchells and Butlers, Ansells, Courage, Watney and Mann all fell into this category – and there was a smaller group (Bass, Worthington, Ind Coope) which had based themselves on Burton because of the water and which, lacking a large conurbation for a base, were forced to become the merchant adventurers of beer. The contrast was quite sharp: whereas a locally-based company like Ansells at one stage did very little trade outside a fifty-mile radius from its Birmingham brewery, Ind Coope did a very low proportion of its business within fifty miles of Burton.

When the wave of mergers began, the two groups sought to remedy their weaknesses by moving in opposite directions. Ind Coope joined forces in 1961 with two regional brewers (Ansells and Tetley Walker, the latter based on Leeds and Liverpool), while Mitchells and Butlers moved into Burton in 1961 by taking over Bass. Ind Coope gained outlets, Mitchells and Butlers national brand names, in the shape of Bass and Worthington.

Whitbread, based largely in the south-east and depending heavily on sales through the free trade – in 1960 it did only a quarter of its turnover through tied outlets – chose a different and, it hoped, less painful, method of expansion. In 1950, it began to build up a circle of 'friends', associated companies in which it had a shareholding (initially ten per cent). This gave Whitbread the wider distribution it wanted for its products; the 'friends' were supposed to gain a certain security from unwelcome take-over attacks and the benefit of Whitbread's advice on technical and financial problems – two Whitbread

[1] Guinness, described by one brewer as 'the cuckoo in the nest', has no public houses in Britain, partly because it had a fair distribution before houses became tied and partly because it gained access to many more during the First World War. During the war, the Government limited the average gravity of English beer to 30°, but Guinness was allowed in at 40°–45°–partly because Guinness only brewed stout and partly because Lloyd George did not want to exacerbate the Irish situation.

men normally joined their Boards. By 1961, there were already seventeen associated companies, controlling over 10,000 public houses between them and Whitbread continued to make further alliances.

At this stage, the company does not seem to have had any intention of progressively undermining the independence of its associates: a loose federation served its purpose. But it rapidly became plain that such a structure would not be able to compete effectively against the centralized power of groups like Allied Breweries; and there was always the possibility that Whitbread would find its friends snatched from under its nose if it did not secure a greater degree of control. The result was that, by early 1969, Whitbread had taken over more than twenty of its associated companies, and clearly intends to mop up the rest at an appropriate moment. It has also jettisoned the earlier ideal of not disturbing either the management or organizations of its partners.

Not all the locally-based brewers were so successful in moving out of their original bases. Courage remains essentially a regional brewer, though it has pushed west and north from London; Watney Mann (produced by a merger of 1958) is still weak in many parts of the country – it was frustrated by Bass from taking over Bent's and thus establishing a strong base in Liverpool and the Lancashire towns; and Scottish and Newcastle is similarly weak in terms of a national chain of tied outlets – roughly sixty per cent of its sales are through the free trade, which yields thinner profit margins.

Not all the mergers which took place were anything like so purposeful as they might appear in hindsight; many were contracted almost casually. Courage, for example, found itself in 1946 with 1,500 public houses in a wide swathe between London and Southampton. In the mid-1950s, Barclay Perkins, which had a line of pubs extending from London to the south coast, asked Courage to do some of its brewing: eventually there was a merger (opposed, incidentally, by the only non-family man on the Courage Board, Swallow). The next to appear was Simmonds of Reading, which felt that it was unable to survive on its own and asked to be taken over, and finally there were two refugees from Eddie Taylor – Bristol Georges and Hole's of Newark. The acquisition of Hole's was a typical example of the way in which British brewers closed their ranks against the Canadian. During the war, Hereward Swallow had got to know Sir Oliver Welby, who held a controlling interest in Hole's; when Taylor appeared on the scene, Welby eventually turned to Swallow.

Nor did all the mergers prove as pleasurable as might have been expected in an industry which prides itself so much on its friendliness and its *esprit de corps*. The aftermath of the alliance between Courage and Barclay Perkins was a salutary experience for both parties. A massive joint Board was set up, which was basically an amalgamation of the two existing Boards, and at managerial level there were, as Swallow said, 'two or three of everybody'. He himself was joint managing director with a Barclay man: they spent their time issuing joint instructions and trying to act as one person. An internecine war developed throughout the group: it ended in a considerable shake-out and a programme of accelerated attrition by which executive directors were to retire at sixty-one.

Elsewhere, the axe was wielded a good deal more sharply. Roughly half the management of Bass was disposed of within a fairly short time of its take-over by Mitchells and Butlers. In that instance the alliance had not been formed on such a cosy basis.

The struggle at Board level was only the first stage of upheaval. Equally painful was the process of integrating local satrapies into a cohesive commercial structure. Although some mergers did not demand major initial reorganization so far at least as the pattern of breweries was concerned (the one which produced Allied is a case in point), the majority brought fundamental change. Courage found that its new acquisitions were still happily under-cutting each other where their sales overlapped, and it had too many brand-names and too many breweries. Whitbread was even more heavily encumbered once it began to take over its associated companies. It had twenty-odd breweries where four or five large units would have been adequate. The price of having so many small units is high: Whitbread's new brewery at Luton can brew at two-thirds the cost of its next most efficient unit. (Two of Bass Charrington's eighteen breweries produce fifty-four per cent of its beer.)

For a time old orders were allowed to survive. The Whitbread chief executive, for example, was scheduled to spend fifteen days of every month visiting the far-flung corners of the empire. This compromise position lasted longer at Whitbread than it did in some other places but even there it could not persist indefinitely. Some of the subsidiary company Boards have now been merged with others; six breweries have been closed in two years; and the Whitbread name has gone up on all the group's pubs. Control of key matters now rests at the centre. The same kind of process has been going on at Courage. The names of all its beers have been changed to Courage, the original independent companies have been replaced by Courage (Eastern), (Central), and (Western), and head office controls cash, product policy, prices and personnel: nobody who earns more than £1,500 a year can be either moved or promoted without reference to head office. In the first year after Bass, Mitchells and Butlers took over Charrington, five breweries were closed.

The same sort of weeding-out process has also been taking place among the brewers' retail outlets. The reasons were equally compelling. For one thing, the maintenance and replacement of public houses and off-licences represents an enormous drain on cash resources, particularly because no depreciation is allowed on them and the money has to be found out of taxed profits. Allied, for example, lays out roughly £9m. a year on maintenance and improvements and admits that it under-spends because of shortage of cash flow. (The industry makes about nine per cent on capital employed.)

With property values rising, it has been a considerable temptation for brewers to sell off those of their outlets on which they could see a good profit; Allied's rule of thumb is that it sells out when the property value is twice the licensed value. Ind Coope had already realized over £10m. from property by the time of the 1961 merger, and Bass Char-rington (which prefers to sit on property rather than money, according to Alan Walker) collects between £1m. and £1¼m. a year from the sale of tied estate. In this respect, it is well endowed because a large proportion of its outlets are urban (Charrington probably has a better collection of sites in London than any other brewer). Those brewers (such as Watney Mann) which have a large proportion of their proper-ties in rural areas, do not find them either so rapidly marketable or so lucrative.

Equally, since the average public house represents a capital invest-ment of between £30,000 and £40,000, brewers have been anxious to improve their turnovers. This has not proved easy, particularly since Britain is littered with villages which have three or four public houses, each of them selling not much more than a hundred barrels of beer annually. The brewers who are strongest in the Midlands and the industrial North are often more fortunate, because public houses in those areas tend to be larger and sales per outlet higher; groups with their strength mainly in the South usually have a large number of rural public houses with small throughputs. Whitbread is now closing outlets at the rate of 120 a year, and the same process is evident in other groups. The pace is likely to be stepped up rather than to slacken.

Mergers have undoubtedly produced economies of scale (with more to come) in production and distribution. As in other industries, it has also brought a reduction of choice as local beers have disappeared.[1] On the other hand, there are still very few genuinely national brands: despite the large amount of money spent on promoting them, brews such as Watney's Red Barrel and Whitbread's Pale Ale are still semi-national in character. Regional preferences remain strong. Double Diamond, one of Allied's pasteurized beers which has achieved national distribution (its production probably equals that of Bass and Worthington put together) was still outsold in 1968 by one of Allied's regional brews, Ansell's Mild.

Nevertheless, the brewers are increasingly breaking out of a mould which had become too parochial. Several had sizeable overseas interests before the Second War (many of them in Imperial territories),[2] but were slow to exploit growing European markets. Now, vigorous efforts are being made to build up European empires, and the favourite method of advance has been to buy up foreign brewers. Allied is now the second largest brewer in Holland, Watney Mann the third largest in Belgium. It is a belated beginning for an industry which, in 1905, already included twelve of the largest twenty-eight companies in Britain.[3]

[1] The brewers point out that there are still 3,000 different beers available in Britain, roughly the same number as in the United States.

[2] Guinness is particularly strong in Nigeria and Malaya.

[3] 'The Emergence of the Large-Scale Company in Great Britain, 1870–1914' by P. L. Payne; *Economic History Review*, Second Series, Volume XX, p. 539.

CHAPTER 11

In the Wake of Empire

The British shipping industry – which, before the turn of the century, carried more than half the world's goods in its bottoms[1] – was in large part the creation of the British Empire. Almost all the biggest companies grew up to carry its colonists, its administrators and its soldiers as well as its goods and its mail. Only Cunard (of those which survive as major independent entities) depended for the greater part of its business on a route – the North Atlantic – which was not marked with Imperial staging-posts and on a country (the United States) which was not coloured red on the map.

The curious fact is that, despite the virtual disappearance of the Empire, it is the companies which based themselves on the old Imperial routes which have survived best. P and O is comfortably the largest shipping group in the world – Ocean Steam and British and Commonwealth are also among the biggest – while Cunard has been fighting for its life after having made a loss in five of the last eight years.

The desire of newly independent nations to have their own shipping lines may have helped demote the British to what one chairman calls 'the rank of junior vice-admiral', but it has not prevented them from retaining a sizeable foothold in every important trading area. British companies now share the Indian and Pakistani trades with national lines; British and Commonwealth has a large holding in Safmarine, South Africa's biggest shipping group, and acts as UK agents for the East Africa National Shipping Line, owned jointly by Kenya, Tanzania, Zambia and Uganda; while Elder Dempster and Blue Funnel (both parts of Ocean Steam) hold the strongest positions in the West

[1] Although Britain's merchant fleet still amounts to 2,500 ships of $20\frac{1}{2}$ million tons, her share of world trade is now little more than one-eighth.

Peninsular and Oriental Steam Navigation

Leadenhall Street, London. Turnover for 1968, £172m. 257 ships, 2.8m. tons. Includes British India, New Zealand Shipping Company and the Union Steam-Ship Company of New Zealand, Hain-Nourse, the Strick Line and Trident Tankers. A member of the Overseas Containers consortium. 20 per cent of Air Holdings.

Ocean Steam Ship

India Buildings, Liverpool. Turnover in 1968, £64.9m. 104 ships, 880,000 tons. Blue Funnel Line, Elder Dempster, Glen Line. Also a member of Overseas Containers.

Cunard

St James's Square, London. Turnover in 1968, £56.5m. 68 ships, 733,000 tons. Owns Queen Elizabeth 2. Cargo interests include the Port Line and Cunard-Brocklebank. Member of the Associated Container Transportation and Atlantic Container Line consortia.

British and Commonwealth Shipping

St Mary Axe, London. Turnover in 1968, £50m. 67 ships, 638,000 tons. Clan Line, Union-Castle. Member of Overseas Containers Limited. Also owns British United Airways and 46 per cent of Air Holdings.

African and Far Eastern trades. Furthermore, it is the British who are most frequently asked to chair international shipping bodies and many of the 300–400 'conferences' which fix freight rates in their own areas.

It is, therefore, little wonder that the chairmen of companies which have relatively little to do with the New World count their blessings and recall the lines which have foundered on the South American trade. They themselves hardly earn a luxurious living – shipping's return on capital has been amongst the lowest in British industry for a number of years – but at least they have to suffer neither South American governments which add thirty per cent to customs duties for goods carried in foreign ships nor the US Federal Maritime Commission, which busies itself ensuring that ships which run on the North Atlantic do not operate a cosy cartel.

Nor is the imperial past entirely dead. Mementoes remain : one of the panoramic seascapes in the foyer of Cayzer House carries the subscription 'from the ends of the earth at the Empire's need'. There are memories, too; P and O directors can remember when Calcutta was the second city of the Empire, when the British India fleet alone contained 122 ships and when shipping nabobs who made their fortunes in the East retired at forty-seven; and the tradition has only recently been broken that the chairman of P and O should have been reared in the offices of British India's managing agents in Calcutta, Mackinnon Mackenzie. Sir Donald Anderson is the first chairman who was not 'bred' in India. Nor is ingrained tradition easily forgotten: 'we are all trailing clouds of colonial duty somewhere along the line', said a director of one shipping company.

The impression is perhaps all the stronger because the big shipping companies now seem to attract young men who might in earlier times have become functionaries of Empire. 'If you like,' said Anderson, 'they're the sort who might have run Mashonaland,' and Ford Geddes, one of P and O's deputy chairmen, did not believe he could have found such an interesting job anywhere else, except perhaps by becoming a District Officer in Tanganyika. Anderson and Geddes are both wealthy men, but the shipping business has more than its share of people who would be prepared to work for lower salaries, who look down on stockbrokers as commission-grubbers, who have been drawn to an industry which – despite the coming of giant oil tankers and container ships – still retains some aura of romance.

Lindsay Alexander, now a director of Ocean Steam, was one who joined 'by romantic vision'. He arrived in Liverpool after the war with a First in History from Oxford and having done extremely well in the Foreign Service examination. A clerk gave him two documents to read while he waited: one was the Fleet Book and the second the Cable Sheet. Among the cables, Alexander found one which had been sent from Sourabaya and which said that the 'Tyndareus' had called at Panarukan, Pasarukan and Banjuwangi on the 20th and was due in Sourabaya at daylight on the 21st loaded with 1,282 bales of tobacco. It made Alexander think of Conrad and the Spice Islands. Even finance directors can be moved by the same emotions: John Mitchell of P and O, although aware that the company's ships did not carry apes and peacocks, was still conscious of 'a romantic something'.

But men are also drawn to shipping by a variety of other motives. One is a complex kind of snobbery. Compared, for example, with the retail trade or manufacturing industry, shipping is very acceptable socially. This may have something to do with its imperial heritage, but it may also be connected with the fact that it is a service industry which does not soil its hands with anything so sordid as selling shoes or making washing machines: until recently, shipping men preferred to talk about 'canvassing for cargo' rather than use the word 'selling'. 'It's more like a regiment than a factory', as one director put it.

Again, shipping is more closely allied (geographically and in spirit) to the City of London than it is to manufacturing industry. Most of the big companies are grouped within a quarter-mile radius of the Baltic Exchange, their directors generally belong only to the Boards of banks and insurance companies, and the club which they commonly use – the City of London – was founded by the Duke of Wellington as a place where he could conveniently meet City gentlemen. It was founded for the benefit of merchants, shipowners and bankers, but does not, I was told, take in drapers.

In the case of P and O, there is the added cachet of being a chartered company – the first charter was granted by Queen Victoria in 1840. As one director pointed out, the charter puts P and O in the same bracket as the Bank of England.

All this has helped make a number of the big shipping companies something of a class preserve, a cross between clubs and regiments, a place where a Scottish accent is acceptable but not a Northern one, and where the director of one large group can say that 'nobody who grates will find a home here'.

Critics within the industry believe that these attitudes may help to explain why some shipowners still treat their businesses as a sort of hobby and why there has been such a widespread indifference to levels of profitability. Among shipping men, certainly, professionalism has tended to be equated with mastery of the logistics of ship operation; in this respect, it resembles other transport enterprises, like British Rail. The industry has also been backward in introducing techniques such as marketing and budgetary control.

Yet, to be fair, there is no evidence that the big Continental shipowners produce any better return on capital than their British counterparts (all Americans used to be dismissed as 'third-rate operators' and most still are) and the resignation which some shipping men are apt to display when the subject of profitability comes up should not be put down entirely to apathy. The truth is that they often feel themselves in the grip of circumstances over which they have little control: Shell, they say, may be able to achieve results by 'belly-aching about profits', but the best they can do is to achieve the highest possible load-factor.

They are certainly at the mercy of accidents both of nature and of trade: a late fruit season in Tasmania or exceptionally heavy purchases of Australian wool by the Japanese can seriously affect returns. A ship expecting to carry 25,000 bales of wool from Melbourne to an English destination is suddenly struggling to fill its holds with something else. Reverses like this make it virtually impossible to set realistic profit targets.

Again, the conference system acts not only as a safety-net but also as a strait-jacket. The major British firms grew by offering 'liner' services, analogous to Corporation bus companies, in that they represent an undertaking to run regular journeys over a set route.[1] Shippers may promise to bring all their goods to companies within the conference and, in return, the shipowners not only give a discount on the rates fixed by the conference but also shoulder the burden of carrying some cargoes which they know will be unprofitable.

The shipowners are, of course, free to opt out of the arrangement at any time, but they tend to show the same reluctance as railwaymen in cutting lines. This is partly because they feel an obligation to continue the service, partly because the trade in question is providing a steady business and will, they hope, turn out to be profitable in the long run and partly because they have a heavy investment in the ships involved: as one P and O director put it, 'you can't scrap ships like petrol stations'. There is, in some cases, the additional point that, like railway managers, shipping men develop a love for their routes and services which is based on the sheer pleasure of being able to operate complicated schedules. (Cunard has always been looked upon as little better than a trans-Atlantic ferry service.) This rapture in their own virtuosity only tends to confirm a natural conservatism.

At the end of the war, companies like P and O and Ocean Steam set about rebuilding their pre-war liner businesses. This involved heavy new investment – a large proportion of their fleets had been destroyed – but it was where their expertise lay. The P and O group had been essentially a collection of cargo liner companies with one big passenger operator, in the shape of Peninsular and Oriental itself, while Ocean Steam had consisted almost entirely of cargo liners.

In the first years after the war, traditional liner businesses seemed to fare well enough. There was a world-wide shortage of transport vehicles of all sorts and the shipowners managed to earn a useful return on their

---

[1] Tramps, on the other hand, are much more like taxis: they are chartered for particular journeys or a particular period of time. Cruise liners, oil tankers and bulk carriers are all tramps in that sense.

capital: as late as 1957, British and Commonwealth was earning fourteen per cent (before tax), Ocean over eight, P and O almost nine per cent.[1] To companies like P and O, which had failed to pay a dividend in several of the pre-war years, this seemed like a very reasonable living indeed.

But it soon became clear that the post-war years had brought a fundamental change in the climate in which shipping had to operate. For one thing, more and more governments (as operators of national lines) began to force their way into the conference system: every country wanted its own mercantile marine. They were not only concerned to take part of the trade for themselves – a demand which the other shipowners were hardly in a position to resist – but they also wanted to keep down rates for balance of payments reasons. This introduced a completely new motive into the price-fixing debates: before the war, the merchants with whom British shipowners then dealt had generally been more concerned with the quality of service provided than with the rates. In some cases, governments also seem to have felt that they were merely recouping what had been taken from them during the years of 'imperial exploitation'.

Whatever the motive, European liner operators have come under intense pressure in a number of areas. They complain that, although they are a service industry, they cannot be expected to provide the service for next to nothing – and resent approaches from governments which demand that rates be kept down so that they can remain competitive in overseas markets.

Some companies have been luckier than others. Ocean Steam, which collects roughly two-thirds of its revenue from trading in an arc which begins in Ceylon and ends in Japan, has found itself in an area which has proved comparatively prosperous and stable and in which it has not suffered unduly from governmental interference; it also has a monopoly of the trade from the Far East to Britain's west coast. Its greatest challenge came in the mid-1950s when the Mitsui Line was fighting to capture business. The Far Eastern Freight Conference (of which Ocean's companies are leading members) cut its rates to hold off the attack and then finally allowed the Japanese into the ring, but with only a modest proportion of the business.

P and O, with its much more widely spread empire, found itself with a heavy involvement in the Indian sub-continent,[2] and while its trades

[1] By 1961, P and O's return had sunk to 0·4 per cent.
[2] British India still has no less than 25 liner trades.

based on India are still profitable in shipping terms, the returns are hardly exciting. The same is true of some of the trades between Britain and the Far East. P and O has also been forced out of the business of carrying migrants to the Antipodes by the Italians and the arrival of the big jets has reduced its passenger business to Australia by roughly fifteen per cent: rather over-optimistically, perhaps, it thinks the worst is now over.

Loyalty to the liner trades may have had something to do with the fact that both P and O and Ocean Steam at first tended to respond rather inflexibly to the new post-war situation. Ocean Steam, for example, seems to have completely missed the increasing importance of the oil tanker. This was probably because it regarded itself as a specialist operator: its staffs, it believed, were not trained to run cheap ships for bulk cargoes. P and O, for its part, was late into the tanker business: its first ship was not ordered until 1955, which left it with approximately three years of good chartering rates and a fleet of small ships. (Ironically, it would have been even worse off if it had been able to order more of the 30–50,000 tonners which it wanted to build. These are now uneconomic, whereas the 18,000-tonners which made up the bulk of P and O's early tanker fleet are in good demand for the carriage of products.)

The same charge, on the other hand, cannot be levelled at British and Commonwealth, which had its first oil tankers on charter to British Petroleum in 1952. The company's flexibility owes a good deal to its presiding genius, Sir Nicholas Cayzer, who is dedicated to profit rather than to shipping. British and Commonwealth was cutting down on oil tankers at roughly the same time as P and O was becoming more interested.

P and O has shown itself progressively more willing to change its traditional pattern of operation. It soon became aware that it would have to operate its passenger ships as 'tramps', and now has the largest cruising business in the world.[1] In the 1960s, it formed a new business division and by 1970 roughly forty per cent of the book value of its fleet will consist of tankers and bulk carriers, activities which did not exist in 1957.

It has also committed itself wholeheartedly (in consort with Ocean Steam, British and Commonwealth and Furness Withy – they have formed a new joint company, Overseas Containers Limited) to a process

[1] Its cruises from Australia and the United States, and the new Pacific routes which it began to open up in 1954, are among the most profitable parts of its business.

which will mean a revolution for most of the important cargo liner trades: the introduction of container ships. In the Australian trade, for example, where the change-over has already begun, there will be only nine ships instead of about forty and the speed with which ships can be unloaded and loaded (forty-eight hours instead of two–three weeks) means that each ship can make five round-trips a year to Australia instead of two-and-a-half.[1] The partners are hoping that the container ships will show a return on capital of perhaps fifteen per cent.

Cunard has found itself faced with greater problems than any of the other big shipping companies, and it has been least successful in coping with them. Its predicament sprang from the fact that, in 1956, over half its revenue came from passenger traffic on the North Atlantic: it was not prepared for the devastating impact which the big jets were to make on its business and, although it tried to cushion the blow by means of a short-lived partnership with BOAC, the price of unpreparedness was high: between 1961 and 1967, Cunard lost over £17m. on its passenger ships. In these circumstances, rapid retreat was essential and in 1969 only twenty per cent of its revenue will be earned by its passenger services. P and O and British and Commonwealth have managed to pare down their passenger businesses rather more gracefully, but the decline has still been marked: British and Commonwealth, which had fourteen passenger vessels in 1962, now has only three, and by 1970 P and O will have halved the number of passenger ships which it owned in 1957 (forty-four).

The P and O group used to be an extremely loosely-knit affair. Its architect, Lord Inchcape, collected companies and then granted them almost complete independence: they kept their own colours, competed with each other, preferred to consult Lloyd's rather than P and O and did not even tell Inchcape when they proposed to build new ships. This, presumably, was his method of harnessing the tribal loyalties of his various acquisitions and at the same time keeping at bay the jealousy they felt towards the big company which had taken away their sovereignty. His successors do not doubt his good sense and point to Owen Phillips, Lord Kylsant, as an example of a similarly ambitious man who bought up the Royal Mail, Elder Dempster and White Star

[1] The typical container ship carries over 1,100 containers – aluminium and steel boxes capable of holding twenty tons of cargo. They are obviously a good deal easier to handle than, say, 200,000 boxes of fruit, which had to be sorted into perhaps 350 marques.

Lines, but then came to grief partly because he tried to create a highly centralized group.

P and O did gradually increase its power of financial surveillance, but attempts to extend its influence were bitterly resisted. Sir Donald Anderson, who became chairman in 1960, clearly regards himself as a physician rather than a surgeon. 'With the bosses of the lines in the group,' he said in 1967, 'I don't give orders, I try to persuade them. If a man disagrees, he doesn't get the sack, he just isn't persuaded. There are strong tribal feelings and you must draw people along with you. If you try to push them, they simply won't play, they'll just be bloody surly. It is impossible to get competent men to do things they don't want to do – you either persuade them or wait until they die.'

This may sound like an extreme *laisser-faire* philosophy, but there are few shipping men inside or outside P and O who doubt Anderson's wisdom: as the director of another group put it, 'if it hadn't been for his restraint, the centrifugal forces would have dragged P and O apart'.

The result is that progress towards making P and O into a recognizable entity has been slow and is only now beginning to bear fruit. Anderson has been helped by the fact that a number of the group's companies have been going through difficult times and that new business ventures – such as the tanker-building programme – have been group projects. The coming of the container ship will also progressively reduce the power of the individual cargo liner companies: the Overseas Containers consortium will take over most of their functions.

The atmosphere at the new P and O headquarters in Leadenhall Street is now beginning to reflect this process of unification. There are group executives who do not belong to the individual companies and a group executive committee on which the chairmen of the companies sit, some of the companies have their offices in the headquarters building instead of being scattered about the City in separate premises, and the senior staff of all the companies belong to the headquarters luncheon mess; the result is that they now meet each other, which happened only rarely in the past. P and O has also begun to recruit managers on a group basis.

Anderson has not allowed these problems to deter him from a consistently expansionist policy at a time when others have been either holding back or even getting out of the shipping business: P and O now has on order a greater tonnage – 1.6m. – than is currently *owned* by any other shipping company in Britain. None of this is merely a replacement for existing ships: it represents expansion into fields unknown to

P and O ten years ago. The hope is that the new tankers and bulk carriers will yield better returns than its liner businesses;[1] Anderson's bench-mark is ten per cent.

His major concern is that P and O will not reap adequate reward for its optimism because the market is flooded with ships built on cheap, borrowed money. Anderson looks back with pleasure to the days when shipowners paid cash for their new ships; now they put down only twenty per cent and borrow the rest at $5\frac{1}{2}$ per cent and this, in his view, has led to over-building. But although P and O would now prefer the end of credit if only to keep less well-endowed competitors out of the field, its own ability to borrow is one reason why it has been able to move from a shortage of cash to a surplus. Indeed, its cash flow – which rose from £18m. in 1966 to £33 m. in 1968 – is now almost embarrassingly large and, since the money is not needed to finance the shipbuilding programme, Anderson will have to find something else to do with it.

In Ocean Steam's case, the power of headquarters has always been paramount, and Ocean's managing directors – who operate not merely from one building but from one room – have traditionally exercised a tight control over all parts of the business. Each day at noon, the directors and departmental heads in Liverpool gather in a meeting sometimes known as Morning Prayers to check the movements of the fleet. The meeting, which generally lasts between four and seven minutes, enshrines an established company principle: everybody connected with shipping management should know what everybody else is doing.

Ocean Steam also has a reputation for doing things in very much its own way and for not only being right in the majority of cases but for behaving as though it could scarcely be otherwise given the intellectual abilities of its managers. This quality is known in the shipping world as 'Holtishness'.[2] Alone among the big groups, Ocean Steam does not insure any of its vessels because it does not see why it should subsidize other companies who do not run their shows as well as it runs its own.

---

[1] One of the major problems of operating a tanker fleet is assessing charter rates accurately enough to ensure the projected return over what is often a thirteen-year period: three for building the tanker and ten for the charter period. This means, for example, estimating Pakistani wage rates thirteen years ahead (most of P and O's ratings are Pakistanis) and since the cost of provisions in various parts of the world also has to be taken into account, owners in 1969 have to try to guess the cost of eggs in Rio de Janeiro in 1982.

[2] The company was founded by Philip and Alfred Holt.

So far as losses go, the policy has paid off; in the last ninety years, the group has lost only a handful of ships in peace-time. 'Holtishness' has also shown its worth in hard cash terms. In most recent years, it has had a better return on capital than the other big shipping groups, although its average – at something over $4\frac{1}{2}$ per cent – is still only modest.

Ocean Steam's reputation for intellectual arrogance and for rightness is founded on high intelligence, a style of management unique in British industry and specialization in cargo liners. It has been hiring top-class brains for over fifty years – the first non-family recruit, Roland Thornton, who had taken a First in Greats at Balliol, was typical of those who followed – and the company is now liberally sprinkled with Firsts in subjects like zoology, classics, English and history. Its Etonians include a former President of Pop. The annual additions to this élite are put through a stringent vetting procedure – a 'black-ball' from any of the eleven managing directors is enough to disqualify a candidate – and an equally thorough training which lasts seven years.

If and when they eventually become managing directors, they take their place in what is variously described as the Common Management Room or the Quarter Deck. The room, which houses all the managing directors – they sit facing each other at pairs of desks – has no doors and its only symbol of elevation is a six-inch step up to a false floor. The managing directors have only one telephone each and must abide by strict rules: no smoking in offices between nine and half-past five, no tea-cups on tables.

The process of management is based on a series of open debates, with every idea submitted to the interplay of argument. Six of the eleven are responsible for one of the group's main areas of profitability and each of them has a deputy, and this in itself leads to what is effectively a series of small and informal sub-committees. Nor is there very much in the way of hierarchical structure among the eleven: the senior director is merely *prior inter pares*. The high level of noise makes it difficult for newcomers to settle down, but they eventually learn to fit in the paper-work between discussions. There are facilities available when debates turn into rows; the contestants retire to one of a series of interview rooms – 'behind the fives courts sort of thing'. The system clearly has its annoyances, but it means that everything is thrashed out in the open and it gives each of the managing directors an awareness of all the activities of the group.

Ocean Steam has kept its business as simple as its style of management. It has ignored oil tankers and only moved outside cargo liner ships for the first time in 1969 when it joined up with P and O on the building of two chemical bulk carriers. This concentration on cargo liners means that, once the Far Eastern trade is containerized, the management of something like three-quarters of Ocean Steam's business will have been taken over by Overseas Containers: it will be left with a large investment in OCL and its West African trade. It is already prepared for this fundamental change: large parts of its fleet will become obsolescent in the early 1970s.

Whatever changes the future may bring, both Ocean Steam and P and O are committed to shipping; British and Commonwealth is not. 'We do not make a fetish of being in shipping,' said Sir Nicholas Cayzer, who compares the group with conglomerates like Thomas Tilling. British and Commonwealth has built comparatively few new ships of its own in recent years and – apart from its share in those now on order for OCL – it has no new tonnage building. Indeed, it has made a practice of chartering where this seems to make economic sense. The reason for this retrenchment is simple enough; Cayzer is convinced that, for the moment, he can earn a better return on the company's money by expanding in other fields (although he did make twelve per cent on his shipping capital in 1968). He is also reconciled to the thought that virtually all B and C's shipping business will eventually take the form of trade investments, either in Safmarine or OCL.

Certainly not all B and C's shipping ventures have proved as profitable as Cayzer hoped. Although it made a handsome return on the twenty-six standard war-built ships which it picked up after the war, the take-over of the Union-Castle Line in 1955 is now rated to have been 'neither a good buy nor a bad one'. What it meant was that the Cayzers added a big investment in passenger services to their traditional Clan Line cargo business only a few years before those passenger services had to be severely contracted; it did, however, give them control of the major line in the South African trade, a trade in which the Clan Line had considerable interests.

The Cayzers, however, were quick to move their money into a variety of other activities. They have had an investment in aircraft since 1951, when they bought a half-share in Hunting Clan, which ran trooping services among other things; British and Commonwealth now owns British United Airways, and has a substantial interest in three large (and profitable) travel agencies. In the early 1950s, the Cayzers began to build up the investment side of the business and now have a considerable portfolio.

The Cayzer Group also owns a collection of diverse industrial businesses – including companies making microscopes and plastic boats – and it has, in the past, made gramophone records with a fair degree of success. Not all these ventures have produced quick results – Sir Nicholas is hoping that BUA will make its first profit in 1969 – but his general principle is to dispose rapidly of investments which do not seem likely to produce good returns in the short run.

Some traditional shipping men seem to find this approach both distasteful and rather disturbing: Cayzer, they imply, is no longer really one of them. More to the point, they think British and Commonwealth is too dependent on one man; whether it will be able to produce an adequate replacement when Cayzer retires remains to be seen.

Cunard, on the other hand, is regarded as something of an outsider partly because of its poor record in recent years. Sir Basil Smallpeice, who became chairman in 1965, could hardly have begun to learn the business at a more difficult time: Cunard had been making losses on its passenger ships for four years and it was questionable how many could survive. It had also just decided to build the Queen Elizabeth 2, a project which Smallpeice was 'happy to go along with' though doubting whether such large ships could be economic in the long term. Other passenger liner operators had (and still have) even greater doubts. Fully aware that P and O's largest ships (Canberra and Oriana) find it hard to make a good living, they cannot see how the QE2 will succeed once its initial glamour has worn off.

Until 1957, everything had seemed to go right for Cunard: the old Queens (Mary and Elizabeth) were making a quarter of a million pounds' profit on many of their voyages. Cunard's prosperity, however, also served to obscure some serious weaknesses both of organization and management, weaknesses which were to become only too apparent when business turned down.

To begin with, after the death in 1947 of Sir Percy Bates (who had brought both the Queen Elizabeth and the Queen Mary into service), the succession to the Cunard chairmanship had become unclear. Because the man who had been groomed was in poor health, Bates was succeeded by his brother Fred, a banker. When Fred Bates died in 1952, Colonel Denis Bates (who was already sixty-eight) was pressed to move in as a stop-gap. He was followed in 1959 by Sir John Brocklebank. During much of this period, the day-to-day running of the company was left to a series of general managers who wielded considerable authority.

The organization of the company also had curious features. Cunard's head office, for example, remained in Liverpool despite the fact that between eighty-five and ninety per cent of its passengers sailed from Southampton. This hardly helped the relationship between sea and shore staffs. Again, it maintained a chain of branch offices in cities like Bradford and Birmingham despite the arrival of the travel agencies.

When Smallpeice took over, he scrapped the general manager system, moved Cunard's passenger line headquarters from Liverpool to Southampton, cut down the number of branch offices both in Britain and the United States and brought in a number of outsiders. He also pointed out in his first annual report that the company had only been kept going by sales of investments and property which had raised £13m. and tax recoveries which had brought in another £11.8m.

Nor did the future look any brighter. By 1965, the number of passengers travelling across the North Atlantic by sea had fallen to 650,000 (in 1957, one million had made the voyage) and the proportion of transatlantic journeys made by sea had fallen from fifty per cent to only fourteen per cent. The Queens had lost more than £1½m. between them in 1964.

Smallpeice eventually set about selling off five of the passenger fleet; only Carmania and Franconia are now left of the ships which he took over in 1965, and the first Queen Elizabeth was sold for more than £3½m. to an American company in 1969 for use as a holiday centre. But Smallpeice now rests considerable hope in the QE2, which he believes will have operating costs twenty per cent lower than her predecessor and will yield an annual profit of the order of £1m. after paying off interest of £900,000 on the Government loan which financed her construction.

On the cargo side of the business, which has become an increasingly large part of Cunard's declining turnover, Smallpeice has joined two container consortia and has put Cunard's best property – the Port Line, which has proved a modest profit-earner over the years – under the management of Blue Star.

Whether the QE2 justifies Smallpeice's optimism or not, Cunard evidently has plenty of other problems. It is still short of management and its morale has received a severe battering. When the new men moved in, old company servants began to feel that their experience in Cunard stood them in bad rather than good stead. Apart from anything else, Smallpeice has to re-establish some sort of *esprit de corps*: at the moment, Cunard is a formless and (despite the fact that it managed to make a profit again in 1968) struggling enterprise. Smallpeice is fortunate that he is blessed with low blood-pressure; it is a characteristic which has been useful in the past and is likely to be just as useful in the future.

But the upheavals which have taken place in the shipping world so far are merely a beginning. A merger between P and O and Ocean Steam, for example, is a possibility, if only because Ocean Steam will have little of its own left to manage by the time the container revolution has run its course; P and O certainly has plenty of cash in its purse. Prophets within the industry make more far-reaching predictions: they suggest that Overseas Containers may become the basis of a British Shipping Corporation. Whatever happens, the independent shipowner is becoming more and more a figure of the past: consortia and joint projects are the order of the day. Like the British Army, the shipping industry has fewer and fewer regiments.

CHAPTER 12

The Engineers

The engineering industry is now as crucial to the economy as textiles once was. No other industry, however, was so affected by the end of the sellers' market and the arrival of competition in the later 1950s, and none has gone through a more profound upheaval in the last decade.

The old world, in which competition had been reduced to a minimum, disappeared in those years. It had been the golden era of the trade association, when the standing of men related to their standing in the association, and when – as Kenneth Bond, General and English Electric's present deputy managing director, put it – 'people associated with their competitors rather than their customers'. Unpleasantness was thereby avoided. 'In the old days,' said the director of one large engineering company, 'if a chap had been doing a piece of business for a long time, that contract was his preserve and other companies never did anything unethical like offering better terms.' The occasional mavericks who tried to take away business from other firms – like Sir Allen Clark, who built up Plessey – were referred to as 'pirates'. The existence of a network of gentlemen's agreements provided no spur to greater efficiency in the factories.

It was a world of comfortable conformity, in which everybody did well enough and nobody upset the apple cart. There was the company aeroplane, for the chairman's use only, hunting and fishing rights for the privileged few on the Board, and ample expense accounts. The chairman was treated like God, and since those who ruled in a highly dictatorial or idiosyncratic style tended to surround themselves with weaker men, they were often not confronted with the distasteful situations which occurred in their businesses. Incompetent as managers

British Leyland Motor Corporation

Berkeley Square, London. Turnover £974m. in 1968. Cars –
Austin, Morris, Triumph, Jaguar, Rover – trucks and buses.
Construction equipment.

General Electric and English Electric Company

Headquarters, Stanhope Gate, London. Turnover, £950m. in
1968–9. Everything from turbo-generators to electric light bulbs.
Behind Osram, Hotpoint and Morphy-Richards. 40 per cent
shareholding in British Aircraft Corporation, 18 per cent in
International Computers.

Ford Motor Company

Warley, Essex. Turnover £500m. (estimated) in 1968. Cars –
Escort, Cortina, Capri, Corsair, Zephyr, Zodiac – trucks, vans and
tractors. Subsidiary of Ford USA.

Guest, Keen and Nettlefolds

Smethwick, Worcestershire. Turnover £433m. in 1968. Huge
range of engineering products from giant forgings to office furniture and 80,000 varieties of nuts, bolts and screws. A third of turnover goes to the motor industry – wheels, propeller shafts, etc.

Hawker Siddeley Group

St James's Square, London. Turnover £382m. in 1968. Largest
aerospace group outside the United States: including the Trident,
Comet and Buccaneer aircraft and the Firestreak and Seaslug
missiles. Also diesel engines and locomotives.

Rolls-Royce

Derby. Turnover £319m. in 1968. Aero engines, cars, diesel
engines, industrial and marine gas turbines. 20 per cent share in
British Aircraft Corporation.

Tube Investments

St James's, London. Turnover £250m. in 1968. Largest manufacturer of precision steel tubes in the world, biggest maker of pedal
cycles. Also domestic appliances. Behind Radiation, Raleigh,
Creda, Baco.

Vauxhall Motors

Luton, Bedfordshire. Turnover of £216m. in 1968. Cars – Viva,
Victor, Viscount – and Bedford trucks. Subsidiary of General
Motors of the United States.

British Aircraft Corporation

Pall Mall, London. Turnover £191m. in 1968. BAC 111, VC 10,
Concorde, Jaguar, Lightning. Owned 40–40–20 by General
Electric and English Electric, Vickers and Rolls-Royce.

The Engineers

Rootes Motors

Devonshire House, Piccadilly. Turnover of £176m. in 1968. Cars – Hillman, Sunbeam, Singer and Humber – and Dodge trucks. Subsidiary of the Chrysler Corporation of America.

Plessey

Ilford, Essex. Turnover £165m. in 1968. Mainly telecommunications and electronics – systems, equipment and components. Holds 18 per cent shareholding in International Computers.

Vickers

Millbank, London. Turnover £154m. in 1968. Ships, including nuclear submarines, heavy engineering products, printing machinery, office equipment, chemical plants and medical engineering. 40 per cent share in British Aircraft Corporation, 12.6 per cent in International Computers.

International Computers Limited

Putney, London. Turnover of £92m. in 1968. Computers, data processing equipment.

Ferranti

Hollinwood, Manchester. Turnover of about £55m. in 1968. Transformers, meters, electronics, avionics, numerical control machines. Holds 5.7 per cent of shares in International Computers.

themselves, they often did not recognize the managerial dead wood which surrounded them so that their Boards, and the Boards of their subsidiaries, were frequently stuffed with old retainers and incompetent friends.

It was also, in many companies, the heyday of the engineer. At a time when products sold themselves and prices were rigged, companies concentrated on that technical excellence which had always been an important part of the British engineering tradition. 'All the standards,' said Sir Joseph Latham, who was struggling to pull AEI round when Weinstock of GEC made his take-over bid in 1967, 'were engineering standards.' In some companies, engineers became general managers almost overnight, with no formal training and frequently little in the way of natural ability. Having arrived, their first priority was to turn out their own idea of 'fine gear': profit was incidental.

Conversely, the arts of selling and cost control scarcely existed, and both accountants and salesmen were thought of as lesser breeds of men. Amongst the heavy engineers this was perhaps not altogether

surprising, but it was similar even in some of the big motor manufacturers. 'In the old days,' said a former senior executive with one of
them, 'salesmen were simply regarded as order takers or glad-hand
men. They were never consulted about new models – they were simply
told, there's the car, now bloody well sell it.' When the end of the sellers'
market came, new skills as well as new philosophies had to be learnt.
'The environment of the company and of the country was so engineer-
dominated,' said Lord Nelson, formerly chairman of English Electric
and now chairman of General Electric and English Electric, 'that it
took a long time to switch over to being price-oriented.'

This implicit contempt for the salesman in a number of companies
amounted to a complete separation between the men who produced
goods and the men who sold them. Kenneth Bond recalled the sort of
thing that used to happen: 'The salesman might say he could sell 1,000
of a particular item, and he was told by the works that the ex-factory
price would be £10. He replied that the price must be £5. All right,
the factory people would say, but you must have 5,000 of them. He
took them – 4,000 couldn't be sold and stayed in the store-room. This
sort of thing made the salesmen very bitter.' There was the same
separation in the old English Electric company. 'Our works were not
businesses,' said Viscount Caldecote, who was a director of the company. 'They only knew they'd made the stuff at the price they'd been
told – selling it was somebody else's responsibility.'

The dominance of engineers and the rarity of influential finance
directors meant that work was taken on because it was technically
interesting rather than likely to yield a profit. Contracts for atomic
power stations which turned out to be highly unprofitable were
celebrated. 'If anybody wanted us to make something that hadn't
been made before,' said Sir Jack Scamp of General Electric and English
Electric, 'we regarded it as a compliment. If anybody had asked whether
it was going to be worthwhile in terms of profit, the reply would probably have been "somebody has to do it".' At Vickers, whose management felt constrained to try and fill the massive capacity developed in
wartime, there was the same craft pride. 'In the past,' said a senior
executive at Barrow, 'if somebody asked "can you make this?", we said
"by God we can!"' At Accles and Pollock, for a long time the most
profitable of Tube Investment's tube-producing subsidiaries, products
were sometimes developed for their own sake rather than because they
were going to be profitable, according to the present managing director
Dr John Sawkill. The result, he added, was that 'we could do tubes

for the insemination of queen bees, but not the products of tomorrow.'

Many companies became jacks-of-all-trades. 'We took the line that we could do anything,' said Sawkill, 'and the result was that we got anything. All kinds of orders were taken on – two feet here, fifty feet there – I think at one time we had 1,000 customers under £5 and not one in six figures.' Frequently the trouble was that profit was calculated on the output of an entire works and not on the basis of individual products. John Barber, who moved to AEI as finance director from Ford, recalls visiting one factory turning out two hundred different products and discovering that the manager had no idea which were profitable. There was sometimes surprising inaccuracy about even basic information, as English Electric discovered when they set about taking over one of AEI's small subsidiary companies. 'We asked them to give us their figures,' said George Riddell, now joint deputy managing director of General Electric and English Electric 'and when they did finally produce something, we found that the turnover figure was out by £100,000 on a total of less than £500,000.'

Particularly among the heavy engineering companies which prided themselves on their paternalism, there was the same laxness on labour costs – even when profits began to decline; factories turning out unprofitable products and operating at a fraction of their capacity were allowed to continue in business. Even in the viable plants, there had been substantial hoarding of labour; AEI was able to lose 9,000 workers without major complaint from anyone, and production actually rose – 'people were always tucking something away as a safeguard,' said Sir Joseph Latham. At one Midlands engineering company, for example, twenty carpenters who had arrived to put a new storey onto the office block stayed on. 'Engineers are very keen on the idea of continuity', said George Boswell, who was director of personnel at English Electric. 'Once they have got Joe trained, they want to keep him – they want a good reliability factor even when the return is low. This is particularly so if they are insulated from the market.'

Some companies – such as Vickers – prided themselves on offering stability of employment at almost any cost and – like an army unit – seemed more concerned with morale and *esprit de corps* than with the impact on profits. 'Barring accidents,' a Vickers senior executive at Barrow told me, 'you're here for the duration. We don't kick people out who make mistakes. If a man made one mistake, you'd put your arm round his shoulder and call him a silly bugger. If he did it a dozen times, then you'd give him a new job.' Vickers was not alone in its tolerance.

Ray Brookes, now chairman of GKN, recalls that when a man was sacked from the forgings plant which he was running, he could always get a job at a nearby GKN plant, then known locally as 'the Convalescent Home'.

Organization and management had also not kept pace with the rapid post-war growth of many companies. By the end of the 1950s, they were different enterprises and bursting at the seams. The loudest creaking noises came from those, like Hawker and GKN, which were run as holding companies but with nothing very much in the way of headquarters staff to hold them. Sir Kenneth Peacock, at GKN, had more than ninety people reporting directly to him, and sat on the Boards of each of the numerous subsidiaries. Others with small headquarters staffs, like Tube Investments, seemed to spend a great deal of time on the acquisition of new subsidiaries and the chairman, Sir Ivan Stedeford, was consequently not often seen in some parts of his empire. The TI subsidiaries which wanted cash for capital investment wrote to Sir Ivan and, in due course, received a reply, by letter : there was no established procedure for discussing new expenditure proposals.

It also occurred to many companies only late in the day that they needed to plan the recruitment of managers to run their expanding empires. (Ford and Rolls-Royce were among the exceptions.) There was a strong prejudice against going to the universities for graduates : they, it was thought, were likely to be idle young men with ideas above their station, a prejudice no doubt reinforced by the fact that many chairmen had not themselves been to university. Some companies which did recruit graduates in considerable numbers (like AEI and GEC) often did not seem to know how best to use them.

At the British Motor Corporation, the road to the top often started with an apprenticeship : a prospective boss ought to have had 'swarf in his shoes' at some time. Even those companies which did take a handful of graduates in the 1950s soon lost a high proportion of them. 'TI lost almost every graduate it took on in those early days,' said Sir David Watherston, the group's director of personnel. 'People did not know how to deal with them.' At Vickers, one of the senior executives in Barrow was frank about his approach to young university men. 'In those days,' he said, 'my attitude was "let the buggers learn the hard way". Now, we're giving them more responsibility.'

Some managements were also learning the hard way. Many companies which had had the time of their lives in the early 1950s found profit-making thereafter a much less automatic procedure. None suffered a sharper reversal of fortune than the British Motor Corporation and Rootes. In 1959–60, BMC had made a profit of almost £27m. on sales of £346m.; seven years later, it turned in a loss of £3m. on sales of £467m. Rootes Motors, which had done very comfortably in the 1950s, lost almost £1m. in 1965, over £3m. in 1966 and over £10m. in 1967. The company faced collapse and Chrysler, the third largest American motor company, was allowed to step in.[1]

The same sort of decline, though not so marked, was evident elsewhere. The General Electric Company was in a serious plight by the early 1960s: profits had halved between 1956 and 1961, although sales had increased every year; Vickers' net profit in 1967 was not much more than a third of the 1958 figure, although sales were higher; Tube Investments' profits fell by forty-five per cent between 1961 and 1967 although sales had increased slightly. In the cases of GKN and AEI, turnover went up steadily enough, but profits did not. GKN's turnover rose by seventy per cent between 1958 and 1967, profits by less than ten per cent. AEI's record was much the same – sales up seventy-seven per cent from 1957 to 1966, profits only fifteen per cent better.

This was the general experience, but there were exceptions. Plessey, for example, increased its sales by almost six hundred per cent between 1958 and 1967 (mainly by acquisitions), and its profits by 964 per cent. The arrival of Arnold Weinstock at General Electric helped produce a rise in profits of 262 per cent between 1962 and 1967, although sales

---

[1] The company for a long time remained tightly in the control of the Rootes family – they made decisions on the most minute features of new models – and Lord Rootes and Sir Reginald (as they became) were followed into the business by their three sons.

Its troubles began when Lord Rootes decided to take on the militants at the company's British Light Steel Pressings plant at Acton, where there had been persistent strikes: Rootes thus became the first of the car makers really to stand up to the unions. The resultant strike lasted thirteen weeks, Rootes got rid of many of the trouble-makers, collected a £1½m. loss for 1961–2 and earned the congratulations of the other manufacturers: 'everybody patted Billy on the back', recalled one company executive, 'but nobody sent him a cheque.' Then the Hillman Imp, which was the company's attempt to break into the small car market, never quite lived up to expectations – the Linwood plant at which it was built was only operating at a third of capacity in 1966. Finally, when BMC bought Pressed Steel in 1965, Rootes decided that it could not afford to have virtually all its car bodies made by a firm owned by a competitor, and paid Pressed Steel £14m. for its body plant at Linwood.

All these factors left Rootes short of cash and short of sales. Before Lord Rootes died at the end of 1964, he had sold a £12,300,000 stake in the company to Chrysler, with the promise that it would not mean a take-over by the Americans. He was wrong.

were only about a third higher. Leyland, too, more than trebled its profits between 1962 and 1967, while turnover only doubled.

There were also human casualties. Chairmen famous for their perennial optimism appeared bewildered, indeed almost paralysed, by the reversal in fortunes: they made the same cheerful noises, but their smiles looked more and more strained. Some who, during the 1950s, had advised other people how to run their businesses had less to say for themselves. Others again, appointed as compromise candidates, were helpless to halt the slide of their companies, and cast around for outside advice. Some felt the time had come to retire: others were forced out of office in palace revolutions.

Many of the old bosses had distrusted neat organizational structures and operated on their hunches. Lord Hives, chairman of Rolls-Royce until 1957, once jokingly warned one of his staff that he would sack him if he saw an organization chart on his desk.

That so many had proved incapable of adjusting to the new conditions is also a reflection on standards of managerial competence: one chairman and managing director, according to a colleague on the Board, could not even read a profit and loss account. But the apparent helplessness of so many captains of industry reflected the change brought about by the end of the sellers' market and the collapse of the price rings. The transition was as profound, if not as sudden, as between peace and war: it simply lacked the conventional sounds of battle. Just as Chamberlain proved inadequate for the siege conditions of 1940, so the peacetime chairmen of some British engineering companies looked ill-at-ease in the more competitive world with which they were confronted.

An upheaval of organization followed. There was, first of all, the take-over in 1967 of Associated Electrical Industries by the General Electric Company and then, in the following year, the merger between GEC and English Electric. The result is an alliance which compares in size with the European electrical giants.

In the motor industry, a merger movement had already been under way. The Leyland Motor Corporation, which produced trucks and buses, had steadily bought up other truck companies during the 1950s and early 1960s and moved into cars by taking over, first, Standard–Triumph and then Rover. Meanwhile the British Motor Corporation, itself the result of a merger between Austin and Morris in 1951, had taken over Jaguar and the only remaining independent mass-producer of car bodies, Pressed Steel. Leyland then set its sights on British Motor

Holdings, as it had become, and was prepared to fight a take-over battle. In the event, a peaceful marriage was arranged and the IRC made available £25m. to the new company. British Leyland is now the only British motor company of any size.

The third important merger which took place in 1968 was the formation of one British computer company in an attempt to combat the massive market power of the American companies, and IBM in particular. The Government took a 10½ per cent shareholding in the new company, International Computers Limited, which brought together International Computers and Tabulators, the computer interests of English Electric and a financial stake of £18m. from Plessey: it also agreed to put up £13½m. to back ICL's research programme.

Elsewhere in the industry, substantial structural changes were taking place. Vickers, for example, exchanged its troubled aircraft business for a forty per cent share in the British Aircraft Corporation in 1960, and lost its steel business when much of the industry was renationalized in 1967; its battle then was to find a new *raison d'être* and it bought printing machinery and office equipment companies. Hawker, afraid to keep too many of its eggs in the aviation basket, moved strongly into diesel engines and electrical engineering; Guest, Keen and Nettlefolds and Tube Investments (which also lost major steel interests in 1967 when large parts of the industry were renationalized) expanded rapidly through acquisitions. TI's assets, which amounted to only £10m. in 1944, stood at £182m. in 1964, while GKN's assets had grown from £22½m. in 1943 to £227m. in 1963. Meanwhile Plessey doubled in size in 1961 when it took over two of Britain's biggest manufacturers of telephone equipment, Automatic Telephone and Electric and Ericcson Telephones.

This upheaval of organization has brought with it a new generation of bosses, often very different in background and approach from those who went before. It is not merely that long-standing company traditions have been broken – with an all-round businessman running GEC instead of the engineers who had traditionally led it, a salesman at British Leyland instead of production men, a former Professor of Aviation at Hawker Siddeley, Civil Servants at TI and Vickers – but also that a different style has emerged. The blood-and-guts merchants (like Sir Roy Dobson) have gone; so have the men who came up from the shop floor and were proud of it; and the autocrats who remain at least make a point of taking their decisions by some criteria other than hunch, even if it is only what the newspapers will say about them.

The new men tend to pride themselves on their rationality: the few who possess buccaneering instincts take care to cloak them in at least an appearance of urbanity. The result is that the engineering bosses are a blander, smoother, overtly more reasonable group of men than those who preceded them.

Companies also became increasingly aware that they were short of potential managers of quality and in desperation turned to the universities. Plessey, which had taken on five graduates in 1960, hired 250 in 1968; TI, which had recruited only a dozen in 1959, took on 150 in 1968; and British Motor Holdings expected to recruit seventy in the year in which it joined forces with Leyland. The results of this revolution in attitudes were soon noticeable. The made-up chargehands who had formed a significant part of the subsidiary Boards of many companies were slowly being replaced by men who had not spent all their working lives in the business: but, for those who believed that the act of recruiting graduates would solve a good many problems, it was disappointing to see how few actually rose to the top.

Many engineering companies have also developed a passion for organization charts, for what Weinstock disparagingly refers to as 'pattern-weaving'. They began divisionalizing and centralizing or decentralizing, and it is a poor company these days which does not have its pack of charts or its handbook to explain how it works.

Some companies are like ailing savages who have been told about a new medicine on the bush telegraph: unsure of the precise benefits, they are still prepared to try it. At the worst, this serves a useful defensive purpose. If the company does not become any healthier as a result, its bosses can at least claim that they have tried the fashionable remedies.

Mr Weinstock's Trinity

'Some of us here,' said Arnold Weinstock, managing director of the General Electric and English Electric[1] Company, 'have the feeling that we are involved in a crusade. 'The crusade is the reform and reorganization of the British electrical industry, which Weinstock believes has been in some of its parts 'a blot on the national life'.

The evangelism is rather less unfashionable than it used to be in

[1] This cumbersome name can scarcely last for long.

British industry, but Weinstock still excites not only admiration but also widespread disapproval, even among businessmen. He has moved with indecent haste; he has, on occasion, been ruthless; he has disturbed the status quo; he has been extremely successful; in short, his approach to business cannot be reconciled with the view that if British industry needs change, it ought to be a gentle and gradual process. Even now, his critics are hopeful that it may all prove to have been just a flash in the pan.

The man himself is taller and leaner than you might expect, with high, square shoulders and an invisible neck. He is also a good deal more boyish; his voice (in laughter or anger) becomes high-pitched, his movements can be self-conscious and even ungainly, and his grin is that of a young man. He sits, in a corner of his office, behind a tiny, curved desk which is a replica of the one used by S. S. Eriks, who built up the Mullard valve business. 'He was a cold sort of man,' said Weinstock, 'but he was the most intelligent businessman I ever met and dead straight, and I liked him.' The other adjective which Weinstock uses about businessmen he approves of is 'manly'. He himself is straightforward, passionate in his views – he has an almost physical revulsion against inefficiency – and with a real warmth and generosity for those he likes.

Weinstock was born in North London, the son of a tailor who had come to Britain from Poland in 1906. His speech is full of recognizably Jewish turns of phrase ('brains we have always got room for'; 'make no decision without you know the details') and although he has not lived in an Orthodox Jewish household for many years, he believes in what he calls 'the religion of Abraham'. This involves a simple and fundamentalist view of the universe – 'good and order and God go together, and so do evil and chaos and the Devil' – and it goes along with a desire for rationality in all things. Waste, says Weinstock, is not only wicked but also irrational.

At the age of fourteen, he was evacuated to the Midlands, where he lived in the home of a man who, ironically enough, worked for Associated Electrical Industries, the company which Weinstock was later to take over. He went on to read statistics at LSE and then at Cambridge ('I hadn't enough background to do mathematics') and was then drafted into the Admiralty at Bath. There, he supplemented his £420 a year by lecturing for the Workers Educational Association. After the war, Weinstock joined a small business which specialized in property development and in the renovation and resale of small

General Electric and English Electric
220,000 employees.

PRODUCT GROUPS

Turbo-generators (fifty per cent of the British market); switchgear (fifty per cent); transformers (forty per cent); electrical machines (forty per cent); cables (twenty per cent); industrial electronics (fifty per cent); defence electronics (fifty per cent); telecommunications (forty per cent); locomotives (ninety per cent); electrical consumer goods (thirty per cent), including a third of the cooker market, and rather over a quarter in refrigerators, lamps and washing machines.

companies. He was personal assistant to the chairman, Louis Scott, and in his seven years with Scott he learnt about balance sheets and profit and loss accounts, and about dealing with the problems of sick companies. He also married Netta, the daughter of Michael Sobell.

Sobell had started in business in the 1920s by importing American refrigerators and radios. Then he had begun assembling radios on his own account and, after the war, produced television sets which sold through furniture stores. In 1933, Sobell sold out his firm, Sobell Industries, to EMI – he was their sub-contractor in the manufacture of TV sets for Great Universal Stores – and, as part of the deal, EMI agreed to sell back to Sobell his factory and plant. Sobell then set up Radio and Allied (Holdings) and brought in Weinstock as manager.

Weinstock was again *in statu pupillari*: he sat opposite his father-in-law in the same office for eighteen months, but he rapidly made an impact on Sobell's business. At the outset, he knew nothing about television receivers but ordered a detailed analysis of the cost of the components, and then sought ways of reducing it. He spent two days a fortnight in the factory, at least one in the laboratory; every single item of expenditure was queried, every avenue of technical advance explored. The result was that, in 1955, Radio and Allied produced a seventeen-inch set for a fourteen-inch price; the number of valves had been reduced, £2 had been saved by producing the first moulded plywood case and the total cost had been brought down by fifteen per cent. In its first seventeen months, the company made a profit of over £600,000. Radio and Allied then produced a 21-inch set which sold for eighty-six guineas instead of the standard 115 guineas, and followed that up by marketing the first fourteen-inch portable.

Radio and Allied grew steadily every year at a time when the number of firms producing television sets was falling from twenty to five and when companies like EMI, Ferranti, Ultra, Ekco, English Electric and Cossor were getting out of the business. By this time, with his father-in-law still keeping an eye on him, Weinstock was running the company: he (or Sobell) signed every cheque – 'I wanted to see what we were spending'. In 1958, Radio and Allied went public and three years later it was bought by GEC[1] for £8½m.; he and his father-in-law moved onto the GEC Board and collected a sizeable chunk of the company's equity.

Some of the GEC directors may have thought they were simply buying useful profits; in fact, they had also acquired a saviour. Saviours, however, are frequently uncomfortable to live with and Weinstock was no exception. Weinstock joined the management committee in 1961, and, from that point on, some of its meetings became acrimonious. There were also major clashes of personality, and the upshot was that he became increasingly irritable. Frequently the arguments centred on approval of some new piece of capital expenditure and Weinstock, who was acutely aware that the banks were anxious about the size of the company's overdraft and who felt that they were not tackling GEC's fundamental problems, kept insisting that they did not have the money for such schemes.

After the fiercest of these rows Weinstock decided to throw in the sponge, for the time being at least, and announced that he was going back to Radio and Allied at Slough. There is no sign that this was the petulance of thwarted ambition: at this point, indeed, it seems clear that he had no aspirations to supreme power. 'I didn't want to meddle in what I didn't know about,' he said. 'The consumer goods side was all I was aspiring to.' (He had stopped the GEC television business losing money inside three weeks, going out himself to sell the sets which were in stock.) One of the senior members of the management committee had already suggested privately that Weinstock should become managing director, and Weinstock had turned down the idea.

His withdrawal did not solve GEC's problems. When the financial director, E. H. Davison, who had been brought in from Courtaulds, left the company, members of the management committee sought Weinstock's advice, with the result that Radio and Allied's finance director, Kenneth Bond, moved into head office. Bond was (and is) an

---

[1] Until 1960 the company had been run by relatives of the men who had built it up between the wars, Lord Hirst and Max Railing. In 1960, Sir Arnold Lindley became chairman and managing director.

extremely clear-minded accountant who had acted for EMI in the deal with Sobell. Eventually, a palace revolution at Magnet House saw Weinstock brought back as managing director, with Arnold Lindley as chairman and Robert Millar as managing director (technical). Lindley left the company in 1964 and Millar took control of GEC's affairs in the Far East.

By the time Weinstock took over, GEC was – in his own words – 'on the brink of ruin'. The company was still essentially a giant wholesaling business with thirty-two Magnet Houses dotted round the country selling everything from sockets and plugs to switchgear. The headquarters of the company, in Kingsway, also doubled as a warehouse, with 250,000 square feet of space and over 2,000 people. 'Magnet House,' Weinstock said, 'was ridiculous. It was a rabbit warren with people shut away in hutches making work for each other. The basement was packed with goods which nobody wanted – there were enough lightning conductors there to last the whole of Europe for fifteen years. My heart fell six inches when I went out of the back door at night and looked around. It was a great tomb in which the business was stifling to death.'

Weinstock's first move was to close down and dispose of all thirty-two Magnet Houses: the one in Kingsway brought in over £3m. 'It was rather like the dissolution of the monasteries,' recalls Bond, whose own role in the affair was almost equivalent to Thomas Cromwell's. The head office was moved to more modest premises in Stanhope Gate and the staff cut from over 2,000 to less than two hundred; altogether, the company's labour force fell initially by about 7,000. A proportion of the 7,000 were managers, many of whom apparently departed without argument. 'You don't need to fire them,' said Weinstock. 'Just tell them what's expected of them, and they'll go.' A small number of factories were closed (including one which made one-off light fittings and which was working at one-fifth of its capacity), the turbo-generator business was sold to Parsons in exchange for shares and several part-interests in companies were disposed of.

A good deal of the company's stock was scrapped when the Magnet Houses disappeared, and everywhere costs came under sharp scrutiny. 'Every time you see a piece of wool,' said Weinstock, 'you pull. Sometimes the knitting ends in a knot. Sometimes the fabric falls apart altogether.' One particularly bad piece of knitting was the 12,000 catalogue items offered by the groups which covered lighting, heating and installation, more than half of them bought in from outside. The result of the early economies was that GEC's bank overdraft came down from £11m. in 1961 to £1m. in 1964, while its profits went up from just over £6m. in 1962–3 to £11¾m. in the following year.

There were also fundamental changes in philosophy and practice. Henceforth, GEC's engineers had to learn that 'it is as much an art to produce things which people want as it is to produce goods which measure up to a standard of perfection'; its research effort had to be 'directed towards meeting the needs of commerce' and not towards satisfying somebody's curiosity; and, most important of all, so far as Weinstock was concerned, the business had to be based not on the head office but on the product and the market.

This meant breaking down GEC into what in effect were a series of Radio and Allieds – separate businesses which could develop, make and market their own products. This in turn meant the death of many of the old groups into which GEC had been divided (and which were often conglomerations of businesses), the dispersal of some of the head office staff into the operating units and the stripping away of the superstructure of shared services and joint costs which were allocated to the different groups and over which they had no control – 'they simply fell from the sky', said Bond.

The exercise was not a complicated one, but it proved extremely revealing. 'The process of forcing the businesses into geographical separation helped us find out what was viable and what was not,' said Bond. 'It was rather like peeling an onion – sometimes, when you got to the middle, there was nothing there.' But it did a good deal more. The formation of individual enterprises which had to sell what they made removed one set of excuses for failure; the elimination of joint costs and shared services another. From now on, the managers could properly be held accountable. Weinstock and Bond had decided very early that they were prepared to suffer the extra cost of allowing each business to have its own services: 'the economies,' said Bond, 'are not worth loss of control of the business.'

When the process was complete, there were fifty-three separate businesses in GEC, some of them – like telecommunications – large, and some of them small; the smallest unit had a turnover of under £250,000. To some of the managers, their new-found independence and accountability came as something of a shock: not all survived it.

Weinstock now had a structure through which he could exercise effective control; the decks had been cleared and he had to apply to a large number of enterprises lessons learnt in one.

The key was to be constant pressure from the top. 'We must make people feel that somebody who really knows is watching them all the time,' said Bond, 'that their operations are fully exposed.' The disciplines introduced by Weinstock and Bond were demanding, but far from unique. Cash balances were to be reported every day – 'we wanted an early consciousness of things going wrong,' said Bond, 'and that way they couldn't hide till the end of the month' – and every month detailed reports (including key financial statistics) had to be sent to Stanhope Gate. The reaction to inadequate performance as revealed in these reports was sharp and instantaneous; both Weinstock and Bond can be extremely waspish, and a telephone call or a letter from one or the other invariably leaves managers wishing that they had done better.

This, however, is merely the sort of discipline which might be expected in any well-run holding company. What was unique at GEC was the way in which the system increasingly reflected Weinstock's own characteristics, in particular his attention to detail and his self-critical nature: he has a detailed knowledge of the products of a good many of GEC's businesses and a conviction that he has done nothing in his life which could not have been done better, which he expects his manager to share. 'There has to be the constant belief,' said Bond, 'that you are not doing things the way you should. Sometimes you have to make yourself bloody-minded, and in the end the likelihood is that something will change for the better.'

'Bloody-mindedness' can easily shade over into ruthlessness. Bond told the story of one business which was fighting for survival and whose managing director claimed that he had done everything possible to cut costs. He was told that twenty-four people would have to be sacked if the business were to continue. The managing director complained that he could not spare them, but did as he was told and although eight of the twenty-four had to be hired again, he had saved the labour costs of the rest.

Weinstock's role was roughly comparable to that of Chairman Mao. 'The most important thing I do,' he says, 'is to think and watch and see the way things ought to be going. Without that, the mechanism of control is quite irrelevant. My job is to lay down the framework in which the companies operate – to suggest, regenerate, castigate, encourage, stimulate.' He also sets himself to provide guidance on strategy for the individual businesses. 'I depend very much on the generals in the field, but they look to me for certain things – I should let them know what battles they are fighting, I should give them a sight of the enemy, provide them with reconnaissance reports of where they are likely to run into trouble. They also want more troops and more money and they expect me to supply those too.'

The pressure from Stanhope Gate was not wholly effective at first: Weinstock had to find managers who could work with him. Soon, however, the liaison improved and there developed a steady flow of people coming to headquarters for help and advice. The individual managers gradually became aware of the terms on which they were welcome. Weinstock did not want to see them if they were asking permission to go ahead with a project which was within the agreed budget – that was their decision. He did expect to be consulted when they wanted to go ahead, but were not sure if they should. For their part, they came to respect the rigorous analysis to which they were subjected. 'We know what the score is at Stanhope Gate,' said Peter Jones, who manages a number of light industrial businesses. 'When we go there, it's a washing process.'

The flow was (and is) very much a one-way affair. Weinstock does not like travelling – he regards it as a waste of time – and his trips to factories are infrequent. With fifty-three businesses, he feels he cannot know enough about them in detail to be able to make a significant contribution on a brief visit, and is aware that these affairs all too easily degenerate into a state procession. His natural curiosity also fits him ill for such occasions. 'When there's an organized visit, and they say "turn left",' he says, 'I invariably turn right, and finish up looking into the store bins or talking to a foreman about why there are four bends in a fabrication instead of two.' His colleagues make it plain that the managers of the plants visited usually enjoy the occasion as little as Weinstock: since he tends to go when the business has run into difficulties, they may not always be exactly morale-boosting visits. David Lewis, who is in charge of administration at Stanhope Gate among other things, is equally critical of what he calls 'the mad dog approach'. 'The trouble with regular visits to the factories,' said Lewis, 'is that you have to do it all the time, you can't sit and watch half the time and then turn into a mad dog for the rest.' He conceded that the visiting boss may 'see the odd man snoring' but added that 'chaps snoring show up in the monthly figures anyway.'

So Weinstock brought about the revival of GEC largely from the fifth floor of Stanhope Gate. The organization which he built up around him there was remarkably informal. To begin with, all the committees – including the management committee – disappeared. (To Weinstock, committees are simply a way of avoiding responsibility and he regards formal management structures with distrust because of their tendency to become self-perpetuating.) Instead, he gathered around him a few men whom he trusted and respected. In the days before the take-over of AEI, the inner group consisted of Weinstock, Bond, Lewis and Tom Kerr. Bond was the financial boss, and Lewis – an Oxford mathematician who had become Radio and Allied's lawyer – dealt with the administration and legal side of the company, as well as vetting major contracts. Kerr was a veteran of the company who had lived through several palace revolutions.

In a sense, this group – with help from Lord Aldington, the new chairman, and Sir Jack Scamp – formed a committee which was constantly in session; like the Special Committee at Unilever, they moved freely into and out of each other's rooms. It was the sort of environment which suited Weinstock: he liked the simple geometry of Stanhope Gate. The arguments continued to be fierce, but Weinstock does not operate as an autocrat, and is ready to listen to every point of view. 'I think that everything I do is likely to be wrong,' he says, 'and that makes me more careful.' He was, however, the central figure in the operation and, apart from anything else, he initiated a sort of corporate parsimony which marks out GEC from many other British engineering companies: Bond, for example, submits no expenses, *pour encourager les autres*.

GEC's profits continued to rise – by 1966 they were £19½m. and Weinstock and Bond were beginning to conduct regular *tours d'horizon*. One of the companies whose faltering progress they watched with interest was Associated Electrical Industries, which had a sizeable investment at the heavy end of the electrical business and major interests in telecommunications and cables. Weinstock, however, was not sure that he was ready to tackle the problems which AEI would bring, and in any case the AEI directors kept making optimistic noises about their prospects.

In the spring of 1967, Ronald Grierson, the IRC's first managing director (he has since become one of GEC's vice-chairmen), told Weinstock that he wanted to take a look at the electrical industry with a view to rationalization. Weinstock replied that, so far as he could see, AEI was the stumbling block. Grierson agreed and took from his pocket a scheme which involved a merger between the two. Weinstock, however, declined the proposition. 'We gave him the piece of paper right back,' he said, 'but it did bring the question into the forefront of our minds.' AEI also turned down the idea point-blank. GEC then waited for the AEI interim statement, which it hoped would give it something to get its teeth into. It did: the figures were poor, the statement pessimistic, and the next day Weinstock and Bond were with their merchant bankers discussing take-over tactics. Worried by rumours that American General Electric was about to put in a bid, they wasted no time; the following Thursday, GEC made its offer.

The bid was received with dismay at AEI headquarters in Grosvenor Place: the company was ill-prepared to do battle. At once grander and drabber than Stanhope Gate, the atmosphere at Grosvenor Place was a fair reflection of what AEI still, in many respects, remained: an old-style British engineering company. The rooms were impressive, even grandiose, the corridors ample, and in the chairman's waiting room were hung a series of hunting prints entitled 'Chances of the Steeple Chase'. Behind the traditional façade, however, a desperate and belated effort was being made to pull the business into shape.

The new chief executive, Sir Joseph Latham, was faced with appalling problems. One was simply that AEI had never become a company in the normal meaning of the word. Its two largest parts, Metropolitan Vickers at Manchester and British Thomson Houston at Rugby, operated as separate entities, and indeed some of the men at Metrovick both felt themselves superior to their bosses in Grosvenor Place and were determined to keep them in their place. One of the first things which Latham did when he became chief executive was to put a Metrovick man in charge at Rugby.

This lack of unity within the group was partly a reflection of the fact that the influence of AEI's head office had often been weak although it was large in numbers, partly that the company's headquarters had for long periods adopted a consciously *laisser-faire* attitude to the activities of the operating units. Before he was appointed chief executive, Latham had pressed for a strengthening of the Board, and in 1965 two new functional directors had been appointed. John Barber came from Ford as financial director, Nigel McLean from the Motherwell Bridge company as commercial director.

But Grosvenor Place was far from being the only part of AEI where the management needed strengthening. Many of the men with senior executive posts in the divisions, although they were of high intellectual calibre, had not proved successful as managers. The organization of the groups also left a great deal to be desired – the Motor and Control Gear Division alone had ten different factories. There was insufficient in the way of constructive planning for the future, there was a complete split between production and sales (Weinstock found that the people producing the goods did not know how prices were fixed or how tenders were handled), and there was massive over-manning.

Latham felt that his first job was to establish his own authority over the group and to take a personal grip on its affairs. He himself took over responsibility for four of AEI's six product groups and he was also chairman of British Domestic Appliances, a company jointly owned with EMI. He agreed at the time that this represented an excessive centralization of power in his own hands, but felt it was necessary for the time being because he believed AEI had been suffering from a lack of certainty in direction – before his appointment as chief executive he and Sir Charles Wheeler had not always seen eye to eye on how the company should be run.

Latham then set out on a tour of all the company's main plants. At each, he outlined the seriousness of the situation to the management, and told them what was expected. At Trafford Park, where 150 senior executives were gathered to meet him, there were – he recalled – no questions. This was to be the first of many visits. For example, Latham flew to Manchester every month to meet the top managers and discuss with them their major problems. Always he took with him up-to-date reports on their performance: he wanted it to be quite clear that he knew precisely what was going on. In addition, the general managers of all the main groups came to Grosvenor Place once a month and, for those who wanted to consult more often, there was an open invitation to turn up on the fourth Wednesday of every month. If meetings and hard work could have solved AEI's problems, this furious burst of activity would surely have done so. Latham also took a tough line with managers whose performance did not satisfy him – he replaced a few senior men in the group – and he continued the process of eliminating the duplication of products between Metrovick and BTH which Lord Chandos[1] had begun in 1958.

Meanwhile, John Barber was trying to tackle the group's financial and planning problems. These had been in many ways one of the weakest parts of its operation. Lord Chandos had hired a man from Ford to help the Board assess new capital expenditure proposals from the divisions, but Barber felt that the staffing still needed strengthening. He discovered that although AEI had more than 3,000 people in its finance staffs, the vast majority were clerks and concerned with looking

[1] Chandos was chairman from 1945–51 and from 1954–63.

at the past rather than the future. There was also so serious a shortage of information about costs and profits in the divisions that, in his view, 'the profit-consciousness of some individual companies must have been virtually nil.'

Barber quickly brought in a number of outsiders from Ford, Shell and Esso and set up a finance planning office and an economics unit. He drew up a finance manual to show managers how to prepare a profit budget and how to analyse and present projects: it also contained a guide to the techniques of discounted cash flow.

Barber then began to seek detailed information from the individual units about their operations. He was conscious that he was moving in an arbitrary way but felt, like Latham, that something drastic had to be done. He asked, among other things, what cost reductions each of the general managers was planning, so that they were forced to spell out in detail their targets for the year ahead. The exercise had another particular point. Barber felt that AEI ought to be able to get rid of roughly 20,000 of its home labour force of 80,000 and that when figures were revealed, the general managers would have to explain how it was that they had so many men.

It took Barber almost a year before he succeeded in collecting enough useful information from the groups. When the information did begin to flow to Grosvenor Place, the company's labour force started to decline markedly. In the following year, AEI lost 9,000 men and production actually increased.

In the event, all these efforts proved to be of no avail. After a bitter battle, AEI was taken over by GEC and Wheeler, Latham and Barber shortly left the company. But Weinstock and Bond were not satisfied with what had been done to reform AEI: 'everything that was wrong at GEC, only worse', was Weinstock's view. He described the efforts to get more information from the operating units as 'a lot of figures flying about'; their only effect, so far as he could see, had been to add £1m. to AEI's overheads. The separation of production from sales provided what Bond called 'the perfect alibi system – if anything went wrong, somebody else was always responsible', and the question of joint costs had not been solved. In AEI, said Bond, more time seemed to have been spent on allocating overheads than on reducing them.

Rationalization now went ahead swiftly. GEC had already broken down AEI's business into thirty rough product groups and these were swiftly brought together with the comparable businesses in GEC. The

barony of Trafford Park was divided into separate businesses – switchgear, traction and turbo-generators – and a GEC man, Douglas
Morton, moved in. Then Weinstock and Bond tackled the question of
overheads – there was, said Bond, £8m. of expenditure in AEI before
you got down to the hard core of the business. Several layers of management – the groups, the home sales and international departments –
were disbanded, and Grosvenor House sold. Weinstock even managed
to make a profit out of the pictures in the Board room and he himself
examined closely the smallest expenses of the company. 'Why do they
need two copies of the Financial Times,' he asked, 'and ought we to
pay for people's newspapers anyway?' AEI's shooting rights in Nor-
thampton were also sold off.

Barber's estimates of the extent to which the labour force could be
reduced proved, if anything, an underestimate. In the first year after
the take-over, the labour force of the new joint company fell by 18,000.
Some 10,000 of these were actual redundancies, and the remainder
came from natural wastage.

Weinstock had by this time already begun talking to the other large
electrical company, English Electric, about a possible rationalization
of some parts of the heavy end of his newly-acquired business: there
was speculation that he might be willing to sell off some of GEC-AEI's
activities to Lord Nelson. At one stage in the talks, Weinstock suggested
the possibility of a full merger, but got no response from Nelson. He
also mentioned the thought to the IRC, but was told to wait. Then, on
August 21, 1968, Plessey made a bid for English and, in so doing,
helped drive the company into Weinstock's waiting arms.

English Electric was a very different sort of company from AEI,
but its best years had been in the 1950s and, since that time, its performance had looked less impressive. After the war, it had been
flooded with orders from the railway and electricity supply industries,
and often its main problem was to find enough capacity to satisfy
them. On the aviation side of the business, the Canberra had proved
extremely successful. The company's position, however, became less
rosy as the years went by, and there were costly ventures.

One was the Eland aircraft engine, which English had undertaken to
build with Government backing. The Government gradually withdrew
support, but the company went ahead with the Eland's development
and did not give up the project until 1963. By that time, it had lost
£6½m. 'We should have got out three years earlier,' said George
Riddell, now General Electric and English Electric's joint deputy

managing director. The first Lord Nelson,[1] however, had refused to abandon the Eland, partly out of a feeling that his company had obligations to potential customers, partly out of native pig-headedness. 'I'll build a bloody aeroplane to put it in,' he told one of his colleagues.

It was Nelson again who decided that English should go into television receivers – 'I'm not asking you, I'm telling you.' It soon became plain that it was a serious error to make only one size of receiver, but the only way in which the business could be dropped was by going behind the chairman's back. Nelson's colleagues simply refused to sign the next stock authorization and, when he asked how the business was doing, they told him blandly that they were no longer in it. The merging of English Electric's aircraft interests into the British Aircraft Corporation also proved to be a painful experience. It was agreed to on the Government's promise of more orders – 'a piece of sheer blackmail', according to one of the company's directors.

Nelson had saved English from disaster in the 1930s and he had continued to show remarkable prescience in those areas which he knew well. For example, he was designing 500-megawatt generating sets at a time when the electricity supply industry was saying that the largest it would ever want was 60 megawatts.

His autocratic style, however, became increasingly inappropriate as English Electric continued to grow. 'In the middle 1950s,' said one of his colleagues, 'you couldn't move a chair without George. He didn't have the time to sift the facts on every new venture and he wouldn't let others do it for him.' As a result, the structure of English began to creak increasingly loudly. Partly because it was centred so strongly around Nelson's own person, it was still organized geographically: it was based on works and not on products.

This created some curious anomalies. Lord Caldecote, for example, was the director of English Electric's aircraft equipment business, but he could not give orders to, say, the manager of the factory at Preston, which did aircraft work among other things, because the manager was in turn responsible to a general manager in Bradford. As Caldecote said: 'We had grown very fast, and the relationship between head office and the places where the work was done had become very nebulous.'

The arrival of the second Lord Nelson as chairman produced a major

---

[1] He had had a crucial part in putting the business together in the 1930s and was once introduced to a visiting Russian general by the then Chancellor of the Exchequer, Sir Stafford Cripps, as 'the greatest autocrat in England'. He retired in 1962, at the age of seventy-four.

reorganization and a period of rapid growth through acquisition. Nelson attacked the problem of the Eland by forming a joint company with Rolls-Royce and then selling out altogether. He also, in 1965, called in McKinsey. The result was that the company was divided into nine product groups, each of which was given a considerable measure of autonomy. At the top, the company was run by a triumvirate which consisted of Nelson, George Riddell, a Scottish chartered accountant, and Bernard Banks, who had joined the company as an apprentice just after the First World War.

The reorganization, however, created new problems and did not solve old ones. For one thing, there developed a considerable duplication of effort between head office and the new groups. While the group heads busily set up their own staffs, there still remained at headquarters a considerable number of functional bosses responsible for such things as purchasing, commercial policy, engineering, manufacturing services and so on. This was quite plainly nonsensical in a number of instances, and even members of the triumvirate admitted that it was difficult to define what was the job of some of the functional bosses. This duplication of effort also contributed to a second major problem: there were still too many joint costs, and bitter battles were fought between the groups and headquarters as to how these should be allocated.

These weaknesses were all the more critical because English Electric more than doubled in size between 1962 and 1967 through a series of major acquisitions, which included Elliott Automation and Ruston and Hornsby, makers of diesel engines. Nelson was determined that English should not be thought of as 'just one of the heavies' and had, before the merger with GEC, predicted that half the company's business would be in electronics by the 1970s: it already accounted for one-third by 1967. However, not all English Electric's ventures into high technology had paid off. It had lost well over £4m. on its Systems 4 range of computers by the time it exchanged its interests in the field for an eighteen per cent shareholding in ICL; this was another difficult experience for Nelson.

After the merger Weinstock was the moving force in the new joint company. He was ready to make concessions to English Electric in the interests of creating unity, but determined to press ahead with rationalization. He regarded Lord Nelson, who became chairman, as the company's public spokesman and the man to handle relations with national buyers, Governments and other industries: himself as responsible for actually running the company.

The first stage of rationalization consisted simply of dividing up English Electric by product and joining the businesses with their counterparts in GEC. The alliance had produced what in many ways was a remarkably compact group, a good deal less diverse than either General Electric of America or Westinghouse, although neither of them is in the telecommunications business. Roughly thirty-five per cent of Weinstock's turnover now comes from electronics and telecommunications, under twenty per cent from the heavy end of the business, less than ten per cent from consumer goods, and the balance from cables, the industrial division and plants overseas. One of the unresolved problems left by the merger was that GEC acquired English Electric's forty per cent shareholding in the British Aircraft Corporation. Weinstock may or may not want to take upon himself the massive cares of the British aircraft industry: he will certainly not wish to remain a minority shareholder in BAC for any length of time.

In terms of organization, Weinstock soon began to look critically upon English Electric's imposing headquarters in the Strand. He determined to find out what the operating businesses felt they needed at head office: the rest would have to go. English Electric House has now been disposed of and those of its staff who remain have moved to Stanhope Gate – which nevertheless still has a complement of less than two hundred. Furthermore, while some of English Electric's parts – Marconi, for example – were in good health, it soon became plain that large-scale redundancy could not be avoided at the heavy end of the business. There had been a serious falling-off of orders generally: new orders for switchgear placed by the electricity authorities in 1968 amounted to one-third of those in 1964, in the case of transformers to only one-sixth.

But, for a man who admits to being impatient by nature, Weinstock moved with remarkable circumspection in dealing with English Electric; the problems were more complex and he had to take account of a greater sensitivity about rationalization and redundancy on the part of the trade unions.

The extraordinary thing about Weinstock and his colleagues is the ease with which they have made the transition from running a small business to controlling an extremely large one (by British standards). They have made mistakes. There has been a high turnover of senior managers in some areas; and Weinstock himself has the image of a cold and distant person who is more interested in figures than human beings. For the rest, he has so far succeeded in negotiating the political and structural problems of large-scale business remarkably well. There is still an informal air about the operation at Stanhope Gate and apart from the months when he was struggling with the problems which the merger with English presented, Weinstock always seems to have plenty of time: nevertheless he concerns himself not only with the strategy of the business but also – to a surprising extent – with its detail. He always seems to be talking to Bond or Lewis about the minutiae of individual orders or contracts.

As a manager, he can be unpredictable: one of his colleagues said that 'nobody can ever tell what Arnold is going to think'. He certainly rejects many fashionable ideas. He has, for example, little time for management consultants and takes a sceptical view of the business schools. The former students he has met, he observes, have been either very able, moderately good or quite useless, as in any group, which suggests to Weinstock that their abilities have little to do with the schools. He is also conscious that the company is still short of good managers and that he needs to do more about management development. His current solution to the problem is based on his own experience. Recently, he took into his office a young man in his early twenties whom he liked and trusted: this gave the young man much the same experience as Weinstock had been given by his own father-in-law. He was able to watch Weinstock at work, and he was given a constant stream of problem situations on which to report. Then he was sent to one of the company's plants. The scheme is still in its experimental stages but, if it works, Weinstock intends to make all his managers follow suit.

Weinstock has so far refused to join the scramble for recognition in Whitehall, a disease which afflicts a very large number of British businessmen. He belongs to no committees, goes to few official dinners, makes no speeches. By his abstinence, he may even increase his unpopularity: not only does he not say the right things or do the right things, he does not even want the right things. In his own words, he minds the business. This concentration of effort has proved not unprofitable. He has acquired a 1200-acre estate in Wiltshire, a flat in Grosvenor Square, and a third share in a string of racehorses (which he owns jointly with Michael Sobell) and which, apart from his family, is his main interest outside the business.

Weinstock's problems are, of course, far from over: for one thing, he will probably have to sustain the heavy end of the business mainly on the strength of export orders for some years, in the hope that home orders will pick up in the mid-1970s. Another question is whether he can retain the passion for efficiency which has driven him thus far. On the face of it, he is unlikely to lose the messianic streak in his character – Jews, he says, often like to try to do difficult things which are for the general good – and he is certainly a great deal less likely to be diverted from his purpose than some other successful Jewish businessmen. In his desk, he keeps a piece of paper which acts as a constant spur. On it are the key statistics of two of the big American electrical companies, together with those for his own firm.[1] It is constantly brought up to date. The gap is still so wide that Weinstock is unlikely to want to give up for some time yet.

Astride the Thresholds

The companies which have ventured into what is sometimes loosely called high technology give off an odour all their own. Compared with ICI or Weinstock's empire (which has a very substantial interest in advanced technology) it is a more precarious, more volatile, less institutional world. Indeed, a number of the companies which remain sometimes appear to be as much survivors as conquerors. The most venerable of them, Ferranti, has a history of brilliant invention, technical prowess and financial vicissitude; the company was put in the hands of the Receiver in 1903 and in 1904 a petition was entered in Court to 'wind it up',[2] but Sebastian de Ferranti's grandfather was able to raise money from the bank by pledging his shares to another company. That, no doubt, is why Sebastian always lists as the first of his achievements 'being solvent now'.

Most of the others have had their moments too. ICT (the principal forbear of ICL) was for a long time an extremely shaky enterprise and had to be propped up with Government money, albeit repayable. The company, which eventually became Elliott Automation (now safely under Weinstock's umbrella), was on the verge of collapse when Leon Bagrit moved in at the end of the Second World War. Plessey, too, had its financial difficulties in the early years: Allen Clark, who ran

---

[1] Average output per head in the American electrical industry is between £5,000 and £6,000; in the British industry, £2,700.

[2] *Life and Letters of S. Z. de Ferranti*, Gertrude Z. de Ferranti and R. Ince, London, Williams and Norgate (2nd edition, 1956), p. 151.

'High Technology' Companies

Plessey

Turnover of £165m. in 1968 from 123 manufacturing and research centres. Telecommunications accounts for thirty-three per cent of its business, components for twenty per cent, electronics twenty per cent, dynamics seven per cent, automation six per cent, overseas fourteen per cent. Largest producer of telephone systems in the Commonwealth, largest supplier of memory systems in Western Europe. Wide range of components, including fixed capacitators (largest producer in Europe) and integrated circuits. Garrard record-playing turntables and changers. Also hydraulic gear pumps and aerospace equipment.

International Computers

Turnover of £92m. for 1968. Ninety per cent of its business is in computers, ten per cent in punch-card equipment.

Ferranti

£55m. turnover in 1968, factories at Hollinwood, Wythenshawe, Barrow, Edinburgh, Bracknell. Third of business is in instruments, transformers and meters; a third in defence contracts; a third in civil electronics, including integrated circuits and numerical control tools.

---

the company from 1925 until his death in 1962, managed it at such a stretch that he had to borrow money from employees, including the man who was in charge of the company's tool room.

The memory of these crises seems in some cases to have entered the collective company consciousness, and now acts as a spur. But the rather highly-strung enthusiasm which is evident in these companies owes a good deal more to the fact that, in many of their activities, they seek to operate on the frontiers of technology, to be – in the words of Arthur Humphreys, managing director of ICL – 'astride the thresholds'. Frontiers have a habit of moving with alarming suddenness, and this may to some extent account for the observation of one of Plessey's senior executives that 'many of our people are beyond the average border line of commitment'.[1] Certainly it helps to explain the curious language which they use, reminiscent occasionally of wartime RAF slang – 'press-on types', 'sweet contracts', 'the current gas'.

The commitment may also be heightened by evidence of the success of American corporations like International Business Machines and Texas Instruments. Despite the insecurity, it has certainly helped to

---

[1] A cynic might say that it related more directly to Plessey's hire-and-fire reputation. This reputation, however, is far less justified than it was.

draw forth an almost obligatory gold-rush mentality in British companies operating in the same fields. In 1967, for example, ICT had perhaps 2½ per cent of a world computer market worth £2,000m. a year, but its ambitions were unlimited. 'In ten years' time,' said Arthur Humphreys, 'the market will be worth £10,000m., and if we only have ten per cent of that, we'll be bigger than ICI is now.' The millennium is both distant and elusive and ICL, about a twentieth the size of IBM, has a feeling of treading where other saints have already trod. 'IBM,' as one ICL man puts it enviously, 'has years of motivation behind it.' The British do not take kindly to finding themselves cast in the role of Johnny-come-latelies.

While the Americans continue to spend roughly ten times as much on research and development as Britain, they are unlikely to improve their status, and indeed the truth is that the British companies are trying to find those patches of soil which American giants have omitted to till. As Michael Clark, Plessey's deputy managing director, put it: 'We are looking for niches where the Americans have not put vast sums of money.' Sir Leon Bagrit was equally frank about the fact that 'Elliott Automation was based on the idea of getting between the legs of the big giants.'

Just how dependent on the Americans most of the British companies have been, and for their innovations as much as their omissions, is plain from their history. When Bagrit moved into Elliott, it was in difficulties: in his first year, the company lost £230,000. Elliott had nothing to sell – 'there was no hope for the instruments we were making' – and it could not afford to re-design and re-tool. There was only one way out and Bagrit took it. He went to America and collected licences – so many, indeed, that at one time more than fifty per cent of Elliott's products contained a sizeable dose of trans-Atlantic technology. Nevertheless, the expedient enabled the company to survive.

ICT's ancestry illustrates the point even more forcibly. Its largest parent, British Tabulating Machine, was until 1949 licensed to market IBM equipment in Britain; no less than forty per cent of its turnover came from sales under the licence. At that time, British Tabulating had very little in the way of technology – the company was essentially a producer of punch-card machines – and, as Humphreys admits, 'we, like a lot of others, thought of computer people as long-haired boffins who wanted to do astro-physics.'

When ICT (formed in 1959 by the merger between BTM and Powers-Samas Accounting Machines) did produce its first computer in 1962, it was three years behind schedule, and in the meantime the company had been forced to make arrangements with both the Radio Corporation of America and Univac. 'It was a case of back to the breast', said Humphreys. These arrangements helped save ICT, however, and Humphreys regards the deal with Univac as the best he has made for the company.

Plessey's early dependence on American licences stemmed largely from Allen Clark's unwillingness to finance a large research and development programme of his own; he was, he said, more interested in cash than prestige. The result was that, in the early 1950s, Plessey was probably spending less than £500,000 on research and development, and as late as 1955 as much as twenty per cent of its business was being done on licence. Only Ferranti can claim that it has hardly ever taken American licences. 'Our business,' said Sebastian de Ferranti, 'is to do it ourselves. You can't attract good people if you are merely licensing from the Americans.'

Plessey has at least emulated the Americans by growing at a rattling pace: between 1959 and 1968, its turnover went up almost seven times, its profits more than eight times. Unlike IBM or Texas, however, the growth came not from within but from a series of major acquisitions, many of them cleverly negotiated.

These began in 1960 (while Sir Allen Clark was very much alive) with the purchase of Garrard, makers of record-playing turntables and changers amongst other things. Then, in 1961, Clark doubled the size of his business overnight by buying Automatic Telephone and Electric and Ericcson Telephones. With them, he also won for himself a seat at the 'telephone table', the group of manufacturers who, under the bulk supply agreement which then operated, shared Post Office telephone equipment contracts between them. After Allen Clark died, Plessey acquired sizeable companies in Australia and South Africa, and in 1965 took over Decca's ground and heavy radar business and the Telegraph Condenser Company.

For a large, established company with a settled management structure such a list of acquisitions would have created problems. In the case of Plessey, which had grown up as a one-man band and which had not even an agreed succession to replace that man when he died in 1962, it produced a series of upheavals which sometimes left the management looking like performing seals trying to stay on a slippery ball which was growing all the time and taking them further and further from the ground.

Plessey, for example, was still a national company but it had no marketing organization worth the name, because Clark's philosophy had been based on Board-room selling, with himself negotiating many of the big deals personally; he would march into a man's office and offer to make a part for a good deal less than the man was paying. Products had in the past tended to proliferate for similar reasons: Clark took Plessey wherever the contracts led. So far as research and development was concerned, spending had increased, but the sums were still relatively modest: a sizeable part of the business was in components. The company, furthermore, had little in the way of formal structure, and its management was thinly spread. There was also the question of morale. Even to senior members of the headquarters staff, Clark had been an intimidating figure – he favoured Stetson hats, big cigars and monogrammed shirts – and created in many parts of his empire an environment of either apprehension or fear.

In his latter years, however, Clark (who was painfully conscious of losing touch with the company he had built) had begun to modify some of the attitudes which had made him one of the most successful entrepreneurs of his time. He was aware, for example, that the rapid expansion of Plessey demanded a fundamental reorganization of the business. Unfortunately he died before he had had the chance to implement his plans. What was worse, he left behind him two large and undigested acquisitions (the telephone companies) and a Board-room split over who should succeed him.

He had clearly groomed his elder son, John, for the job (he had become joint managing director during his father's illness), but there were several on the Board who did not think John was up to it. His younger son, Michael, was also a director. John and Michael between them held less than five per cent of the Plessey shares, but they were their father's sons and they represented thereby a link with a successful past. It has never been clear whether they won the battle of the succession because of their demonstrated ability or because other directors backed them out of loyalty to their father: but win the battle they did, though only by the narrowest of margins and at the cost of three resignations.

It was an uncomfortable inheritance. Allen Clark had run Plessey in a highly personal way, and his two sons (both still in their thirties) had to impose their own style of leadership, rebuild the Board and at the same time take a grip on what was rapidly becoming a different sort of company, both in size and in nature: moving increasingly from components into complete products and systems, from its jobbing shop past into proprietary products. Within the old Plessey company, they had to retain the loyalty to himself which their father had built. The new acquisitions, on the other hand, presented an entirely different problem: ATE and Ericcson had loyalty neither to Plessey nor to the Clark family and, moreover, were themselves rivals.

Temperamentally the brothers Clark were perhaps not ideally suited to the job. John is a burly man who, in many ways, looks, thinks and acts like his father; he did his early training at Metrovick and Ford and is an extremely hard worker but he also has an unusual mixture of flamboyance and reserve. Michael, on the other hand, is brisk and brusque and probably has the more analytical and the quicker mind. Neither is a natural diplomat, but both were determined that command of the company should remain in Clark hands. In some ways, they complemented each other – John is more interested in day-to-day management, Michael in long-range planning – but both were essentially production men.

Perhaps their most immediate problem was what to do about the telephone companies which, in terms of asset values, amounted to something approaching half the business. Allen Clark had bought ATE and Ericcson both because he wanted to get in on the bulk supply agreement and because he had decided to move strongly into the field of communications. He could hardly have bought at a better time. The later 1960s were to see a very sharp increase in Post Office investment in the telephone service, and by 1968 Plessey alone was doing more work under the bulk supply agreement than had been done by the entire British telecommunications industry in 1964.

Allen Clark, however, had acquired two companies for a very specific reason: he wanted to achieve the savings of rationalization. Under his successors, this is precisely what did not happen. Perhaps because of the hiatus left by his death, no decisive move to merge the two operations was made in the early years, and ATE and Ericcson were allowed to go on running side by side. The policy was to make each one tidier and more efficient, and the result was considerable duplication and an unabated rivalry between the two. When a decision was made in 1965 to try to bring them together, the first efforts at joint management were a failure, and John Clark concedes that 'in the past, we've not been smart in that we've lacked people who could move in and ride a situation hard'. Eventually, after Michael Clark had taken on the job himself, Plessey brought in a Massey-Ferguson man to complete the amalgamation.

But the telephone companies were the symptoms of a much larger problem. Essentially, Plessey was faced with the need to plan and control a business which was both growing and spreading with enormous speed and which had previously been heavily dependent on one man. In a sense, it was a situation analogous to that of adolescence. 'We are still in our teenage years,' said one of the company's senior executives in 1968, 'and we're still changing from a village store into a major departmental store.' During the 1960s, Plessey had become a store which sold over 4,000 different products – everything from magnets and car radios to gas turbines and air defence radar systems – and it was clearly impossible to try to manage it, as often in the past, on the basis of *ad hoc* decisions.

Its history gave it certain advantages in facing up to these issues. Its jobbing shop past, for example, provided a tradition of tight production engineering, and Clark had gathered round him a group of men to whom money was not an abstraction. Furthermore, Plessey had restricted itself to relatively unsophisticated products – 'we kept out of guided weapons and the really big systems,' said Michael Clark – and had made its way more cautiously with what Clark described as 'nice, pedestrian things' like army radio equipment. This had at least helped to steer the company clear of major cancellations (like TSR 2) which had a serious impact on firms like Elliott.

On the other hand, Plessey had come late to the idea of corporate planning. Indeed, in many ways, it had become a collection of Topsies, with decisions on the manufacture of new products being taken not at headquarters, which had an inadequate staff, but in the operating units – sometimes with the minimum of consultation. There had been too little concern with strategy and long-term objectives, with where Plessey wanted to find itself in the world.

The Clarks resorted to the most fashionable of solutions: in 1964, they called in McKinsey. The result was that Plessey was carved up into a number of groups – Automation, Components, Electronics, Dynamics, Telecommunications and International – each with a considerable degree of autonomy; and the headquarters staff was strengthened, not least by the formation of an Office of Corporate Planning. Plessey became one of the most heavily documented companies in the country, with rules and procedures for everything. In addition, there had already been a sharp increase in graduate recruitment. Although a good many were lost in the first years,[1] John Clark took the view that it was cheaper in the long run for a company to grow its own timber.

The reorganization had at least one unfortunate side-effect: it served to stretch still further a top management which had not yet been adequately replenished since the Board-room row of 1962. In 1967 Plessey at last filled one of the more obvious gaps by taking on Thomas Hudson, formerly managing director of IBM's operation in the United Kingdom, to take charge of both finance and corporate planning. In one way, it seemed a curious choice. Hudson's experience was that of a man who had spent most of his business life in a company with a limited range of products. Plessey, by contrast, had a mass of products – far too many – and the profusion had been made the worse by the acquisitions.

The new task represented a considerable challenge to Hudson. Plessey (with the stimulus of McKinsey) had already begun to do the essential groundwork before he arrived – a five-year plan was slowly coming into being – but Hudson set out to isolate strategic objectives against which basic decisions could be taken: which products to back, which to drop, where to invest the available cash. He was conscious that Plessey were novices in the art of planning, but determined that the Topsies should be brought under control – 'the horses must be put on the rein' – and that the company should be clear in its own mind where it intended to go.

All decisions on the manufacture of new products are now taken at headquarters, an important limitation on the groups' autonomy, and Hudson is working hard on a comprehensive product strategy. When it is complete – and he did not expect to have 'a really good projection' until 1970 – it should make considerably less arduous the continuous process of weeding out products which Plessey has to suffer at present. It may also help the company to deploy its management more effectively.

Hudson's arrival and the work of his staff have undoubtedly helped to focus Plessey's ideas about its own future. The Clarks are clear that they want to specialize rather than become a widely-spread conglomerate; to make further acquisitions overseas as a hedge not only against deflation but also against the possibility of bad management in Britain; and to be three times as big by 1975. Hudson is also insis-

---

[1] Over the five years 1963–8, however, Plessey has lost only thirty-seven per cent of its graduate intake, compared to a national average of sixty-two per cent.

tent that the company should get out of those of its parts which do not contribute to its technological strength – which means concentrating in the main on electronics and communications. (He was a strong advocate of Plessey taking a share in ICL – it had decided to drop its own computer, the XL 12 – and is now on the Board of the International Computers holding company.) This refining process is bound to lead, at the least, to hard debate because in Hudson's view it means eventually getting out of products which happen to be highly profitable.

Hudson is also convinced that these things are not a matter of choice: the facts of international business life demand that Plessey should become more selective. For one thing, the Americans are now much more reluctant to grant licences in Europe than they were, which means that Plessey is driven willy-nilly into much heavier expenditure on research and development on its own account. More than half Plessey's spending on this comes from its own funds – that half amounted to about £10m. in 1968 – and it must concentrate its attack if it hopes to compete with the vast resources which the major American companies can command. One of its most crucial problems is to make micro-circuits more reliable. Success or failure will have a decisive effect on almost every part of the business, since the micro-circuits will replace a whole range of components now in use, and almost a third of Plessey's research and development staff are involved.

The other way of increasing the resources available for R. and D. is for Plessey to grow rapidly in size, giving it bigger bulk profits and more money to spend, and this the company has been struggling to do. The abortive bid for English Electric was one effort in that direction, and it will not be the last: Arnold Weinstock's absorption of both AEI and English must have left the Clarks feeling a little like Lord Cardigan after the charge of the Light Brigade, but they are a resilient pair and there is little doubt that they will produce alternative plans. Nor, of course, is it only R. and D. expenditure which hangs on good acquisitions. Plessey's remarkable profit growth between 1956 and 1964 (which ran at an annual rate of thirty-five per cent, taking the pre-tax figures) was to a great extent due to the acquisitions which the company made: if it wants to move back towards that rate of growth, it will clearly have to buy very successfully indeed. It has already acquired one American company, and intends to take over others with the shares of the first.

John Clark has worked hard to establish his own personal authority over the company. Unlike Weinstock, he is a strong believer in the peripatetic approach, and faithfully pounds the shop floor – 'making fatuous comments, if you like' – because he thinks this is the best way of identifying Plessey's people with its management. In 1967, he spent 165 days out of London. He reviews one of the groups each month, choosing a site outside London, and likes to begin with a walk round the factory.

But, although the second generation Clarks are from one point of view an improvement on their father – they do not cause quite the degree of apprehension that he did – Plessey has still not fully found its new self; 'when AG died,' as one old retainer remarked, 'it was like dropping a religion.' What John and Michael have given Plessey is something of their own drive and briskness, together with a real sense of urgency that the company must keep on growing swiftly if it is to mean anything in the world. At the moment, although it is the 135th largest company outside the United States, it is really significant neither on a narrow front, like IBM, nor on a broad front, like General Electric and English Electric.

IBM is clearly the enemy so far as International Computers is concerned, but it also dwarfs the three or four other American computer manufacturers which are larger than ICL. Massive American dominance is just one of the uncomfortable facts of life which ICL has to face: even now that it has succeeded in drawing unto itself virtually all the other British computer companies, its prospects do not look particularly rosy.

To begin with, despite its name, it is weak internationally. It has not so far felt strong enough to begin marketing its computers in America, which accounts for almost sixty per cent of world sales, nor does it seem likely to do so for some considerable time. Its only business there is a tiny one in peripheral equipment. In Europe, it was also slow to move forward – for several years, it had no product to sell, let alone the resources with which to exploit it – and it is only now beginning to make significant inroads into that market. Consequently, the company has been heavily dependent on Britain, where it has roughly held its own with IBM.

Even here, however, it was unlucky enough to put its first computer on the market shortly before a period of almost continuous economic restriction: in a country which contains a very large number of small companies, who need persuading even in good times that it is worth spending between £50,000 and £60,000 to buy a computer and well

over twice that to put it into effective operation, a long period of deflation is a considerable handicap.

In the circumstances, it is astonishing that ICL has survived at all.
During the 1950s, as IBM and other American companies were advancing with considerable speed, both its parents-to-be (BTM and Powers-
Samas) were left far behind. When the two did decide to come
together, in 1959, it was not in response to the American challenge: a
request from the joint stock banks, who wanted some new equipment
developing, acted as the trigger.

Having decided to merge, BTM and Powers-Samas agreed that the
marriage should be consummated with the minimum of pain and unpleasantness. One of ICL's directors summed up the spirit of the affair:
'Let's put these two together and not really decide who's going to be
boss'. British Tabulating Machine, which took 62 per cent of the equity
of the joint company, ICT, did not use its power. The idea – in the
words of one of ICL's directors – was that 'neither should raise any
subject first and that both should reach the same conclusion precisely
together'. Sir Cecil Weir, the chairman of the new company, had
promised that nobody on either side would lose his job, which effectively blocked any prospect of rationalization: since the two companies
were making much the same things, there was a long period when ICT
had two of everything.

Its efforts to develop a computer of its own were equally inept. The
1301, a product of BTM's liaison with GEC, had been scheduled to
arrive late in 1959. The electronics of the project (GEC's contribution
to the partnership) went well enough, but there were problems in
mechanical engineering with the result that the computer was not first
delivered until the autumn of 1962. This left the company without a
product, and while the acquisition of GEC's engineers in 1961 and of
EMI's computer interests in 1962 gave ICT additional skills, it also
burdened it with largely unrelated product ranges.

In 1961, ICT signed an agreement with RCA, which enabled it to
market the RCA 301 in Britain as well as giving it access to the American company's development work. Then, at the end of 1962, after
engineering snags, this time with work on a new calculating tabulator,
Arthur Humphreys acquired rights to market the Univac 1004. The
1004 earned a very large proportion of the profit which ICT made
between 1964 and 1967.

At this stage, it was still a disunited array of products and people,
largely occupied in selling other companies' products, and morale fell

steadily. In 1963, however, again on the advice of Humphreys, a crucial gamble was taken: ICT decided to drop both its own computer and that of RCA, and to adopt the FP 6000, a computer which Ferranti was developing in Canada – a prelude to the acquisition of Ferranti's computer division.

The history of the 6000 had been, to say the least, curious. Ferranti had spent a good deal of time and effort in building the large Atlas computer and the frustrations inherent in this process provoked one of the company's salesmen to write a specification with the heading 'A computer I could actually sell'. Since the salesman's name was Harry, his brainchild was nicknamed Harryvac. Ferranti's Canadian company picked up the specification, and it eventually became the FP 6000. By 1963, however, Ferranti realized that it had neither the resources nor the sales force to make a full-scale attack on the computer market: it therefore decided to sell out its business to ICT.

From ICT's point of view the link with Ferranti proved to be a life-saver. The Ferranti technology was sound, and the appearance of ICT's own 1900, developed from the FP 6000, not only helped restore morale but also fused the various tribes of technologists who had been acquired over the years. The 1900 made a company out of a consortium. It was announced in February 1964, and a year later there were twenty in use. It was a modest beginning, but impressive by comparison with early ventures.

The problems of management structure took even longer to resolve, for sick as ICT was, the terms of the partition of power continued to be meticulously observed. When Sir Cecil Weir died suddenly in 1960, another ex-BTM man (Cecil Mead) was made deputy chairman alongside Colonel Terence Maxwell, and a former Civil Servant, Sir Edward Playfair, was brought in from outside to hold the balance. The logic of what went on beneath this delicate equipoise seemed to receive less attention. There were only two executive directors on the Board, and while some functional bosses reported to the chairman, others reported to the deputy chairman and others again to a group of deputy managing directors.

By the time Ferranti's computer interests were acquired, ICT was in desperate straits, and there was a widespread decline in confidence. It was in these circumstances that Basil de Ferranti became managing director. In some ways, he appeared to be a fall-guy: he was rich, for that reason he was expendable and if somebody had to stick out his neck, it might as well be him. Although a small profit had been forecast for 1965, ICT in fact made a loss. Playfair then left the company, and although Basil de Ferranti retained the title of managing director, Mead did the job.[1]

In the years that followed, the business made a slow and unspectacular recovery. The 1900 sold well and when Humphreys took over as managing director of operations in 1967, some of the more obvious organizational nonsenses began to disappear, including the system by which the functional bosses reported to different people. Humphreys, who looks and speaks like a pugnacious London docker and began life as a solicitor's clerk in Kent, decreed that they should all report to him.

By the time ICT joined forces with English Electric's computer business in 1968, it was recognizable as a company and cohesive enough to take upon itself the problems which the new recruit brought with it. Ironically, English Electric's Systems 4 range of computers was, in effect, a cousin of RCA's Spectra 70, the machine which ICT had rejected in favour of the link with Ferranti. The Systems 4 range had run into serious difficulties. Announced in 1965, only a trickle had reached the market by 1967, and delays in delivery had driven important customers to take their orders elsewhere. The struggle to iron out the system's weaknesses had also begun to weigh heavily on English Electric's staff at Kidsgrove: they had run into what appeared to be a series of circular problems – once one snag had been freed, another appeared – and in the end they could be forgiven for feeling punch-drunk.

Fortunately, however, the ICT/English merger did not repeat the BTM/Powers pattern. Humphreys was plainly the operational boss, and his job was made easier because there was no counterpart in English for many of ICT's functional bosses, nor did it have a large sales organization outside Europe. The result was that the ICT men rapidly took command: within months of the merger, only one of ICL's eight most senior executives came from English Electric.

The one organizational oddity which remains is that a Holdings Board has been set above the ICL Board to represent the major shareholders: General Electric, Plessey, the Government, Vickers and Ferranti. There is nothing unusual about the powers which the Holdings Board possesses – the ability to remove the ICL management, to

---

[1] Ferranti had played a vital role in achieving the ICL-Ferranti merger; in the adoption of the 1900; and in securing the backing of the National Research and Development Corporation when the company's credit-worthiness was at its lowest.

vet capital expenditure items over £200,000 and appointments at salaries over £6000. The peculiarity rests in that International Computers (Holdings) holds nothing but International Computers: it is a classic one-over-one situation.

There are a number of other, more specific anomalies. For one thing, Sir John Wall is chairman of both the ICL and Holdings Boards, but acts in effect as a non-executive chairman in the case of ICL so that he is free to criticize the company when he is wearing his Holdings hat and does not look as if he is criticizing himself. Basil de Ferranti also sits on both boards, in one case as a director of ICL, in the other as a representative of the Ferranti interest. Not unnaturally, in the first months of its existence, the members of the Holdings Board tended to be spokesmen for their own particular interests, rather than an independent team. As one of ICL's directors put it: 'Like a large computer system, the Holdings Board will take a little commissioning.'

Organization apart, ICL is still far from out of the wood. In the short term, sales of the 1900 fell below expectations in 1968 and although the Systems 4 was expected to double its 1968 sales in 1969, it was still suffering from proving delays. ICL also has the trickly job of producing future models which can incorporate both the 1900 and the Systems 4. This will be no easy task.

Looking to the longer term, it could well be three years before ICL is earning a reasonable return on its assets and even that will depend on the buoyancy of the European market. The disadvantages of its relatively small size become apparent in the high cost of components (ICT buys out only over sixty per cent by value of its machine – compared with over fifty per cent in the car industry), and Humphreys wants to tackle the problem by persuading the smaller American manufacturers that one way to combat IBM is for each of them to specialize in particular peripherals. ICL's labour force is also large in relation to sales compared to that of IBM (which does twenty times the turnover with only seven times the number of workers).

In one sense, ICL is still overtly convalescent – at least until 1971 it will continue to lean heavily on the Government for its research and development funds – but it is probably not yet strong enough to survive a major flop unaided. At least it is in a business which the Government regards as strategic, and it now has both a range of computers of its own and a determined management with strong nerves: they may need them.

A selection of Sebastian de Ferranti's *obiter dicta* help to suggest both the spirit of his management and the nature of the enterprise:

> 'I think the head office is in Manchester.'
> 'If we had a financial director vetting applications for cash, he'd mess the thing up in five minutes.'
> 'All that matters in management is that the average age of your men must be less than that of your rivals.'
> 'I'd sooner become smaller than raise public money.'

De Ferranti is at once one of the ablest and most personable men in British industry. He has electric energy, a sharp wit and a buccaneering spirit. He has frequently been wooed by other companies – as much for himself as for the business he runs – and he has the genuine respect of men like Arnold Weinstock. Beneath the carefully maintained veneer of amateurism lies sharp judgement, but de Ferranti runs his business as far as possible in a way which suits his own personal inclinations and enthusiasms and not according to approved business conventions. In this sense, he is a survivor from a past age who has, ironically enough, found himself involved in the most advanced technology.

His idiosyncratic style would scarcely be possible were it not that he and his brother Basil between them retain a majority of the shares. (Now that their uncle Denis has sold his twenty-six per cent shareholding, a large chunk of the equity is in public hands, but not enough to disturb family control.) Both are determined to learn the lessons of the past: to keep the business solvent and to avoid the sort of family disagreement which led to a split between their father, Sir Vincent, and his younger brother, Denis. Basil has always felt that it was incumbent upon him not to rock the boat and after he had fought the 1955 General Election (as a Tory),[1] he took over the jobs of managing the company's Canadian subsidiary and of running down the domestic appliance side of the British business. That left the field clear for Sebastian to take charge of the mainstream of Ferranti's affairs, and avoided the danger of a personality clash.

In many ways, Sebastian runs the business much as his father did. Sir Vincent had broken down the company into profit centres in the 1930s – each of them with very considerable autonomy, each with its own research and development facilities. Several of the present Ferranti Board, indeed, are men who worked with Sir Vincent, but it is not an executive body and has never been the power-house of the company.

[1] He won a by-election in 1958 and in 1962 was appointed Parliamentary Secretary at the Ministry of Aviation.

The power rests in the individual businesses and Sebastian himself acts as a catalyst in his contact with the individual managers. He also keeps a very close eye on the company's cash flow, and it is he who makes the final decision as to how the available money shall be allocated.

It is a difficult balancing act he has to perform. Ferranti regards its niche in the world as 'the advanced technological scene', which currently means an involvement in numerical control equipment, computer-aided design equipment, microelectronics, process automation and the navigation and attack systems for the RAF's Phantom aircraft. It is, unfortunately, a scene which tends to create a considerable appetite for capital, but since Ferranti is unwilling to go to the public for money – Sebastian says the company would not be able to have so many 'sporting swipes' at things if there were shareholders constantly looking over its shoulder – capital is painfully short. This means running a very large bank overdraft – over £11m. in 1968 – paying small dividends (traditionally six per cent, though more recently it was raised to twelve per cent), and hasty withdrawal from any product which is either unexciting or too cash-consuming.

Ferranti must have retired from a score or more of such businesses since 1882. They include cables, switchgear, alternators, domestic cookers and water heaters, heating irons, electric fires, clocks, commercial radio and television and computers. In some cases, it felt it could neither continue to finance its losses nor hope to raise the resources to compete in the market: the computer business was losing £1m. a year when it was sold to ICT. In other cases, a weakness in marketing proved Ferranti's undoing. Its electric fires, for example, were both excellent and expensive, but it never bothered to explain to the public why they were so expensive. It was the same story in radio and television. 'We thought people would understand that our sets had good valves,' said Basil de Ferranti, 'but they didn't.'

The omission seems to spring from a genuine and quite profound lack of interest. 'We have never had an understanding of how to interpret the public's desires,' said Basil, 'and frankly we are not really interested.' Any disdain for salesmanship may spring partly from the fact that Ferranti believes it is impossible to mount a marketing operation in some of the things in which it really is interested, like microcircuits: the best that can be done in that field, in Sebastian's view, is intelligent guesswork.

The list of failures has inevitably been costly. It has not only brought sizeable losses, but has also reduced the flow of cash available for advanced projects – which have had to be fed from the steady profits earned by older and less glamorous businesses, like meters. Because of these failures and the refusal to raise public money, Ferranti has grown only at the modest pace of seven per cent a year. It was already a sizeable business when Plessey had scarcely been heard of: this does not worry Sebastian, who insists that he is not in business to achieve what he calls 'sheer vulgar size'.

What does anger him is the failure of successive Governments to grasp the importance of advanced technology firmly enough to offer adequate support to the British companies involved in it. He sees this failure as a straightforward sell-out to the Americans. 'We didn't cancel the TSR 2 and save the money,' he said. 'We bought the F 111 instead, and that is financing American technology out of the pockets of the British taxpayer.' Defence contracts are vital to a company like Ferranti, not merely because of the profits (excessive or otherwise) which it may earn, but also because the knowledge they yield can often be transferred to applications in the civil field. It was the fateful Bloodhound contract – on which Ferranti will be making payments until 1970 – which gave the company its excellence in control engineering and put it into the process control business: the Argus computer which is at the heart of Ferranti's process control systems was first built for Bloodhound. Here again, the falling off in defence orders must inevitably both hold back growth and take away from the company the prospect of 'spin-off' into civil work.

Ferranti has notable achievements to its credit. Its computer technology gave ICT the basis for the 1900. It is among the world leaders in numerical control machines, and is confident enough of the future in them to have refused to sell out to the American Bendix Corporation. In the field of microelectronics, it did not waste time by exploring germanium, but went straight to a silicon base and now claims to be only a few months behind Texas Instruments.

As for the future, Sebastian de Ferranti maintains a determined air of optimism. Although profits were halved in 1968 – largely because Ferranti made a mess of the highly complex system which it is building for the Phantoms – Sebastian believes that there will be a growth in commercial electronics and that nothing but a national economic disaster will put the business at serious risk.

In one sense, perhaps, Britain is fortunate to have a company like Ferranti which is genuinely concerned with the advance of technology, even at the expense of profit. On the other hand, it is also questionable whether the country can afford the luxury of a company run by men who are proud of being engineering snobs and who scorn the normal commercial rules. It is quite possible that with a major injection of public money Ferranti could by now have been a much more significant force in the world. Family control has kept its standards high, but its turnover low.

Manipulators of Metals

The three largest general engineering companies in Britain – Guest, Keen and Nettlefolds, Tube Investments and Vickers – have all been searching their souls in recent years: GKN and TI, in particular, conscious of the arrival of 'industrial logic' as the new Ark of the Covenant, have had more than a suspicion that they were rag-bags of assorted enterprises accumulated over the years from a mixture of self-defence, ambition, optimism, benevolence and temporary loss of faculty. Vickers, on the other hand, saw its role as arms-maker to the nation disappearing once the Korean War was over, and was compelled to carve out a new niche.

Lord Plowden, who became chairman of TI in 1963, faced the problem with the equanimity which you might expect of a most distinguished ex-Civil Servant of exceptionally tidy mind; and if, at that point, TI had no convincing explanation for the shape of its empire, Lord Plowden was just the man to discover one. His depression at the range of TI's interests – which included aluminium, steel, bicycles, coffee pots and road signs as well as precision tubes – did not prevent him from producing an answer: TI, he declared, were 'manipulators of metals'. Plowden knew perfectly well that creating an artificial logic on an *ex post facto* basis would not solve any of TI's problems, but he hoped it would provide a sense of direction for the future. With this guide-line, as one of the company's managing directors pointed out, Tube Investments was unlikely to start making rubber balls out of discarded tyres.

Guest Keen's search for a consistent philosophy has run into still greater obstacles. Its product range is even wider (one of its deputy chairmen jovially admitted it was such a complicated company, they sometimes didn't understand it themselves); it has had large spare resources – and, therefore, a temptation to extend its interests; and, it has nobody with Plowden's flair for the portmanteau phrase. Ought it to try and isolate a common purpose for the group? In 1967, as part of the debate, the senior directors took themselves off for three days to a good hotel and golf course in Ayrshire to look, from afar, at where GKN stood and where it was going.

Vickers has been in the unhappiest position of all; armaments had given it both an objective and a philosophy and it gradually lost both – even though, as late as 1958, it still included a clause in its contracts which warned that they might be cancelled in the event of national emergency. What Vickers required was a massive shift of resources into new activities.

All three companies therefore found themselves faced with similar dilemmas. All three, for example, were essentially sub-contractors: they produced things to the specification and often to the design of others and, in the case of Vickers, the customer (in the shape of the Government) even laid down the profit, on the basis of cost-plus. Guest Keen, heavily committed to the motor industry, moved at the behest of the car makers; Tube Investments was at the mercy of industries stretching from electricity generation to office furniture; and although the bits which Vickers banged out – in the shape of warships, tanks and guns – were larger and more impressive, they were still produced mainly to blue-prints provided by the military. Vickers and GKN, in particular, had far too few products of their own which they could promote and market independently; over ninety per cent of Guest Keen's turnover still comes from components which are not unique to the group. This dependent posture makes all three companies vulnerable despite their size.

Furthermore, with order books bulging in the 1950s, there was no pressing incentive to spend large sums on research and development programmes. All too often, they found themselves taking licences and, since they had little of their own to promote, their marketing remained either weak (as in the case of GKN or TI) or almost non-existent (as in the case of Vickers). As harder times exposed these weaknesses, all three became increasingly aware of the need to develop their own products, to market them independently, to be masters in their own house; and all three began to wish they were nearer to the final consumer.

Their other problem was, they scarcely existed as entities. TI was a collection of companies some of which had been encouraged to fight each other, and it would hardly have been surprising if they had little

esprit de corps; GKN's subsidiaries were loosely connected to the group
largely by the fact of a common chairman and directors; and although
Vickers men did possess a real pride of belonging, individual plants
often felt cut off from headquarters. From the 1920s, Vickers had been
run by a succession of soldiers and bankers and since (until 1949) they
were also part-timers, they seemed as remote as the sphinx to all but
the most senior managers. Vickers, indeed, did not have (and, in some
parts, still does not have) the feeling of a commercial enterprise at all;
it gave the impression of a military unit filling in time until it received
its call-up papers again.

Guest, Keen and Nettlefolds was still little known in Birmingham,
even after the Second World War. One potential recruit who came for
an interview found that neither taxi drivers nor the telephone operators
in his hotel had even heard of the company. When he eventually found
his way to its headquarters in the back streets of Smethwick, he was
ushered into dingy offices which were, in fact, part of the old bolt and
nut works. The head office staff consisted of a chairman and managing
director, a financial director, a chief accountant and his staff, and a
handful of office girls – fifteen or sixteen people in all. The company's
books were written by hand.

Guest Keen still depended heavily on its fastener business – which
had accounted for perhaps half its turnover in the pre-war years – and
on steel. It had a monopoly of the wood-screw, a very strong position
in bolts and nuts, and it belonged to all the appropriate cartels; it
was both profitable and complacent.

Partly because of its protected position, it had also failed to modernize
much of its plant. The heart of the empire, the giant Heath Street works,
built in 1854 and turning out 50m. gross of screws a year in 17,000
different varieties, was 'straight out of Dickens', according to Claude
Birch who arrived there in 1954. Some of the machines had been installed in the 1880s, the belts for the steam engines ran underneath the
floor, and it had not seen a coat of paint for years. Birch, coming as he
did from Rolls-Royce, found it hard to believe that such a firm existed.
Heath Street was still making excellent profits, but it was by that time
desperately in need of new investment.

The organization of the business also left a great deal to be desired.
Traditionally, Guest Keen's Board had consisted largely of descendants
of the original founding families and their relations, together with
fathers and sons who had been acquired with their companies. Sir
Anthony Bowlby, who joined GKN in 1929 and is now a director, recalls

that he felt very much the odd man out because he had no sort of family connection. Suitable jobs were found for able young men of the right family, but outsiders had to give evidence that they would fit in with the style of the existing bosses, a number of them country dwellers addicted to country pursuits.

Bowlby was the son of a surgeon to King George V; William Fea, who arrived in 1935, and is now a deputy chairman, had spent his early years on his father's *estancia* in Argentina and then returned to take a First in mathematics at Oxford. They joined young men like Stephen Lloyd, a son-in-law of Neville Chamberlain who had been invalided out of the Indian Civil Service and whose father was general manager of the Heath Street factory, and Geoffrey Sankey, who had read for the Bar at Cambridge as well as taking an engineering degree and whose grandfather had built up the Sankey business. GKN reckoned to be a company successfully run by gentlemen.

Kenneth Peacock, who became chairman in 1953, was in some ways eminently well qualified to lead a company such as Guest Keen then was. His background and interests were both impeccable. His father had come to GKN when the bolt and nut works of which he was part-owner was taken over by the group in 1919; the elder Peacock had been a director for twenty-seven years and latterly vice-chairman. Kenneth himself, who may very well have joined GKN only at his father's insistence, had driven at Le Mans and eventually bought himself a fine estate in the Cotswolds where he was able to indulge a love for horses. He was modest, had considerable charm and an elephantine memory, and he worked extremely hard: he was also unusually generous by nature, and his humanity has left a mark on GKN which is still discernible.

Peacock set out to manage in much the same fashion as his predecessors. The forty or so subsidiaries were given a great deal of autonomy, and the group was held together by a series of inter-locking directorships: Peacock sat on every one of the Boards himself, and his senior colleagues at head office each took their quota. Peacock also involved himself deeply in the whole range of the group's affairs and the subsidiary company chairmen wrote constantly to him about their problems. It was a style of leadership in which benevolence and hunch played a great part, and it brought the most rapid period of growth in Guest Keen's history; the company moved away from its dependence on fasteners and took a much larger stake in the motor industry. But the Peacock era also left behind it many problems. Managers who were either incompetent or time-servers were allowed to continue in office; the fact that the chairman was always prepared to hold their hands did not encourage the development of strong and self-reliant bosses; and Peacock's insistence on working by instinct meant that the main Board often had the minimum of information on which to judge investment proposals which were put to them. Nevertheless, his instinct was often good and, in any event, the group's financial resources were an adequate cushion against error.

Guest Keen began to grow and spread in an unplanned, indeed almost casual way. Peacock's popularity and known taste for acquisition inevitably attracted a number of men who, for one reason or another, were ready to sell their companies, and who came to him because they were sure he would treat them gently. There was often, however, no close analysis of either the record or the management of these suitor firms: Peacock's hunch would be that GKN should acquire the company – 'my seaweed tells me' – and he would send somebody off to buy it. The willing sellers frequently had management problems of their own, and this merely served to stretch the resources of a group whose own management talent was already thinly spread.

Just how passive GKN was in this process may be judged from the fact that, although the later 1950s and early 1960s saw a steady stream of acquisitions, no take-over battle was fought in Peacock's reign and it was not until 1963 that GKN made its first approach to another company.

These regular additions inevitably put pressure on GKN's tiny headquarters staff. Peacock himself moved onto the Board of each new acquisition, and spent a good deal of his time in orbit round the country trying to attend the appropriate meetings. At weekends, he regularly took home two briefcases. By the early 1960s, no less than ninety people were reporting directly to him. Nothing major could be done without his approval; but once Peacock had been convinced, carrying the Board was seldom difficult.

Nevertheless, profits continued to be high. The fastener business had still not felt the full force of competition from Japan and Red China, steel was in its heyday, the motor industry was booming. In 1956, GKN earned nineteen per cent on net assets, and in only one year between 1951 and 1960 did its returns fall below fifteen per cent. Not until profit margins began to decline was there any demand for major reorganization within the group.

Such significant changes as had taken place before 1960 were financial rather than structural. The most important sprang from an idea which the group's accountants picked up from Unilever: the centralization of cash. Until 1956, all the subsidiaries were allowed to hold separate cash balances at the bank and, since they were kept on current account, they did not even earn interest. As they amounted, at times, to between £5m. and £6m. this was an incredible waste of resources; and the fact that centralization seemed novel to GKN reflected the group's isolation as well as the great autonomy granted to subsidiary companies. Furthermore, the raising of cash within the group had always been an arduous affair, involving an apparently endless series of telephone calls. The process of persuading the subsidiary companies to pay their cash balances into a central account daily was also long and difficult – they feared, quite rightly, that it would make inroads into their autonomy – but they eventually allowed themselves to be persuaded.

More fundamental reorganization, however, could not be long delayed. By the end of the 1950s, GKN was bulging at the seams; the interlocking directorships had ceased to interlock in any effective way. A restructuring of the group was under discussion from 1960 onwards, and the 1961 results were no doubt a spur to reform. Largely because of a sharp fall in steel earnings (from £11.8m. to £6.4m.) GKN's profit fell by thirty per cent, and its return on net assets sank from 17.6 per cent to 11.3 per cent in one year. The expertise of the Guest Keen Board was financial rather than technical – it had (and still has) more than its fair share of accountants and less than its fair share of trained engineers – and it was the accountants who led a movement for the creation of a stronger head office.

The new structure which emerged divided GKN into eight sub-groups with a number of appendages left unattached. Some of the eight made obvious sense; others, like engineering equipment, were ill-assorted, and their collection under one roof seemed little more than an effort to make GKN look reasonably tidy. The new shape of things also relieved the chief executive by cutting the number of people reporting to him from ninety to eight, but whether it has added to efficiency is still in question. It looks impressive, but the new groups have simply added a further layer of management without substantially undermining the autonomy of individual companies and without necessarily improving head office control.

When Peacock retired in 1965 from bad health and overwork, he handed over to his successor (Raymond Brookes) a company which was no longer in rude health. 1964 had been a better year – steel profits had staged a minor recovery, the motor industry had done well – and Guest Keen had drawn benefit from important new acquisitions (such as the three sizeable drop-forging companies) : the net result was to put the return on net assets above thirteen per cent. The group was also strong financially, with large and unused borrowing powers, and it was capable of considerable further expansion.

The long years of Peacock's rule had, however, helped dull the decisiveness of some of those around him. GKN's Board was large and elderly and beneath it the management was patchy. This was due partly to Peacock's reluctance to get rid of dead wood, partly to the fact that GKN had never had an adequate management recruitment policy; not until September 1967 did it begin to recruit university graduates on a group basis and – although it seems to be an extremely pleasant company – its attractions were evidently not obvious to graduates. In 1967, roughly five hundred were interviewed, but of the 160 to whom jobs were offered, only eighteen accepted.

Other sins of omission were also only too obvious. Marketing was primitive in many parts of the group – market research had been done for the first time at Heath Street in 1962 – GKN was in too many small businesses, it had too few sophisticated products of its own, it was too dependent on the British market, its research and development expenditure was pitifully small. On a more personal level, Brookes had to contend with deeply entrenched interests within Guest Keen which wanted change to be as gradual and graceful as possible.

Brookes is a short, stocky Midlander of a rougher cut than some of GKN's other directors : he describes himself as 'a Staffordshire lad and a hot forger'. He had started his working life as an apprentice engineer in West Bromwich and during the war had taken over as manager at Garringtons, one of GKN's forgings plants. Significantly, one of his first moves was to take Garringtons out of the Drop Forgers Association : he wanted, he said, to 'take the opposition to the cleaners'. There was a considerable row when his intentions became known – not all GKN's directors (Peacock included) agreed that cartels only held back good firms and kept the small and inefficient in business – but Brookes insisted.

He also boasted that, after the war, he would build a forgings plant like a modern dairy, with electric furnaces and presses in place of hammers. The plant was duly built, and lost £750,000 in the first three years but thereafter gave Garringtons a considerable price advantage over its competitors; the company became one of GKN's star performers. Brookes managed it with the minimum of frills, and strict control of costs.

As a result, he made steady progress up the GKN hierarchy. For some of the old guard, however, he moved rather too abruptly, and, when the time came to find Peacock's successor, Peacock himself was not one of Brookes's supporters. He nevertheless got the job and very shortly made his presence felt. When Birfield (which is, among other things, one of the largest independent producers of transmission drives in the world) decided that it was going to resist GKN's offer of a merger after at first appearing to be willing, Brookes made it plain that he was not going to withdraw gracefully, as Peacock might have done. Birfield was the first shotgun marriage in GKN's history.

The Birfield acquisition gave GKN opportunities of precisely the sort which Brookes wanted: at once it provided the group with a real foothold in Europe, and an opportunity to develop unique products. Equally plainly, Birfield was just a beginning. Brookes was looking for a major switch in the balance of the group's activities. He had no emotional attachment to the past – he once said that he did not particularly like screws – and he wanted business which helped give GKN its own technology and which moved it nearer to the consumer. The best way to do that rapidly, so far as he could see, was by spending more on R. and D. and by further acquisitions. At one stage, he even cast envious eyes in the direction of Rolls-Royce.

In 1969, Brookes committed Guest Keen to a further major investment in Australia — where it already owned a company (John Lysaght) which had a virtual monopoly of sheet steel production. Brookes was concerned at Lysaght's dependence for its semi-finished steel on Broken Hill Proprietary, Australia's largest company, and he was also afraid that, unless GKN moved, somebody else might begin to build a new steelworks in Victoria, Australia's fastest-growing State. He has therefore linked up with BHP in building a new steelworks at Westernport Bay, south of Melbourne. The first stage of the project is a cold reduction mill which could lead to an integrated steelworks costing £360m. It gives Guest Keen a larger investment in a growing market (and Lysaght has always produced good profits); and it could give the company some sort of leverage in negotiating prices with the British Steel Corporation (GKN is its largest customer). Too much ought not to be made of this point, however, since Guest Keen already has all the leverage it needs in a world of surplus capacity and with European and American producers ready to step in.

For all his determination, it would not be surprising if Brookes had sometimes felt weighed down by the colossal range of GKN's problems. The group's patchy management has forced him to intervene more often than he would have liked – he is not a member of any of the sub-group Boards – and he moved Claude Birch into Forgings and Castings because he was not happy with the way things were going. He readily admits that, although he wants to be 'a thinking chairman', he has been forced to act too often as a mobile fire brigade. In some ways, too, he seems to feel restricted by Guest Keen's benevolent past: he waited for eighteen months after the Birfield take-over before integrating the company fully into GKN, largely because he wanted to demonstrate that GKN was nicer than the opposition had painted it. Similarly, he has failed to sort out the more obvious anomalies in the group's head-quarters organization – GKN has both a chief executive and a managing director – and, although he wants to move the head office to London, his colleagues have so far refused to be persuaded.

Brookes is still looking for suitable acquisitions with which to keep the group moving forward: despite all his efforts, he has not yet been able to push the return on net assets above 12.1 per cent and GKN has thus not yet fully lived up to the prophecy of one of Brookes's colleagues: 'Kenneth made the group nice, Ray will make it efficient.' At least Brookes has many of the right instincts and a determination which too many British chairmen lack.

Lord Plowden, the chairman of TI,[1] came into an inheritance no less daunting than that of Brookes. The heart and original base of TI was the steel tube business, which in the past has regularly turned in between forty and sixty per cent of the group's profits from around a quarter of the capital employed: in good years, it earned over twenty per cent on its net assets.

Sir Ivan Stedeford, the son of a Methodist minister who set up his own car sales business in Birmingham and was persuaded to join TI only reluctantly by its first head, John Aston (who was also Stedeford's father-in-law), developed this side of the business brilliantly.[2] Possessed of what he describes as 'a rather acquisitive instinct', he bought com-

---

[1] Plowden has his headquarters in Bridgewater House, which once housed a mistress of Charles II.

[2] Stedeford was the dominant figure in TI from 1939, when he became managing director, until 1962, when he retired as chairman.

panies steadily at the rate of two or three a year – and TI held what was virtually a monopoly of precision tubes in the British market for a good many years.

Nor was there anything paternalistic about the way in which Stedeford ran TI. He judged the tube-producing companies sternly by their results and if their bosses did not produce adequate results, he got rid of them. 'I wanted men to stand or fall by their own decisions,' he says. Partly because of this uncompromising demand for results, partly because he became a rather distant figure after he had moved his headquarters to London in 1940, partly because he is a somewhat taciturn man, Stedeford inspired fear in some of his managers. But 'a *soupçon* of fear', he felt, was no bad thing.

From his tube-producing base, Stedeford had moved out into other fields, but with less apparent shrewdness than had marked his earlier acquisitions. In 1953, he bought Round Oak, a small steel producer, to secure supplies of raw material. Still troubled, perhaps, by the danger of a steel shortage, he then acquired Park Gate, a works producing bar steel which needed modernizing and which (together with Round Oak) turned out more than TI needed: Stedeford had to spend £32m. on re-equipping it.

The move into steel was followed in 1959 by the purchase of a controlling stake in British Aluminium (price, £20m.) and in 1960 by the acquisition of the cycle firm of Raleigh for another £12½m. To Stedeford, they seemed logical enough. He bought Raleigh because he was afraid of over-capacity in the declining British cycle industry and Raleigh (with a forty per cent share of the market comparable to that of TI's Hercules and Phillips), was the company which threatened it. British Aluminium he bought partly as a defensive measure: aluminium might become a danger to steel in the manufacture of tubes.

To critics within the company, both these purchases seemed like acquisitions for acquisition's sake; Raleigh represented 'a big corner in a dying market', and British Aluminium a large stake in a complex industry very different from those in which TI had traditionally been involved. The price Stedeford had to pay also seemed inflated. If return on capital is any criterion, the critics are right: the aluminium division has never produced a return better than 5.7 per cent in the last six years and although the cycle division topped ten per cent in its best year, it has also fallen below five per cent.

Plowden also took over a very mixed bag of engineering and electrical businesses, and he moved into TI at a time when its overall return on assets had fallen from thirteen per cent in 1961 to 7.2 per cent in 1963, and its profits from £21m. to a little over £12m.

As a good organization man, Plowden noted the sketchiness of the group organization – Stedeford had mapped out a breakdown of the group into divisions, but it was not yet functioning efficiently – and its disparate nature. 'There was a lot of empire,' he said, 'but nobody seemed quite sure where it all was.' On the one hand, he acknowledged that the extreme decentralization which had been practised was perfectly sensible at a time of monopoly; on the other, he felt the time had come for the TI chairman to perform 'a service of cohesion'.

Plowden therefore began a series of tours which took him to every plant in the group, dutifully shaking hands with the longest-serving employees and, so far as possible, letting other people do the talking. He made it plain that he did not want to be thought of as the king of TI: 'I spend my time not being God,' he said. He also took care to explain to those who were closely concerned the logic behind decisions.

This preoccupation with *esprit de corps* inevitably meant that Plowden moved only slowly in tackling the structural weaknesses of the group. He refused to operate as a 'hatchet man' and preferred (when he could) to wait until people retired. He also delayed moving into situations where retrenchment was clearly needed and himself conceded that he should have tackled Loewy Robertson, an engineering company which designed heavy rolling mills, two years before he did; the business was losing almost £1m. a year when TI sold it off in 1967. Some of his colleagues felt that he was too sympathetic and that he placed too much emphasis on planning: it was all very well spending time understanding where you were going, but you had to actually go there at some point. In 1967, TI's return on net assets was still only 7.3 per cent. At that point, Plowden had little to show for his efforts apart from an improvement in morale and the outward signs of a greater team spirit: everybody was now writing letters on TI notepaper.

Nonetheless, some of the more intractable situations in the group had begun to resolve themselves. The decision to sell Loewy was, in itself, a major step forward: it showed that TI's patience was not inexhaustible. The renationalization of steel (which Plowden had known about well in advance through friends in Whitehall) brought about the sale of Park Gate and half of Round Oak in return for a payment of £53m. and provided the resources to buy Radiation, with its strong domestic cooking and heating business. This move closer to the consumer was precisely what TI had wanted.

Raleigh's labour force, meanwhile, had been steadily run down from 12,000 to 7,500 and other products moved in to replace the declining cycle business (total output in the United Kingdom had fallen from 4m. in 1951 to less than 1½m. in 1967). TI bought a company which turned out car seats for the motor industry, closed its factory at Watford, and moved the work into Raleigh: Raleigh has also turned its hand to toys, perambulators and push chairs. By 1968, roughly one-third of its capacity was taken up by goods other than cycles: its target is a half. The result is that in 1968 Raleigh's profits doubled and its return on capital again crept closer to ten per cent. In aluminium, Plowden decided to sell off TI's interest in British Aluminium's Canadian company, and to invest £37m. on a new smelter in Scotland, which will give TI a vertically integrated operation in Britain for the first time and may raise the derisory returns which the aluminium division has been producing.

The old mainstay of the group, steel tubes, had unfortunately not been doing so well; in 1967–8, the division's profits were less than half what they had been two years previously. Part of the decline was due to lower orders for power stations and heavy chemical plant as investment fell away; part also to the persistently high overheads of a division which has no less than seventeen different companies.

The problems of reorganizing the traditional core of TI's business has proved particularly intractable. In some ways this is a legacy of the historical rivalries which existed between the individual companies, but it also reflects a failure on the part of TI's management. The two founding tube companies, Accles and Pollock and Tubes Ltd., had always regarded each other with unashamed dislike. 'In the old days,' said Peter Stedeford, Sir Ivan's nephew,[1] 'it wasn't downright warfare, more like the Cardiff-Swansea rugger match.' A and P was known by its rivals as 'the Oldbury Gang', Tubes Ltd. as 'the Rocky Lane Gang'. The Rocky Lane Gang held their heads particularly high because Sir Ivan kept his headquarters there before he moved to London.

Accles and Pollock had been run for a good many years by the Hackett family. Walter Hackett, senior, whose father had been an ostler at Guest Keen and had himself started at A and P as a labourer,

[1] Two other relatives of Stedeford are on the TI Board: Michael Boughton, his son-in-law, and John Aston, his wife's brother.

was followed by his son, Walter junior, who became general manager in 1933. Walter junior had risen from the shop floor, had held a union card, and was a Midlands businessman of the old school. He arrived at work at 7.30 a.m., went through all the mail himself, favoured knitted waistcoats, and ran A and P with a grip of iron. In many ways, he was also a one-man band, and since people did not contradict Hackett lightly, even senior executives waited upon his orders. Hackett was shrewd and inventive and he was soon appointed assistant managing director of TI.

Before and after the war A and P became rapidly larger and more complex: it accepted even the smallest orders, its development departments mushroomed and its overheads grew. In the easy times of the 1950s, all this went largely unremarked. Hackett himself could not give his full time to the company because he was involved in other TI jobs (he was, at one time, not only A and P's joint managing director, but also chairman of the tube division and a managing director of TI itself), and a succession of other men were appointed as joint managing directors. A and P's problems were made all the worse when the stainless steel side of the business – which had a high value and a high turnover – was hived off to another company. Eventually Peter Stede-ford was moved in to try to sort it out. He found that there were far too many small customers and that the overheads of the business were 'ghastly'; in particular, vast quantities of staff were needed to handle all the small orders. He decided that A and P should stop trying to compete with 'the back street merchants', got rid of a good many small customers by fixing a minimum limit of five hundred feet on orders for ordinary tube, and cut the labour force by between seven and eight hundred. His successor was Dr John Sawkill, a scientist who had begun life at Tube Investments in the research laboratories and who was appointed despite the doubts of some of the old guard: 'he's only been here seven years,' complained one.

But A and P, like many of TI's other tube companies, is very far from solving all its problems. In 1967 it still had a staff of 1,100 in a total labour force of 3,200. and its Board was still an incongruous mixture of men promoted from the shop floor and importations from outside TI, some of them the fruits of its graduate recruitment programme. The decision to drop unprofitable small orders has been partly successful – eighty per cent of the tube division's output now goes to a hundred large customers – but a great deal remains to be done not only at A and P but also to the organization of the division as a whole. The rivalries of the past – when company A put in a stainless steel plant because company B had already done so – have left their mark, and although the advent of new tube plants in very large sizes has forced some degree of rationalisation, it has not gone anything like far enough.

Plowden has undoubtedly made TI a happier army than it was before: he inspires confidence down the line and he has steadily developed a team at headquarters which is capable of assembling facts and of taking rational decisions on them. They believe that the worst is now over, though much still remains to be done. Indeed, they seem relieved that things have turned out as well as they have. As Brian Kellett, one of TI's managing directors, put it: 'We have a better future than we deserve.' But the group's return on net assets in 1967–8 was still only eight per cent.

Only an optimist would describe Vickers' future as bright, although the 1968 results showed a modest recovery and may be the start of better things. Nevertheless, Sir Leslie Rowan, who took over the chairmanship from Major-General Sir Charles Dunphie in 1967, has one of the most difficult tasks in British industry. During the post-war years Vickers staggered from one disaster to the next, not entirely sure whether it ought to remain a camp follower of the armed services or whether it ought to shrug off the past and become a business like any other. Its after-tax return on capital employed sagged from a modest 5.8 per cent in 1956 to a disastrous 2.8 per cent in 1967; its prospects have frequently been hopeful, its actual results continually disappointing since the end of the 1950s.

Rowan, another ex-Civil Servant with a distinguished record of public service, puts down Vickers' poor record partly to the fact that 'in a family, people tend to be too kind', to a failure to be ruthless enough in closing down surplus capacity, and to a lack of its own products. There is little doubt that, to some extent, Vickers has been a victim both of circumstance and of bad luck, but it has also paid the penalty of long years when it was almost totally dependent on Government orders, and when as a result the normal skills of business atrophied within the company. It has, in effect, been a nationalized industry, but without the protection and the perquisites which a nationalized industry can expect.

After the war, Vickers found itself with a declining armaments business and a heavy investment in shipbuilding, steel and aircraft.

Many of its works were the relics of a time when it had preferred to make its own components rather than buy them from outside: Dartford had been acquired so that it could produce its own gunpowder, the Ioco company so that it could make fabric for its airships. It was a combination of interests which imposed enormous burdens on the company's resources. At first, however, all went reasonably well, and the late forties and early fifties brought good profits. Korea renewed the demand for armaments, there was a buoyant market for steel and for new merchant tonnage, and the Viscount proved to be one of the most successful aircraft built in Britain since the war; 480 were sold.

But the hectic activity was all too short-lived, and in many parts of the company there was again a desperate effort to fill capacity. Paint machinery, winding equipment for gold mines, machines for washing bottles and for manufacturing cement and soap flakes – all helped to fill the gap left by the decline of armaments. Vickers, did not have enough products of its own and, particularly at Barrow and at Elswick on the Tyne, it took a good many licences; 'when you have 3,000 men to employ,' as a senior engineer at Barrow explained, 'you can't start doing R. and D.' The trouble was that the alternative to R. and D., in the short term at least, was little more than odd-jobbing.

Vickers' own efforts at diversification frequently ended in disappointment, and its attempt to enter the tractor market was a disaster. The story began in 1947 when the Labour Government asked Vickers to convert one hundred Sherman tanks into earth-moving equipment for the ground-nuts scheme. The politicians then pressed Vickers to produce a heavy-duty tractor: at one stage, they said they would want 1,000 a year. The idea seemed a good one, and Rolls agreed to develop a diesel engine. Unfortunately, however, the ground-nuts scheme collapsed and Vickers was left without an adequate base-load. Roughly two hundred large tractors were produced, but the development time allowed (given Vickers' inexperience) was too short – only one year from prototype to model, compared with a five-year period for tanks – and they proved to be 'no bloody good' in service, according to a man who was to be general manager of the tractor division: Vickers decided to take them all back and offer compensation to their owners.

The company then developed a second tractor, the Vigor. It was not competitively priced (costing roughly £10,000) and by that time Vickers was faced with strong opposition from American companies like Caterpillar, which had begun to manufacture inside the Sterling Area. Estimates of sales proved over-optimistic and in 1962, Vickers decided to call it a day: by that time, the tractor venture had cost it over £10m.

By the early 1960s Vickers was in serious trouble: steel profits had fallen, the ship-building boom was over, and it had suffered costly financial failures in aviation. The successor to the Viscount, the Vanguard, had been overtaken by a new generation of pure jets: only forty-three were sold, and the loss on a project which Vickers had financed entirely from its own funds was £13m. Its next venture, the VC 10, proved little less expensive, despite its early promise as a money-earner: the company made a loss provision of £15m., and although that has been steadily whittled down, there is no prospect of the project getting out of the red. Vickers continued to carry the heavy development costs of the VC 10 even after it had exchanged its aviation business for a forty per cent share in the British Aircraft Corporation. Furthermore, the company had decided to build the VC 10 at roughly the same time as approving construction of a new melting and rolling mill in Sheffield, at a cost of £26m.

The effect of this heavy outflow was to leave Vickers desperately short of cash: its borrowings amounted to almost £70m. by 1963, and were still over £60m. in 1965. This both held up the re-equipment of many of its plants and delayed the diversification into new products which was by now imperative; for the works at Barrow, it meant that the engineers still had to tool each job individually, instead of investing in numerical control equipment.

By 1965, with its cash burden rather lighter and the prospect of compensation for its steel interests, Vickers felt able to begin diversification: it bought (among other things) printing machinery companies and an office equipment group (Roneo). Some of its new ventures looked odd beside its old businesses. For example, it had made a film to demonstrate some of the sophisticated hospital equipment which its medical group was producing: on the walls of the film theatre were posters of the Vickers Mark I and II tanks.[1] Nonetheless, by 1966, almost a quarter of its capital had been invested in new products.

Soon, what one of the directors of the medical group called 'the great big lump from the past' had been still further reduced by the

[1] The cinema had been used shortly before for a 'presentation' of Vickers' Battle Tank and the 'posters' were 'fairly sophisticated charts'.

sale of Vickers' seventy-five per cent share in the English Steel Corporation – the compensation amounted to over £16m.; its loss-making
shipyard on the Tyne was sold to a consortium in exchange for an
eighteen per cent share-holding in the new company; old plants
working far below capacity were closed, and others streamlined. The
results obstinately refused to improve, however, and indeed in 1967
Vickers' net profit was its lowest since the war, and less than a third of
what it had been in 1962. The new businesses were doing well enough,
but Vickers' Canadian company had made very heavy losses on its
new shipbuilding. In 1968, however, the Canadian company turned in
a profit and Vickers made its best return on capital employed since
1962.

Rowan continued to see a silver lining somewhere ahead as Vickers
entered its second century. The son of missionary parents, he was
brought up in India, but then found his way via Cambridge (and
captaining England at hockey) to the Government Service, where he
became permanent private secretary to both Churchill and Attlee.
Vickers, curiously, hired him to handle both personnel and finance –
'God and Mammon,' said Rowan.

He was astonished by what he found – he recalled visiting one plant
where he was successively shown the manufacture of four-inch guns and
bottle-washing machines[1] – but eager to build a new Vickers. He supported the hiring of McKinsey and had learnt from Churchill that
people must be brought into the centre; the result was that managers
who had previously lurked in their Northern fastnesses for much of the
year were invited to come to Millbank for weekly progress reports. He
also became convinced that greater toughness was needed in pruning
dying enterprises – 'somebody has to be a son of a bitch even in a
family' – though *not* at the cost of serious damage to the Vickers team
spirit.

The changes required were immense. Vickers had a management
dominated by engineers educated in a cosy atmosphere of cost-plus,
and with little idea of how to sell products on the open market. Like
their labour force, many regarded Vickers as a permanent institution,
such as the monarchy, and were convinced that they had taken
a job 'for the duration'. They believed that they were in business to
employ people and to fill their works, rather than to make profits and

---

[1] A ten per cent improvement in the engineering of a gun might, he reflected, be
significant because it would yield a better price – while the same sort of improvement
in bottle-washing machines would not bring the same scale of reward.

serve the shareholders. They also felt a great loyalty to the company, and continued in the gentlemanly and benevolent style of their predecessors: newcomers were struck by what 'awfully good chaps' their colleagues were.

McKinsey helped to stir more interest in the principles of scientific management. It encouraged greater consideration of the likely returns from an investment before money was spent, it suggested that Vickers should be organized on the basis of businesses which made profit instead of works which employed people, and it helped instal a system of budgets and targets. Vickers, it said, had been works-oriented: it should now become market-oriented.

The sentiments were excellent; their practical achievement more difficult. The older managers had been moulded in a different era and the physical facts of life had to be faced. At Barrow, for example, Vickers had 13,000 men (over a third of the male working population), and perhaps 45,000 of the town's population of 64,000 depended on the company. Given Barrow's extreme isolation Vickers could not easily resign from its considerable responsibilities.

In the years before the First World War, two small villages – Vickerstown North and South – had been erected to house the workers who went there to build dreadnoughts. The names of the streets – Baden Powell, Lord Roberts, Juno, Powerful, Naiad – show how deep are the company's roots in the area. In the years that followed, Vickers not only provided work, it also supported the community's social life – subsidizing Barrow's theatre and football club, contributing to local charity, carrying far more than its share of the town's disabled. The employees, as one manager told me in 1967, thought of each other as comrades.

Contraction of the business was bound to be painful in these circumstances. Men who should have been laid off did odd jobs and, when work was short, all sorts of contracts were taken on which would have been regarded as unsatisfacory in other circumstances. There were some which provided long production runs – at the height of British Rail's programme of dieselization, Barrow was producing between two and three hundred engines a year – but the majority were all too short; in 1967, one of the managers of the general engineering division estimated that at least eighty per cent of its work was on runs of six or less. Rationalization and the fact that Barrow remains the 'lead yard' for the Navy's nuclear submarine programme have helped in some respects, but it is still a struggle.

Other plants, like that at South Marston, near Swindon, have also taken in a hotch-potch of products. Thirty per cent of its production consists of bits for aircraft – it does major sub-assemblies for the VC 10 and the BAC 111 – another thirty per cent in hydraulics through an agreement with an American company, ten per cent in medical equipment like nursing incubators and hyperbaric beds, between ten and fifteen per cent in nuclear and radiation engineering (rings and loops for reactors, cobalt radiation plants) and the balance in general engineering and automation. In areas like these, Vickers is faced with a constant battle to fill the space which it occupies.

Its problems, therefore, remain formidable. It has some excellent businesses – its printing presses and its brewery equipment are among the finest in the world – but it is still carrying the frightening burdens of the past. Rowan believes that the corner may soon be turned. If he is right, then Vickers must be a prime target for take-over by another company which would aim to sell off the assets it did not want.

Last of the Few

Rolls-Royce, whose image – as represented by its magnificent motor-cars – is the ultimate in Britishness, is nevertheless more American in its basic attitudes and atmosphere than any other British company, and even than some British subsidiaries of US corporations.

Once the traditional image is discarded, this is not in any way surprising. Although, in one sense, Rolls is the most provincial of Britain's big companies – the aero engine division, which accounted for eighty per cent of sales and eighty-three per cent of profits in 1967,[1] has only a handful of people in London – it lives in a world which is dominated by the United States. Its only competitors are American (it is one of three manufacturers of gas turbines left in existence) and its future rests in large part on its ability to compete in the US. Although (at present) Rolls has no American base, only a very modest share of the US market and its major competitor – Pratt and Whitney – is twice its

[1] Although the telegraphic address of Rolls' Derby headquarters is 'Roycar', motor-cars are no longer made there and they account for five per cent or less of the company's sales.

size in terms of sales,[1] its long-term objective is not merely to chip the corners off American supremacy, but to achieve the leading position for itself.

Long before it won headlines by landing a £180m. order to put turbo-fans into Lockheed's 1011 trijet airliner, Rolls was convinced that nothing could stop it making a major breakthrough into the United States or capturing a large slice of the world's markets.

These aspirations produce an unceasing flow of people between Derby and the United States. Rolls' chairman and chief executive, Sir Denning Pearson, and Sir David Huddie, the head of the aero engine division, each cross the Atlantic half-a-dozen times a year and its salesmen and engineers pay regular visits to all the major American airlines and airframe companies; one of Rolls' senior executives reckons to have crossed the Atlantic two hundred times since the war. Hundreds of Americans travel in the opposite direction, many of them because Rolls-Royce engines power six types of American aircraft in current production. Pearson's language is coloured by the terminology of American business – he refers to himself as the 'chief paid official' of the company, thinks in dollars and, when he makes comparisons, instinctively chooses General Motors or Pratt and Whitney.

So far as Pearson is concerned, the trans-Atlantic influence is more a matter of choice than chance. Unlike the heads of some large British companies, he has no chip on his shoulder about adopting American styles of management: he wants Rolls-Royce to take unto itself the best which the United States can offer and takes the view that 'if it's American, it's likely to be pretty good, because the Americans are pretty good at business'.

Rolls borrowed the basic concepts for its cost control system from American models. In 1961, Huddie went to the United States with the man who was to be chief cost controller, and they spent six weeks apiece at General Motors, Boeing and Westinghouse to find out how they operated. Rolls-Royce's research, development and design organization, which employs 18,000 people, matches the best in American industry in its scale and ambitions, the company has a battery of thirty-nine computers which provides a system of production and management control as sophisticated as anything in the United States

[1] Rolls is not dwarfed by its American competitors to anything like the same extent as Britain's two largest airframe companies. Boeing (sales of £1,200m. in 1967) is more than three times the size of Hawker Siddeley, while Lockheed (sales of £970m.) is five times as large as the British Aircraft Corporation.

and it has a willingness to buy outside advice which is unusual in British industry. Pearson's maxim is simple: 'When in doubt, hire a consultant – you don't have to pay him a pension.'

This transformation has been forced upon Rolls by the intensity of American competition, and it is now almost unrecognizable as the company of even fifteen years ago, let alone the one Pearson joined in 1932. At that stage, although Rolls had first produced aero engines in 1915 and had just decided to put its money into developing the Merlin, by far the largest proportion of its business was in motor-cars. Its ambitions, however, were already trans-Atlantic: it had set up an American company to market its cars, but realized it had made a psychological error and abandoned the venture. In Derby, its reputation was like that of other car makers – 'Rush 'em and Rest 'em' – because of sharp seasonal fluctuations in demand.

In these years, Rolls was managed from London: its managing director lived there, and visited Derby when he had to. It was an appropriate enough style for a company which was selling its product to tycoons and the titled. When the Board did come to Derby, it seldom demeaned itself by meeting at the works, but repaired instead to the comfort of the Midland Hotel. One of the war's beneficial effects, so far as Rolls was concerned, was to bring the managing director to the Midlands. His staff persuaded him that it was too dangerous for him to stay in London, and he lived for the duration at the company's guest house.

The war turned Rolls-Royce into a sizeable aero-engine business. Since it was involved almost entirely in the production of Merlins, it was also virtually a one-product business. The end of the war inevitably brought a slump in demand – the labour force fell from 47,000 to 24,000 in fifteen months – and a strong conviction on the part of men like Pearson that Rolls had to break into civil aviation; until 1945, its efforts had been restricted to military engines.

It proved to be a painful apprenticeship. Since Rolls had not previously developed engines for regular airline use – with over ten times as many operating hours a year as a typical military aircraft – the modified Merlins which went into Trans-Canada's DC 4s gave considerable trouble in the early years;[1] their cylinder blocks were being changed every six hundred flying hours. (One of Rolls' current engines regularly flies more than ten times that number between major overhauls.)

But Rolls' wartime experience left it with one priceless advantage:

[1] The engine was ultimately developed into a reliable unit and is still in airline service.

it was the only company in the world which had experience of producing and maintaining jet engines in operational service. Its development engineers had been working since the end of the war to produce a gas turbine for civil use. Their eventual triumph, in the shape of the Dart, gave Rolls most of the world market for gas turbines until the late 1950s: Pratt and Whitney had to take a licence from Rolls to manufacture its Nene and Tay military engines in order to get into the jet business after the war.

With military orders booming – they accounted for the bulk of Rolls-Royce's business during the early 1950s – these were easy years: aero engine companies were turning in even better profits than the makers of airframes. For the designers, in particular, it was an exhilarating atmosphere in which to work. Rolls, then as now, was teeming with brilliant engineers ('even the lavatory cleaner had a degree') and the company was committed to the pursuit of excellence at a cracking pace.

Naturally enough, under the circumstances, there was little concern for organizational structure. The planning of projects tended to be vague and, since the designers had the whip hand, there was more emphasis on the size and power of engines than on the profit they might make, more concern with technical feasibility than commercial value. Cost control was primitive. The chairman, Lord Hives, who had joined the company in 1908 to supervise experimental work on cars, was a superb manager and gave young men major responsibilities at an age which would still seem lunatic in the staider British companies. Huddie was given charge of development work on a complete engine project at the age of thirty, and Claude Birch (now with GKN) was appointed chairman of the training committee at twenty-seven.

Hives also distrusted neat organization; the more tightly you defined responsibility, the more you created water-tight compartments, the more you ran the danger of killing inspiration. The result was what appeared to be chaos. 'He used to coin idiotic titles,' said a man who worked under him, 'such as, for example, chief designer, brackets, civil, brackets, projects – when there were six of them already – and the people concerned were left to battle it out!' Huddie insists that Hives never allowed the chaos to go too far and always ensured that the fight for money and power was a fair one. It was a system which allowed engineering genius to flourish.

But a different era was beginning, governed by a new set of circumstances. For one thing, Rolls-Royce had lost its monopoly of the gas turbine: it could no longer afford to rest on superior technology.

Furthermore, the decline of military orders – and, by the later 1960s, Rolls-Royce's business was becoming increasingly civil – also brought with it a decline in the number of projects for which the Government would foot the entire development bill (even though, like the Avon, they were later sold in civil versions) and a decline also in the longer runs which military business often provided.

Development costs for engines were mounting as rapidly as they were for aircraft, and Rolls had to be prepared to spend more of its own money for returns which were a good deal less predictable. Its decision, in 1957, to build the Spey, meant an initial investment of £20m., a total long-term outlay of £30m.; the Government was only prepared to cover a third of the bill, on the usual repayment basis. By the later 1960s, the total development and production cost of a big new engine (including modifications in service) had risen to nearer £60m. and Rolls was inevitably driven towards greater dependence on Government funding; it is reported to be putting up seventy per cent of the launching cost of the basic engine for the medium-range version of the Lockheed 1011.[1]

A more competitive market and a sharp increase in total launching costs have pushed up the break-even point for new engines. Rolls says it is impossible to generalize on how many engines must be produced before the break-even point is reached, but one estimate suggests that while sales of 1,000 covered launching costs in the 1950s, the figure is nearer 1,600 today. The runs provided by civil business were frequently all too short. 'If this is civil business with seventy aircraft,' one of the older Rolls-Royce men said to Pearson, 'give me war with a thousand!' Rolls has not yet been able to repeat the phenomenal success of the Dart, which sold over 6,000 and is still going strong and which now powers more airliners than any other turbine engine. There were also commercial failures like the Clyde, while the Medway, built at a cost of £4½m. to fit BEA's original concept of the Trident, did not go into production. (It was not a complete write-off, however, because the Spey was closely modelled on it.) The runs of even reasonably successful engines tended to be measured in hundreds rather than the thousands on which the big American companies could frequently count.

Rolls had come hard up against a basic dilemma – how to compete with the Americans without actually breaking into the American market. The obstacles appeared enormous. To begin with, although

---

[1] Presumably the Government will want a more rapid return on its money now that it is lending more than half the sum involved.

Rolls produced technological advances – it was first with both the propjet and the turbofan (fan-jet) – such breakthroughs were unlikely to be crucial once the basic design of the gas turbine had stabilized.

There was also the natural American bias against buying jet engines overseas. This was not merely a question of resistance on the part of the American airlines and airframe manufacturers, but of the reluctance of United States Governments to allow strategic contracts to go abroad, damaging the national balance of payments into the bargain. The administration's view influences the decisions of operators if only because it holds patronage over the allocation of new domestic air routes.

Above all, there was the question of meeting the Americans on cost and fuel economy. With a tariff of ten per cent on imported aero engines, and taking into account the assorted influences on the American industry to buy at home, Rolls effectively had to undercut Pratt and Whitney by twenty-five per cent. It had the advantage of lower labour costs – even though, in a highly labour-intensive industry, its wage bill takes up over forty per cent of its earnings – but it was not helped by the lack in Britain of the competitive sub-contracting industry which exists in the United States. Costs were also inflated by the need to build up volume by selling to scores of foreign airlines and governments: satisfying their individual requirements meant – as Pearson put it – producing in '57 varieties'.[1]

The crucial need, therefore, was a full-scale attack on costs: Rolls had to become more commercial in its attitudes and less indulgent towards its engineers. It also had to learn how to plan.

The changes which followed amounted to as profound a revolution in management methods as has ever been carried through by a British company. There had been piecemeal reorganizations before Hives retired: a motor-car division had been separated off and based at Crewe in 1954, an oil engine division at Shrewsbury in 1956. In 1958, after Pearson had taken over, divisional Boards were set up for each part of the company, and given complete responsibility for day-to-day operations. Pearson then began trying to formalize what had previously been informal, and eventually produced Rolls-Royce's Blue Book,

---

[1] The industry's time-scales are long ones. For example, the studies which led to the RB 211 started in the early 1960s, the engine was being ordered in 1968 and will enter airline service in 1971. Production will continue throughout the 1970s (and possibly beyond) with a spares business going on long after that. The first Dart ran in 1946; its spares business will last until at least 1980.

which defines the functions and responsibilities of each manager.

The attack on costs followed. Huddie, who became general manager of the aero engine division in 1962, was quite clear about the need. 'You don't have to sell engineering here,' he said, 'they'll do that without you. What we dedicated ourselves to was finding ways of making engines not to a standard of perfection but to the right standard at the lowest possible cost.'

The creation of a cost control organization began in 1961, and the system steadily increased in sophistication and effectiveness. General Motors had warned Huddie that he might not see major benefits for ten years; in fact, it had begun to pay off significantly by 1967.

The basic framework is simple enough. The financial controller, who is responsible for all the accounting, costing and financial forecasting of the aero engine division, has an office next door to Huddie's. Functionally responsible to him are several senior controllers working for directors with specific responsibilities to the division – engineering, production, commercial and experimental – and each of these controllers has his own staff covering separate work centres, defined as geographical locations allied to certain types of work. The financial controller also has a profit plans manager, responsible for drawing up plans in great detail.

The work centres were created in 1963 as an effort to break down the division into manageable units. 'We're not like some people, we don't have hundreds of products,' said H. E. Trevan-Hawke, Rolls' director of finance. 'We've got one damn great product, which we make in one lump, and we found it very hard to split up the colossal amorphous mass which the division had become. We decided eventually that we couldn't put a price on everything, or measure profits on everything, but that we could set cost per hour targets.' McKinsey were called in to help Rolls implement its ideas on work centres.

The financial controller's main job is to co-ordinate the creation of one-year and five-year plans which lay down cost and profit targets for each area of the division. Every four weeks, a financial control statement is produced which reports on progress against the one-year plan and singles out exceptions – anything which is five per cent or more above or below target. Huddie gets a rough result a week before the end of the four-week period, with one page in red showing the major variants; the first half of each divisional Board meeting is taken up in dealing with them. Huddie finds the process indispensable. 'Without it,' he said, 'there's no way of knowing that scrap is costing you forty per cent more than you planned. Then you're off like a scalded fly trying to do something about it.'

Huddie admits that, when Rolls first started drawing up an overall plan, it committed the error of not bringing the individuals concerned into the process – 'it was made in a corner away from them, and the result was that we kept being surprised.' Now, in an effort to push a sense of responsibility as far down the line as possible, every area of the business is given a part in creating it, including foremen. Huddie sets the task – the number of men to be used, the length of time to be taken, the cost per hour – and each area signs for itself. Rolls now has a profit plan for all projects, existing and new. Each major area also has to name its improvement objectives – which Huddie limits to six – and the cost savings they intend to achieve. The key, according to Huddie, is a simple set of figures, which are known right down to the foreman level. 'The further we have gone down the line,' said Sir Denning Pearson, 'the more we have under-spent our budgets.'

Rolls has been spending heavily to make sure that its management techniques match its engineering talent. About two per cent of the aero engine division's turnover goes on computers, and there are 1,300 people involved in data processing and computer work. Roughly forty per cent of the capacity of Rolls' thirty-nine computers is taken up with engineering and technical work, sixty per cent with management systems. The computers have, among other things, helped speed up what were once tedious engineering processes. A computer now designs die blocks for compressor blades and then produces the tapes to operate the automatic machines which cut them. It also designs and makes tapes to manufacture the inspection tools needed to test the compressor. This process used to take six months; it can now be done in a day. The computers can also test an aircraft's performance before either it or its engines have left the drawing board by matching tapes which reflect the design characteristics of both.

Huddie, a brilliant engineer from Northern Ireland who runs the division with phenomenal energy and enthusiasm (a man who knew him in his early years described him as 'a frightfully able nut case': Huddie thinks of himself as a 'controlled enthusiast'), believes it would be wrong to use the system as an absolute tool. The overall plan makes allowance for shortfalls although, for obvious reasons, very few people are told about them. Huddie's success has been in communicating to his staff his own passionate belief in the new way of doing things, and the involvement of the designers in the fight to cut costs brought savings which helped Rolls to undercut Pratt and Whitney by £42,000 an engine (£208,000 to £250,000) in the bid to get the RB 178 into Boeing's jumbo jets. Rolls still failed to get the order, but it won the next round at Lockheed.

Huddie has collected around him a team of six trouble-shooters – an executive assistant, and five staff officers – the oldest of whom is thirty-six. They have, he says, 'no authority, but all the authority in the world.' Their job is to make sure that the inter-faces between projects do not interfere with progress; when there is a hold-up, they have to resolve it quickly. In the event of failure, they appeal directly to Huddie.

Rolls-Royce is also experimenting with incentives of its own devising. Key men in the aero engine division are on a bonus which is broken into two parts, and which makes a large part of their salary dependent on their personal performance. The first is related to a man's success in hitting the target set for his area of the business. The second is based on his performance against a series of personal objectives, a combination of qualities vital to the job in which he is most deficient. Huddie writes the objectives himself, but allows each man a certain freedom in formulating his own – 'I allow him to substitute one quality for another, but not more than that.'

When Huddie took over, there were other organizational problems. One was that many engine parts were still being produced at both the company's main plants, in Derby and Glasgow. By the end of 1962, Huddie had drawn up a plan to cut out the major areas of duplication, and by the end of 1965 it had been carried through. Now, for example, compressor blades for all engines are made at Glasgow, all wheels at Derby. The only duplications which remain are in small items of less than 10-inches cube.

These changes were carried through in a period which included extremely difficult years. With the future uncertain, the decision to invest £20m. in the Spey had been bold : Pearson told the Board that he could not guarantee success if they decided to go ahead, but that he could guarantee failure if they did not. Then, in the early 1960s, a slump in orders hit Rolls severely. The result was that sales fell by £20m., the labour force by 7,000. In 1962, 2,000 men were sacked, and 30,000 more put on short time. In 1961, Rolls had trouble in showing a profit at all, and it only produced its £1.8m. by a revision in accounting practices. Fortunately, the return to 'Rush 'em and Rest 'em' was short-lived.

Its steady sellers, the Dart and the Spey, helped the company through the crisis, and in addition its efforts in the United States began to bear fruit. The Spey, for example, was chosen for eight types of British and foreign aircraft, including the Corsair and the Grumman Gulfstream II in the US, and the Conway was used for a number of Boeing 707s and Douglas DC 8s. There were also disappointments, like the loss of the jumbo-jet contract. In the battle to win the Lockheed order, Huddie himself took a flat in America for several months, and Pearson said that – with every engine worth over $500,000, and perhaps as much again for spares[1] – he would gladly have shipped the entire Board to New York with gold-plated Rolls-Royces to clinch the deal. Rolls spent over eighteen months working on the bid, one version of which weighed sixty-three pounds.

The Lockheed order is very much the beginning of the road so far as Rolls is concerned. Its share of sales in the United States is still small but increasing, and it is aiming to capture thirty per cent during the 1970s. At least the acquisition of Bristol Siddeley has given Rolls a larger stake in European markets (with the engines for the Concorde and VFW 614) and given it an entrant in the civil supersonic field. It must also have relieved fears that Pratt and Whitney would snap up Bristol Siddeley: the idea of P and W manufacturing in Europe at British wage rates was not one to cause pleasure at Derby.

Rolls still has weaknesses. Its labour force, for example, is too large – it has more people than Pratt and Whitney, yet produces fewer engines[2] – but Pearson can now fairly boast that its engines and techniques are as good as anything in the world. Its margin on sales is also desperately thin – 2.7 per cent after tax in 1968 – but better, even at that, than the returns of the United Aircraft Corporation, which produced only 2.6 per cent in 1967. For the future, Rolls is as confident as ever. 'We've put down the fertilizer,' said Huddie. 'The real returns are just coming.'

Rolls-Royce has somehow managed to avoid much of the clamour in which the British aircraft industry has been involved since the war. Perhaps, with the gas turbine, it was better placed than the airframe manufacturers; perhaps it preferred not to embroil itself – Lord Hives was never willing to become president of the industry's trade association, the Society of British Aircraft Constructors, on the ground that someone had to mind Rolls' business.

[1] Some airlines reckon to spend $1 on spares for every hour of flying time.
[2] One reason for the larger labour force is Rolls' wide range of engines, with shorter production runs than in the US – coupled with the fact that engine work is more widely sub-contracted by American manufacturers.

Certainly no other industry has suffered a series of such profound shocks. The Comet disasters of the early 1950s not only depressed de Havilland's business (and morale) for several years, but also seriously affected other companies, including Rolls-Royce, which was to have put its Avon engine into the Comet II. In 1957, the Sandys White Paper seemed to sound the death-knell of manned flight, except for the sort of mundane jobs which transport aircraft and helicopters could perform, and with the exception of a replacement for the Canberra. In 1960, at the point of the Government's gun, came the reluctant mergers which produced the British Aircraft Corporation and the Hawker Siddeley Group.

As if these upheavals were not enough, from 1960 onwards the industry had to survive major cancellations in both missiles and aircraft – Blue Streak in 1960, the TSR 2 (a strike and reconnaissance aircraft), the HS 681 (a short take-off transport) and the P. 1154 vertical take-off fighter in 1965 – not to mention reductions of orders by Britain's nationalized airlines. The cancellations only served to enhance the industry's sense of insecurity. As Sir Arnold Hall, Hawker's chairman, pointed out, they did not involve merely 'tearing up a few drawings': the end of the HS 681 and the P. 1154 meant the loss of £1,000m. of potential sales for Hawker, and an incidental £2m. in the redisposition of capacity.

Not even the most acquiescent of industries would have allowed these events to pass without protest and the aircraft companies' complaints rent the air at frequent intervals. In more recent times, the din has abated. The structure of the industry is more stable; some of the explosive pioneers who led the protests have passed on; and the remaining companies, increasingly dependent on the Government for launching aid as development costs continue to soar, are inclined to take a cooler view of their calling. In Hall's view the aeroplane business had become far too emotional an affair; to him, it is simply a branch of engineering.

During the war, the Americans had been allowed to retain a virtual monopoly of transport aircraft. Britain's efforts to fill the gap in the early post-war years were both costly and disastrous: the Government lost £15½m. in financing the Brabazon and the Princess alone. Nevertheless, the Korean War produced a world-wide revival of military demand, the Viscount proved extremely successful, and in the years from 1949 to 1956, the industry earned an average return on capital employed of about eighteen per cent; in 1955 and 1956, Hawker made over thirty per cent. Thereafter, profits went steadily downhill and by 1964, the industry was making little better than six per cent; the big American companies showed the same trend.

The industry was still primitive in its organization, with too many small firms fighting for too few orders; it was interested in sophisticated machines but not in sophisticated management; and its concepts of cost control were elementary. Far too many of its leaders still believed that enthusiasm and technical prowess could conquer all.

By the late 1950s, military orders had fallen away and a number of companies – some of which had put their own money into civil projects – were in serious trouble. Vickers, faced with heavy losses on the Vanguard, turned to the Government for financial aid. The Government agreed to put up twenty-five per cent of the development costs of the VC 10, not without apprehension.

The return on its investment in the industry had, after all, been lamentable; of the £88m. which it spent between 1945 and 1959, it had recovered only £25m. by 1965, less than thirty per cent.[1] This reflected the weakness conferred on the British industry by its small home market, and also its failure to break out into world markets: too many aircraft were tailor-made for the nationalized airlines, and little effort was made to canvass the requirements of overseas operators. The Plowden Report of 1965 pointed out that every one of the sixteen aircraft introduced between 1955 and 1964 had been a flop in export markets, and that sales abroad (in terms of numbers) had amounted to only $7\frac{1}{2}$ per cent of those at home. The overall post-war record in the civil field had been scarcely less depressing. Of the thirty-six different transport types produced by the end of 1965, only eight had sold more than one hundred aircraft.

Apart from the Viscount and the Rolls-Royce Dart engine, the Americans – with their massive home base – had swept the board. They had overwhelming advantages: more than sixty per cent of the world's air traffic has a North American origin (US domestic airlines alone account for forty per cent of all the miles flown) and seventy per cent of the world's airframes are built in the United States. This ensures very long production runs – Plowden estimated, for example,

[1] After 1960, the money was repayable on a pre-arranged formula, but the Government generally only gets back a quarter of the profit margin on each sale until the company has covered its share of the launching costs. Thereafter, the Government takes a larger share. It is, in effect, an interest-free loan which does not have to be repaid in full in the event of failure.

that (taking civil aircraft introduced between 1955 and 1961), they were $4\frac{1}{2}$ times as long as those for comparable British models, and that despite higher labour and raw material prices, American production costs were twenty per cent lower.

The Government was thus faced with the choice of leaving the field to the Americans or paying up in increasing amounts. Despite the constraints imposed by a precarious balance of payments situation, it has felt compelled to take the latter course (even though on a narrower front), not only from considerations of pride or strategy, but also because Britain has the second largest aircraft industry and because £4,000m. a year is likely to be spent on aircraft equipment during the 1970s. Despite the cancellations of 1965, the Government has backed the Concorde, the world's first supersonic airliner, to the tune of several hundreds of millions of pounds, and the Ministry of Technology estimated in 1967 that it would be providing two-thirds of the cost of *all* development projects up to 1970.

The British Aircraft Corporation, a merger of Bristol Aeroplane with the aircraft interests of Vickers and English Electric, has been heavily dependent on the Government from birth.[1] The Government, on the other hand, did not have the job of producing one enterprise from three companies. The fact that two of the three (Vickers and English Electric) had equal stakes in the business meant that it lacked a dominant partner with a clear-cut supremacy, and that it was therefore more likely to produce a compromise than rapid rationalization. This is precisely what happened at first.

Another of BAC's initial weaknesses was a shortage of products. The Bristol Aeroplane Company had, by 1960, fallen on difficult times, with production of its Britannia stopped and only the Bloodhound missile earning profits. Vickers, with sales of the Viscount past their peak, brought to BAC the Vanguard, which went into service at the end of 1960 although its commercial prospects were far from bright. Only English Electric, with the military work provided by the Canberra and the Lightning, was doing well.

English Electric had also drawn up plans for a 'super-Canberra', but had agreed with Vickers before the merger that the airframe work on it should be divided between them. English, however, resented the decision to put Vickers in charge of that part of the project (which

---

[1] Its directors say that only twenty-seven per cent of its business now comes from Government orders: without Government money for development, it would not be in business at all.

became the TSR 2) because Vickers had never produced a supersonic aircraft. From 1960 to 1965, BAC was heavily dependent on TSR 2, while not being in control of the project as a whole; the Government, for example, dictated the choice of engine and engine manufacturer. Furthermore, since two-thirds of the cost was to go on the engine and the sophisticated equipment, BAC was contractually responsible for only one-third.

The cancellation of TSR 2 came as a considerable shock but by 1965 work on the Concorde – in which BAC was to work with the French firm of Sud Aviation – was well under way, with the Government footing one hundred per cent of the bill; another Anglo–French project, the Jaguar tactical support and training aircraft, had also been launched. BAC contributed to its salvation by developing the One-Eleven as a private venture, building (at its own cost) the multi-role version of the Lightning, and developing and selling the BAC 167 ahead of the RAF requirement for a pressurized Provost. From that point, it has made a modest recovery. In 1966 it paid a dividend of six per cent, in 1967 of seven and a half per cent, and it is doing well abroad – eighty-four of the first 107 One-Elevens were sold to overseas customers, and about sixty per cent of its £341m. backlog of orders is for export. It is now approaching the break-even point of two hundred for the One-Eleven, which looks like being in production until 1975.

For the future, it desperately needs an entrant in the sub-sonic field larger than the One-Eleven – a Two-Eleven was turned down by the Government – and its hopes rest heavily on the Concorde, which represents the biggest gamble in the history of the industry. At present, although a number of airlines have taken out options, some are less than enthusiastic because of the problems of going supersonic. BAC, on the other hand, remains convinced that if one airline goes supersonic the rest must follow, and predicts that 250 sales by 1975 will mean earnings of £1,500m. It points out that European man-hour costs are only one-third of those in America, but that if the Americans' lower unit costs (because of bigger initial runs) can be matched by European collaboration, Europe can lead the world. It also admits that while such collaboration brings a reduction in research and development costs per country, it also adds to the overall bill by about twenty-five per cent.

At some stage, BAC may find itself working in harness with the other major surviving airframe company, Hawker Siddeley. In November 1966, the Government said there should be a merger between the airframe interests of the two companies; more than two years have now passed, but nothing has yet come of that decision. Sir Arnold Hall says the Government asked Hawker for information, but that he has talked to neither the Government nor BAC about such a deal. In the meantime, he is neither for nor against the idea; everything would depend on the terms.

Hall's insistence that he has no ideological bias against a heavier involvement in aircraft seems to be contradicted by the way Hawker has developed over the last fifteen years. Aerospace, which includes missiles and sales to other aircraft companies by subsidiaries like High Duty Alloys (its biggest customer is Rolls-Royce) now accounts for more than half its sales and over two-thirds of its profits (before tax and interest) but while the proportion of its capital committed to aircraft has remained relatively static, it has moved smartly into a variety of other fields. To take the most striking example: it is now one of the largest makers of diesel engines in Europe, whereas fifteen years ago it did not produce any. What is more, diesel engines probably provide an average return on capital at least twice as high as Hawker's aircraft business.

The group's first burst of diversification came in 1957, immediately after the Sandys White Paper. Like the bosses of virtually every other aircraft business, Sir Roy Dobson began hurriedly looking for other baskets in which to put some of Hawker's eggs. He bought the Brush Group, makers of diesel engines, generators and steam turbines (against the advice of his financial director) and a seventy-seven per cent shareholding in the Dominion Coal and Steel Corporation of Canada (Dosco) which gave Hawker twenty per cent of Canada's steel-making capacity, as well as ship-yards and coal and iron ore mines. Shortly afterwards, Dobson acquired an Australian business producing, amongst other things, timber and bricks for the building industry.

The process went on after Hall had taken over as managing director in 1963, but in a more controlled fashion. He bought a diesel engine company (Lister) and Crompton Parkinson, manufacturers of electric motors, transformers and switchgear.[1] Hall insists that he did not, like Dobson, buy them as a reaction to the perils of the aviation business, but because he wanted to consolidate Hawker's diesel and electrical interests.

Not all the newer ventures provided the comfort intended, and indeed

[1] In 1968, the electrical division accounted for thirty-one per cent of Hawker's capital employed, but only nine per cent of its profit.

Hawker's £26m. investment in Canada turned out to be a messy and (so far) only marginally profitable affair. 'We've spent a lot of time trying to stop leaks in buckets,' said the group's financial director, John Robertson. Hawker has closed Dosco's iron mines, been relieved of its coal mines by the Canadian Government and (after building a new steel mill) sold off its steel plants. It has also shut down the traditional carriage and wagon section of another of its acquisitions – Canadian Car.

The aircraft side has, so far as Canada is concerned, survived rather better. Avro's business was ruined in 1959 when the Canadian Government cancelled both the Arrow supersonic interceptor and the engine which was to power it, but de Havilland has done well enough with its Twin Otters and Beavers. Like Hawker's Canadian aero engine company (which has sold out forty per cent of its shares to the United Aircraft Corporation, parent of Pratt and Whitney), de Havilland has done some useful horse-trading with the Americans to fill spare capacity. It built tails and wings for the DC 9 and then sold Douglas its tooling and a lease on the factory space.

Hall's major job, however, has been the rationalization of the group's aircraft interests in Britain. The chiefs of Hawker's constituent companies had always resisted any attempt to limit their autonomy and when Hall suggested that the time for rationalization had come he was bitterly opposed – by Dobson among others. The mergers of 1960 merely complicated an already untidy situation. They had more than doubled Hawker's aircraft labour force (from 36,000 to 73,000), and dumped in its lap not only the results of diversifications by each of the companies[1] – it acquired factories making steam rollers, lawn mowers, gas meters and lamp posts – but also their development schemes for new aeroplanes. On the aircraft side alone there were thirty factories, offices and stores scattered over the country. By the time Hall took over, some initial reorganization had been carried through – the de Havilland and Blackburn engine companies had been sold – but the major part remained.

Hall began the operation with distinct advantages. One was that he was in an unquestioned position of power: Hawker Siddeley had taken over de Havilland, Blackburn and Folland rather than form a consortium, as BAC had done. Furthermore, although Hall had worked for Hawker before (he was technical director from 1955–8), he came back to the group in 1963 as a new man, unencumbered by old

[1] De Havilland, Folland and Blackburn were added to the group.

relationships and involvement in the squabbles which negotiation of the mergers had brought. On the other hand, those wounds still festered – some de Havilland men in particular felt that they had belonged to the superior company and yet been poorly treated – and not surprisingly, there was precious little feeling for Hawker while the new acquisitions retained much of their old shape and autonomy.

Hall's solution was relatively simple. He formed one aircraft division, hiving off missiles and aerospace to Hawker Siddeley Dynamics, and the steam-rollers, ¡amp posts and other odds and ends into a holdings division. Once there, he thought, they could be weeded out and the survivors used as a nursery for young managers. The internal organization of the aircraft division was an interim solution, a halfway house to full integration. For the time being, it was to have three sub-groups; de Havilland was to handle civil projects, Blackburn and Folland were absorbed by Hawker in a group to produce fighters, Avro-Whitworth was to deal with heavy military orders like the Vulcan.

In 1965, taking the cancellations of the HS 681 and the P. 1154 as his opportunity, Hall completed the reorganization. Hawker Siddeley Aviation became one company, with its centre at the old Hawker headquarters at Kingston. Of the directors of the seven original companies, fourteen out of forty-eight remained; of the thirty factories, only twelve survived. This deft piece of butchery put the remaining directors in no doubt as to the source of further promotion – Hawker Siddeley Aviation, and not de Havilland or Blackburn was now the sole purveyor of top jobs – and this, of course, may have helped to redirect loyalties. Furthermore, the aircraft which Hawker was building were no longer in the possession of one company – work was divided around the group. The HS 125 executive jet, for example, was designed at Hatfield, built at Chester, and the parts for it sub-contracted to half-a-dozen different factories.

Hall's own authority within the group steadily increased. His intellect, as a Fellow of the Royal Society and former director of the Royal Aircraft Establishment, was not in question; the fact that he could fly and had worked with Whittle on the jet engine also gave him standing with the engineers. But his greatest virtue, so far as his colleagues at head office were concerned, was his willingness to listen and to plan on the basis of assembled fact. This was a blessed relief after the volcanic eruptions and the barnstorming which had characterized Dobson. It soothed their bruised feelings, restored their confidence and, at the same time, nourished their loyalty towards Hawker.

Despite all the departures from subsidiary Boards, no one came or left at the highest levels of the company. Instead, Hall took the men who were there and, in some cases, redirected their energies. For example, Sir Aubrey Burke, former chairman of de Havilland and an aircraft man all his life, happily took over supervision of the diesel engine business and the holdings group. It was not surprising that Hall came to be regarded as a super-man by many of his colleagues – 'the most brilliant man in England', in the view of more than one. For the first time Hawker had become a united group, and the opposition party which had existed in Dobson's time disappeared.

The aircraft which were on the stocks also gave promise of a future less ulcerous than the past – they were both less fraught with risk and less politically vulnerable than BAC's Concorde and Jaguar. Once the cancellations had been weathered Hawker was left with a business which, if it does not seem likely to yield fat profits, at least has the prospect of steady and continuing sales. The HS 125, the HS 748 turbo-prop airliner, the HS 810 (a replacement for the Shackleton), the Buccaneer strike and reconnaissance aircraft, the Twin Otter and the Beaver are all good bread-and-butter lines; the Trident has obvious potential; and there is plenty of work in refurbishing Hunters, Shackletons and Vulcans. The HS 125 has already passed its break-even point and Hawker can foresee a market for the HS 748 for the next forty years. The group also has useful contracts for the P 1154 fighter, the Nimrod (an advanced reconnaissance plane for the Navy) and the Harrier, the first vertical take-off aircraft to go into service.

Hall's chief concern was, and is, for the future. BAC is currently doing the more advanced work in the civil field, and it has the best long-term military contracts. On the military side, Hawker has nothing clearly in sight to carry it through the middle-1970s: in the civil sector, it was disturbed by the Government's decision to withdraw from the European airbus project, for which it was to build the wings and instal the engines (it has now agreed to continue to participate in the venture). If, as seems likely, the merger with BAC ultimately takes place and Hall becomes boss of the combined enterprise, some of these problems would be solved, although Hawker would also inherit the massive uncertainties which surround BAC's present prospects. Till then, he is content with what he has: an order book of £380m. and an aircraft business as stable and free of risk as any in the world.

To that extent, Hawker is left waiting for the Government. Hall's ambitions in fields other than aircraft are comparatively modest. He can see the advantages of size as a defence against take-over but is also aware of its limitations for improving the bulk of Hawker's operations, many of which are concerned with the production of batches of goods and therefore will not yield economies of scale so easily as high-volume businesses. He is therefore more likely to be looking for medium-sized enterprises in mechanical engineering and electrical products rather than for larger purchases, such as Vickers. He would like to have got his hands on parts of English Electric's empire, but resisted Plessey's suggestion of a joint bid partly because of possible taxation snags and partly because he thought the opposition from GEC too strong.

Hawker is therefore comfortably placed for the modest expansion which Hall seems to have in mind, though its profits are also likely to remain modest. Its main weakness is that, like so many other British companies, it appears to be too dependent on one man. There is no obvious successor to Hall and the group has a rather elderly Board. The aircraft industry has only recently been forced to cultivate professional management and many of Hawker's best men are probably still in the second line.

So far as the industry as a whole is concerned, many of its anxieties centre on the danger of European (mainly French) domination – although the British industry is currently about $2\frac{1}{2}$ times the size of the French. Concorde and Jaguar, its spokesmen point out, are French-led and Britain is now (temporarily or permanently) out of the airbus; if airframe control goes to Europe, so does engine control, and Britain will be merely a junior partner (if partner at all) just as the market really takes off. 'By 1975,' said one of them, 'there will be no UK-led aerospace produce left on the world scene, except perhaps the fag-end of One-Eleven and Harrier production and we shall be technically dependent on an industry whose only aeroplanes of any note have been the Caravelle and the Mirage.'

The Car Makers

If there is one basic difference between the motor industry and other big engineers, it is that for much the larger part of its business it is dealing with millions of customers: it is a mass-production industry turning out fashion goods. It is also therefore a very convenient tool with which the Government can regulate consumer spending, and between 1957 and 1968 hire purchase terms on cars were changed eleven times, the rate of purchase tax on seven occasions.

For a good many years after the war, the optimism of the industry's leaders was consistently justified. As late as 1960 it was making an average return on capital (before tax), of almost twenty-five per cent (the aircraft industry was already earning less than ten per cent) and it was in the van of the export drive,[1] making less and less profit on its overseas sales as the years went by, but bringing in dollars and at least helping to cover its overheads.

But 1960 proved to be a high point of its earnings, and in 1967 the industry was still making less cars than in 1964. By 1967, its before-tax return on capital had slumped to 1.8 per cent (taking the average for the companies now in the British Leyland group, together with Ford, Vauxhall and Rootes); and its total income had fallen from a profit of £46.6m. in 1964 to a loss of £2.4m. in 1967. Ford's vehicle production was down by 100,000; British Motor Holdings' by almost 200,000, even allowing for the fact that it had, in the meantime, taken over Jaguar; while Rootes made a loss in five of the seven years between 1962 and 1967. By that time, Britain had slipped from second to fourth among the world's car manufacturers. Nineteen sixty-eight brought a sharp recovery, particularly for British Leyland and Ford, although 1969 is very unlikely to be such a good year overall.

The industry has put down a good deal of its troubles to frequent changes in hire purchase,[2] and pointed out that its competitors in West Germany have never had to contend with similar restrictions, the Italians for only a short period in the middle 1960s. Yet, although sales in Britain had been falling away between 1964 and 1967, the industry still had faith that boom times would return and went on investing at a very high level – the rate of growth in its fixed assets was almost double that for manufacturing industry as a whole between 1960 and 1966. The heaviest spender, Ford, invested three times as much between 1961 and 1967 as it had from 1954 to 1960.

This combination of falling sales and rising investment meant that the industry was using less of its capacity as the years went by; in 1964 the figure was eighty-eight per cent, in 1967 only sixty-four per cent.

---

[1] The motor industry accounts for about seventeen per cent of Britain's exports of manufactured goods.

[2] Roughly a quarter of car sales are made on hire purchase contracts.

Since the break-even point for big British motor companies usually comes when they are employing around sixty-five per cent of their capacity, the industry was at that time clearly running close to the border-line of profitability.

There was a serious threat to morale at the British Motor Corporation, the largest company in the BMH empire. I happened to visit the Longbridge headquarters only a few days before the merger with Leyland was announced, and found a company which was trying hard to make up lost ground. The roads around the plant were clogged with unfinished cars parked three and four deep in the snow, and there were thousands more at nearby airfields. BMC had decided to give its 1100 and Mini ranges a face-lift for the 1967 Motor Show and, partly because of strikes, some component suppliers had been unable to meet their target dates. By the end of the year, BMC was turning out incomplete vehicles which had to be stock-piled until the components arrived.

Gone were the halcyon days when the company was making engineering history with the Mini and the 1100 and when its chiefs could be justifiably expansive in predicting the future. At the time of the merger with Morris in 1951,[1] Austin alone was selling more cars in Britain than Ford; by July 1967, BMH's share of the market had fallen within a few years from forty-two per cent to 27.7 per cent, and it was scarcely ahead of Ford. John Kelly, then its head of market research, felt that the company had tended to rest too much on its laurels; now, he said, there were no laurels to rest on. It was also perfectly ready to try any remedy which promised better things; indeed, some of the suggestions sounded fanciful. One senior executive told me he would

---

[1] Its first boss was Leonard Lord (later Lord Lambury) who had become managing director of Morris Motors in 1932 and was then appointed chairman of Austin after the war. Lord, a blunt man, who suffered from a sizeable inferiority complex, was a virtual dictator and believed in encouraging vigorous competition between Austin and Morris, whom he referred to fondly as 'those buggers in the country'. Lord chose Sir George Harriman to be the Elisha to his Elijah, and Harriman took over as chairman when Lord retired in 1961. Harriman (who, like Lord, had started as an apprentice) had grown up in Lambury's shadow and the old man continued to exercise a considerable influence upon him: Lambury's room at Longbridge was left unoccupied and unchanged until the day he died in 1967. Harriman developed a close partnership with his chief designer, Alec Issigonis, and real power at Longbridge rested with these two men. BMC's headquarters' staff was quite large but uneven in quality, and Harriman continued to involve himself in many of the day-to-day details of the business.

like to 'sprinkle a few classics graduates around the place', whole men, as he called them. He, like others, was in a mood to confess his faults.

One of BMC's senior executives admitted that, over the previous six years, new or modified models had sometimes appeared on the market too late and in inadequate numbers, with the result that everybody had been 'out of breath'. He also felt there was need for more stringent timing and cost disciplines in the company's engineering division. Frequently the price of new models drifted upwards – the price of the Austin 1800, launched in 1965, had to be raised by £53 shortly after it had been put on the market.

The case of the 1800 also demonstrated BMC's seemingly cavalier attitude towards its rivals – Lord Lambury had joked on one occasion that its initials stood for 'Blast my Competitors'. Alec Issigonis, BMC's chief designer, said in 1965 that he had never specifically thought about a competitor in creating the car, and Sir George Harriman (at that time, the chairman and managing director) added that they had not compared the 1800's performance and cost with that of the probable competition because they were so confident of the car's potential. The hope was that sales of the 1800 would steadily build up to perhaps 3,000 a week; on the eve of the Leyland merger in 1968, more than two years after its launching, it was running at about one thousand.

BMC also offered a vast number of variations on its range of models, many of them different in little more than the badge they bore, apparently with the idea of keeping volume high: there were sixteen different varieties of the Mini alone.[1]

Some of these models were eventually discovered to be losing money (the Austin Westminster lost the company £17 on every sale); others, like the A40, were making tiny returns. Nor did BMC seem to have calculated with any degree of accuracy the extra costs it was incurring in producing so many varieties of the same basic model. Ford, which is widely used as a bench-mark of efficiency in the industry, reckons that the 'complexity cost' of putting a different model onto a line turning out forty indentical cars an hour is $1,000 for each different part fitted.[2] One of BMC's other weaknesses, or so some of the Leyland men felt after they moved in, was insufficient management information. John Barber, British Leyland's director of finance and planning, thinks

[1] Transport costs on the movement of parts within the group ran at an exceptionally high level – well over £2m. a year.

[2] Volkswagen boosts its profits partly by producing identical models on six of its production lines, and using a seventh for all the variations.

it was so serious that it would have been difficult to know that anything was wrong until it stuck out like a sore thumb.

Ron Lucas, who returned from the United States to be BMC's director of finance in 1965, also found the structure of the business confusing. There were three main operating companies – Austin, Morris and Fisher Ludlow – each of them with its own board of directors and its own books. But there was also a good deal of inter-company business between the divisions, and cars bearing the Morris badge were sometimes assembled in the Austin plant at Longbridge. Austin then had to sell the car to Morris, who in turn sold it to the trade. Lucas thought the books of the three companies were rendered meaningless by this cross-traffic, and the system also meant that none of the men in charge of the three operations could be held fully responsible. Harriman had produced a scheme, with the help of Cooper Brothers, to divisionalize BMC and Lucas was given the job of implementing it.

Nor was BMC's sales organization any more rational. It had 6,000 outlets across the world, but a quarter of them sold twenty models or less each year and they seemed to have been collected on the principle that the company would try to sell cars wherever there was a petrol pump. BMC was strong in the country districts, and comparatively weak in many big urban areas.

The company, however, had to examine its weaknesses because of the disastrous slump in sales. A product planning team for commercial vehicles had been started towards the end of 1965, and although it was another two years before the company duplicated the idea on the car side, there was every intention of putting the new director of planning, Geoffrey Rose, onto the BMC Board. At the time of the Leyland merger, Rose had twenty-eight people in his team and it was their job to set a price bracket for each model, and then make sure that it hit its timing, cost and performance targets. It was they who had to point out to the engineers that they could not afford a particular door lock or those lovely cotter pins. An accountant had been moved into the engineering division to try to ensure that cost control was effective. It was still a primitive organization compared to that which had existed at Ford for years, but it was a beginning.

Similarly, a market research department of thirty (seventy-five per cent of them graduates) had been built up and was beginning to make its presence felt. Both teams had begun to produce reports which underlined BMC's more glaring shortcomings. One pointed out that good engineering alone was no longer enough, that the motoring public was becoming increasingly fashion-conscious.[1] Another, produced in January 1967, said flatly that BMC would have to 'move away from the approach that our customers are anonymous people who have the opportunity to purchase our goods.'

At the centre, J. R. Edwards, who had returned from Pressed Steel in 1965, was drawing up a plan for the rationalization of the group's plants, and he had a number of closures in mind – one of which would have resulted in an immediate saving of £8 on each body produced by the plant concerned, with no loss of output whatsoever. For financial accounting purposes, Lucas had formed four new divisions – home sales, export sales, engineering and manufacturing – and put all the budgets on a clear-cut basis.

Edwards and Lucas estimated that they needed a breathing-space of eighteen months to allow these reforms to take effect. Some of the management was afraid that a take-over bid by Leylands was in the offing, and hoped that the 29.8 per cent of BMH's shares which could be mustered through the holdings of the Nuffield Foundation and Sir William Lyons of Jaguar, would provide a good basis for defence. It was not to be. The Government was strongly in favour of a merger and in the event BMC decided that it would be wiser to agree. Leyland men involved in the negotiations said that Sir George Harriman behaved like a gentleman, and that he often seemed as concerned that the undertakings he had given Lyons when BMC merged with Jaguar were honoured, as with the actual terms of the deal.

Sir Donald Stokes, who thus became chief executive of the new company, British Leyland, had spent most of his life in the truck and bus business. He had made his name with Leyland[2] principally as an export salesman, and was its sales director when it entered the car field by taking over Standard-Triumph in 1961. Triumph was losing money heavily and according to George Turnbull (then general manager of its manufacturing subsidiary, now boss of the Austin-Morris division of British Leyland), the directors had not decided which new models they wanted and the cupboard was 'all but bare'.

The Leyland men soon made their mark at Triumph. Three hundred

[1] There was also concern in the company about the austere appearance of many BMC models. Lucas made the point that, in a car with a north-south engine, fifty-five per cent of the cost went on body and trim, forty-five per cent on the engine; with a transverse engine, on the other hand, the figures were reversed and Lucas said that an austere body and appointments were essential if the selling price was to be right.

[2] A Lancashire-based company which had been built up by a series of engineers, of whom the most important was Sir Henry Spurrier.

senior staff were fired, including every member of the Board except one; there was a brisk drive to improve the quality of existing models; and the first new model under Leyland management, the 2000, was considerably up-graded from the competitor for the Ford Consul which Triumph originally had in mind.

When Stokes took over as managing director at Leyland (and Triumph) in 1964, he found himself with a specialist car business which was making useful profits. It had never needed any injection of cash from Leyland, although it might very well have had trouble raising further finance from the banks if Leyland had not moved in. Triumph's basic philosophy was to produce cars 'a little bit more sophisticated' than Ford or BMC, at a higher price, and with larger profit margins. It broke even when it could sell 100,000 a year, and since it turned out 125,000 in 1967, when BMC and Ford were either losing money or not making very much, it was a steady money-earner.

Stokes himself played a considerable part in setting up its product planning committee and in starting regular meetings on model policy. He also continued in the style which he had developed as sales director. He was in continuous motion round the company's plants (two days at Leyland, two at Triumph, one in London), involved himself in the detail of every side of the business and depended on a small group of trusted plant managers rather than on a headquarters staff. He was helped by the fact that the Leyland business was a relatively simple one with a small number of large plants – and he knew all the men concerned intimately.

Leyland's next acquisition in the car field, in 1967, was another specialist company, Rover. Rover was a successful business which had managed to extend the sellers' market for its products long after it had disappeared for the volume producers. Having made thirty per cent on its capital in the mid-1950s, it was still earning 11.7 per cent in 1965–1966, when the industry's average had fallen to 7.8. Its break-even point was about 65,000 models a year, and since it was consistently making 80,000, it regularly turned in profits of between £3 and £3½m.

Its most recent success had been the Rover 2000, which for long periods outsold Stokes's own 2000. Initially planned to cost £1,000, it had eventually appeared on the market at £1,275. The Rover bosses took the view that price was not a crucial factor in their bracket, and proved the point by selling the 2000 at well over twice the rate which they had forecast (eight hundred a week against an original expectation of 350). They modestly remarked that they were nothing like so professional as Ford, and that Ford could no doubt have made the 2000 in larger quantities at a lower price, but that it was not in fact doing so.

Rover had changed somewhat from the pre-war pattern – when its highest annual output had been 11,000 and when it did not need a sales department because almost all its models were sold for it by Henlys, the large distributors – but it had begun to 'bump up against the problem of volume' when Stokes made the first approach. It was finding the expenses of its overseas operation – it either manufactured or assembled in thirty-six countries – increasingly onerous and it had discovered that since component manufacturers tended to design parts for the volume producers, it was forced either to take the same parts or pay astronomical prices for one-offs.

Having accepted the Leyland offer, it did not find the sequel particularly pleasant. Stokes lost little time in tidying up the company; three-quarters of Rover's overseas operations had been merged with Triumph's inside a year and 400 men had been sacked. These were mild enough disturbances but enough to upset some of the Rover chiefs. Stokes was regarded as 'a very remarkable man', but not perhaps universally loved.

The acquisition of British Motor Holdings was a very different matter for Stokes, in type as well as in size. It put him, and Leyland, into the volume car business and direct competition with Ford for the first time. He was also aware that, on this occasion, very substantial reorganization would be needed and before very long fifty fact-finding teams, drawn from the two companies, were looking at what had to be done in particular areas of the business. The exercise was designed not only to get at the facts but also to find out which of BMH's managers were going to be useful.

Stokes and Barber had to face the fact that in February 1968, Ford had for the first time out-sold BMH on the British market. On the other hand, it soon became clear that Leyland could not have acquired the company at a more opportune moment. There was an enormous backlog of orders to be satisfied, and a booming consumer demand for much of the remainder of 1968. The company could not produce enough cars to meet it and, as Barber said, 'we simply couldn't help coining money'. It was an ideal atmosphere in which to begin reorganization.

Barber himself spent a good part of the early spring and summer fighting to reduce the huge stocks of vehicles which BMC had accumulated during the previous winter; by the holidays, stocks were virtually nil. Meanwhile, Stokes had decided to carve up his empire into seven divisions – one covering the high volume cars; another gathering together the three specialist producers, Triumph, Rover and Jaguar; and others dealing with trucks and buses, Pressed Steel Fisher (making car bodies), the overseas companies, foundries and general engineering and the construction equipment business. Of British Leyland's turnover of over £900m. well over £400m. came from volume cars, and roughly £225m. each from specialist models and trucks and buses.[1] Stokes preferred the divisional structure to a simple partition between manufacturing and sales, with sales responsible for product policy.

By the autumn of 1968, Stokes had also taken a number of other major decisions. As new models appeared, the old marques of Wolseley and Riley were to disappear: only the Austin and Morris lines were to continue, with de luxe and GT variations as high profit earners. Turnbull was moved into the volume car division to continue the attack on costs. British Leyland also began to reduce its enormous labour force by natural wastage and by not recruiting in certain areas and a new model policy began to emerge. Stokes had decided to wait six months before undertaking basic rationalization of the group's sixty-seven factories and gigantic dealer network.[2] He believed the delay would pay off in the shape of better relationships.

Despite the increased size of the group, Stokes continued to run the business on the same principles by which he had worked at Leyland. His dislike for head office staffs – because they were apt to build empires for themselves and find work for each other – had not diminished and Leyland's London office became, if anything, even smaller with the departure of many of the export sales division. It consisted of Stokes and his staff; Barber, with a small staff; Michael Shanks, as the new director of marketing services and economic planning; and the public relations department. Stokes continued to depend heavily on a small group of line managers reinforced by constant personal pressure upon the key areas of the business.

Nobody in the company was allowed to spend anything – even £25 for a new typewriter – unless it had been authorized by him.[3] He

---

[1] British Leyland's share of the British car market has fluctuated between 39 and 43 per cent; Ford currently (June 1969) has almost 30 per cent.

[2] BMC had been spending £2.1m. a year in stationery and printing, divided between three hundred suppliers: they were reduced to three.

[3] Stokes has recently become a little more liberal in delegating authority for expenditure.

checked every item personally – from investments costing £1m. to batteries for fork-lift trucks – arguing that it took little of his time. Additions to the staff and all salary increases for men earning £1,500 or over had to be approved by him. He continued to involve himself in every detail of the business – calling for the chief inspector at Triumph to help him answer letters of complaint personally and having reports sent to every foreman which told him, by Wednesday of the following week, how well he had performed against budget.

Stokes, of course, is fully aware that he is unable to contribute a great deal at many of the detailed meetings which he attends but believes that his busy presence around the company helps keep everyone on their toes.

He still continues to travel round the group at regular intervals. Shortly after the negotiations with BMH were completed, he set off on a five-week tour of the world, with very precise and detailed objectives: 'I shall go to Nairobi, where I shall beat up the outfit, get orders and see Ministers, and then on to other parts of Africa to do much the same thing. In Australia, we have some big deals brewing – I'll make a million there. Then to Nissan and Toyota in Japan – that's educational. In India, I shall go through the figures and the accounts, but that won't take more than two or three days.' Stokes also visits each of the company's biggest plants in Britain at least once every three weeks.

When colleagues suggested that he was trying to do too much and that he interfered excessively in day-to-day affairs, Stokes would reply that he hadn't been to AEC for a fortnight. As for the reorganization which was taking place in the truck and bus division,[1] Stokes remarked that he only spent two days a fortnight at the Leyland plant – 'apart from that, I let them get on with it.'

To what extent Stokes will be able to continue in this autocratic style, and how far he will be persuaded by colleagues that he must build up his head office staff, remains to be seen. Clearly, far too much still depends on him. That he has survived so far (and remained in the running for the title of Britain's most prestigious industrialist, despite a late challenge from Arnold Weinstock) is due to a unique

---

[1] The sellers' market lasted much longer in trucks and buses than it did for cars. For many years, Leyland was able to sell all it made, and fixed its prices by computing costs and then adding an appropriate percentage. The result was that its financial control needed tightening, and an ex-Ford financial controller has now been moved in. Although there has been a good deal of rationalization of Leyland's early truck acquisitions, the company still makes engines and gear-boxes in too many places.

combination of talents. Stokes deals with day-to-day problems with great deftness and skill; he makes decisions crisply; his hunches about model policy are usually shrewd; he is absolutely dedicated; he has the knack of saying precisely the right thing, whether to shop stewards or managers; and he uses newspapers and television more effectively than any other British industrialist.

Whether he will prove so efficient as the boss of an enormous empire and as a long-term planner has yet to be proved. Even at its present size, British Leyland is going to find it hard going against the American and European giants: it is still smaller than Volkswagen, not to mention General Motors, Ford and Chrysler. It has to introduce a range of new models which prove to be both attractive and competitive (too many of the present range leave much to be desired in both performance and styling), it has to cut down a labour force which is still far too large compared with those of its principal rivals,[1] and it has to rationalize its factories and its dealer network. It is impossible to make a judgement on the basis of the first year's performance – things have been far too easy on both the home and export markets to show how genuinely competitive British Leyland will be. By the early 1970s, however, it will be clear how successful Stokes has been.

Ford had developed in a style and tradition which was as American as BMC's was British. It had expanded almost entirely by internal growth and not by acquisition; it was a highly centralized business, based on Dagenham and indeed remained a one-plant operation until after the Second World War (its second major car plant, at Halewood on Merseyside, was not built until 1963). Whereas BMC had been run almost entirely by production men and engineers, the most powerful influences at Ford in the post-war period were either buyers or finance men. Sir Patrick Hennessy, who was the dominant force in the business from 1948 until 1963, had been a buyer and so had three of the four managing directors who followed him.[2]

Ford's engineers have always been regarded, and regarded themselves, as being very much part of a team which worked to tight financial disciplines. For many years the company's models have been

---

[1] Just how poor is the productivity of the car side of British Leyland can best be judged by comparing its performance with that of other major companies. Ford UK, Volkswagen and Chrysler all produce about eleven cars per employee per year: the car side of British Leyland turns out only about six cars for each of its workers.

[2] Ford, like Marks and Spencer, offers a free consultancy service to its suppliers, to help them bring down their costs.

developed by a product planning committee whose job it is to make sure that the right cars are put onto the market at the right price and time. The Cortina, launched in 1962, has become a classic example of near-perfect planning.

When the specification was drawn up, every part – even those costing less than a penny – were listed in a Redbook. The dimensions of the car were laid down to the nearest tenth of an inch. Each manager who was responsible for developing, manufacturing or buying parts, signed the Redbook as a mark of his personal commitment to its objectives. The engineers adhered rigorously to these objectives: the Cortina's steering wheel was redesigned four times because it was exceeding its target by 1d. (The cost-control on some items, such as the instrument panel, was too severe, and it had to be modified later, at considerable expense.) The result was that the Cortina was launched on exactly the day planned, the capital investment required was eight per cent less than had been expected, and the car weighed only 1.8 per cent more and cost only a few shillings more than the targets laid down in the Redbook.

Ford's product planners work to a ten-year programme and in 1968 they were arguing about the price of a model due to appear in 1972 in terms of cents rather than dollars and in terms of a possible variation in weight of fifteen pounds. Since Ford reckons that its cars cost about two shillings per lb. to make, a variation of fifteen lbs. can affect its profit by £450,000 a year on a model with annual sales of 300,000. Stan Gillen, the American who was once Ford of Britain's managing director and is now vice-president of manufacturing in Ford of Europe, was confident in 1968 that the 1972 car would reach the market at within $10 of its target. It is a system which has produced a number of significant engineering innovations, but Ford's design lay-outs are usually highly orthodox.

Ford's organization also differed markedly from BMC's in other ways. For a number of years, it has been recruiting as many graduates as it can lay its hand on: in 1967, 170 were hired, and the company was looking for 200 in 1969. Far from believing that it now has too many, Gillen is convinced that Ford in Britain has not gone anything like far enough in buying brain-power: he is influenced by the fact that twenty-two per cent of the entire labour force of his last Ford division in America had university degrees.

Yet, despite the excellence of its management machine (and graduates of 'The System' now adorn the board-rooms of a dozen other companies), Ford's results in the years up to 1967 were very far from exciting. Its average return on capital, after tax, for the three years 1965–7 was a meagre 3.1 per cent. 1968, however, was the most profitable year in the history of the company.

One reason for its poor returns in earlier years was that Ford had spent £265m. on capital investment since 1960. Its chiefs admit that they made a miscalculation about the speed at which the market would develop, gambling on an expansion which did not materialize when they expected it: they estimate that car sales have fallen roughly two years behind their projections. The result was a great deal of spare capacity which Ford tried to fill by making components for other companies (crankshafts for Rootes, for example).

Nevertheless, particularly with the justification of excellent 1968 figures, the Ford men are not repentant, and argue that they would not have cut back the investment programme by much even if they had known that sales would actually decline in earlier years. Their reasoning is that there is little point in installing new capacity 'in small packets': so far as car assembly is concerned, they say only a line producing forty cars an hour is worth building, because anything less drives unit costs too high. Similarly, they would not build an engine transfer line making less than 160 engines an hour; Gillen said that, even if the line were only producing eight hundred engines a day, it would still be cheaper because of savings in manpower, among other things. Ford is confident that the returns will continue to come – even if later than expected – and it is planning to continue spending at an annual rate of £40m. for the next five years.

The second factor which led to poor results up to 1967 was a serious misjudgement in the timing of new models. Largely because it had not paid enough attention to its commercial vehicles and allowed the range to run down,[1] Ford tried to do too much at once. Within three years, it produced a completely new range of commercial vehicles, a new range of tractors, a new big car (the Mark IV range of Executive, Zephyrs and Zodiacs) a new small car (the Escort), a Cortina with between 1,200 and 1,300 new parts, and a revamped Corsair. In this scramble, it brought out the Mark IVs too early and the Escort too late.

The result was that the sales of the Mark IVs, the first of which came out in 1966, were extremely disappointing during a period of

[1] Two-thirds of Ford's turnover comes from cars, twenty per cent from commercial vehicles and fourteen per cent from tractors.

austerity, and Ford admits that it might still have sold just as many, or more, of the old Mark IIIs, even in 1968. Meanwhile the decision to replace the Anglia with the Escort had been taken too late – partly because (like Vauxhall) Ford has always been rather afraid of thin profits at the lower end of the market. (Ford has always reckoned that BMC made little out of the Mini for a long time, and has been apt to over-compensate in its efforts not to repeat the mistake.) In the event, the Escort proved very successful.

The third factor in Ford's failure to earn more respectable profits on its capital has been minimal earnings on its much-vaunted export business, which accounts for forty per cent of all the vehicles it sells. Overall, before devaluation, sales abroad were probably not doing much more than make a useful contribution to overheads; in that sense, Ford was using its excess capacity on the basis of marginal profit. But the company takes the view that, even it if is not now earning big profits in most overseas markets, it is much better to stay in business there for the sake of the future.

Ford, naturally enough, has always been strongly influenced by the wishes of its American parent. The influence has become increasingly apparent since Ford of America bought out the remaining British shareholders for £130m. in 1961, and particularly after the retirement of Sir Patrick Hennessy from the position of chief executive in 1963. Hennessy was a man of stature and strong conviction who had considerable standing with the bosses at Dearborn. During most of his years of office, no American held a senior job at Dagenham and the number of trans-Atlantic visitors was much smaller than it subsequently became. Since 1961, Ford's chief designer has been an American, and Stan Gillen was appointed managing director in 1965. The total number of Americans was at first not large, however, and in 1964 they occupied only four of the top twenty-eight positions in the company. American ideas have had little influence on the mechanical parts of Ford's new models (although the engine for the Mark I Consul was designed in Dearborn), but a noticeable effect on their styling: the 'dish' tail-light of the Cortina, for example, bore a striking resemblance to that of an earlier Thunderbird.

In 1967, the parent company took a much closer grip not only on British Ford but also on the entire European operation when it set up a new body, Ford of Europe, with headquarters (at Warley, in Essex) in the same building as Ford of Britain. Ford of Europe is responsible to Dearborn not only for Ford of Britain and Ford of Germany but also for Africa (excluding South Africa) and the Middle East. Its president, three vice-presidents and four other members of its policy committee of twelve are American; and there are roughly 120 more at Warley offering a wide range of specialist advice – everything from an architect service for new dealers to expertise on outlets in the major European cities.[1]

The object of the exercise was perfectly sensible – to ensure that Ford's widespread operations in Europe were more closely co-ordinated than they had been by Overseas Automotive Operations, based on Dearborn – but given the political animus which Ford has attracted in the past as a spearhead of the power of the dollar, the company naturally wants to play down as much as it can the diminution of national authority which is the inevitable consequence of Ford of Europe.

A European product committee – made up of men from Ford of Europe and the two national managements – is already planning new models on a continental basis. The Escort is being made in West Germany, largely with parts shipped from Dagenham, and Ford intends that all its new models shall, in future, be launched simultaneously in every Western European country. By making sure that there is as little duplication as possible in the two model ranges, it expects to make major savings on development costs; by arranging its sources of component supply on a European basis, it expects to be able to buy a good deal more flexibly and economically. The Ford men point out that really tight co-ordination is essential because of the company's very high wages bill: 76,000 of its 90,000 employees in Europe are engaged in manufacturing.

Each of the two countries, however, will keep its own styling studio in an effort to retain a 'national personality' in the two model ranges. In most cases, they will have different bodies and Ford is concentrating its drive for rationalization on the internal parts of the car, which the public cannot see and which its salesmen do not have to sell. It also insists that the national managements will continue to have the last word, but Ford of Europe can exert very considerable pressure when its advice is not accepted. Its power as against that of the national managements is illustrated by the amount of money which its bosses can spend without reference to Dearborn: its president, John Andrews, can authorize expenditure of up to £1m. within an agreed budget, the managing director of Ford of Britain only £250,000.

[1] There are also about thirty Germans working at Warley.

But a European structure also makes sense for Ford in other respects. Its greatest anxiety for the future is that strikes among the component suppliers in Britain will continue to upset delivery dates;[1] its bosses say that they are only able to sell effectively in the United States because of pressure by the parent company on American dealers, and reckon that if strikes continue at the rate set in recent times (six major suppliers had three or more strikes in the period from April 1967 to March 1968), the company could lose £100m. worth of sales in the next four years. A European purchasing system will give it much more flexibility in moving its business to West German component firms (much less strike-prone than their British counterparts) when any situation becomes intolerable.[2] Indeed, that new flexibility is already being demonstrated in practice.

For example, all the Escort's parts were initially shipped to West Germany from Britain: now seventeen per cent of its bought-out parts have been transferred to German firms. Similarly, all but a few dozen of the 340 items which were originally supplied by British manufacturers for the company's Transit range of medium commercial vans have now been switched to West German companies. Ford can scarcely be expected to put its business at risk when deliveries from British sources are so frequently disrupted by industrial unrest; in this sense, Ford of Europe will simply help to ensure that Britain pays the price for its failures in labour relations.[3]

While Ford is Ford everywhere, General Motors is Vauxhall in Britain, Opel in West Germany and Holden in Australia; and David

[1] Ford's own labour record, once one of the worst in Britain, has shown a startling improvement in recent years. In 1962, over 793,000 man-hours were lost through industrial disputes; only 614,000 were lost in the next four years. A serious strike in the spring of 1969 somewhat marred this performance.

[2] The motor industry in the United States has far more control than the British over its component supplies. General Motors has for many years made all its own bodies and most of the important internal parts, and Ford and Chrysler have followed its example by buying up their component suppliers or building factories of their own. American subsidiaries in Europe tend to take the same approach. For example, GM has built a factory at Strasbourg to make automatic transmissions for both Opel and Vauxhall. By comparison, a company like British Leyland is extremely dependent on its outside suppliers – of whom there are perhaps 2,000.

[3] Ford says that its policy is to buy high-volume components in both countries and very low-volume components in one or the other (where possible): the low-volume components are bought in both however. The company also says the amount of money it will spend in Britain with British suppliers will not decline in any way in the future.

BUSINESS IN BRITAIN

Hegland, the American managing director of Vauxhall, has stated categorically that its parent company, General Motors, will not follow Ford down the road which leads to an integrated European operation.

For many years, Vauxhall seemed to be something of an after-thought so far as General Motors was concerned.[1] Until it launched the Viva in 1963, its models were competing for only about fifty per cent of the British market, – 'we did not design cars for the young, for wives or for the second-car family', said Geoffrey Moore, the sales director – and one can scarcely believe that a company as professional as General Motors would have allowed this state of affairs to continue if expansion in Britain had had any priority in its thinking.

Vauxhall's explanations for why it was so slow to enter the small-car market – sticking instead to a satisfactory business in trucks and medium-sized family models – centre round the fact that it did not have the capacity to do so. (Its new plant at Ellesmere Port did not open until 1962.) This answer begs the question: why did it not have the capacity? There the answers stop, and one is left wondering whether corporate conservatism was not at the root of the matter. This diagnosis certainly seems to be borne out by the fact that Opel in West Germany was also slow off the mark in the small-car field.

Since the first Viva was launched, and then most effectively face-lifted in 1965, Vauxhall has made a more considerable impact on the British market. Its share of sales has risen from ten per cent to almost twelve per cent (June, 1969) and Hegland claims that it could have reached fifteen per cent in 1967 had it not been for strikes and the introduction of the new Victor.

As might be expected from part of Alfred Sloan's empire, Vauxhall was already using long-range forecasting and annual budgets in the 1930s, and even then offered a business advisory service to dealers. But the curious thing is that, despite the progressive nature of its management techniques, Vauxhall has always seemed a cosy, pro-vincial sort of outfit. This may have something to do with the fact that GM has never seemed to interfere in its affairs to any marked degree. Three of its last four managing directors have been Americans – they are normally drawn from the pool of talent in the corporation's overseas operation – and the quantities of chrome which adorned many of its models in the 1950s suggested that advice from the designers in

[1] Whereas Ford of Britain's sales of cars and trucks represented fifteen per cent of Ford's total world sales (in terms of units) in 1967, Vauxhall's output was only 4.6 per cent of GM's world-wide production.

Detroit had had its effect, but by and large Vauxhall has been allowed to run its own shop.

The intriguing question is where – if anywhere – General Motors intends to take Vauxhall. Now it has a fuller range of cars, its present volume of sales must leave it in an uncomfortable position; to earn respectable profits, it will surely have to push its market share nearer to the twenty per cent which Hegland has been somewhat optimistically predicting for 1970.

Even so, Vauxhall's position is not nearly so uncomfortable as that of Rootes, now controlled (with a seventy-seven per cent holding) by the third American motor giant, Chrysler. Its new bosses managed to produce a modest profit in 1967–8 after three years of heavy losses, but Rootes still had little better than ten per cent of the market for most of 1968 (its market share was down to less than nine per cent in June, 1969) and almost £2½m. of the £3m. profit came from the sale of properties and investments which, in their nature, are a non-recurring bonus.

A considerable revolution has already been carried through within the old Rootes' empire. The most obvious changes have occurred at the top. Lord (Geoffrey) Rootes (previously managing director) remains as chairman, but he is not a member of the eight-man administrative committee which runs the company; Brian Rootes, who had been in charge of home and export sales and service, is no longer with the company; Timothy Rootes has also left and has since bought up several Rootes' distributorships. These departures, and others, have given a new nickname to the executive floor at the Rootes' headquarters in Piccadilly. Once known as 'The Green Belt' because of the colour of its wall-to-wall carpeting, it has now been dubbed 'The Garden of Remembrance'.

Chrysler found the company in a perilous state, with neither the Government nor the banks willing to put up money and none of the other motor companies in a position to take it over. Rootes was still very much a family business, and a family business with a philosophy consistent with that of a company which had started by selling cars and then moved into their manufacture.[1] At the time of the take-over, Rootes still owned dealer- and distributorships which handled roughly thirty per cent of its sales in Britain, and it was noticeable that whereas independent outlets were capturing (on average) over twelve per cent

[1] It was built up by William and Reginald Rootes, who began as car salesmen and had by 1926 become the biggest distributors in Britain.

of the car market, those owned by the company were achieving a penetration of only ten to $10\frac{1}{2}$ per cent.[1]

The principal reason for this discrepancy seems to have been that the Rootes-owned distributors – who controlled its sales over a very large part of London, Birmingham, Manchester and, to a lesser degree, Glasgow – earned an additional discount for the company by wholesaling; they therefore had no incentive to build up the retail side of their business, and were consequently retailing twenty per cent less than comparable Ford and Vauxhall distributors.

The men from Chrysler were also worried by the fears which independent dealers might harbour about the way in which Rootes could have operated its own outlets. Might it not be suspected of channelling profitable fleet sales to them, and of giving them preference in times of short supply? It was therefore decided to sell off the entire chain and to concentrate on manufacturing.

The network of owned outlets was one inheritance from the past. Another, or so it seemed to the new management, was that the company had been divided up into a number of separate family empires, without close co-ordination between them; and that the autocratic reign of Lord William Rootes had been followed by a period of less decisiveness.

Rootes, for example, had no profit plan which fully spelled out how its objectives were to be achieved; instead there was a broad target, say an annual improvement of £2m. or £3m. Nor did Chrysler men feel that the company had an adequate system of financial control.

Its difficulties extended into other fields. Its manufacturing capacity was even more under-utilized than that of other companies. The plant at Linwood, for example, had been built on the theory that the Imp would sell at the rate of 3,000 a week, but it had never done better than 1,700 (even including models sold in the form of completely knocked-down parts), and by 1968 Rootes was lucky if it sold 1,200 a week. The Imp had been launched far too late (three years behind the Mini), and it was in a declining segment of the market. In these circumstances, Linwood was beginning to look even more of a white elephant than it had done previously. Rootes' profits were also affected by its inflated labour force: each of its cars, its new bosses discovered, took forty-eight man-hours to produce, compared with between twenty and twenty-five hours for the Chrysler operation in America.

As if these problems were not enough, the attitude of the general

[1] Eight hundred of the Rootes dealers were selling less than twelve cars a year.

public to Rootes' products had been deteriorating. A survey completed in 1967 revealed that the company had a stodgy image and that, although people over fifty were loyal to it largely on the grounds of reliability and comfort, many potential younger customers felt that the performance of its models and their styling left a good deal to be desired.

Chrysler had recruited a new British boss for Rootes in the shape of Gilbert Hunt, formerly with Massey-Ferguson, on the understanding that he would run the business with direct access to the American bosses. Hunt rapidly won the admiration of his American colleagues by the speed and directness with which he began to tackle the company's problems.[1]

Its plants at Acton, Cricklewood and Kew were closed, and 2,500 men sacked. While the long-term plan is for the plants at Linwood and Coventry to have greater flexibility in the car models they produce and for the manufacture of commercial vehicles to be centred at Dunstable, the gaping hole of spare capacity at Linwood was partly plugged by moving in the Arrow models as well as the Imp derivatives. A whole series of new models and face-lifts was rushed out – eleven in 1966–7 alone – to replace the more outdated members of the Rootes' range. Plans to fill the gap in the Viva-Escort-Cortina segment of the market were pushed ahead. At the same time, the organization was considerably simplified by merging the previous divisions into two, manufacturing and sales, and by giving the advertising to two agencies instead of four; and in the autumn of 1968 the company's first five-year plan emerged.

Its target, to win seventeen per cent of the market, is one which Hunt and Rootes are going to find extremely difficult to meet. Even with booming demand in 1968 and a number of new models, its share of the market has declined markedly. Its new model in the 1100–1500 cc class, when it comes, will have to cope with established competitors, and the fact that Rootes has never made a real mark in that particular price-bracket. Its bigger competitors all have to make heavy investment pay off, and for the moment Rootes has a smaller share of the home market than any other major company.

---

[1] Chrysler likes to have its overseas subsidiaries run by nationals and the brief given to the twenty-seven Americans now at Rootes is to work themselves out of a job.

CHAPTER 13

The Slow Salvation of Textiles

One of the great drawbacks of the environment in which British industry operated during the forty or so years after 1918 was a widespread lack of competition on the home market: in its absence many British companies grew complacent and moribund. Anyone who proposes this thesis, however, has to explain why it was that the cotton textile industry – which failed to rig the market in Britain and was largely unprotected from global competition of the fiercest kind – should have suffered the most disastrous decline.

But the cotton industry's failure to respond to the stimulus of competition, although partly attributable to its own lethargy and incompetence, was not without important mitigating circumstances. The first sprang from the fact that, until 1914, Lancashire had completely dominated the world market, indeed had been – to all intents and purposes – the world's cotton cloth industry. Even India was reserved to it by virtue of Britain's imperial power. By comparison, the home market was insignificant: it was said that the mills worked before breakfast to satisfy demand in Britain, thereafter for export. This was clearly an artificial situation. The industry was suffering from dropsy: it had grown to a size which it could not hope to maintain once other countries began to develop their own industries.

These unavoidable consequences were particularly serious because of the nature of the textile industry. Whereas very few countries are today capable of emulating IBM (which dominates the world computer market in much the same degree as Lancashire dominated cotton textiles)[1] because of the complex technology and heavy investment

---

[1] One reason why the technology was fairly rapidly acquired was the willingness of Lancashire machinery makers to supply highly-skilled advice and the willingness of Lancashire managers to go overseas to run the new plants.

Courtaulds

headquarters, Hanover Square, London. Turnover, £576m. in 1968–9. Man-made fibres, including rayon and modified rayon (ninety-eight per cent of the British market), nylon, acetate and triacetate, and acrylic. Textiles – largest company in Britain, with yarn spinning and processing; woven, knitted and bonded fabrics; dyeing, printing and finishing; furnishing and household textiles; hosiery, knitwear and other garments. Names include Susan Small, Bairnswear, Wolsey, Meridian, Lyle and Scott, Ballito, Kayser, Aristoc, Gossard, Christy. Owns about one hundred shops. Other interests include chemicals, packaging, paints and plastics (among them Lego toys).

Coats Patons

Glasgow. Turnover in 1968, £210m. Largest manufacturer of sewing thread in the world (twenty-five per cent of the entire market), largest maker of hand-knitting yarns and children's clothes in Britain. Names include Ladybird. Also four hundred shops in the Scotch Wool, Bellman and Jaeger chains.

English Calico

Manchester. Turnover in 1968, £156m. Thread (including American Thread Co.), Fabrics (Tootal Thomson, Cepea and Winterbottom Book Cloth), Men's Wear (Tootal, Raelbrook Shirts, Pyramid Handkerchiefs), Household Textiles (Osman sheets and towels, Easifit stretch covers, Stiebels net curtains), Knitting & Garments (Raysil, London Maid, Judy). Vertically integrated, uses all textile processes and over fifty per cent man-made fibres. Also owns four hundred shops and stores: non-textile activities, plastics, printing, paper-making, polyester foam.

Viyella International

Savile Row, London. Turnover in 1968, £70m. Knitting and yarn processing; spinning and weaving; bleaching, dyeing; finishing and printing; garments; home furnishings; tufted carpets; seventeen per cent of branded shirt market through Van Heusen, Mekay, Peter England and Aertex.

---

involved, it was both cheap and easy to emulate Lancashire. The capital required for plant and machinery was small, the skills needed to operate them modest. Lancashire was thus faced with the task of trying to compete with countries whose wage-rates were a fraction of its own: to beat them on their own ground (with the transport costs involved), and to keep them out of a British market which was largely unprotected, first out of adherence to Free Trade and then to the Commonwealth spirit, as expressed in the Ottawa Agreements of 1932. It was an impossible task, although rapid and thorough-going rationalization would have eased the decline. In other words, the competition which Lancashire was asked to face, far from being stimulating, was so over-whelming as to be debilitating to all except the most valiant spirits.

Unfortunately, Lancashire contained all too few of these. Indeed, few other major world industries can have grown up on such a narrow base of management ability. The vast majority of its proprietors were enterprising artisans capable of running a relatively simple, one-stage manufacturing operation, but seldom guilty of any wider vision: it was a cottage industry writ large. Their descendants, often of the same modest ability but with less initiative and pertinacity, found themselves caught up in a swirling downward spiral of trade; bewildered and afraid, they clung to the fortunes which they had. Their money, they judged, was better employed earning three per cent on deposit at the bank rather than being invested in new machinery. Only too frequently they retired to the country or the seaside, leaving behind them an accountant and a mill manager of the sergeant-major variety.

The organization of cotton, moreover, remained essentially that of a small man's industry. Spinning, weaving, finishing, wholesaling, making up into garments and retailing were specialized activities performed by separate enterprises: each man took his cut. The various processes were often geographically separate, with whole districts concentrating on one activity – which helped to make the industry extraordinarily parochial. Each section lived in its own world and there was little thought of trying to cut costs and prices by making the process vertical: the industry, indeed, was obsessed with processes rather than products. Such rationalization as did take place about the turn of the century was simply a gathering together of specialists (thread producers, spinners or finishers) not for the purpose of greater efficiency but simply to try to ensure the survival of all.

The industry, in fact, seemed more like a collection of sub-contractors than a group of businesses. The manufacturers, who spun and wove but did not sell, were often completely out of touch with fashion and demand: they did as they were bid. The merchants, comfortably ensconced in Manchester, expected customers to come to them, with the result that there was no adequate network of distribution through the rest of the country. This, of course, was partly a reflection of the relative unimportance of the home market and it meant that even a giant of the industry, English Sewing Cotton, preferred to let its main competitor, J. and P. Coats, do its selling for it: this arrangement continued in every market except the American until long after the Second World War.[1]

Furthermore, although the organization of the large groups (ESC, Calico Printers and so on) became slightly less clumsy with time, if only to permit them to survive, they were frequently still a legitimate attempt on the part of original vendors to secure the interests of themselves and their families. Often, therefore, no decisive, reforming element emerged, and indeed the object of the exercise was to maintain a delicate balance of power on the Board. Sir Cyril Harrison became English Sewing's first managing director in 1948, more than half a century after the company's birth; until then, it had been run by a committee of three executive directors, none of them managing.

In the inter-war years many Boards had come to include either descendants of the original vendors or their friends. In these circumstances, Board meetings could be extremely low-powered gatherings – 'eighty-five per cent bromide, fifteen per cent work,' as one managing director put it – and they occupied themselves in curious ways; the Board of one company spent part of one meeting signing cheques and, on another occasion, called a special meeting to enable them to sign stock certificates. A dreadful paralysis settled over the industry. Many of its leaders were not only incompetent but also self-seeking (a knighthood was regarded by some as the supreme prize), and there was no catalytic influence from outside to spark off a transformation.[2]

Some companies made more vigorous efforts than others to ride out the storm. Calico Printers, for example, tried to hang on to its threatened overseas markets (and, before 1914, ninety per cent of its business had been abroad) by setting up plants in China and Egypt, among other places. It even built spinning and weaving mills in these countries to avoid being at the mercy of native producers; at home it moved into garment manufacturing – in a small way and by chance rather than intent – through the acquisition of Brook Manufacturing, which was one of its bad debts. Nevertheless, CPA did not pay dividends to its

[1] From Coats' point of view, the Central Agency, which acted as distributor for a number of other companies besides ESC, made a very useful contribution to profits.

[2] The Yorkshire woollen industry, on the other side of the Pennines, was suffering from many of the same problems, but since it was nothing like so dependent on overseas markets, it succeeded in weathering the period between the wars with less tribulation.

preference shareholders for the greater part of the 1930s. Its salvation was to come in the 1950s, with the success of Terylene.

English Sewing Cotton, on the other hand, lost markets and did not respond by setting up overseas plants before the war. Abroad, it rested heavily on the profits of its subsidiary, the American Thread Company, which was larger than the parent until 1963; at home, it succeeded in capturing a large share of the domestic thread market with the help of the Coats salesmen, and also took a small stake in spinning and knitting.

There were two partial exceptions to this general tale of woe, and both were based outside Lancashire: the first was Coats, the world's largest thread producer, and the second Courtaulds, which had made its fortune out of rayon. Even here, the posture of the two companies between the wars was largely defensive.

Coats, for example, which had moved into a score of countries (including Russia, Italy, Canada, Japan and Brazil) between 1890 and 1914 under the influence of the brilliant German, Philippi, seemed to have lost its dynamic thrust after Philippi's death during the First World War; the founding families were no longer providing enough first-class talent. The company was extremely conservative financially – it did not go to the market for money from 1919 until 1967, although it had huge unused borrowing power not only in Britain but also in the United States; the overseas expansion which took place between the wars was very limited; and there was scarcely any change in manufacturing methods between 1905 and 1945. Incredibly, Coats' profits were lower in 1947 than they had been in 1902. The company had simply clung to what it had, a good thread business whose requirements could be met out of its own cash flow: more than ninety per cent of its assets were in thread.

Courtaulds was, in one sense, much more comfortably placed than the cotton manufacturers: until the middle-1920s it still had control of all the key viscose patents and by then had collected a large slice of one of the greatest bonanzas in industrial history. Its subsidiary, the American Viscose Company (set up in 1910), earned well over $500m. in profits during the thirty years of its life from an original investment of less than $1m. In its best years, it made 280 per cent on its capital and seventy per cent on its selling price; it eventually became as large as the parent company. During the boom years, it was much the same story in Britain, with rayon being produced for 2s 6d per lb, and sold at twenty shillings. Members of the Courtauld family made vast fortunes and so, too, did the non-family managers who had persuaded them to move into rayon: one of these was earning an annual bonus of almost £55,000 by 1912.

Unfortunately, however, the company – and Samuel Courtauld was chairman from 1922 to 1947 – tended to rest on its laurels. The basic viscose patents which Courtaulds held ran out in 1926 and profits declined very sharply during the 1930s – but the enterprise stood still. Then, in 1941, intense pressure was put on Courtaulds to sell the Viscose Corporation (as it had become) to pacify isolationist elements in America who opposed financial aid to Britain. It duly sold ninety-five per cent of its holdings to the British Government for just over £27m. – a figure, as Winston Churchill said, very much below its intrinsic worth.[1]

Yet it was Courtaulds, spurred on by the take-over bid from ICI, which was to be the major force in the reorganization of the old cotton textile industry. It was destined to sweep north into Lancashire just as Coats was to move south across the Border into Yorkshire woollens. In the early post-war years, however, there was little sign of any movement at all; the industry was prospering (English Sewing Cotton, for example, earned twenty-nine per cent on its capital in 1948), but Courtaulds scarcely seemed able to recover a sense of direction for itself, let alone take on Lancashire.

Its main object was to rebuild rayon, the source of its past glories, and although it had involved itself, somewhat gingerly, in nylon (through its partnership with ICI in British Nylon Spinners), its leading lights thought of nylon as being cold, clammy and rather sleazy: who, they asked, would wear such stuff? In one way, their revulsion was simply the reaction of textile fibre men[2] to a chemical fibre, which, in its early manifestations, was a form of extruded plastic. In another, it was a reflection both of profound conservatism and a sense of superiority. Courtaulds' bank was the Bank of England (where it had normally kept £30m. or £40m. on deposit) and it therefore felt little need to worry about the opinions of the City. Its chairman, Sir John Hanbury-Williams (who had succeeded Samuel Courtauld in 1947), the son of a Marshal of the Diplomatic Corps who himself became Gentleman-Usher to King George V. He had a strong sense of protocol: Press enquiries were almost invariably met with 'no comment'.

[1] Winston S. Churchill, *The Second World War*, Vol. 2, p. 506. Cassell, London, 1951 edition.
[2] Cellulosic fibres, of which rayon is one, are derived from wood or cotton linters.

Courtaulds' disdain for the prospects of nylon seemed justified at first: British Nylon Spinners did not prosper in the early post-war years, and relations with ICI became strained. They were stretched almost to breaking-point by ICI's refusal to put its latest fibre, Terylene, into BNS – quite reasonably, since Courtaulds had had nothing to do with its development. An argument then developed about access to nylon technology, and in the end it was agreed (in 1952) that BNS should be run by an entirely separate management and that neither ICI nor Courtaulds should have technical access to the company's processes.[1] The prohibition was strictly adhered to: while the Courtaulds' Board discussed questions like the price at which nylon should be sold and gave approval for extensions of capacity, even the company's research manager was not allowed to tour the BNS plants. Courtaulds was thus excluded from the technology of the second great fibre bonanza.

The result was that, by the late 1950s, it was left with little more than rayon. It had spent the previous years buying up smaller rayon companies (without exception, at their own request) and in 1957 it took over its largest competitor, British Celanese, whose profits had slumped. The Courtaulds' management also acquired a number of assorted sidelines—including cardboard boxes, tin cans, aerosols, lipstick containers and plastics. This diversification reflected a nervousness about the future.

To some of the younger men on the board, however, it was already clear that the company had no future with a mixture of rayon and plastic toys: on that basis it might continue to be gentlemanly, but it would be doomed. Their dissatisfaction encouraged them to experiment. One of the incidental items which had come to Courtaulds with British Celanese was an acetate warp-knitting plant. Warp knitting eliminated several stages in the old cotton manufacturing process: with it, fabric would be produced directly from fibre. One of the younger directors, Frank Kearton (a scientist who had begun life as a process operator with ICI) asked if he could take over the Celanese plant[2] after being told by the company's textile experts that there was no future in warp knitting. He also talked the Courtaulds' Board into buying Gossard, which made women's underwear: the company was tentatively feeling its way towards a much broader involvement in textiles.

Kearton also reopened the door to nylon technology by persuading

---

[1] Courtaulds had already agreed some time before to transfer all its nylon technologists into BNS. Sir Frank Kearton says this left it 'picked clean as a bone'.

[2] Celanese also put Courtaulds into the garment business: it owned half a dozen small companies making lingerie and nightwear.

ICI to let Courtaulds continue to operate a small polyamides plant which, again, it had acquired in the Celanese deal. Such a move appeared to be against the BNS agreement, and ICI initially wanted the plant closed down, but Kearton apparently succeeded in convincing it that the research done there might be of benefit to BNS. When the break-up of BNS in 1964 left Courtaulds free to move independently, it was able to mount its own nylon operation very quickly indeed:[1] six factories were built in four years and Courtaulds soon became the second largest producer in Britain.

However, it took the tremendous shock to Courtaulds' nervous system provoked by the ICI take-over bid to produce a decisive change of direction. Some of the older directors, who had come to believe that Courtaulds was not viable as a long-term proposition and that surrender to ICI was the most sensible course (they had, indeed, agreed the price of it), found their views sharply rejected by the younger men: eventually they departed and Kearton emerged as the new power in the company.[2] He was the prime influence in convincing the Courtaulds' Board that it should put its faith, and its money, into textiles. It was one of the largest industries in the country (with a total turnover, including garments, of £2,700m.) and Kearton rightly predicted that it was due for an upturn. Nor was it a small investment which he had in mind: he wanted Courtaulds to command twenty-five per cent of Britain's textile capacity.

By March 1962, Courtaulds knew it had survived the battle with ICI, begun at the end of 1961. By Christmas of the same year, Kearton had all but settled the details of a Grand Design for Lancashire. He had persuaded five of the most substantial companies – the Lancashire Cotton Corporation, Fine Spinners and Doublers, English Sewing Cotton, Combined English Mills and Tootal – to agree to a giant merger. The companies were to exchange shares and Courtaulds was to pump in new capital and take a large equity interest. Then came the first hold-up: one of Courtaulds' outside directors suggested it would be wise to tell ICI about the proposal. ICI eventually proved receptive, and agreed to put up forty-five per cent of the new capital, with Courtaulds providing the remaining fifty-five per cent. A second and, as it

[1] Courtaulds exchanged its half of BNS for the thirty-eight per cent of its shares acquired by ICI in the take-over battle: since Courtaulds' original investment in BNS was £4m., the swap represented a tax-free capital gain of £100m.

[2] Kearton was one of two Courtaulds' men to be offered a seat on the ICI Board, under the deal which ICI was proposing.

proved, fatal snag now emerged; one of the parties demanded a bigger share in the equity of the new company. Kearton and Chambers thereupon agreed that the scheme would have to be called off: if one company was given a larger stake, the others would undoubtedly want the same. The Grand Design had fallen through.

The failure of this ambitious project was, however, the beginning rather than the end of the affair. In 1963, English Sewing, with money from ICI and Courtaulds, bought Tootal; in the same year, a relative newcomer, Viyella, bought Combined English Mills; and in 1964 Courtaulds itself acquired the Lancashire Cotton Corporation and Fine Spinners and Doublers.

These gave Courtaulds over a third of Lancashire's spinning capacity, but they were simply to be the largest of the ninety-odd textile, hosiery and garment companies which Kearton bought between 1963 and 1968. He took over dyeing, printing and finishing firms; weaving and knitting plants; scores of hosiery and garment makers, most of them small; seven wholesalers; and collected one hundred or so shops along the way.[1]

These assorted purchases cost Courtaulds well over £150m. and, in addition to making it the biggest spinner in Britain, gave it twenty per cent of filament weaving, thirty per cent of warp knitting capacity and twenty per cent of the market for women's underwear and stockings. They also dumped a fair proportion of Lancashire's problems on Courtaulds' doorstep. Kearton had reckoned that it would take six years to rationalize and re-equip the spinning empires; in the spring of 1968 he still regarded their profitability as 'derisory', but believed the corner had been turned.

There were problems, too, in fishing waters which contained such a large proportion of small companies: there are, for example, no less than eighty-eight warp knitters in Britain. Kearton was looking for companies which were run down and badly managed, but which had considerable profit potential. With that rule-of-thumb, he knew he had to expect to buy overdrafts as well as potential, and large numbers of small units also meant a further stretching of scarce management resources. There was one compensation, so far as Kearton was concerned. Since most of the companies he was acquiring were small, it did not matter if one or two turned out to be what he calls 'lemons'.

During these years, Courtaulds also put massive investment into fibres and decided to build new weaving sheds; examined the possibility

[1] The shops represent less than one per cent of turnover, and are regarded as 'quite incidental': Courtaulds see themselves as manufacturers rather than 'shop people'.

of moving into the Yorkshire woollen industry, and had talks with Montague Burton, which has a chain of six hundred men's wear shops as well as fourteen factories; made a careful appraisal of the carpet industry, where its Courtelle and Evlan yarns have been so successful; and sought (and failed) to make other major alliances. ICI turned down Kearton's proposal of a fibre union, and discussions for a Courtaulds/Viyella merger eventually fell through, even though Kearton had previously agreed a price with Viyella's architect, Joe Hyman. Then, in 1969, Courtaulds withdrew an offer for English Calico – produced by a merger between ESC and Calico Printers in 1968 – at the request of the Board of Trade.[1]

Viyella was the second catalytic force which helped transform the textile industry in the 1960s. In many ways its beginnings were similar to the circumstances of Courtaulds own re-entry into the field, in that Hyman made his money and his name by backing the warp-knitting process when few other people had seen its possibilities. By the early 1960s he had a solid base, which included every process from knitting to finishing, his profits had more than trebled from 1961 to 1963, and his ambitions had become imperial: he wanted to be big, and he wanted to demonstrate that Lancashire could be made to pay. He lacked only one thing – ready cash – and this he asked for, and got, from ICI.

Hyman was gratified that ICI, the biggest company in Britain, should want to back him. He felt that perhaps the chemical giant needed him to help get Terylene off the ground, and he took it to his bosom as a partner: ICI bought twenty per cent of the Viyella equity, a holding equal to Hyman's own. Hyman used the ICI money to help him buy British Van Heusen, a vertically organized group with everything from spinning to shops; he also acquired Combined English Mills, which had twenty-eight spinning plants, and the Bradford Dyers Association, the largest dyeing and finishing company in the world. The acquisition of CEM was a typical piece of Hyman quixotry: a desire to do something for Lancashire was mixed with, on the one hand, a determination to show that spinning could be made to pay as part of a vertical group and, on the other, a desire (which exists in Hyman as in many others) to be recognized as a public-spirited industrialist.

His honeymoon with ICI was, in the event, short-lived. ICI had made money available to English Sewing Cotton before giving it to Viyella,

---

[1] The Board has now called for a temporary standstill on mergers between the big Lancashire textile companies; the standstill applies to Coats Paton as well as to Courtaulds, English Calico and Viyella.

and as it backed more and more textile groups, it seemed more and more evident to Hyman that Viyella was a vehicle for ICI's purposes rather than the reverse. ICI, he charged, was trying to balkanize the industry; in 1967, he paid off the loan and severed the link.

In the meantime, he had moved with considerable speed and skill to rationalize the two hundred manufacturing units he had acquired. The non-textile assets which many of his purchases had gathered about them – British Van Heusen owned pig farms – were disposed of, Van Heusen's Aertex shops were sold off (Hyman does not believe that textile companies should operate in the retail field), other properties disposed of, fifteen of CEM's mills closed, stock figures reduced, Boards retired, manpower cut, marketing overhauled. Hyman moved with apparently effortless ease through a tangle of difficulties and swiftly created a group with ten per cent of Britain's spinning capacity, seventeen per cent of warp knitting and seventeen per cent of the branded shirt market.

In the process, unfortunately, he did not endear himself to a good many people in the industry, not least some of those who had been struggling with only indifferent success to run textile businesses in Lancashire. For them Hyman talked too much; he was apt to express his ambitions in a somewhat Napoleonic style; he moved too quickly and, most important of all, it was obvious that he would dominate most companies in which he operated.

This lack of rapport with some other company bosses was to be a factor in thwarting many of Hyman's plans for further acquisitions: in Britain, companies seeking a merger are apt to look for the most comfortable partner. When Hyman announced a merger scheme with English Sewing Cotton early in 1968, he received a sharp rebuff. ESC announced that the Calico Printers Association was its intended, and had been for some time: English Calico was duly formed. This was an alliance between two of the last sizeable Lancashire-based companies; they lived on each other's doorstep in Manchester and neither had a particularly exciting record.

ESC had emerged from the war much too heavily dependent on its American business (which regularly provided between a third and sixty per cent of its profits) and on thread. Furthermore, its British plants, its methods and much of its management were old-fashioned. The Coats selling organization had helped give it three-quarters of the British domestic thread market, which was declining, but less than twenty per cent of the industrial market, which was expanding, even though slowly. It was a curious situation: even ESC's commercial director had no access to the firm's customers and his job was basically to liaise with Coats. Any thought of breaking away was checked by the fear that Coats might overwhelm it.[1]

ESC's earliest efforts after the war were concentrated on building up overseas thread business in India, Australia and elsewhere; on increasing its spinning capacity – it was one of the pioneers of three-shift working; on the purchase of weaving mills – it bought seventeen after 1947;[2] and on reducing the 32,000 different varieties of thread which it sold in Britain before the war – it cut them to 8,000 (with the help of the sellers' market) in the two years after the war. As its return on capital continued to fall (it was down to six per cent by 1958), ESC began to feel that it ought to move nearer to the consumer, that it was no longer sufficient to be an anonymous sub-contractor. It was shaken into action by two further factors: one was a fear that it might be taken over by Sir Isaac Wolfson's Great Universal Stores, the second, alarm at the implications of the ICI-Courtaulds battle. If Courtaulds was not large enough to be safe, thought ESC's directors, who was?

When these alarums without forced ESC to move, its Board plumped heavily for a deeper involvement in Lancashire textiles. Again the choice seems to have been partly motivated by misguided local patriotism. Among a spate of acquisitions made between 1963 and 1965, the most significant were Tootal and Barlow and Jones. This took ESC into traditional textiles with a vengeance and also into paper and plastics, by virtue of Tootal's previous diversifications. A small part of these new assets earned reasonable returns, but others – such as men's wear – proved troublesome and altogether ESC burnt its fingers badly. On the thread side, it had more than doubled its share of the industrial market and probably held not much less than half the total British market for all thread. Helped by a price increase and devaluation, its overall profits had been steadily improving.

Its future partner, Calico Printers, had decided to diversify a good deal earlier than ESC – in its case, moving away from traditional textiles – but the policy was not pursued with any urgency until the end of the 1950s. CPA's problem by that time was straightforward

---

[1] When ESC finally broke away from the Coats arrangement, it had not a single man on its staff who had ever sold a reel of thread: within six weeks it had hired two hundred.

[2] Only four are now left.

enough. It was earning fat royalties from Terylene (over £3m. in some years) and these frequently provided the bulk of its profits.[1] Profits from its traditional business, on the other hand, fluctuated between £2m. and zero. It wanted therefore to assure itself of a stable profit base against the time when the Terylene royalties should decline. The best way to do this, it decided, was by moving closer to the consumer; in CPA's case, that meant buying retail outlets.

Its first venture into the retail field, in the early 1950s, had been a failure – it had bought shops and then tried to pump into them goods from its garment company, Brook Manufacturing. Its second attempt, which was launched towards the end of the decade, did not seek such a tight relationship between fashion goods and outlets. It acquired a considerable assortment of shops – including 150 Van Allan shops, the Hide Group of department stores and shops and the Harry Fenton's men's wear chain – together with the Rael-Brook shirt company and a mail order business. In some areas, the expansion proved extremely effective – half the shirts sold in CPA's shops are its own – but in women's garments the proportion is a good deal less than twenty per cent. The venture into retail trading has not yet proved any more profitable for CPA than it has for most other textile companies which have used the same strategy.

The motives for the coming together of these two businesses are still not entirely clear but Neville Butterworth, the chairman of English Calico, says he wanted CPA for its men's wear (it had fourteen per cent of the shirt market) and to help create what he calls 'the biggest fabric organization in Europe'.

A Cambridge graduate in economics and mathematics, he describes himself as 'a tidier-upper'; he has certainly justified the description since the merger. He sold CPA's mail order business for £1m.; £3m. had been paid for it, but Butterworth says it would have lost £900,000 in 1968 if it had been allowed to continue for a full year. He also sold one of CPA's trade investments in South Africa for £2.3m.; the CPA head office; and a variety of its shops (one site, at Wood Green in London, brought in over £1m.). Butterworth says he would also be willing to consider a good offer for the other shops, although he wants to retain the men's-wear outlets. Only one of the old CPA Board is still with the company.

Butterworth has undoubtedly made a brisk beginning, but English Calico still has a long way to go. One of its problems is that there will

[1] Almost seventy per cent in 1964 and 1966, over half in 1965.

now be a sharp decline in Terylene royalties, because the patents to a large extent ran out in 1968. This decline will have to be met by increased trading profits. Nevertheless, Butterworth is confident enough: he wants to move into knitting for men's suits and takes comfort from the fact that about two-thirds of English Calico's profits come from areas – thread, retail and non-textiles – not subject to the normal fluctuations of textiles.

As for the prospect of a closer link with Courtaulds (which already holds eight per cent of the Calico equity), Butterworth would prefer a joint company involving the Lancashire interests of both groups.

Courtaulds was driven into textiles by the need to seek a new *raison d'être* after narrowly fighting off the ICI bid, Viyella by the ambition of one man. A third force, J. and P. Coats, was forced out of its traditional thread preserves by the slow growth (currently four per cent a year) which the thread business offered.

Just as Courtaulds had spent the post-war years trying to refurbish rayon, so Coats devoted itself to expanding its thread operation. It moved into South Africa during the war and into Australia and a number of South American countries thereafter. By the end of the 1950s, however, its directors were beginning to feel that the company had far too high a proportion of its assets in thread and far too high a proportion overseas; after over a century of the most extreme specialization, the Coats Board began to discuss the virtues of verticality and the merits of moving out of their secure thread fortress. They looked around for suitable areas of expansion; in that search, they had the inestimable blessing of being liked, of being regarded as a gentle giant which had generally conducted itself impeccably.

Their first thoughts were of taking an interest in Lancashire, but the idea proved unattractive. The woollen industry, on the other hand, seemed a more promising and indeed natural line of advance. For one thing, Coats had already taken a twenty-five per cent interest in a Greenock company which it had supported during the 1950s; Fleming Reid had a yarn, knitting and garment business together with some three hundred Scotch Wool shops. The other seventy-five per cent was taken by Patons and Baldwins, which did a sizeable trade in woollen, acrylic and nylon yarns. P and B was yet another firm whose products had been distributed through Coats' Central Agency.

Gradually, it became apparent that a complete partnership would suit both sides. Patons would give Coats a large investment in Britain; Coats would strengthen Patons abroad. Patons also sensed that it might be vulnerable to attack from Courtaulds[1] and preferred what it thought would be a more congenial union with Coats: the two chairmen were already personal friends.

The marriage (in 1960) and the manner of its consummation (or, more accurately, non-consummation) seriously held up Coats' move into woollens. Patons fully expected to go on running its own show, and Coats men who tried to interfere were told bluntly to mind their own business. Patons also succeeded in taking four of the ten seats on the joint Board, a higher proportion than its size (its turnover was about a third of Coats') strictly justified. Nine years after the merger, Patons has only three of the eleven places on the holdings Board and Charles Bell, the chairman of Coats, is also the chairman of Patons.

After this long hiatus, Coats began to strengthen its bridgehead in wool, and also to move nearer the consumer. In 1965, it took a controlling interest in Pasolds,[2] which had the largest children's wear business in the country besides knitwear and underwear companies: in 1966, it bought ninety-two Bellman wool and clothing shops; in 1967, it acquired Jaeger, which owned retail shops eighty per cent of whose goods were manufactured at the group's own factories, and also mills owned by Jeremiah Ambler which produced yarns from synthetic fibres; in 1969, it took a majority interest in West Riding Worsted, a vertically organized group which is very strong in spinning but handles every process from the raw wool to the finished cloth. Bellman was bought because it was hoped that it might provide management to pull round the Scotch Wool shops, which have been seriously wounded by Marks and Spencer: Bellman was making as much profit on less than one hundred shops as Scotch Wool was making on three hundred. Coats has also extended its interests outside textiles, mainly into die-casting and associated processes: this has produced very useful profits.

So far as Charles Bell is concerned, these investments are only a beginning. He wants to strengthen the spinning base which Ambler and West Riding have given him, and then continue the progression through weaving and knitting into the shops. He does not want to become completely vertical, because he feels he is in a volatile business,

[1] Sir Frank Kearton had been trying to persuade Coats *and* Patons to link up with Courtaulds.

[2] Again, Kearton had been talking merger terms with Eric Pasold; he could not, however, persuade the Courtaulds' Board to pay Pasolds' price. Kearton says that in the case of both Pasolds and of West Riding (a later acquisition by Coats) one of the factors was Coats' willingness to take initially a partial holding.

but prefers instead the notion of an inverted pyramid, with Coats doing one hundred per cent of its own spinning, fifty per cent of its own weaving and knitting, and owning shops twenty-five per cent of whose goods are made within the group. He is only too well aware that the Bellman-Scotch Wool chain falls far short of this target, with only ten to fifteen per cent of its turnover home-made.

But Bell's major problem is the nature of the Yorkshire woollen industry. It is made up of a mass of 1,850 companies,[1] eighty per cent of them privately owned and with only three which are capitalized at over £1m.; there is the added complication that many of the biggest companies also produce the poorest returns. Traditions are not easily broken in the Yorkshire woollen trade and the idea of handing over control of their own destiny, let alone the Rolls and the annual visit to the Antipodes is something which many of the family-controlled empires would be loath to accept, even for sweet talkers from Scotland. Bell, however, is not prepared to talk for ever: he would prefer to keep the take-overs friendly, but is quite prepared to fight for any crucial pieces in his jig-saw. He is also convinced that time is on his side and that, with the advance of synthetic fibres, many small businesses will have to surrender if only because they do not have the cash for new machinery.

In any event, Coats has at last begun to come out of its shell. Only five-sevenths of its assets are now in thread, although eighty-two per cent of its profits are still earned abroad,[2] and even if its investment in shops has so far been a flop, there is good hope of growth from Pasolds and Patons.

Thus the textile industry, and particularly the Lancashire end of it, has gone through a more profound revolution of organization in the last decade than it had during the previous six. The Yorkshire industry is facing change of the same magnitude. This transformation is partly due to the fact that the industry has also gone through a management revolution. The major companies have now, at last, been mercifully rescued by a new wave of autocrats. Kearton is the fastest-talking, and one of the fastest-moving, autocrats in the whole of British industry; Bell is the first autocrat whom Coats has produced since Phillipi; and Hyman, although not quite the one-man band which his reputation suggests, is still monarch within his own kingdom. (His description of

---

[1] There are 120 privately-owned spinners who employ between ten and 120 people, and 140 private weaving companies with between ten and one hundred employees.

[2] The British market accounts for only five per cent of Coats' thread sales.

himself as 'the only proprietor left in the business' seems, however, rather presumptuous in view of the fact that at the time of writing he has only seven per cent of the Viyella shares.) All three have an entrepreneurial instinct and a ruthlessness which are extremely welcome.

The obsessive specialization of the industry is also fast disappearing, except among the legions of lilliputian companies which still remain in both Lancashire and Yorkshire: verticality (more or less complete) is the new god. This fundamental change of ideology has been partly dictated by the ability to turn raw material directly into cloth and partly by a conviction that companies can no longer afford to be obscure sub-contractors lost in a multitude of inter-dependent processes. It has to be added that the passion to end anonymity has been accompanied by some extremely ill-judged ventures into the market place. Nobody has yet proved that retail shops are a proper occupation for a textile manufacturer and at this point the evidence strongly suggests that Hyman (and Marks and Spencer, for that matter) are right to keep manufacturing and retailing strictly apart. Having a face is all very well, so long as it is not a bloody one.

The process of rationalization is very far from over, the Government and the Monopolies Commission permitting. Bell and Hyman are both hungry for further acquisitions, and they have good businesses at their backs.[1] Courtaulds has shed its old dependence on rayon (production of viscose filament is now down to about a third of what it was in the mid-1950s), and although the fibres industry is volatile and precarious, the company has achieved a fair balance between that side of its business and textiles: both now probably account for rather more than forty per cent of its turnover. Its organization is either very flexible or very untidy, according to your point of view, but Kearton insists that a tidy organization would be out of date within three months in a group which has been moving so fast and in so many different directions. Nevertheless, if it was headed by anyone less deft, its lack of shape might well be a liability. But Courtaulds is no longer a mass of committees, and Kearton has succeeded in imbuing it with something of his own commercial sharpness.

Coats' return on capital has slipped back somewhat since it awoke from its long sleep, but is still high compared with other big textile groups, and with its base firmly planted in an extremely efficient thread operation and huge borrowing power now at the ready, it has tremendous latent power. A persistent tradition of clinging to overseas

[1] Kearton says he has ceased to be hungry, for the time being.

thread businesses which make losses or yield only poor returns, in the belief that they must pay off in the end, will not affect its results really significantly, but it may well have to think again about its retail shops.

For Hyman, much depends on the success of his gamble that polyester-cotton mixtures will expand in Britain as rapidly as they have in the United States, and on his ability to make his large investment in Lancashire earn a good deal more than the profits it is currently providing. His return on capital fell back sharply between 1964 and 1967, but picked up again in 1968. Viyella is also more dependent on the British market than either Courtaulds or, of course, Coats. In one sense, it is a good thing for the textile industry that Hyman's talks with both Courtaulds and ICI have not led to a merger: Hyman would have achieved his desire to operate on a larger stage, but he would not have been driven (as he now is) to use his very considerable talent to the limit. He has so far been more efficient as a practising prophet rather than as a saint, and is likely to remain so.

So far as the industry as a whole is concerned, a great deal still remains to be done. For one thing, rationalization has not yet gone far enough, despite all that has been achieved; a Textile Council study published in 1969 said that the number of units in the Lancashire industry was expected to decline from over seven hundred to under three hundred within the next six years. The report also pointed out that the industry still had too many high-cost firms; costs varied by 40–45 per cent between the best and worst companies in particular sections. The salvation of textiles is a slow and laborious process.

CHAPTER 14

The Newest Profession?

If management consultancy is a profession – and even its leading practitioners are divided on the point[1] – it is surely the only one where member firms plan to grow at fifteen per cent per annum. Its expansion over the last five years has, in fact, been so rapid as to astonish even the most optimistic operators and, having previously spent a great deal of energy in trying to give their activities greater standing (the Management Consultants Association was formed in 1956, the Institute of Management Consultants in 1962),[2] they find that their lack of professional credentials has been forgotten in the rush. Many are only too delighted to be free to think of themselves as businessmen.

Management consultancy has none of the accepted marks of a profession. To begin with, anyone can set up as a consultant; as in the case of estate agents, all that is required is a plate on the door. Nor are there any examinations; the Institute has drawn up what it calls 'The Body of Knowledge', but although it enjoins this, it does not as yet examine on it. Finally, although members of the official bodies must not advertise or tout for business in unseemly ways (by circular letter, for example), they are free to offer their services through letters to individual businessmen and seem to find no difficulty in obtaining the introductions they need.

Many consultancy firms, indeed, market their wares with a zest

[1] For example, John Tyzack – who, until recently, ran his own consulting firm – says: 'Management consultancy is not within a thousand miles of being a profession. It's a business.'

[2] The MCA is basically an employers' association, made up of nineteen firms which do about two-thirds of the consulting business in Britain (McKinsey and Booz, Allen are not members), while the Institute is for individual consultants.

PA Management Consultants

Albert Gate, London. Income in fees, £6½m. world-wide in 1968; over 800 consultants world-wide, 500 in Britain.

Inbucon: including Associated Industrial Consultants

Knightsbridge House, London. Subsidiary of American Leasco World Trade. Income £4½m. Over 800 professional staff.

Urwick Orr

Hobart Place, London. Income £4m. 525 consultants.

P-E Consulting Group

Grosvenor Place, London. Income, £3.3m. world-wide. Over 400 consultants.

McKinsey

St James's Street, London. Income in Britain, £1¼m. (estimated). 75 consultants.

Booz, Allen

New Bond Street, London. Income in Britain, £1¼m. (estimated) out of global total of £20m. 80 consultants (1,200 professionally qualified staff world-wide).

---

which would put most professional salesmen to shame. PA Management Consultants, which has the reputation of being the hardest seller in the business, has a manual entitled 'Selling Our Work' which includes sections on 'Persuasion', 'Rules for Persuasion', 'Preparation for Persuasion' and 'Creating Enthusiastic Clients' as well as hints on voice, bearing and manner; the company also pays a sales royalty for each 'consultant week' sold (ranging from £25 for less than five weeks sold to £200 for over a hundred weeks sold) and budgets for a target profit on each man in the field; the attitudes of some of the other groups suggest that they pursue business scarcely less fiercely.

The directors of the largest firms are all expected to be (to a lesser or greater degree) salesmen as well as administrators or specialists, and are rated partly according to their ability to attract business. The most successful styles might be described as ascetic/intense (particularly effective with the larger public companies) and bedside/benign (more suitable for smaller, family-type businesses) which requires grey hair, and a mild and fatherly manner concealing keen commercial judgement. The consultancy firms (such as Urwick Orr) which appoint outside directors often pick them partly because of their reputation and con-tacts – contacts are vital in the consultancy world – and the assignments which those contacts may produce.

At a lower level, methods vary. PA employs survey consultants who are exclusively concerned with selling the firm's services, while other groups tend to make one man responsible for both sales and supervision in a particular area. Even the non-consulting services provided by firms yield a bonus through their ability to bring in business. AIC, for example, is among those which run management training centres, and although it loses money on the operation it says that – apart from its value as a service to clients – the centre is a useful source of contacts from which future assignments may flow. Similarly, most groups run departments to help clients find executives;[1] these normally yield higher profits than the general run of consulting.[2]

There are a number of perfectly valid reasons for this eager salesman-ship. One is that consultants, like advertising men, are selling an intangible expertise: their ardour, many feel, therefore needs to be all the greater. Another is that consultancy – at one time, an extremely insecure occupation – has traditionally offered both high rewards and the prospect of rapid promotion. Booz, Allen, for example, expects its men to be capable of earning £5,000 a year at the age of thirty, and very successful consultants in large British firms can be paid as much as £10,000 by the time they are forty. This means that fixed costs are high – fifty-five per cent of fees normally go towards the payment of salaries – and the impact of unemployed consultants on profits is immediate and can be serious. In the past, when both fees and salaries were paid by the hour, having men 'off the clock'[3] was worrying enough; now that consultants are on fixed annual salaries,[4] the dangers are all the greater. No doubt this is why consultants sometimes talk in terms of 'weeks sold' rather than of problems solved.

[1] The big consultant firms say they do not 'head-hunt' in the sense of seeking out managers and making tempting offers on behalf of a client; they normally operate through press advertising. But, as Brian Smith of PA says, they have on record details of men who replied to previous advertisements and who might be suitable for another job being advertised. PA, he adds, can check through the records of some 15,000 men and let those likely to be interested know of vacancies advertised.

[2] Twenty per cent seems to be the standard gross return at which the large British consultancies aim.

[3] The phrase still survives.

[4] Consultants with the big firms are often also on long engagements, another legacy of the insecure past. PA, for instnace, generally offers its staff three-year contracts.

The rapid growth of the big businesses – at an average rate of about twelve per cent per annum over the last decade – has only made the situation more difficult. In 1950, PA had perhaps thirty consultants; now it has over 800, many of them with a considerable degree of specialization.[1] Keeping them all profitably employed in work which fits their particular skill is the management's greatest problem.

These pressures help to account for some of the curiosities of consultancy. In particular, a large number of firms like to describe themselves as 'the Rolls-Royce of the business', which seems to mean that they not only claim to provide a more effective service but also charge more for it. Charles Allison, the managing director of Booz, Allen in Britain, says that it is probably among the most expensive in the world; whereas most British consultants charge between 250 guineas and 370 guineas per man per week (depending on the man and the assignment), Booz, Allen asks about £200 a day for its best performers,[2] and a senior member of its staff could have a rate almost twice the British average. (McKinsey's rates are believed to average £400–£500 a week.) But fees are not kept at these levels on the theory that expense lends enchantment: although high charges are undoubtedly something of a status symbol in the consultancy business, they also enable firms to buy the best talent available. Furthermore, in the view of at least one managing director, the cost encourages clients to pay attention and to act on his firm's recommendations.

But the urgent need to sell also accounts for some of the less satisfactory features of the management consultancy business. When order books are low, it is extremely difficult to turn down work, even when the consultant is being asked to solve what he believes to be the wrong problem. Consultancy firms may protest that they would never accept jobs whose outcome might damage their reputation, but senior executives admit that their firms have sometimes done what clients wanted (rather than what they needed) at times when they had consultants 'off the clock'. Often they hope they will be asked to stay on and solve what they conceive to be the real problem.

For similar reasons, some consultancy firms are only too willing to stay in client companies for very long periods. The average assignment probably lasts between six months and a year, and Allison of Booz,

[1] In 1950, there were only about 250 consultants in Britain, compared with the current figure of 3,500.

[2] American firms relate their charges to the salary of the consultant involved, and since salaries are fixed at US levels, charges are correspondingly high.

Allen believes that if it goes on for more than eighteen months, there is something wrong either with itself or the client. Nevertheless, Bill Mitton, the chairman of AIC, said that his firm had once worked in one company for nineteen years and PA has been retained by another company for fifteen, with only brief intervals between jobs. Accepting that both did valuable work for the whole of that time, when consultants become a near-permanent fixture of the landscape in this way they also run the risk of stunting the growth of the existing management.

Long assignments can also pose problems of diplomacy, as the former managing director of another firm explained: 'The sort of job you want is the one which goes on for years and years, but there can be difficulties when it comes to switching consultants. The first consultant – let's say he was a production engineer – may get tired after a few years, and ask for a change of company. At that particular time, you might have several accountants waiting for jobs, and the tricky thing is to persuade the client that he also has a costing problem.'

There are other curiosities about the business, at least to the outsider. One is that management consultants are not, like consultants in many of the professions, successful operators in their own fields who turn freelance to market their skill and reputation at higher rates: the Boards of the big British consultancy firms do not include among their full-time directors the name of one businessman of national reputation, and indeed the great majority held executive posts of modest importance before becoming consultants. Brian Smith, now the managing director of PA, which he joined in his late twenties, had previously run a small tool-making business in Cumberland; Anthony Frodsham of P-E was an electrical engineer with a middle management job in ICI; Bill Mitton was a colliery manager; and even Hugh Parker of McKinsey came to the firm twenty years ago from a job as assistant manager of a jute mill in India – a modest beginning for a man who has since prescribed on the ailments of Shell and ICI.[1] John Tyzack, formerly director of administrative services for BEA, is one of very few British consultants who have previously held really senior jobs in industry.

The fact is that, in management consultancy as in many other businesses, the most successful are those who join young and climb the ladder from within; firms like PA have no outside directors at all. But

[1] Parker points out that while many consultants of the present generation are 'converted line managers', this is less true today to the extent that men are going straight into consultancy from the universities and business schools.

although PA and others can (in my view) be fairly criticized for being too ingrown, it is also a fact that the roles of the consultant and the executive are profoundly different.[1] Frodsham of P-E gives one consultant's eye-view of the contrast: 'The executive is a man who gives orders, a man of quick decision and action. He is also an emotional man who relies a good deal on instinct. The consultant, on the other hand, is essentially a quiet research worker who does not need to give an answer today. He is an analyst and not an entrepreneur, and he has no executive power.'

The lack of authority to enforce their recommendations is one of the frustrations of the consulting life – Brian Smith believes the business is 'thirty per cent getting it right and seventy per cent getting it across';[2] another is that, never having run large companies themselves, consultants have to be content with telling others how to do it. They would argue, however, that as dispassionate outsiders they exercise what one consultant described as 'clean power' and in some ways their activities are intellectual and even academic in nature: Hugh Parker, who describes consultancy as 'the scientific method applied to business', occasionally uses a blackboard when talking to clients.

McKinsey, indeed, has had a profound influence on management consultancy in Britain; in the view of a number of highly-placed British consultants, it has put the business on the map for the first time. McKinsey's growth has been rapid – from two consultants in 1959 to seventy-five today – but others have expanded just as quickly (Booz, Allen, for example, now has eighty consultants compared with five only six years ago), and its most significant impact has undoubtedly been upon the status of consultancy in this country; largely because of McKinsey, the consultant is now accepted as the chairman's companion.

This is an eminence undreamed of by most British consultants only ten years ago. All the biggest British firms sprang from a company started in Britain in 1927 by the American, Charles E. Bedaux; its main concern was labour cost-control, its most prominent tool was the stop-watch and it was not favourably regarded by the trade unions. AIC was one of British Bedaux's subsidiaries, while the founders of PA

[1] The point is not invalidated by the fact that a good many young men spend five years or so in consultancy to broaden their experience before going back into industry: they do so at an early age (generally between twenty-eight and thirty-four) and on a short-service basis.

[2] Frodsham of P-E said in 1969: 'The consultant must be like the Japanese General Yamashita who could make a huge bell ring by applying a pulsating pressure with his forefinger on the bell's rim.'

and P-E and one of the founders of Urwick Orr all worked for Britih Bedaux.

Most of the big consultancy firms have found it difficult to raise themselves from these humble origins. They have always been (and, in many cases, still are) dominated by engineers; and a large proportion of their work is still centred on the factory floor. There are exceptions – Urwick Orr says that more than half its assignments include company reorganization and that it does 'no works study or routine stuff' – but in 1968 the nineteen members of the MCA earned little more than double what McKinsey alone made from 'company appraisal and overall policy development'. They console themselves with the thought that they are concentrating on the practical – 'we produce improvements on the shop floor', said Frodsham, 'McKinsey can't do that' – but they would dearly love to find themselves in the Board-room more often than they do. Not only do they feel up-staged by McKinsey in terms of prestige – the Americans will not tackle any problem which is not 'the proper concern of the chief executive' – but also deprived of work which pays much more handsomely than the ordinary run of consultancy. PA set up a Corporate Strategy Division in 1965 and other companies have similar departments, but they have not even begun to eat into McKinsey's lead in its chosen field.

The wound has been deepened by the enthusiasm with which British newspapers have followed McKinsey's activities. When PA was called in to help reorganize the Metropolitan Police, one carried a story which began with the line: 'A big firm of British consultants (*unnamed*) are to do a McKinsey-type operation on the Metropolitan Police.' This sort of coverage has aroused understandable complaint, but the harsh truth is that McKinsey is news and they are not.[1]

McKinsey (which has been called in by Dunlop, Rolls-Royce, the BBC and the Bank of England as well as by Shell and ICI) owes its success – and it is worth remembering that no other American consultancy has been anything like so successful – to a combination of circumstances. It arrived at precisely the right moment (when company growth was beginning to lag and chairmen were ready to look to American ideas of efficiency for an answer),[2] it has had remarkably

[1] When British consultants work abroad for national bodies – Inbucon for example, had an assignment from the Swiss Post Office – the Press of the country concerned almost invariably has something to say about the use of foreign consultants.

[2] Companies sometimes ask McKinsey for American members of its staff, who usually account for twenty-five per cent or less of its consultant strength in Britain.

effective leadership (in the shape of Hugh Parker) and its conservative style has blended admirably with the British scene. From the beginning, it eschewed the hard-sell – Parker claims that it has never approached a single company for work and employs nobody who is charged with developing new business; it limited itself to high-level consultancy, usually for large organizations – Parker says its services are not economic for small businesses, although he does work for a few; and it offers what Parker claims is 'the best collective experience of any consulting firm in the world'. Once McKinsey had become fashionable, its attractions were almost universal.

Parker's own style is distinctly ascetic/intense. He has deep-set eyes and an earnest manner, regularly goes sculling at Henley and brings to his work the dedication of the evangelist. His men are the Mormons of the consultancy world, in appearance at least: they almost always operate in pairs and they invariably seem to wear clean raincoats. Their calibre varies but their general standard is impressive.

Because McKinsey is a specialist organization taking on a relatively small number of very remunerative assignments, Parker himself is able to spend over half his time as a practising consultant and is often there when recommendations are presented to the client. By comparison, Frodsham of P-E spends only five per cent of his working week as a consultant, Smith of PA perhaps ten per cent. Furthermore, whereas McKinsey spends almost all its time in large organizations, the big British firms carry out a large proportion of their assignments in small businesses; in 1967, three-quarters of the clients served by firms belonging to the MCA had less than 1,000 employees.

These differences in philosophy and practice are partly accounted for by the shape of the consultancy business in Britain. It has traditionally been dominated by four very large firms; PA, the biggest of the four, claims to be the second-largest management consultancy firm in the world (Booz, Allen is the largest), but whereas Booz – with 1,200 consultants and an income four times as great as PA's – has only two per cent of the American market, PA accounts for fifteen per cent of all the consultancy work done in this country. Over the years, these four have become department stores, providing everything from automated warehouse design and machine tool advisory services to 'think tanks' capable of solving complex mathematical problems.

Consultants who work for them are apt to suggest that they were forced to offer a comprehensive service, but while this may have been true to some extent in the early post-war years, it has not been true in more recent times. The fact is that, as new areas of knowledge have developed, the big British firms have usually chosen to diversify rather than risk losing potential business. Each new fad (and the British market, as one managing director says, is still something of a fad market) has found them ready to add to their range: network analysis, computer feasibility studies, management development, their appetites have been omnivorous. Nor were they deterred by the rise of large numbers of smaller and more specialized consultants, although some firms have occasionally found it useful to be able to pass on business (sometimes for an introductory fee of ten per cent) and to be offered assignments in return.

There are, of course, advantages as well as disadvantages in size and spread. The main benefit of the department store consultancy is that it can claim to be able to handle under its own roof any problem which may crop up during an assignment (Booz, Allen employs atomic scientists and probability statisticians). The danger is that, as size and spread increase, quality may suffer. A firm like PA, for instance, has to find over one hundred new consultants each year to cope with the growth of its business and the natural turnover of staff. The problem is not necessarily to find enough people of adequate intellectual calibre – the vast majority of consultants are either graduates or have a professional qualification – but to get them properly trained and supervised by experienced senior consultants who are themselves in short supply and under considerable pressure.[1] The problem could well become more acute as business continues to expand. The MCA estimates that there will be 8,000 consultants in this country by 1980, and this seems a reasonable forecast since Britain has only sixty consultants for each million of population compared with 140 in the United States.

The other danger which confronts the big British firms is that, with increasing size, their top men will drift further and further from the front line, becoming remote not only from their clients but also from knowledge of the latest techniques. There is already evidence to suggest that some firms have been held back in their penetration of new areas of business by directors who find it difficult to break their mental attachment to the stop-watch era. These are problems which need to be faced if the big firms are not to become flabby and over-extended.

[1] The big British companies generally give new recruits about six months' initial training, while McKinsey men go through an intensive three-week course in the United States. Thereafter all McKinsey's consultants spend one Saturday each month in training meetings; this includes Parker himself.

So far as the recipients of their advice are concerned, there are welcome signs that the larger companies in particular are using consultants' services in a much more sophisticated way than was formerly the case. Certainly consultants are not offered *carte blanche* as often as they were; they are given tighter briefs and companies usually insist on meeting the consultants who will actually carry out the assignment rather than taking whoever they are sent.

Furthermore, while it is clear that the efforts of consultants sometimes produce results which are neither adequate nor lasting, there seems to be a fair degree of satisfaction with their work to judge by the figures which they quote for 'repeat business'. Urwick Orr and McKinsey say that two-thirds of their assignments come from companies for whom they have worked before, the figure given by PA and AIC is sixty per cent. Taking a wider sample, the MCA produces impressive figures to demonstrate the effectiveness of consultants in achieving higher productivity and lower labour costs.

Apart from any more specific benefits, however, the principal value of consultants in Britain is that they can provide an external impetus towards change in companies which have either lost their way or become too ingrown to generate it for themselves. Nor is the typical company complaint that it has only been told what it already knew a valid one; if the answer was so obvious, it is all the more guilty in having paid so dearly for it. The fact is that the right solution for an organization's problems is almost bound to exist already in the minds of some of its managers: the problem is to isolate it and get it accepted.

Consultants can also perform another particularly useful function; they provide a cross-fertilization service between companies, acting in effect as pollen-carriers in the spreading of new ideas and techniques. The trouble is that the degree of cross-fertilization which they can provide is limited by the extent of their own experience; and although the partners of McKinsey finance a Foundation for Management Research and PA spends £350,000 a year on research and development, consultants are – by and large – the purveyors of existing knowledge rather than innovators in their own right.

Many firms, moreover, seem to develop a management theory of their own and frequently recommend much the same sort of solution. For example, in nine cases out of ten, on Parker's own estimate, McKinsey advises the division of companies into profit-accountable areas under the control of one man, and the replacement of committee rule by that of a chief executive. It may well be, as Parker says, that this is the right solution and not merely a stock answer, but it is also interesting that he can recall a time when he was favourably disposed to the idea of committee management, because he had seen some particularly effective committees in action. He still recognizes their uses.

Nevertheless, even if management consultants succeed in encouraging self-criticism, preventing stagnation and passing on the best accepted management practice, they will have performed a useful service. It will be all the more useful if British companies do not assume that fashionable techniques are a substitute for good management.

PART 3

A Half-Hearted Effort

CHAPTER 15

A Half-Hearted Effort

One of the more obvious reasons why many British companies perform unimpressively is that the men who run them lack the will to do better. They aim low and are satisfied with modest performances; exhibit a marked lack of the self-critical faculty; and put a quiet (though not ostentatious) life high on their list of priorities. This is despite a noticeable improvement in some areas of business in recent years.

These, at least, are my impressions after three years spent in observing a fair sample of business life in this country. Others more closely involved than I have noticed the same lack of ambition, the same conservatism, the same acceptance of the mediocre. The former chairman of a large textile company complained that while Americans invariably took the line 'I'm sure we can do this better', the typical British response was 'Thank God it's running at all'; the managing director of a large engineering company, concerned at the complacency in some parts of his group, wrote to managers suggesting that they might (from time to time) like to consider the possibility that they could do things better; while the chairman of a highly successful merchant bank described Britain succinctly as a 'status quo' society.

American businessmen and consultants working in this country are apt to be even more critical.

> 'There is a tremendous in-built hunger for the status quo in your society – how did they do things before, then how can they keep things the way they are? The business leaders over here would love to have things stay just the same for the next ten years, then they wouldn't have any worries at all.'
>
> *American managing director of subsidiary in Britain*

> 'There's a lot of inertia here, the resistance to innovation almost defies

belief. Even though they see a thing is logical and right, they still say they can't do it. So many of the people who run companies are skilled main-tainers of the status quo.'

leading American management consultant

'In the U.S., a great many people feel really religiously about the subject of efficiency. How on earth does one manage to get a lot of people here feeling the same way?'

American managing director in international company

Neither the observations nor the phenomena are new. Indeed, the most striking fact about Britain's industrial history over the course of the last century is that almost every major upheaval in organization has been primarily defensive in intent. The mergers which took place at the turn of the century and the price rings which survived until recent times were both preservationist rather than expansionist in character, and the diversification movement which became fashionable in the 1950s was generally inspired by a desire to protect profits rather than multiply them. Even some of the big mergers of the last few years have looked rather like last resorts.

Equally, the majority of British industrialists have shown (until recent times) little eagerness to copy either the organization or the management techniques of more successful industrial nations. Now, hopeful perhaps of the power of the American ju-ju (and conscious that output per man in the United States is $2\frac{1}{2}$ times greater than our own), many companies carry a rabbit's foot of their own choice. The organiza-tional structure of Allied Breweries, for example, was patterned on that of Standard Oil of New Jersey; Wates shares information about profits on a 'need-to-know' basis copied from Texas Instruments; at Vickers, whose personnel evaluation system is again modelled on that of Jersey, a visitor may observe the occasional 'Think' sign once so beloved of IBM. Even Permanent Secretaries of the Treasury now speak quite unself-consciously of 'motivating' men.

This sporadic adoption of American techniques (and even attitudes) should not, however, be mistaken for a wholesale espousal of the trans-Atlantic approach to business – and more particularly of its reputedly fervent dedication to the corporation. What most British businessmen seem to want is a flavour, but no more; not enough, certainly, to disturb their way of doing things or to threaten the basic tenor of life in this country. As one Permanent Secretary put it: 'We want to have the fruits of American society, but we are not prepared to accept the roots.' This is true even in the largest companies, where international competition is most severe and where the temptation to plagiarize might be thought strongest.

Peter Menzies of ICI, for example, believes that it would be wrong for British businesses to 'take up the American pattern' and that we need consciously to protect our way of life. 'The Americans,' he said, 'are very deep in the rat race and the people of Western Europe want a wider life, they don't just want money to spend. In that sense, we're in something of a quandary – we want to keep our private lives while staying in the first league.' Lord Stokes, too, wants to 'stay half-way' and retain what he considers some of the more admirable features of the British management style. The Americans, he believes, are better at efficiency and cost control and the analysis of problems than we are, but overlook traditions and loyalties. 'A lot of people discount paternalism', he said, 'but everybody yearns for a father-figure.'

Many industrialists also do not like what they see happening to US businessmen as a result of their single-minded dedication. They feel it produces a high percentage of narrow-minded bores who are washed out at sixty; and they do not yet feel able to weep over the excellence of sales figures, as is not unknown at celebratory gatherings in the United States.[1] In other words, they are afraid of becoming zombies. In my view, their fears are justified; a large proportion of the American businessmen I have met display a genial impersonality and a mechanical politeness which is both disturbing and unattractive – they behave too much like parts of a business machine and too little like natural human beings.

But if (as Sir Reay Geddes, the Dunlop chairman, says) British managements want everyone in the business to focus on its success, then the great majority need to think much more ideologically about their enterprises, to consider how to transform them from being mere places of employment, collections of individuals pursuing an assortment of activities – which is all most British businesses are – into entities with *esprit de corps*. This does not mean a cloying paternalism and it does not mean Americanization – as the example of Marks and Spencer makes clear – and it cannot be fashioned either by the occasional distribution of largesse or even by taking two brief-cases home at the weekend.

What it does demand from managements is genuine dedication to

[1] Company songs are used by some corporations in both the United States and Japan as a method of nurturing dedication. This would be unthinkable in Britain. As one British businessman sagely remarked, 'If we had a company song, people would only start putting their own words to it.'

and pride in their businesses. The most notable feature of Marks and Spencer is the profound commitment of its directors to the success of their company; their hearts are not, like those of so many British businessmen, elsewhere. Nor is their constant preoccupation with its performance only a matter of goods and profits; they are deeply concerned with the sort of environment which they offer their workers. The result is a degree of staff involvement unmatched in big British enterprises. This is what other companies ought to be copying, not merely Marks' method for keeping its suppliers up to scratch.

If British managements want to win the allegiance as well as the attendance of their workers, they will have to care enough and plan enough to win it. If they regard their businesses merely as a means of making money, they ought not to be surprised if their workers take the same attitude. Many could do worse than begin by cleaning up the scruffy premises from which they operate and by improving the amenities which they offer their employees. Too many plants are still industrial slums – harsh, ugly buildings unrelieved by any attempt to create a pleasant environment – and far too few could match up to the beautifully laid-out Olivetti and Volvo plants in Italy and Sweden. They look like sweat-shops for the exploitation of labour and elicit a response which is consistent with their appearance. Nor, frequently, is much done to develop workers' loyalty or to encourage them to participate in more than the activity of the production lines. In one large company, a demand from headquarters that overheads should be cut led to an announcement that the Christmas party for workers' children would be abolished; in this case, fortunately, the managing director intervened and told the local managers to look elsewhere for their savings.

Monty Spaght of Shell told a story which interested me more than anything else said to me by an American businessman. When he was President of Shell Oil, Spaght once flew to a drilling rig in the Gulf of Mexico to see how the operation was progressing. He was met by the rig operator, who offered him a greasy palm and asked 'How are the third quarter's results looking?' This degree of interest in the company's progress is something which few British companies can claim. I hope I have said enough to indicate that it is not merely a matter of profit-sharing.

The fact that most British businessmen are not more dedicated is often put down to the absence in this country of adequate monetary incentive, to the paralysing effect of high taxation. There could be no more dramatic illustration of the decline of the executive's spending power than the case of the BP chairman. In 1938 he received (after tax) £10,000 out of a salary of £25,000; in 1968, he was being paid £50,000, but took home only £9,700 (and the pound had slumped to roughly a quarter of its 1938 value).

This sort of deterioration may well have had a considerable impact on enthusiasm, but before accepting that tax cuts are likely to be a sure-fire way of boosting the British businessman's output of adrenalin, it is worth reflecting on the observations of commentators like McKenzie, writing in 1901 – before the days of either high taxation or high death duties. He listed 'indifference' as one of the major problems of British management and remarked that 'here in England, when a man has made a modest competency he as a rule rests on his oars and thinks prosperity an excuse for ease'.[1] If true (and other contemporary observers were saying much the same sort of thing), it suggests that Britain has been what Dr John Treasure calls a 'strongly leisure-orientated society'[2] for some considerable time – long before high taxation could be accused of driving us onto the golf courses. In a period when income tax was only a shilling in the £, there were clearly many who chose greater leisure rather than spend more time adding to their fortunes.

It is also worth remembering that in Britain, unlike the United States, the accumulation of fortunes through trade and commerce has not traditionally conferred the highest social status until consecrated by membership of the landed classes. Ownership of land rather than of money has been the principal symbol of status;[3] indeed, the well-bred Englishman has commonly been taught that it is bad form to talk about 'money matters'[4] and that whereas the professions provide the community with important services, industry is merely concerned with making money. 'When I was at school,' said the personnel director of one large company, 'anybody who made money was considered a bit of a Jew, and they weren't first-class citizens.' I do not suggest that money is an unimportant incentive, but merely that – partly because of these

[1] *Op. cit.*, p. 24 and p. 119.

[2] J. A. P. Treasure, *Company Policy and Taxation*, Industrial Educational and Research Foundation, London, 1969.

[3] 'You don't have to defend land or boast about it,' said John Tyzack. 'It's there for everybody to see.'

[4] The reasons for this curious reticence, which still persists, are obscure. Englishmen will talk freely enough about their homes and their possessions, but not about their salaries.

prejudices – it is likely to be less of a motive force than in America, where it has served as a standard measure of success.

The steady advance of the Welfare State and the egalitarianism which has accompanied it have also discouraged aspirations to wealth among businessmen, and those who covet more than modest fortunes seem to be the exception rather than the rule.[1] For many, money is apparently not even a prime objective. Sir Frank Kearton says he is more concerned to be able to please himself than to amass money; Lord Stokes does not know what he takes home after tax, favours high death duties and is more interested in the exercise of power; and Sir Peter Allen of ICI once remarked that he would prefer more leisure to a higher salary. Perhaps these men are, to a greater or lesser degree, shaping their ambitions to fit the tax laws, but for those who would argue that they are merely examples of thwarted acquisitiveness, there is the case of John Davies, former director-general of the Confederation of British Industry. Davies not only took a salary cut when he moved to the CBI but also turned down the chance of becoming a millionaire by working for one of the family-controlled European oil businesses. Davies says he has never believed in the persistence of large fortunes and has never fancied the idea of either making one for himself or having one made for him. He is by no means alone in this attitude.

Nevertheless, I believe that our egalitarianism has led us into a thoroughly unhealthy attitude towards monetary reward. Businessmen, indeed, often sound apologetic about such wealth as they have, and take pains to emphasize the modest nature of their creature comforts. The chairman of one large company to whom I talked vigorously denied newspaper reports (of which, as it happens, I was entirely unaware) that he owned a £30,000 luxury cruiser. The boat, he assured me, had only cost £2,000, was built before the war and boasted neither hot water nor a platinum bar. One can hardly imagine American businessmen being similarly apologetic about their possessions.[2]

The desire for an un-ostentatious image is perfectly understandable

---

[1] John Tyzack recently asked a selection of high-ranking businessmen over the age of forty what their aspirations were. Security came top of the list, and second was the accumulation of money for their retirement. Tyzack's own mental guess was that the average target was likely to be £250,000; in fact, the £50–75,000 range was typical, £100,000 unusually high.

[2] Some trade union leaders appear to act under the same sort of compulsion, though perhaps for different reasons; one well-known figure, now retired, bought a standard saloon of modest size, but asked for it to be fitted with the interior appointments of the luxury model in the range.

after the outcry which the nationalized industry chairmen faced in 1969 when Mr Aubrey Jones recommended that their salaries should be raised and which Lord Beeching also had to endure when appointed chairman of British Railways at the same salary (£24,000) as he was then earning with ICI. The impression which emerged from this particular brouhaha was that here was an arch-plutocrat, a cigar-smoking tycoon of vast wealth who was shameless enough to accept the same salary in the public service as he had earned in private industry.

Nothing could have been more ludicrous. In fact, Beeching lived (and still lives) in a modest two-bedroom house in Surrey, has never owned a new car in his life and usually spends his holidays not in the Bahamas but at a golfing hotel in Devonshire. He is clearly not well cast as a sort of British J. P. Morgan, and under these circumstances was more than justified both in detecting 'a note of sourness' and in concluding that Britain had become an envious society.

The defensiveness of businessmen about their salaries has been sharpened in recent years by intermittent signs of disapproval from politicians of the Left – and the British businessman is nothing if not sensitive to noises from Westminster. Labour Ministers have drawn a distinction between those who 'earn' and those who 'make' money – this has caused guilty reflection amongst those who have acquired sizeable fortunes by perfectly legitimate means – and Mr George Brown (then Foreign Secretary) was quoted in the *Daily Express* as saying of Sir Paul Chambers (then chairman of ICI) that 'whatever he gets is a jolly sight much too much'.[1]

In my view, it is high time we gave up this sort of sniping. To tax high earnings savagely is one thing: to make men feel guilty about what they have left is quite another. I reiterate, however, that amendments in our tax regulations are unlikely of themselves to be the elixir of life which some people believe. The tax laws may well be a check on enterprise – they certainly, for example, inhibit the growth of small private businesses which prefer to remain modest in size rather than pay over the proceeds of growth to the Government – but I am not wholly convinced by senior company executives who tell me that they would think less about hunting if they were paid more. Given the national character, I doubt it. Amending the tax laws would certainly help, but if we want to give a new impetus to business enterprise in this country, we need to plan for changes in the fundamental nature of our society, some of which have already begun to take place.

[1] 1 November 1967.

The first is to ensure that business operates in an increasingly competitive environment: nothing had more disastrous effects on the quality of our industrial life than the decline of competition in the fifty years after 1914. Until then, British industry operated in a more competitive atmosphere than its American counterpart; thereafter, price rings, the activities of trade associations, the cost-plus mentality induced by the wars and the sellers' market all but buried the competitive spirit and created many of the weaknesses from which we are still suffering.

To begin with, the defensive alliances, the cartels and the gentlemen's agreements helped turn Britain into a 'status quo society'; many firms agreed to sacrifice progress for partition of the market, competition for collusion. This applied not only to the duds but also to sound and potentially powerful companies; between the wars, far too many of these virtually stood still. They talked constantly about the 'harshness of competition' just as 'competing abroad' became a standard cliché after the Second World War: no doubt this reflected a preoccupation with export markets, but it had no domestic counterpart, and for good ason.

In these years, British businessmen lost much of their reputation for secretiveness and became instead distinctly gregarious: it was little wonder that they described their industries as 'very friendly'. The resultant cosiness stimulated neither the skills of marketing and financial control nor the recruitment of professional management. Young men were generally hired on the basis of sound character and the right sort of background: 'if he was a good bloke, he could be a manager', said a senior executive in one big engineering company. They might as well have been joining a club or a regiment.

Conservative philosophies were naturally reflected in the leadership of companies: 'old is safe' became an established maxim which endures even today. Furthermore, shareholders were as undemanding as managements were complacent and companies not only got away with paying no dividend on their preference shares for the greater part of the 1930s but got away with it without complaint. As for outside directors, they were all too often chosen to add respectability rather than ginger and frequently came from the directors' trade union of bankers and retired generals.[1]

[1] Even today, no big British company has on its Board the array of talent from unrelated industries which many American corporations can boast. In 1967, for example, the Continental Oil Company Board included the president of Coca-Cola,

In the last decade, this unhealthy situation has been changing. The sellers' market has largely come to an end, competition at home has been increased by the impact of measures like the Restrictive Trade Practices Act and the end of RPM and the battle in world markets has also become very much sharper; the process is likely to continue as tariff barriers fall. Consequently, complacency has diminished, there is an eager search for good professional management as distinct from good chaps and the paternalism is a good deal less pervasive: the chairman of a nationally known company told me with a certain pride that he had sacked twenty-three directors of public companies in the previous three years.

In my view, nothing is so likely to raise the standards of British industry as a highly competitive climate, the economic equivalent of war. With such a climate, we run a serious risk of being badly beaten; without it, we will remain second-rate.

Less progress has been made in curing Britain's second basic weakness – a continuing refusal to recognize that business is the power-house of our society. This is not at all the same thing as politicians distributing largesse to industry in the shape of grants and allowances: that kind of generosity, like so much of our legislation, is aimed at using industry as an instrument of social policy. In the same way, the greater involvement of government in industry springs largely from a realization that it is a handy weapon in the battle to get a higher growth rate or to fend off foreign bankers. In one sense, of course, this new version of mercantilism is a perfectly natural development; but a strong impression remains that for most politicians industry is at best a tool, something to be manipulated for the attainment of other ends rather than being valued as the primary force in the national prosperity. Like a captive bird of prey, it has to be fed so that it can do its work.

Its aims – and particularly the profit motive – are still viewed with considerable suspicion, its activities arouse a widespread distaste on the Right as well as on the Left and although its links with the universities (for example) have improved, it still feels largely cut off from the rest of society. 'Industry', as one chief executive said, 'is a leper.' The contrast

---

a senior Vice-president of IBM, the former president of American Telephone and Telegraph and the chairman of the Owens-Corning Fibreglass Corporation. Sir Denning Pearson of Rolls-Royce thinks a lack of cross-fertilization is one of the reasons why there is a much greater difference between the best and worst in British industry than is the case in the United States.

with the situation in Japan or the United States – where its status is high, where there is a real sense of partnership between business and government and where men like Spaght can speak publicly of profit being 'a God-given moral goal' – is striking.

This ambivalence about the value of industry is reflected throughout British society. It is apparent in the low regard in which business is held compared with, say, university teaching[1] or the higher echelons of the public service;[2] and in a distrust which is evident even among schoolboys. John Tyzack speaks to many groups of school-leavers, graduates and post-graduates at schools, colleges and universities. The questions at the end of his talks indicate to him that many of the boys feel industry is dishonest and run by people who are simply out to make money for themselves; those who join its ranks, they appear to feel, are putting themselves in the hands of financial manipulators.

Tyzack believes these attitudes spring from indoctrination in either schools or homes; whatever the truth, they certainly reflect deep-rooted feelings within our society. Shell's personnel co-ordinator takes a similar view to Tyzack's and adds that Britain suffers more than any other country he knows from a lingering suspicion of business.

The relatively low status of the business life only encourages its leaders to gravitate towards activities which they think will give them more prestige (and perhaps satisfy a latent instinct for public service). They flock on to Royal Commissions, export promotion bodies and economic development committees seeking worthier pastures and (sometimes) a relief from boredom: one chairman I spoke to in the Midlands had more than thirty outside jobs. Sometimes their businesses suffer seriously, but they cannot resist the call. 'You could always flatter businessmen into doing jobs', said a former senior Civil Servant, now in industry. 'Give an Englishman a choice and

---

[1] The strongly élitist bias of our educational system has led to a widespread belief, sometimes fostered by parents or teachers, that a good University degree (preferably at Oxford or Cambridge) is the pinnacle of life's achievement: whatever follows is regarded as something of a postscript.

[2] The situation in the United States would appear to be rather different. While American businessmen frequently seek to crown their careers with a spell in public office, a career in the public service does not always carry the same kudos as it does in Britain. 'If anybody said their son was in the State Department,' said Spaght, 'you'd feel sorry for them because the poor boy would be starving.' He recalls that when he was a boy on the West Coast (he was born in 1909) a career in industry was regarded as being every bit as prestigious as one in the foreign service.

he will always think public service is more important than business.'[1]

Even those who have previously refused a variety of extra-mural appointments and talked earnestly about the need to 'mind the shop' are eventually beguiled. One young and successful managing director told me he could see little use in his company belonging to the appropriate trade association and that he rigorously avoided taking outside jobs. Eighteen months later, this same man wrote apologetically to say that he was soon to become a leading light in the trade association and had accepted an outside post of high prestige in the locality.

The hunt for a title also induces businessmen to act in what they consider to be a public-spirited fashion. This is another way in which the nature of our society 'acts as a drag on business efficiency', in the words of a senior Civil Servant. In trans-Atlantic eyes, too, the distribution of titles does nothing to improve business performance – 'a KCMG', said one American businessman, not perhaps fully conversant with the present honours system or the state of the Empire, but with definite opinions none the less, 'may help to make a better Judge in Kenya, but it doesn't make a better factory manager' – and simply helps to create a hierarchical society, where awe for title and office supersedes respect for the facts. 'If Lord Smith says something,' he added, 'you listen a bit harder than if Mr Smith says the same thing.'

As for the increased intervention of government in industry, a return to mercantilism was a natural consequence of a national economic crisis and it has had some useful results. For one thing, Government and business know a good deal more about each other than they did; and, if the acquaintance has not always proved endearing, at least they understand each other better. Furthermore, some of the newer institutions of government are an advance on their predecessors: the Ministry of Technology, as one of the spearheads of the new mercantilism, has done much useful work and so, too, have the Prices and Incomes Board and the Industrial Reorganization Corporation (although it is worth adding the cautionary note that, in this same period, a good many strategic industrial alliances have been formed in West Germany without the help of an IRC-type body).

However, it is also true that the politicians – in their eagerness – have

[1] Some perceptive Civil Servants feel that the men who rise to leadership in large companies are often more suited to be public servants than businessmen. 'The sort of men I meet,' said one Permanent Secretary, 'are the kind who are willing and able to sit on Royal Commissions and Government inquiries, and they're not the kind who are going to make cut-throat competitors. It's a different motivation altogether.'

generally concerned themselves less with what I believe ought to be their essential task, to try to create the right sort of environment for industry, and more with ensuring greater physical contact, with bringing industrialists into the bosom of Whitehall and despatching Whitehall into the bosom of industry. In other words, the attempt at liaison has been both feverish and meddlesome; there has been too much piecemeal and badly co-ordinated intervention and too little strategic thinking.

Certainly many businessmen are now heartily fed up with the amount of time they have had to spend in dealing with Government-sponsored inquiries (justifiably, in the light of the often modest nature of the results), while some Americans working in this country are appalled at the regularity of liaison with Whitehall which is required of their companies. 'Everything that comes up,' said Spaght, 'you have to run to some damn Ministry or another. I was President of Shell Oil for $4\frac{1}{2}$ years and in that time I didn't visit Washington except once to show my children round. I saw the President and Dean Rusk on social visits, but I was never called before a Minister nor were any of my people. If we wanted to build a $100m. refinery, we'd need a fire and safety permit from the city or State, but we didn't have to ask for federal approval – what the hell would it have to do with them?'

Perhaps the most potentially dangerous result of the closer relationship with Government, however, is a growth of belief in Whitehall as ultimate saviour – in the case of large companies which might otherwise go to the wall – or at least as a manipulator of economic levers which can tide over the ailing enterprise. 'Almost forty years of tariffs, thirty of inflation and even longer of the political myth that the State can do it for us,' said Sir Reay Geddes, 'is too much for a mature industrial country.'

Another undesirable consequence of closer liaison has been a sharp increase in jobs for businessmen in Whitehall; unfortunately a number have been filled not by those who spend their lives seeking opportunites to act 'in the national interest' but by capable industrialists. This is yet another reason for disbanding a high proportion of the gallimaufry of committees which now festoon Whitehall.

Nor has the increasing presence of Government done anything to diminish the naturally acquiescent style of the British businessman when confronted by politicians and Civil Servants. 'When a Civil Servant is merely advancing a point of view,' said one man who has had ample opportunity to observe the relationship at close quarters, 'it is regarded as gospel, a word from the Supreme Power – to such an extent that even the Civil Servants are surprised.' Nor is it unknown for companies to continue to turn out products because dropping them might displease the Government.

While it is going too far to suggest, as one business school professor does, that British industry nationalizes itself, it is true that business in this country has become more and more the art of the politically possible.[1] It is significant that one of the few industrialists who have regularly taken issue with the Government – Lord Robens – is himself a former politician; and it is doubtful whether his protests would have been regarded with such tolerance if he had been chairman of a private company rather than head of a declining nationalized industry.

Nevertheless, there has been a marked improvement in recent years in the performance and style of British business. A new generation of managers is growing up which was not reared in the era of non-competition; there is a genuine interest in professional management; and, apart from the Weinstocks and Keartons, there is no lack of enterprise at more modest levels. There are men, for example, like Roy Annable and Skene Whalley who mortgaged themselves up to the hilt to buy Brockway Carpets, a small company in Kidderminster five years ago. The year they took over, the firm made a loss and had virtually no export business; now they have pushed up the turnover from £200,000 to £500,000, are currently twelfth in the industry's export league (on a proportion of turnover basis) and have spent £100,000 on new buildings and machinery. We need more Annables and Whalleys as well as more Weinstocks. Again, our industrial structure is both more sensible and stronger than it was and, while it is true that the merger is a quantitative rather than a qualitative concept and that the big mergers of recent years still have to prove that they can match up to giant American and continental competitors, their overall efficiency is likely to be higher than the average efficiency of their constituent parts.

Britain's export record, too, is impressive in some respects: the proportion of our gross domestic product which we sell abroad is, in some years, four times that of the United States and well above that of West Germany.

The harsh fact, however, is that major competitors such as the United States, West Germany and Japan have also been moving ahead – and

[1] Aubrey Jones, who personally felt that £25,000 might be an appropriate salary for chairmen of the more important nationalized industries, recommended £20,000 in his report partly because he felt this was the most which was politically practicable.

more rapidly than Britain. The recent increase in productivity in West Germany, for example, has far outstripped anything which we have been able to achieve.

Nor, in my view, will we ever substantially close the gap merely by improving the structure of our industry. The change required is much more fundamental. What is needed is a complete revolution in the attitude of our society to industry and its purposes. Anything less will merely be tinkering with the problem.

It is bound to be a slow and difficult process. We have a society in Britain which in many respects is worth cherishing: Americans who are critical of our business performance still believe that Britain is the most civilized country in the world in which to live and that the quality of our human resources is very high. It is a society which permits a high degree of individual freedom, which is long on tolerance and short on ruthlessness and which – despite some evidence to the contrary – has a high degree of communal sense. I do not believe, however, that we have to sacrifice these virtues in the search for higher business efficiency; there is no reason at all why we should not continue to pursue what a business school professor called 'the British mission – to combine business with humanity'. (Again, Marks and Spencer provides a useful guide to the correct proportions.) What we do have to sacrifice are our complacency, our anti-business snobbery and the tepid commitment of many of our industrialists.

If we do not do so, Britain will continue to justify the verdict of one American businessman on our industrial performance: 'Your society isn't going to hell, but it isn't going any other place either.'

Index of People and Companies

Prinicipal References only